THE TEXT
of the
OLD TESTAMENT

THE TEXT
of the
OLD TESTAMENT

An Introduction to the Biblia Hebraica

SECOND EDITION

Ernst Würthwein

Translated by
Erroll F. Rhodes

WILLIAM B. EERDMANS PUBLISHING COMPANY
GRAND RAPIDS, MICHIGAN

First published as *Der Text des Alten Testaments,*
fifth edition, © 1988 Württembergische Bibelanstalt Stuttgart

English translation © 1995 Wm. B. Eerdmans Publishing Co.
255 Jefferson Ave. S.E., Grand Rapids, Michigan 49503

00 99 98 97 96 95   7 6 5 4 3 2 1

Printed in the United States of America

Library of Congress Cataloging-in-Publication Data

Würthwein, Ernst, 1909-
[Text des Alten Testaments. English]
The text of the Old Testament: an introduction to the Biblia Hebraica /
Ernst Würthwein; translated by Erroll F. Rhodes. — Rev. ed.
p.   cm.
Includes bibliographical references and index.
ISBN 0-8028-0788-7
1. Bible. O.T — Criticism, Textual. 2. Bible. O.T. — Manuscripts.
3. Bible. O.T. — Versions. I. Title.
BS1136.W813   1994
221.4′4 — dc20   94-23307
                                                          CIP

Contents

List of Plates   ix

Preface to the Fifth German Edition   xi

Translator's Note   xii

Introduction   xiii

I. Script and Writing Materials   1

1. Script   1

2. Writing Materials   4

3. Scroll and Codex   7

4. Writing Implements and Ink   9

II. The Masoretic Text   10

1. General Considerations   10

2. The Consonantal Text   13

3. Pointing   21

4. The Masora   28

5. Manuscripts   30

6. Printed Editions   39

III. The Samaritan Pentateuch (ɯ)   45

IV. Preliminary Considerations on the Versions   48

V. The Septuagint (𝕲)   50

  1. Introduction   50

  2. The Letter of Aristeas   51

  3. The Origin and History of the Septuagint
to the Second Century A.D.   52

  4. Revisions and Later Greek Versions   54

  5. Origen's Hexapla   57

  6. Other Recensions of the Septuagint   60

  7. Lagarde's Program   61

  8. Kahle's Thesis   63

  9. The Septuagint and the Hebrew Text   66

 10. Manuscripts   71

 11. Editions   75

 12. The Samariticon   78

VI. The Aramaic Targums (𝕮)   79

  1. Origin and Character   79

  2. The Various Targums   80

  3. The Samaritan Targum (cited in BH as $\mathfrak{w}^T$)   84

VII. The Syriac Version (Peshitta, [𝕾])   85

  1. Name and Literary Problem   85

  2. Manuscripts and Editions   88

VIII. The Old Latin (𝕷)   91

  1. Origin and Problems   91

  2. Editions and Manuscripts   92

IX. The Vulgate (𝕺)   95

  1. Jerome's Version   95

  2. The History of the Vulgate   97

X. **The Coptic Versions** (Ӿ)   100

XI. **The Ethiopic Version** (Ӓ)   102

XII. **The Armenian Version (Arm)**   103

XIII. **The Arabic Versions** (Ӓ)   104

XIV. **The Aims of Textual Criticism**   105

XV. **Causes of Textual Corruption**   107
  1. General Remarks   107
  2. Errors of Reading and Writing   108
  3. Deliberate Alterations   111

XVI. **The Methods of Textual Criticism**   113
  1. General Remarks   113
  2. Establishing the Traditional Text   114
  3. Examination of the Traditional Text   115
  4. The Decision   118
  5. Psychological Considerations   119

XVII. **The Theological Significance of Textual Criticism and the History of the Text**   121

Appendix: Resources for Textual Research   123
  1. Text   123
  2. Concordances   124
  3. Dictionaries   127
  4. Grammars   129
  5. Synopses   130

6. Inscriptions   130
7. Special Literature   130
8. International Organizations   131

Plates   133

List of Sigla   232
Abbreviations   238
Bibliography   242
Index of Authors   277
Index of Subjects   283
Index of Scripture References   290

List of Plates

1. An Inscribed Bowl from Lachish — 135
2. The Stele of Mesha, King of Moab — 137
3. The Siloam Inscription from Jerusalem — 139
4. Lachish Letter No. 4 — 141
5. The Elephantine Papyrus — 143
6. The Nash Papyrus — 145
7. The Entrance to Qumran Cave 1 — 147
8. Two Jars from Cave 1 — 149
9a. A Samuel Fragment from Cave 4 — 151
9b. A Fragment of the Song of Moses — 151
10. The First Isaiah Scroll — 153
11. The First Isaiah Scroll — 155
12. The Second Isaiah Scroll — 157
13. The Habakkuk Commentary — 159
14. Fragments of Leviticus in Old Hebrew Script — 161
15a. A Fragment with Parts of Deut. 29:14-18 and 32:20–31:5 — 163
15b. Part of an Unopened Scroll — 163
16. The Minor Prophets Scroll, Murabbaʿat 88 — 165
17. A Page with Babylonian Pointing — 167
18. A Haphtarah Fragment with Babylonian Pointing — 168-69
19. A Fragment with Palestinian Pointing — 171

20. Codex Cairensis   173
21. The Aleppo Codex   175
22. British Library Codex Or. 4445   177
23. A Torah Manuscript from the Year A.D. 930   179
24. Codex Leningradensis   181
25. A Manuscript with Distinctive Pointing   183
26. The Second Rabbinic Bible of Jacob ben Chayyim   185
27. The Samaritan Triglot   187
28. The Rylands Greek Papyrus 458   189
29. Papyrus Fouad 266   191
30. A Greek Scroll of the Minor Prophets   193
31. Chester Beatty Papyrus 967   195
32. The Berlin Genesis   197
33. Codex Sinaiticus   199
34. The Hexapla Fragments of Milan   201
35. Codex Colberto-Sarravianus   203
36. Codex Marchalianus   205
37. A Syro-Hexaplar Manuscript of A.D. 697   207
38. A Catena Manuscript (Ninth Century A.D.)   209
39. A Peshitta Manuscript of the Year A.D. 464   211
40. The Constance Fragments of the Old Latin Prophets   213
41. Codex Lugdunensis   215
42. A Vulgate Palimpsest from the Fifth Century A.D.   217
43. Codex Amiatinus   219
44. A Coptic Papyrus Codex   221
45. An Ethiopic Manuscript   223
46. An Arabic Manuscript   225
47. The Complutensian Polyglot   227
48. A Chart of the Old Hebrew Alphabet   229
49. The Izbet Sartah Abecedary   231

Preface to the Fifth German Edition

This fifth edition, like earlier editions, has been thoroughly revised in the light of new critical editions of texts, as well as recent contributions and findings in the various areas of the history of the text (especially of the Masoretic text, the Septuagint, and the Peshitta) and of textual criticism.

The "List of Sigla," which shows in parallel columns the sigla used in *Biblia Hebraica Stuttgartensia,* edited in 1967-1977 by K. Elliger and W. Rudolph (BHS), and also those used in its predecessor *Biblia Hebraica,* edited by R. Kittel-P. Kahle in 1929-1937 (BHK), assures the usefulness of this book as an introduction to both editions.

Gratitude is due Erroll F. Rhodes, the translator of the American edition (Grand Rapids, 1979, [2]1985), for contributing many bibliographical references; to Mr. M. Hoffner, Th.M., for valuable clerical assistance, especially in preparing the bibliography; to the Rev. R. Bickert for his gracious help and for reviewing corrections; to the staff of the German Bible Society, and to Dr. J. Lange in particular, for careful editorial assistance.

My wife was a constant source of encouragement and inspiration to me in the preparation of the present revision. It is a matter of deep sorrow that she did not live to see its publication. It is dedicated to her in continuing gratitude.

Marburg, June 1988   ERNST WÜRTHWEIN

Translator's Note

A debt of gratitude must be expressed to Prof. Ernst Würthwein for kindly reviewing the present revision, and granting permission to include a supplementary survey of the resources for textual research; to Harold P. Scanlin, United Bible Societies Translations Advisor, for preparing the supplementary survey, as well as for assisting with counsel on many details; and to Allen C. Myers of William B. Eerdmans Publishing Company for careful editorial oversight. Without their generous cooperation and contributions the present volume would not have been possible.

Greenwich, Connecticut, June 1994   ERROLL F. RHODES

Introduction

When we read a modern book, printed from a manuscript which has been prepared by the author himself and produced under his own supervision, we can study it with confidence that its text represents the author's intention in its wording and even in the details of its punctuation. We can be sure of the text we read. With works produced hundreds or even thousands of years before the invention of printing the situation is quite different. Almost without exception the original documents have been lost. The texts are available only in copies separated from their autographs by several centuries and an unknown number of intermediary copies. We know how easily errors can occur in copying a text. By accident a word may be missed or repeated, groups of words may be inadvertently transposed or replaced by similar or synonymous words, and if the handwriting is difficult to read, an element of guesswork may enter.

Many errors may be due to carelessness, especially if the copyist is a professional scribe who works rapidly and becomes casual, and who further may not be familiar with the subject of the text being copied. But even the scribe who approaches a text with interest and devotion may introduce corruptions. There may be an expression in the exemplar which is felt to reflect an earlier scribe's misunderstanding of the author, and with a concern for the meaning of the text the scribe naturally corrects it, just as we would correct a typographical error in a printed book. But the scribe's correction itself could very well reflect a misunderstanding! It is not only the casual or absentminded scribe who introduces errors, but the conscientious scribe as well. The next stage in the process is obvious. A scribe copying a faulty manuscript — and no manuscript is without errors — will deal with a predecessor's errors either by guesswork or with ingenuity, resulting in a series of intended improvements leading away from the original text.

All the writings which come to us from antiquity, including the writings of the Old and New Testaments, have suffered from just such (mis)adventures.[1] The interpreter of these materials cannot proceed from assumptions which would be accepted without question in the study of a modern book. The text to be interpreted must first be established — it is not already defined. The available witnesses to the text must first be examined in order to reconstruct a single form of the text which we can assert with confidence to be as close to the form of the autographs as scientific principles can lead us, if not (ideally) identical with them. The work of textual criticism is both a preliminary and an integral part of the task of interpretation; its role may once have been overrated, just as now it tends to be overlooked, yet its service remains indispensable.

The purpose and goal of our critical editions of the Bible is to assist in achieving an objective understanding of the text. They bring together in a convenient form a vast array of material, well beyond the capacity of individual scholars to assemble for themselves, to provide the first requirements for a systematic study of the text. But to deal with all this material and use it effectively we must understand its peculiarities and the value of its various elements. When faced with a difficult passage we cannot simply gather together the various readings and select the one which seems to offer the simplest solution, at times preferring the Hebrew text, at other times the Septuagint, and yet other times the Aramaic Targum. Textual witnesses are not all equally reliable. Each has its own character and its own individual history. We must be familiar with these if we hope to avoid inadequate or false solutions. Accordingly we shall first survey the available witnesses to the text in three sections: A. transmission of the text in the original language; B. translations made from the original language; and C. the remaining translations. A fourth section will outline the purpose and procedures of textual criticism, and finally we will consider the theological significance of the history of the text and of textual criticism.

---

1. It is true, as we shall see, that efforts to protect the Hebrew text of the Old Testament from accidental and intentional changes were successful. But this was only after a certain date, and in the preceding centuries it was subject to the common vicissitudes of all ancient texts.

I. Script and Writing Materials

1. Script[1]

Excavations and discoveries of the last hundred years have revealed an unexpected wealth of literary activity in Palestine and Syria. Several different writing systems were invented there during the second millennium B.C., and even foreign systems of writing such as the cuneiform script were in use as well. Here also, presumably, the first step was taken in the transition from complex writing systems with hundreds of letters to the alphabet, that simplest of all forms of writing, with only some twenty-odd letters — a step so significant for human intellectual history. All this was certainly not without significance for the formation of the Old Testament, and must receive due recognition in any consideration of the roles of oral and written tradition among the Israelites and the Jews. We can only allude to this in passing, limiting ourselves here to some comments on those systems of writing which were directly related to the initial writing of the biblical texts and their continuing transmission.

All the manuscripts and fragments of the Hebrew Old Testament which have come down to us from Jewish sources, from the earliest examples, e.g., the Qumran texts (cf. pp. 31f.) and the Nash Papyrus, are with few exceptions written in the script still in use today known as the *square script* (כְּתָב מְרֻבָּע) or the Assyrian script (כְּתָב אַשּׁוּרִי) from its place of origin. This script was in general use in the time of Jesus: the allusion to the letter *yod* as the smallest of the alphabet (Matt. 5:18) would be true only of the square script. This script was derived by a gradual process of development from the Aramaic script which was used extensively (pl. 5). The earliest recorded examples are the ʿAraq el-Emir inscrip-

1. J. Naveh 1987.

I

tion in East Jordan from the fourth or early third century B.C.[2] and the earliest Qumran fragments from about 200 B.C. (4QSam[b] and 4QJer[a]).[3] The Jews were aware, however, that this script was not their earliest. One Jewish tradition attributes its introduction to Ezra, about 430 B.C. The later rabbis were embarrassed by the implication that it was a postexilic innovation. Accordingly they told how the Torah was first given in the square script, but because of Israel's sin the script had been changed, and then in Ezra's time the original form was restored. Although this was obviously special pleading and without any historical value, it clearly reflects the awareness of a change of script in the postexilic period. Most probably the Jews' gradual adoption of the Aramaic language, the lingua franca of the ancient Near East, was followed by their adoption of the Aramaic script, so that by inference it was in this script that the sacred writings were first written, and only eventually in the square script which developed from it.[4]

When the earlier parts of the Old Testament were first written down in the preexilic period, another script was in use in Palestine and Syria. This was the *Phoenician-Old Hebrew script,* the ancestor of all the alphabets of past and present. It is known to us in a later, more developed form in a series of texts, the earliest dating from the eleventh or tenth century. The best-known examples are:[5] the abecedary ostracon from Izbet Ṣarṭah (eleventh century B.C.; pl. 49), the Ahiram sarcophagus from Byblos (*ca.* 1000 B.C.), the farmer's calendar from Gezer (*ca.* 950), the Moabite stone (*ca.* 840; pl. 2), ostraca from Samaria (ink on clay, eighth century), a palimpsest papyrus from Murabba'at (eighth or seventh century), the Siloam inscription (*ca.* 700; pl. 3), and ostraca from Lachish (*ca.* 588; pl. 4) and Arad (sixth century).[6]

2. W. F. Albright 1949: 149f.

3. F. M. Cross 1955: 147-176; 1961a: 133-202.

4. Cf. also G. R. Driver 1954: 250, "This כתב אשורי or simply אשורית 'Assyrian script' was so called because it was the originally Aramean form of the 'Phoenician script' which had been coming into use in Assyrian and Babylonian commercial houses since the 8th century B.C. and which was brought back by Jews returning from the Exile. The 'square script' (כתב מרבע) was derived from this form of the alphabet."

5. The texts have been collected and annotated in H. Donner and W. Röllig 1971-76; D. W. Thomas, ed. 1958; and in J. C. L. Gibson, 1971-82. Selections with linguistic notes: K. Jaroš 1982.

6. Two small sheet silver plaques (possibly amulets; mid-seventh century B.C.?) were found during the 1979 excavation of a tomb at Ketef Hinnom in Jerusalem. They were inscribed with blessings in Old Hebrew script similar to the priestly blessing of Num. 6:24-26, perhaps representing an early form of it. Its use as a private formula is interesting to note.

Its origins must lie far earlier than any of the examples yet discovered. Early examples of alphabetical inscriptions include the *Sinai script* found in a group of inscriptions in the mines of Serabiṭ el-Hadem on the Sinai peninsula and dated by William F. Albright *ca.* 1500,[7] the (related?) *proto-Palestinian script* found on artifacts from middle and southern Palestine of the period from 1700 to 1200 B.C. (Gezer, Lachish, Shechem, etc.; pl. 1),[8] and the cuneiform alphabet of Ugarit in north Syria, *ca.* 1400 B.C. There is no need to discuss here the relationship of these scripts to the Phoenician-Old Hebrew script and the later square script, because it is still largely a prehistory, obscure in its details. Deciphering the scripts, except for Ugaritic, is still at the beginning stages. Only the Phoenician-Old Hebrew script and the later square script are directly related to the earliest written forms of the Old Testament texts and to their preservation as written documents. We need only observe here that when the Israelites settled in Palestine they found in the Phoenician alphabet (although without vowels) a script which was easy to learn and required hardly any improvement; more than four hundred references in the Old Testament attest that the art of writing was widely practiced in Israel.[9]

The transition from the Old Hebrew script to the square script occurred between the fourth and second centuries B.C. — it is impossible to be more precise. For a long while the Old Hebrew script remained in use beside the square script. The coins of the period of Bar Kochba's revolt (A.D. 132-135) bear Old Hebrew letters. Among the texts found in the Dead Sea caves are some written in the Old Hebrew script.[10] "This script . . . derives from the old pre-exilic Hebrew script. Apparently it survived as a book hand and enjoyed a renascence in the period of Maccabean nation-

---

7. W. F. Albright 1948.

8. The so-called Sinai Inscriptions have been collected and studied by W. F. Albright 1966; on the proto-Palestinian inscriptions cf. also F. M. Cross 1954.

9. Cf. D. Diringer 1970: 13; A. Lemaire 1981; B. Sass 1991. S. Warner 1980, suggests the possibility that social barriers militated against its widespread use.

10. According to present reports there are five Pentateuch manuscripts and some fragments of Job (Cross 1961: 43). Cf. pl. 14, pp. 160f. Of special interest is an Exodus scroll with fragments of Exod. 6:25–37:15 which preserves the Samaritan text type almost throughout although it is not of Samaritan origin (it lacks the characteristic addition after 20:17). Cf. P. Skehan 1955: 182-87; and 1959: 22f.; R. S. Hanson 1964; also the major study of J. Sanderson 1986. A badly damaged scroll of Leviticus written in the Old Hebrew script from about 100 B.C. was found by Bedouin in Cave 11 and published by D. N. Freedman and K. A. Mathews (with contributions by R. S. Hanson) 1985. It belongs to the proto-rabbinic textual tradition, later to become the rabbinic standard.

alism and archaism. In any case, at Qumrân it appears in documents contemporary with the Jewish hand."[11] Jewish accounts in the Mishna and the Babylonian Talmud imply that although manuscripts of the Bible in the old script were still circulating in the first two centuries of the Christian era, they were ascribed an inferior degree of holiness — they did not "defile the hands" levitically as did scrolls written in the square script.[12] And yet for a while the Old Hebrew script must have been regarded as especially holy. This would at least explain a peculiar feature of some recently discovered texts: in the Habakkuk Commentary (pl. 13), the Hodayoth, and the Psalm scroll from Cave 11 (11QPsᵃ), the square script is used except for the divine name יהוה and both אל and אלי, which are written in Old Hebrew. Again, the Tetragram is found in Old Hebrew letters in a fragmentary leather scroll containing the Greek text of the Minor Prophets which was discovered in August 1952 by Bedouin at Naḥal Ḥever in the Judean desert (cf. p. 192). It was probably written between 50 B.C. and A.D. 50, and confirms Origen's account of the treatment of divine names, that in the more careful copies of the Greek Old Testament the Old Hebrew script was used for the Tetragram.[13] As late as the fifth century A.D. the divine name was written in Old Hebrew letters in a fragment of Aquila's Greek version.

The *Samaritans* (pl. 27), who contrary to traditional beliefs (cf. p. 45) did not separate themselves from the Jews completely until the Hasmonean period, also preserved their sacred book, the Torah, in *Old Hebrew script,* probably because they claimed to preserve the older and purer tradition, and they may have regarded the introduction of the new script as a flagrant innovation.[14]

2. Writing Materials

Many different kinds of material were used for writing in biblical times. Job wished his words were chiseled in *stone* (Job 19:24); and the successful

---

11. F. M. Cross 1961: 34.
12. Cf. J. Maier 1982: 95; cf. especially p. 16 for the "defilement of hands" by scrolls.
13. Edition: D. Barthélemy 1963; cf. pl. 30.
14. According to F. M. Cross, 1961: 34, the Samaritan script was derived from the (archaizing) Old Hebrew script of the Hasmonean period. The history of Hebrew scripts from the beginning to modern times is illustrated with about four hundred examples by S. A. Birnbaum 1954-57, 1971.

achievement of the tunnel of Siloam (pl. 3) in the late eighth century B.C. was recorded on the smooth surface of a rock in an inscription discovered in 1880. We read in Exod 34:1 of *stone tablets* with the commandments of God written on them, and in Deut. 27:2f. stones were covered with a plaster on which letters were presumably painted. *Wooden tablets*[15] for brief notes may be intended when the prophets Isaiah and Habakkuk were instructed to record their oracles on tablets (Isa. 30:8; Hab. 2:2; perhaps also Isa. 8:1). The *clay tablets* so popular in the rest of the ancient Near East were ideal for the straight lines of cuneiform script, but hardly adapted to the curved lines of the Hebrew script. But the excavations in Palestine demonstrate that *potsherds* or *ostraca* (pl. 4) inscribed with ink were as popular there as elsewhere for routine daily matters. While excavating Tell ed-Duweir (ancient Lachish) in 1935, archaeologists found some ostraca in a room by the city gate which proved to be military dispatches from the last years of Judah, *ca.* 588 B.C. It has already been suggested that individual prophetic statements, proverbs, and the like may have been written on such potsherds before they were collected into books. While this could well account for the lack of continuity found in the order of some biblical books, it remains only a theoretical possibility.

An example of writing material unparalleled elsewhere is the *copper scroll* found in Qumran Cave I; it does not contain a biblical text.

The materials mentioned above were appropriate only for texts of very limited length, and would be relevant only to the earlier stages of the formation of our biblical books. *Papyrus* and *leather* were more suitable materials for extensive books; these must be intended where the Old Testament refers to a scroll, whether מְגִלַּת־סֵפֶר or simply מְגִלָּה (Jer. 36:2ff.; Ezek. 2:9; 3:1-3; Zech. 5:1f.; Ps. 40:8), because only these are adapted to the scroll format.

Papyrus[16] was already being used in Egypt in the third millennium B.C. We know from the famous travel narrative of the Egyptian Wen Amon (*ca.* 1090 B.C.) that this convenient material was exported from Egypt to Phoenicia in exchange for wood. We may infer from the fact that Wen Amon took with him five hundred scrolls of fine grade papyrus (several qualities were distinguished) that the commodity was being manufactured commercially. Egypt was later to be the source of supply for the whole Mediterranean world. Papyrus was made from the stem of the papyrus

---

15. Excavations in Egypt and Mesopotamia show that tablets of two or more panels (diptychs, triptychs) could be prepared for writing with a coat of plaster or wax.

16. Cf. also D. J. Wiseman 1970: 30-32; T. C. Skeat 1969: 54-61.

reed. It was cut into thin strips. A vertical layer was placed upon a horizontal layer; the two were pressed together (the natural gum provided adequate bonding), dried, and rubbed smooth. The sheet was then ready for use. A number of sheets could be glued together to form a scroll of a desired length. The Israelites wrote on such scrolls in columns, from right to left. Usually the inner side of the scroll (recto) with its horizontal grain was used for texts, but some scrolls were inscribed on both sides (cf. Ezek. 2:10). It was probably a papyrus scroll which Baruch wrote on at Jeremiah's dictation, and which King Jehoiakim burned in the open brazier sheet by sheet (Jer. 36). On the whole, the use of papyrus must have been quite common in Palestine. It was cheap and more durable than has generally been recognized, "at least as durable as the best hand-made paper, if not more so."[17] But of course favorable climate and soil, as in the desert sands of Egypt, were required for it to survive through the centuries. This is why very few papyrus fragments have been discovered thus far in Palestine, such as those found in the caves of Qumran and Murabba'at (cf. pp. 31, 146), where the conditions were suitable for their preservation. Among these were found only a few with biblical texts (e.g., Kings and Daniel, and pap4Q Isa[p], pap6Q Ps, pap7Q GrGen).

The palimpsest of Murabba'at deserves mention as the earliest known Hebrew papyrus, ascribed to the eighth (Milik) or seventh (Frank M. Cross, John C. L. Gibson, and others) century B.C. The almost illegible underwriting seems to be a letter, while the overwriting seems to be a list of persons.[18]

As a writing material, it was not until later that *leather*[19] came to play as important a role in Palestine as it did elsewhere in the Near East. Its durability gave it an advantage over papyrus that made it an ideal material for writings which were intended for long or constant use. Jewish regulations still require that a copy of the Torah intended for liturgical use be written on leather made from a clean animal, and this surely represents an ancient usage.[20] The Letter of Aristeas, at the end of the second century

17. T. C. Skeat 1969: 59.

18. Benoit-Milik-de Vaux 1961, no. 17. Text and translation in J. C. L. Gibson 1971: 31f., where the papyrus fragment is dated *ca.* 650 B.C. Legal or administrative documents on papyrus from the Persian period were found in a cave north of Jericho at Wādi ed-Dāliye.

19. T. C. Skeat 1969: 61-65.

20. On the preparation of Torah scrolls the Jerusalem Talmud states: "It is a rule [*halakah*] that was given to Moses at Sinai: write on leather, write with ink, and line with a reed"(*Meg.* 1.9). According to M. Haran 1982 and 1983, the transition to leather as normal for the sacred Scriptures was associated with their canonization.

B.C., alludes to a magnificent Torah scroll with gold writing on leather (parchment?); and the Isaiah scroll found in 1947 (pl. 10, 11) provides an actual example of an ancient biblical scroll which is not much later than this literary evidence. It comprises seventeen sheets of carefully prepared leather (not parchment, as often stated). These were sewn together to make a scroll 7.34 m. long (26 cm. wide). It contains all sixty-six chapters of Isaiah in fifty-four columns, averaging thirty lines of 12.8 cm. width.[21] The lines were marked in the leather with a dull knife, also in accordance with Jewish regulations. This scroll and others found with it were wrapped in linen and sealed in clay jars (pl. 8) — a method of preservation mentioned in Jer. 32:14, and common also in Egypt.

From about 200 B.C. a special technique of treating leather (was lime mordant already known?) was used to produce **parchment** (Greek *pergamon*), named after the city of Pergamon in Asia Minor. This became the principal material for books from the fourth century on, and the dominant writing medium of the medieval period, while the use of papyrus declined. In contrast to the earlier materials, parchment offered great advantages. It is durable, with a smooth writing surface, accepting writing on both sides, and with a light color that lends clarity to the ink. It could be used several times by erasing the text; there are many examples of its use in palimpsests (literally "rescraped," Latin *codex rescriptus* = a rewritten book; pl. 34, 42). The material of the important fragments from the Cairo Geniza (cf. pp. 11, 34) was also parchment. **Paper** made its appearance beside parchment in the ninth century. Paper was invented in China in the first century A.D. or perhaps earlier, and by the eighth century the knowledge of its manufacture came first to the Near East through Chinese prisoners of war, and thence to Europe.

3. Scroll and Codex

The common book format of antiquity was the papyrus or leather scroll — a rather inconvenient form. It takes both hands to use it: one to hold the scroll (the left hand for Hebrew scrolls, because of the right-to-left script), while the other hand draws the sheets out slowly, column by column, and

---

21. The longest of the Qumran scrolls yet discovered is the"Temple Scroll" which was acquired by Israel in 1967 (after the Six Day War): nineteen sheets, 8.6 m. in length. Published: Y. Yadin 1983. Translations: J. Maier 1978 (German); 1985 (English). The original length of the Greek scroll of the Minor Prophets has been estimated at 10 m. (cf. Tov *et al.* 1990).

rolls them up again as they are read (cf. Latin *volvere* "to turn," whence *volumen* "volume" to designate a scroll). After a scroll has been read, it must be wound back on the original roller to prepare for its next use, with the first sheet on the outside again. We noted that the sixty-six chapters of Isaiah required a scroll about 7.5 m. long. For practical reasons a scroll could not be made much longer.[22] Only in exceptional instances of very large scrolls with very small script could the entire Old Testament, or even several of its longer books, be included in a single scroll. Most of the biblical books circulated in separate scrolls, and in some instances, as in the Pentateuch, the division into books seems to have been made with the normal capacity of a scroll in view.

It was the invention of the ***codex*** in the first century A.D., and especially the parchment codex, that made it possible to produce many or all of the books of the Bible in a single volume. Remains of ***papyrus*** codices (pl. 31, 32) containing Greek texts of the Old and New Testament books have survived from the second and third centuries A.D.[23] In the fourth century the codex came into common use. The scroll did not disappear completely, but its importance diminished. The role of the Christian church in this development is of interest. It was the victory of the church which led to the dominance of the codex, which had been used by Christians from the beginning, over the scroll format. Scrolls came to be used only for official records and contracts, while the codex became the normal form for books.[24] Its advantages over the scroll format are obvious: an increased ease of browsing and rapid reference, as well as the use of both sides of the sheet for texts. Even the Jews finally adopted the codex about A.D. 700 for reference works, retaining the use of leather and parchment scrolls for (unpointed!) copies of the Torah and of Esther designated for liturgical use. The majority of the fragments from the Cairo Geniza represent codices (cf. pp. 7, 11, 34); only a few are from scrolls.

---

22. The longest surviving scroll is the 40 m.-long Harris Papyrus in the British Library, which was never intended for practical use. This is far greater than the average, which was between 6 m. and 10 m. for Greek papyrus scrolls. In the Qumran caves there were also found scrolls "of very small format with a tiny script" (Bardtke 1961: 83).

23. C. H. Roberts has shown how completely the codex form came to dominate Christian biblical manuscripts (in complete contrast to pagan and Jewish literature) in the second and third centuries: cf. 1954: 169-204; 1970: 48-66; T. C. Skeat 1969: 65-74; C. H. Roberts and T. C. Skeat 1987.

24. Cf. W. Schubart 1918: 56; and 1921: 122f.

4. Writing Implements and Ink

Writing implements mentioned in the Old Testament include the חֶרֶט (Isa. 8:1) and the עֵט (Jer. 8:8; 17:1; Ps. 45:2; Job 19:24). חֶרֶט corresponds to a *pen* or *stylus* with which characters are inscribed on prepared materials. The same tool is probably intended by עֵט בַּרְזֶל, the iron pen with a diamond point of Jer. 17:1, and the iron chisel of Job 19:24.[25] But again the עֵט סֹפְרִים of Jer. 8:8 and עֵט סוֹפֵר of Ps. 45:2 refer to the *reed pen* of the professional scribe, used with ink on leather, papyrus, and ostraca. In ancient Egypt rushes were used with their ends crushed and frayed like a small brush, or later cut at an acute angle like a quill pen; we may infer similar practices in Palestine. The reed pen *(kalamos),* formed like a quill pen with a split point to permit a flowing cursive script, can be traced to the third century B.C. It has continued in use in the East until modern times.

Ink (Hebrew דְּיוֹ) was used for writing on ostraca, leather, and papyrus. The only mention of it in the Old Testament is at Jer. 36:18 (605 B.C.), where it is referred to as something well known. There were two kinds: *nonmetallic* ink made from lamp black (the soot from an olive oil lamp) in a solution of gum (resin) or oil, and *metallic* ink, usually a compound of gall nuts and vitriol.[26] The use of metallic ink, which was not permanent and was damaging to the writing material, was opposed by Jews in the early Christian centuries, but it became common in the medieval period in spite of Talmudic prohibition. The ink of the Qumran manuscripts was not metallic, but vegetable or carbon.[27] The fact that these inks long continued in use alongside the metallic ink (and are still prescribed for use in Torah scrolls) makes these inks of little use in dating manuscripts, other than favoring an earlier over a medieval date. The inks used by the early scribes did not penetrate deeply, but could be washed off with a sponge or something similar. When it faded the script could be restored. Yet both the Egyptian papyri and the Qumran manuscripts show that the ancient world could produce an ink of remarkable permanence, far more enduring than the later metallic ink.

25. Cf. J. J. Stamm 1953: 302 on this passage.
26. The ink used on the Lachish ostraca has been analyzed as metallic (cf. p. 140). According to G. R. Driver 1954: 86, nonmetallic ink was used for parchment, metallic for papyrus. According to T. C. Skeat 1969: 61, the practice among Greek scribes was practically the reverse.
27. Cf. H. J. Plenderleith in Barthélemy and Milik 1955: 39.

II. The Masoretic Text[1]

1. General Considerations

The Hebrew text of the Old Testament is called *Masoretic* because in its present form it is based on the Masora (Hebrew מָסוֹרֶת),[2] the textual tradition of the Jewish scholars known as the Masoretes. It is designated by the symbol 𝔐 in both the *Biblia Hebraica* edited by Rudolf Kittel (BHK) and the *Biblia Hebraica Stuttgartensia* (BHS).

𝔐   (a) In BHK since the third edition, 𝔐 has represented the text of Ms. B 19^A of the Saltykov-Shchedrin State Public Library of St. Petersburg, written in A.D. 1008 (L, Leningradensis; pl. 24). The fourth edition of *Biblia Hebraica,* the *Biblia Hebraica Stuttgartensia* (BHS), edited by Karl Elliger and Wilhelm Rudolph, is also based on the same manuscript.[3] The first two editions, like most other editions (e.g., Christian D. Ginsburg, 1908ff.),

𝔅   followed the edition of Jacob ben Chayyim (𝔅) printed by Daniel Bomberg in Venice, 1524-25, which was based on late medieval manuscripts. In BHK and BHS, then, we have a text that is centuries older than that of any previously printed edition. But even this manuscript which underlies BHK and BHS is remarkably recent when we consider the age of the Old Testament and compare it with the important fourth- and fifth-century

---

1. I. Yeivin 1980.
2. This broad use of the word Masora to include the whole "philology of the Hebrew Bible," including all the varied activities which go into the transmission of the text (transcription with all its special features, pointing, and the Masora in the narrow sense, cf. p. 28), seems to derive from the Jewish scholar Elias Levita (1469-1549), while in the golden age of the Masoretes it had a special meaning (cf. pp. 13, 28); cf. R. Edelmann 1968: 116-123. M. Gertner 1960 proposes a complex development of the term.
3. On the making of BHS, cf. D. Kellermann (editorial assistant) 1977.

manuscripts of the Greek Old and New Testaments. In fact, we do not have any Hebrew manuscript of the entire Old Testament written earlier than the tenth century. The oldest dated codex (pl. 20) contains only the Prophets and dates from A.D. 895 (Codex Cairensis, cf. p. 35).

In the latter half of the nineteenth century many fragments from the sixth to the eighth century were found in an *Old Cairo* synagogue which until A.D. 882 had been St. Michael's Church. They were discovered there in the *Geniza,* a kind of storage room where worn or faulty manuscripts were kept hidden until they could be disposed of formally (Aramaic גנז "to hide") to avoid misusing or profaning a manuscript containing the holy name of God. Periodically the contents of a Geniza would be buried in the ground with due ceremony. It was only by accident that the Cairo manuscripts escaped this fate: at some time the Geniza was walled over and its existence forgotten.

It is even more coincidental that a number of substantially earlier Hebrew manuscripts, some dating from the pre-Christian era, were hidden during the first and second centuries A.D. in various caves in the Judean desert, especially in the vicinity of the Essene settlement of Khirbet Qumran (pl. 7-15b) near the Dead Sea, and remained there for nearly two millennia to be found in a succession of discoveries since 1947. Among them are found the biblical book of Isaiah in its entirety, the first two chapters of Habakkuk, and fragments of all the other Old Testament books except Esther (cf. pp. 31f.). But despite the importance of these discoveries for scholarly research, the fact remains that for the entire Old Testament we are dependent on manuscripts of the tenth century A.D. and later. This is to be expected because Jewish regulations required the destruction of worn and defective manuscripts. And when scholars had finally established the text in the tenth century, all older manuscripts which represented *earlier stages* of its development were naturally considered defective, and in the course of time they disappeared. It is also true that manuscripts were often destroyed during the medieval persecutions of the Jews, sometimes by their adversaries, but sometimes also by the Jews themselves to prevent their sacred books from falling into the hands of infidels.

In evaluating the significance of surviving manuscripts for textual studies we should remember that although most of them are relatively late, their age is neither the sole nor primary criterion of their worth. When papyrus fragments of the Greek classical authors were discovered which were centuries older than the medieval manuscripts previously known, they aroused high expectations, especially in lay circles; but on examination their texts proved to be inferior. This was because the medieval manuscripts

were based on the careful studies of the great Alexandrian philologists, while the papyri which circulated in the provinces of Egypt represented the range of textual corruption which made the critical work of the Alexandrian scholars so necessary. More important than age, then, is the *textual tradition* represented by a manuscript (Georgio Pasquali: *codices recentiores — non deteriores* "later manuscripts, but not inferior").[4] This holds for the Hebrew text of the Old Testament as well; the history of the transmission of the text must be considered when forming a judgment.

(b) Until the Age of Humanism and the Reformation the Hebrew text and its transmission remained primarily a Jewish concern. In the first millennium A.D., during which the basic lines of transmission were set, we should distinguish between the Jews of Palestine, the *Western Masoretes* (Occidentales, מַעַרְבָּאֵי), and the members of the great Jewish colony in Babylonia, the *Eastern Masoretes* (Orientales, מַדִינְחָאֵי). The Western school centered at Tiberias until the end of the third century, and again from the eighth to the tenth century; the Eastern centers were the schools at Sura,[5] Nehardea (destroyed A.D. 259), and later at Pumbeditha, which were authoritative in matters of Jewish scholarship for centuries. Gradually the Babylonian schools lost their significance, and in the tenth and eleventh centuries they disappeared. Once again the West assumed the spiritual leadership of Judaism, and the Western Masoretes sought to eliminate all traces of textual traditions that differed from their own. The views of the school of Tiberias became determinative for the future, and the Eastern tradition was forgotten for a millennium.

(c) It is well known that for many centuries the Hebrew text of the Old Testament existed as a purely consonantal text. Vowel signs were not added to the text until a later stage, when the consonantal text was already well established with a long history of transmission behind it. The history of the consonantal text and of its vowel pointing therefore must be considered separately.

(d) In the golden age of the Masoretic tradition the scholars who devoted themselves to the textual transmission of the Old Testament were apparently designated by their special functions.[6] The *Sopherim*[7] wrote out

---

4. Cf. G. Pasquali 1952: xvff.

5. The Masoretes of Sura (Sorae) are indicated in BH by the siglum Sor.

6. E. Levine 1982.

7. For the history of the word *sopher,* cf. J. Jeremias 1964: 740. During the Israelite kingdom the word *sopher* indicated the incumbent of a high political office; in Judaism it came to mean a legal scholar, one who knows the Torah, or an ordained theologian. For Josephus (37/38-early second century A.D.) it means a scribe.

Occ
Or

Sor

the consonantal text proper, the *Nakdanim* (from נקד "to point") added
vowel points and accents to the manuscript, and the *Masoretes* added the
marginal and final Masoretic notes (cf. pp. 28f.).[8] The same person could
serve more than one function: for obvious reasons the vowel points and
the Masoretic notes were frequently added by the same scholar. For example, Shelomo ben Buyaʿa wrote the Aleppo Codex, and Aaron ben Asher
was responsible for its pointing and Masoretic notes (cf. p. 174); the same
Shelomo ben Buyaʿa wrote a Torah manuscript in A.D. 930 (cf. p. 178), to
which Ephraim, the son of Rabbi Buyaʿa, added the points and Masora.
According to its colophon, the Leningrad Codex was the work of one man:
Samuel ben Jacob not only wrote it, but pointed it and added the Masora
as well.

2. The Consonantal Text

The consonantal text which is preserved in the medieval manuscripts and
forms the basis of our present editions goes back to about A.D. 100. As part
of the great Jewish revival which marked the decades after the catastrophe
of A.D. 70, the canonical status of certain disputed books of the Old Testament was defined at the Council of Jamnia (late first century A.D.), and an
authoritative text of the Old Testament was also established. Such a text
became a necessity once the canon was defined, and Rabbi Akiba (*ca.* A.D.
55-137) popularized an exegetical method which found significance in the
smallest details and peculiarities of the text. Paul Kahle's suggestion that
an authoritative text of the Torah was established on the basis of early
manuscripts that were then available[9] has been questioned in recent years.[10]
Actually there are many considerations which suggest that the traditional
text of the Hebrew Scriptures was not the result of a planned recension. It
is necessary to distinguish between the Torah and the other books. Even
though there is no known reference in the rabbinic literature to text-critical
or recensional activity such as was applied to the classical Greek text by
the philologists of Alexandria, yet the textual state of the Torah is so
superior to that of the other books that the possibility of its deliberate
revision cannot be ruled out. This is because the Torah was peculiarly

8. R. Edelmann 1968.
9. P. Kahle 1951: 28f.
10. Cf. B. Albrektson 1978. Albrektson does not distinguish clearly enough, in
my opinion, between the treatment of the Torah and the other books.

central to the life and thought of the Rabbis, while the other books were of relatively lesser interest for them. Bertil Albrektson would have to agree that these other books stand in contrast to the Torah by their numerous flaws which belie any careful revision, such as orthographical inconsistency, and the frequency of transposed letters, haplography and dittography, errors of word division and word combination, and the like. Evidently for these books the text which was preserved in the period after A.D.70 was simply that of the dominant group — the Pharisees, while the textual forms favored by other groups of lesser or waning importance disappeared. Thus the standard text of about A.D. 100 should be considered the result of historical developments following the fall of Jerusalem. Since the Torah was always the central concern of the Pharisees, they must have had the best manuscripts available.

Naturally we may assume that this standard text was not completely a new creation: the Rabbis obviously relied on earlier traditions. This fact is demonstrated in an interesting way by the manuscripts from Qumran because there are some among them which are quite close to the Masoretic text. The second Isaiah scroll from Qumran Cave 1 (1QIs[b]), for example, does not differ essentially from the Masoretic text as it is found in the late medieval tradition. This would seem to justify Bleddyn J. Roberts' reference to the "likely existence of a pre-Massoretic 'Massoretic' text."[11] But despite all the superficial similarities there is one decisive difference: the Qumran text of the Masoretic type was only one of several different types in common use (see below), and there is no indication that it was regarded as more authoritative than the others. We may infer that for Qumran, and evidently for the rest of Judaism as well, there was not yet a single authoritative text. It was not until the Jewish revival that one of the existing texts, or a recension of one of these texts, gained a position of authority, eventually displacing almost completely the other forms of the text which were in use among the Jews before A.D. 70. The texts from Murabba‘at show that by A.D. 132/135 this text had prevailed (cf. p. 164). We would know nothing about the varieties of text which circulated in the previous centuries if it were not for the Samaritan Pentateuch (cf. p. 45), the Nash Papyrus (cf. p. 34), the Septuagint (cf. pp. 50ff.), and above all the biblical texts from Qumran. At Qumran three groups of text may be distinguished, related to the Samaritan Pentateuch, the Septuagint, and the Masoretic text respectively.

How this plurality of text types is related to the history of the text

11. B. J. Roberts 1959/60: 144.

has not yet been fully explained. Following William F. Albright, Frank M. Cross would interpret them as local Palestinian, Egyptian, and Babylonian (?) textual forms. Shemaryahu Talmon has responded with the objection that the theory of three local texts can hardly explain satisfactorily the plurality of text types at the end of the pre-Christian era.[12] He regards these as texts which circulated in various social and religious groups, and which were characterized by differences because "the ancient authors, compilers, tradents and scribes enjoyed what may be termed a controlled freedom of textual variation"[13] in the period before the text was standardized. Talmon also assumes that there were yet other forms of the text which have disappeared along with the groups they served. According to Emanuel Tov[14] the problem is not one of text types, but of "independent texts" which were mutually related in a complex web of agreements, differences, and peculiar readings. Cross apparently assumes a Hebrew archetype of the sixth/fifth century B.C. which developed local textual families through the natural processes of scribal transmission (not of intentional recensions),[15] while for Talmon the surviving material leads to the conclusion that "from the very first stage of its manuscript transmission, the Old Testament text was known in a variety of traditions which differed from each other to a greater or less degree."[16] More clarification is needed, some of which may come from the yet unpublished texts from Qumran Cave 4, before reliable conclusions may be drawn about the plurality of texts.[17]

The surviving non-Masoretic texts are more or less distinguished by characteristics that somewhat parallel the relationship of the Chronicler to the books of Samuel and Kings, e.g., they tend to use *matres lectionis* more frequently than does 𝔐, they assimilate words to contemporary spoken forms, e.g., they Aramaize (sometimes using על for אל), they prefer hiphil forms, they replace the imperative use of the infinitive absolute with the simple imperative form, and so on. They also frequently supplement the text with material from parallel passages.

In contrast to these texts the Masoretic text gives the impression of greater age and reliability. Its relation to the ***original form of the text,***

12. Talmon 1970: 198 (= *QHBT,* 40); cf. also E. Tov 1982: 11-28; F. M. Cross 1975.

13. Talmon 1975: 326.

14. E. Tov 1981: 274.

15. F. M. Cross 1966: 85.

16. Talmon 1970: 198.

17. F. M. Cross 1961: 188. For further discussion cf. C. Rabin 1955; S. Talmon 1964; F. M. Cross 1964, 1966; P. W. Skehan 1965; H. P. Scanlin 1993: 27-38.

however, is quite another matter. This becomes evident from a comparison of texts which have a double transmission (2 Sam. 22 = Ps. 18; 2 Kgs. 18:13–20:19 = Isa. 36–39; 2 Kgs 24:18–25:30 = Jer. 52; Isa. 2:2-4 = Mic. 4:1-3; Ps. 14 = Ps. 53; Ps. 40:14-18 = Ps. 70), and the books of Samuel and Kings with their related passages in Chronicles.

The conservative principles of those who established and preserved the text may be observed in some of the features which have survived in 𝔐 to the present day.[18]

(a) **Special points** (puncta extraordinaria). In fifteen passages there are special points found over particular letters or words: Gen. 16:5; 18:9; 19:33; 33:4; 37:12; Num. 3:39; 9:10; 21:30; 29:15; Deut. 29:28; 2 Sam. 19:20; Isa. 44:9; Ezek. 41:20; 46:22; Ps. 27:13. These points register textual or doctrinal reservations on the part of scribes (sopherim) who dared not alter the text they held sacrosanct.[19]

(b) **Inverted nun** (nun inversum). This occurs nine times: before Num. 10:35; after Num. 10:36; and in Ps. 107:21-26, 40. Kahle agrees with Ludwig Blau in understanding it as an abbreviation of נָקוּד "pointed." The נ is inverted to distinguish it from the letters in the text: the question may have to do with the position of the verses marked.

Seb   (c) **Sebirin.** In numerous instances (Christian D. Ginsburg notes altogether about 350 in different manuscripts) a marginal note to an unusual word or usage in the text is introduced by סָבִיר (passive participle of Aramaic סְבַר "to suppose") and proceeds to give the usual form or the expected expression, e.g., Gen. 19:8 הָאֵל for הָאֵלֶּה, Gen. 49:13 the meaning עַל for עַד, Gen. 19:23 the masculine יָצָא for the expected feminine יָצְאָה, etc.[20]

K, Q   (d) **Kethib and Qere.** In many instances the traditional text was felt to be unsatisfactory on grammatical, esthetic, or doctrinal grounds. The solution was found in providing an alternative reading to that found in the text: the distinction was made between the כְּתִיב, the written form which could not be altered, and the קְרִי, the form to be read, with its consonants written in the margin and its vowel points written with the consonants of the כְּתִיב. But not all instances of Kethib-Qere, which number more than 1,300, represent corrections of this kind. In many instances they preserve

18. On the following, cf. Yeivin 1980: 44ff.
19. Cf. S. Talmon 1969.
20. Another (less likely) view is represented by Yeivin 1980: 62f.: the note "Sebir" does not intend to correct the text, but rather to indicate that the reading which would avoid the difficulty of the text (i.e., the Sebir itself) is incorrect; thus it stands in support of the traditional text.

textual variants which were regarded as too important to ignore or forget when the official text was established.[21]

Yet the restoration of the early traditional text, reconstructing and preserving it even where it was open to criticism, is only one of the marks of (rabbinic) occupation with the text. A second mark reveals an opposite tendency. There is clear evidence that no qualms were felt in altering the text when there appeared to be adequate doctrinal reasons. For example, proper names which include the abhorred name of בעל as an element usually retain their original form in the Chronicles while they were altered in the parallel passages of Samuel and Kings.[22] This shows that the second part of the Old Testament, the Prophets, ranked higher in canonical esteem than the Writings, and was subjected to a more thorough revision with doctrinally objectionable elements consistently purged. Jewish tradition preserved the record of these textual alterations in notes known as the *Tiqqune sopherim* and the *Itture sopherim*.

(a) The **Tiqqune sopherim** (תקוני ספרים "scribal corrections"). The tradition of their number is not without ambiguities: a Masoretic tradition indicates eighteen instances where corrections were made with the primary purpose of removing objectionable expressions referring to God. The context of Gen. 18:22 indicates that the original reading was "but YHWH remained standing before Abraham." The idiom "to stand before someone," however, can also mean "to stand in service before someone, to serve" (e.g., Gen. 41:46; 1 Kgs. 1:2), and as this was considered inappropriate at Gen. 18:22, it was changed to the present form. The other corrections: Num. 11:15; 12:12; 1 Sam. 3:13; 2 Sam. 16:12 (בעיני for בעוני);

Tiq soph

---

21. G. Gerleman 1948 has concluded that some of the Qeres represent popular variants, based on his observation that many of the Qeres in Samuel and Kings are found in the text of Chronicles, which preserves a more popular type of text. On the Variant Theory cf. further: R. Gordis 1937; A. Rubinstein 1959; H. M. Orlinsky 1960. Orlinsky suggests that the Jewish scholars of about A.D. 600 who attempted to establish a firm text for vocalization worked with three manuscripts. When these differed, the reading of the majority was automatically accepted for vocalization (Qere), and that of the minority was left unvocalized (Kethib). Yet there are many questions that remain even in Orlinsky's proposal, although there is much in favor of the Variant Theory. An interesting explanation has been proposed by J. Barr 1981. He distinguishes a writing tradition (Kethib) and a reading tradition (Qere): the scribe knew by heart how the text should be read, but the written text could not be altered. The purpose of the procedure was to protect the correct form of the text, i.e., the Kethib. Cf. also D. Kellermann 1980.

22. Cf. 1 Chr. 14:7 בעלידע — 2 Sam. 5:16 אלידע; 1 Chr. 8:33; 9:39 אשבעל — 2 Sam. 2:8ff. איש־בשת; 1 Sam. 8:34; 9:40 מריב בעל — 2 Sam. 4:4, etc. מפיבשת. Cf. Gerleman 1948: 23.

20:1 (לאהליו for לאלהיו, similarly 1 Kgs. 12:16; 2 Chr. 10:16); Jer. 2:11; Ezek. 8:17; Hos. 4:7 כבודם בקלון אמיר for כבודי בקלון המירו); Hab. 1:12; Zech. 2:12; Mal. 1:13; Ps. 106:20; Job 7:20; 32:3; Lam. 3:20 (for details cf. BH apparatus).

Recent studies[23] have shown that actual emendations are found only in 1 Sam. 3:13; Zech. 2:12; and Job 7:20. The other instances represent midrashic interpretation. But many passages not included in the lists attest to early scribal activity with emendations from theological and other motives (e.g., 2 Sam. 12:9, 14; 1 Kgs. 9:8; Job 1:5; 2:9).

(b) The *Itture sopherim* (עטורי ספרים "scribal omissions"). The Babylonian Talmud (*Ned.* 37b) records that the scribes omitted a ו four times with the word אחר (Gen. 18:5; 24:55; Num. 31:2; Ps. 68:26), and once more with משפטיך (Ps. 36:7). Seven passages are also named where certain words are to be read although they are not in the text (קרי ולא כתיב: 2 Sam. 8:3; 16:23; Jer. 31:38; 50:29; Ruth 2:11; 3:5, 17), and five passages where the words in the text are not to be read (כתיב ולא קרי: 2 Kgs. 5:18; Jer. 32:11; 51:3; Ezek. 48:16; Ruth 3:12). Most of these are noted in the Masora of BH.

We can scarcely err in regarding the evidence of these traditions as merely a small fragment of a far more extensive process (cf. also pp. 111f.).

The designation of a particular form of the text as authoritative, to be transmitted thenceforth to the practical exclusion of all other forms, marks a critical turning point in the history of the Old Testament text. The existence of various forms of the text alongside each other, as we find in the situation at Qumran, now became as impossible within Judaism as the free treatment of the text which had given rise to that situation. From this time onward the transmission of the text was to be governed by strict regulations. No pains were spared in preventing errors from entering the sacred text, or in discovering and eliminating them if they should creep in. This was the function of the tradition, the Masora, and it is in this sense that R. Akiba says of it: "The Masora is a (protective) fence about the Law."[24] This was the purpose of the scribes' meticulous work. They counted the verses, words, and letters of the Law and other parts of the Scriptures as a procedural aid in monitoring manuscripts and in checking

23. Cf. the thorough study by C. McCarthy 1981.

24. It is not certain, however, whether in Rabbi Akiba's statement (*Pirqe Aboth* 3:13) the word "Masora" refers to the activities of textual transmission, as it is usually understood (cf. e.g., W. Bacher 1899: 108. H. L. Strack and P. Billerbeck 1922: 693, interprets "Masora" here as the Oral Law. R. Akiba would mean that the Tradition of the Fathers (the Oral Law) was intended to prevent the violation of the Written Law.

their accuracy. One Talmudic passage even derives the name "scribe" from this very practice, suggesting that the ancients were called Sopherim because they counted (סופרים) all the letters of the Torah. They found, for example, that the letter ו of גחון in Lev. 11:42 was the middle letter of the Torah, that the word דרש of Lev. 10:16 was its middle word, etc. It is due to these scribes and their successors that many letters are written in some peculiar way, such as the raised letters of מֹשֶׁה Judg. 18:30 (to be read מֹשֶׁה; cf. the apparatus *in loco*), מִיַּעַר Ps. 80:14 (the middle letter of the Psalter), etc. In fact, it is to them that we may trace the beginnings of those textual studies that later found their formulation in the Masora.

Their greatest importance for the history of the text, however, was their contribution to the universal acceptance of an authoritative, established text which must have appeared to many at the time to be an innovation despite its continuity with an earlier form of the text. The Hebrew manuscripts of the medieval period show a remarkably consistent form of the text, even in the forms of certain peculiarly written letters, and other minor details.

The most plausible explanation of this was long considered to be Paul de Lagarde's theory, first published in 1863, that the Hebrew manuscripts of the medieval period all derived from a single exemplar, an *archetype* made in the second century A.D. In 1797 E. F. C. Rosenmüller was more accurate when he traced the surviving manuscripts of the Hebrew text to a *recension,* but his insight remained ignored even though he repeated it in 1834 in the introduction to the Tauchnitz edition of the Hebrew Old Testament.[25] Yet we have learned today, especially from the material found in the Cairo Geniza, that for centuries there existed texts with variant readings (granting the variants were few); the same inference may be gathered from the biblical quotations (which differ from the text of 𝔐) in the writings of Jewish scholars as late as the eighth century and beyond.[26] Similarly, the fact that a group of medieval Masoretic manuscripts agrees with the Samaritan text in many details, as Johannes Hempel has demonstrated for Deuteronomy,[27] can be explained, in my opinion, by the long-continuing influence of non-Masoretic traditions in the transmission of the

25. The theories of Rosenmüller and Lagarde were long confused with each other; for clarification cf. M. H. Goshen-Gottstein 1967: 254-273, on the forerunners of Lagarde, 1967: 261f. (= *QHBT,* 1975, 53-72 and 60f. respectively). Goshen-Gottstein is right to indicate that in Rosenmüller's time the term "recension" did not yet connote an "almost complete 'official' regulation."

26. Cf. Aptowitzer 1906-15.

27. J. Hempel 1934: 254-274; 1959.

text. We should therefore assume that when the consonantal text was established *ca.* A.D. 100, it did not result in the immediate suppression of all other forms of the text, but that manuscripts with variant texts continued to circulate for a long time, especially in private hands. The impressive unity of tenth-century and later manuscripts is due, as Kahle in particular has shown, to the work of the earlier and later Masoretes who championed the established text and assisted it to victory over all the variant forms of the text.

Divisions. BH indicates various divisions of the Old Testament books which were customary among Jews to a certain extent even at an early date,[28] long before the text was divided into chapters. We should note first the division of the entire Old Testament (except the Psalter)[29] into *open* and *closed paragraphs* (Parashah, plural Parashoth). An open paragraph (פְּתוּחָא) is one that starts a new line after an empty or incomplete line; a closed paragraph (סְתוּמָא) is separated from its preceding paragraph by a short space within the line. Eventually this distinction was ignored in the actual written format, but a prefixed פ (פתוחא) or ס (סתומא) continued to indicate the distinction. BH observes this usage.[30]

ס, פ

A second division of the text into somewhat larger sections of some 452 *Sedarim* (סֵדֶר "order, sequence"). This was of Palestinian origin: it provided a sufficient number of Sedarim (weekly lessons) for the three-year lectionary cycle which was the original Palestinian usage. In Babylonia, where the Torah was read through each year, the division was made into fifty-four (or fifty-three) *Parashoth* (weekly lessons). BH indicates the beginning of a Seder by ס, and the beginning of a Parashah by פרש in the margin (BHS: the inner margin).

פרש ,ס

28. Even in the manuscripts at Qumran a division into Parashoth may already be observed, although it agrees only partly with the Masoretic divisions and occurs with differences in the individual manuscripts (e.g., 1QIs[a] and 1QIs[b]); cf. H. Bardtke 1953a: 33-75; 1961: 91ff. Maimonides (1135-1204) still complained that manuscripts were inconsistent in observing the open and closed Parashoth. In order to remedy the situation he prepared a kind of model Torah scroll, basing it on the authority of the well-known Cairo Codex, which is probably to be identified with the Aleppo Codex (cf. p. 36). Cf. I. Ben-Zvi 1960: 7; M. H. Goshen-Gottstein 1966: 55f.

29. I. Yeivin 1969 reports on a list of open and closed paragraphs in the Psalter which he found in the Geniza fragments at the Bodleian Library, Oxford.

30. J. M. Oesch 1979, after surveying a wide range of materials, including Jewish tradition, medieval biblical manuscripts, texts from the Dead Sea and the Judean desert, and nonbiblical documents from the Near East, concluded that most probably the final redactor of the Torah and the Prophets followed a common custom of antiquity by the use of spacing to distinguish major units and subdivisions of the text. Of course, the assumption of a "final redactor" is open to question.

Verse divisions were also already known in the Talmudic period, with differing Babylonian and Palestinian traditions, but they were not given numbers as subdivisions of chapters until the sixteenth century. The division into *chapters,* a system derived from Stephen Langton (1150-1228), was adopted in Hebrew manuscripts from the Latin Vulgate in the fourteenth century.

3. Pointing

In the matter of vocalization the situation was quite different because there was no written tradition of symbols for indicating the pronunciation or intonation of a text. It is not known when pointing originated. The earlier assignment of its beginnings to the fifth century has come under serious criticism. Bruno Chiesa's study of indirect sources suggests a time between A.D. 650 and 750 as more probable, because the Babylonian Talmud which was completed about A.D. 600 makes no reference to pointing.[31] Moshe Goshen-Gottstein also assumes a time around A.D. 700 as probable. He believes the invention of vowel signs and accents was induced by the Islamic conquests which threatened to extinguish the tradition of precise liturgical recitation.[32] Yet there must have been many factors which necessitated the development of a written system for indicating pronunciation and intonation.[33] Even with the support of a strong oral tradition it was inadequate to have simply a fixed consonantal text together with an occasional use of vowel letters *(matres lectionis)* to indicate pronunciation, as in the proto-Masoretic text. It still left too many words ambiguous in pronunciation and meaning. Further, there was no guidance for intonation, which was essential for liturgical usage.

There was evidently a need felt at an early stage for aids to reading the sacred text. Before the consonantal text was authoritatively established, while it was still possible to treat it with freedom, the proper reading could be indicated by a frequent use of *vowel letters.*[34] A valuable witness for

---

31. B. Chiesa 1979: 36f.

32. M. H. Goshen-Gottstein 1979: 154-156.

33. Cf. M. H. Goshen-Gottstein 1963: 94 (Leimann 1974: 681), n. 52, where he assumes that the development was motivated primarily by internal causes ("dangers of sectarianism, deviating traditions over the centuries, didactic needs, etc.").

34. The use of vowel letters is very ancient; the earliest evidence is in Aramaic documents of about the ninth century B.C. (F. M. Cross and D. N. Freedman 1952) and they are found, although sparingly, in the Siloam inscription (cf. p. 138) and the Lachish ostraca (cf. p. 140).

this stage is provided not only by the Samaritan text, but also by the Isaiah scroll (1QIs^a = Q^a; cf. p. 33), with its abundance of scriptio plena forms. The authoritative consonantal text of the second century followed the earlier usage in reducing significantly the use of the scriptio plena, and ended the practice of inserting vowel letters at will. It seems that another solution was then found. Transliterations were prepared for those Jewish believers who needed them, giving the proper pronunciation of the Hebrew text in the Greek alphabet. Christians also made use of this practice: an example is found in the second column of Origen's *Hexapla,* but Jewish sources also seem to refer to the practice.[35] Eventually from the seventh century A.D. a system of vowel signs written above and below the consonants was adopted, patterned perhaps after Syriac usage. This system was called *pointing,* from the Jewish technical term (Hebrew נָקֵד). At the first stage vowel signs were inserted occasionally in the biblical text to indicate the proper pronunciation required by the liturgical usage of the time (Kahle). This situation is reflected in many of the Geniza fragments, and the Samaritans never advanced beyond it. The next stage was to point the entire text fully. Different systems of pointing eventually developed in the East and the West: the Babylonian, the Palestinian, and finally the Tiberian. The following signs were used.[36]

Babylonian	⊻ ā	⊥ ⸱ } ä	⸱⸱ e	⊷ i	⸳ o	⸓ u
Palestinian	⊷ å	⊷ a	⸳ e / ⊷ æ ⸲ e	⸳ i	⸳⸳ o	⸳⸳⸳ u
Tiberian	⊤ å	⊤ a	⸳⸳ æ	⸳⸳⸳ e	⸳ i	⸳ o	⸳ ּו u

The **Babylonian** system is supralinear. Originally the consonants א, ע, י, and ו were used for the vowels ā, a, i, and u, and in a simplified form they later became the regular vowel signs. This system developed in two stages, an older and simpler stage represented in the fragments of the

---

35. P. Kahle 1959: 158ff. J. A. Emerton 1970 considers the sayings adduced as evidence for the use of such transliterations as unconvincing. But was this a totally new venture on Origen's part? It is improbable.

36. Adapted from P. Kahle in H. Bauer and P. Leander 1922: 102.

seventh century (BHK: Ea, Eb, Ec),[37] and a later, more complex stage appearing in fragments from the eighth and ninth centuries (BHK: Ka, Kb, Kc). The development of the complex system may have been related to the appearance of the Karaites, the sect founded about A.D. 760 by 'Anan ben David. They rejected the Talmud for a more literal interpretation of the text, giving rise to a new interest in the text of the Bible and the necessity for determining its pronunciation as closely as possible. In BHK, pp. xliv-xlvii, Kahle has compiled a list of the Babylonian fragments known to him, derived from more than 120 manuscripts.[38] Variants from the manuscripts which Kahle collected and in part published in *Masoreten des Ostens* (1913) are cited in BHK as V(ar)^{Ka}. The quantity of known material containing biblical texts with Babylonian pointing (but lacking in any uniformity) has since been significantly increased.[39]

The Babylonian tradition was preserved in Yemen into the twelfth and thirteenth centuries. Under the influence of Tiberian pointing a characteristic **Yemenite** tradition was later developed reflecting a simplified Tiberian system with supralinear signs.

The **Palestinian** system, also supralinear, was less adequate. A system found in some Samaritan manuscripts from the twelfth to the fourteenth century was clearly derived from it. Kahle published the relatively few and textually varying biblical fragments (seventh to ninth century) in *Masoreten der Westens,* 2 (1930); they are cited in BHK as V(ar)^{pal}.[40] Their signifi-

37. Manuscripts with this pointing were presumably still available to the editors of the Complutensian Polyglot (1514-1517); cf. pl. 47 and comments.

38. Cf. also the list in *ZAW* 46 (1928) with seventy magnificent facsimiles. Kahle concludes from the fragments Eb 4 and Eb 8 (from a single manuscript) that an older system using only dots and related to the system of the Eastern Syrians antedated the Babylonian system discussed here (P. Kahle 1959: 65f.).

39. Díez Merino 1975 has published a catalogue of all known (Hebrew and Aramaic) biblical fragments. Editions of surviving Babylonian texts in *Textos y Estudios "Cardinal Cisneros"* edited under the supervision of F. Pérez Castro: *Biblia Babilónica. Edicion critica segun manuscritos babilonica: Proverbios* (1976) and *Profetas menores* (1977) edited by A. Navarro Peiro, *Ezequiel* (1980) and *Isaias* (1980) by A. Alba Cecilia, and *Fragmentos de Salmos, Job y Proverbios* (1987; Jewish Theological Seminary, New York, Ms. 508) by A. Díez Macho and A. Navarro Peiro.

40. Díez Macho 1954: 247-265 has published some further fragments from the Library of the Jewish Theological Seminary of America. Besides the biblical texts there are fragments of Targums, Mishnah, Midrash, Masora, and liturgical texts, thus suggesting that this pointing was widely known in Palestine. For further material and a sketch of Hebrew grammar in the Palestinian tradition we are indebted to A. Murtonen 1958-62. Further: M. Dietrich 1968; I. Yeivin 1963; E. J. Revell 1969. Cf. also P. Kahle 1961: 24-31. A list of biblical manuscripts with Palestinian or related pointing is given in E. J. Revell 1977: 7-34. B. Chiesa 1978 has produced a comprehensive study,

cance lies in showing how the vocalized Hebrew manuscripts of the Bible first appeared when the Masoretes of Tiberias began their work. Basically they lack the strict consistency of the Tiberian Masoretes in indicating pronunciation.

Masoretic activity flourished again in the West in the period A.D. 780-930, evidently stimulated by Karaite influence.[41] Tiberias was the center of these studies. The imperfect Palestinian system was inadequate to the demands of this period, and it was found less adaptable than the Babylonian system. So a new *Tiberian* system was created, based on the experience of the Palestinian system, which combined the accent system with a means of indicating finer nuances, and could represent the pronunciation and intonation of the biblical text in its minutest details. This Tiberian system supplanted its two predecessors so thoroughly that their very existence was forgotten for centuries and rediscovered only in the nineteenth and twentieth centuries.

Within the Masoretic center of Tiberias there were several different parties or schools. The Ben Asher family was outstanding among them: its last two members are known today for the model manuscripts Codex Cairensis and the Aleppo Codex (cf. p. 36). But we know that there were
Naft   other Tiberian Masoretes besides the Ben Ashers; Ben Naphtali is the best known among them. The Jewish scholar Mishael ben 'Uzziel in his famous tractate *Kitab al-Khilaf* (eleventh to twelfth century) discusses Aaron ben Moses ben Asher.[42] It was once thought that these two schools were diametrically opposed, because Ben Naphtali's text was identified with manuscripts that have nothing to do with him (see below). But if we read carefully the statement by Mishael, which is our only reliable source for

---

including a survey of research, a catalogue of "Palestinian" biblical fragments, lists of variant readings, etc. He traces this textual family (which is closely related to the Hebrew Vorlage of the Greek version) to priestly groups who went to northern Arabia (Hidschas) after A.D. 70 and returned to Palestine (the southern Jordan valley) under pressure from Caliph Omar (634-644). "Palestinian" pointing flourished, according to Chiesa, *ca.* A.D. 700-850.

41. The Ben Asher family itself apparently belonged to the Karaite community. The arguments demonstrating this relationship have been assembled by N. Wieder 1956/57: 97-113, 269-292, and P. Kahle 1959: 80-82. I. Ben Zvi 1960 challenges this with a reference to A. Dotan 1957: 280-312, 350-362 (English trans. 1977); cf. also D. S. Loewinger 1960: 88-92. In his study of the vocalization of the Qere-Kethib in A (cf. pp. 36, 174), I. Yeivin 1962: 148 also concludes "that the vocalizer of A was most certainly a Karaite." But M. Goshen-Gottstein 1963: 92ff. differs in view of the sharp differences between the rabbinate and the Karaites.

42. Edited by L. Lipschütz 1962, 1964. Cf. J. S. Penkower 1988-89.

Ben Naphtali's text (ignoring as less significant the occasional marginal notes in some manuscripts), it appears that Ben Asher and Ben Naphtali are quite closely related. They differ only eight times in their consonantal text, and these differences are slight. The majority of their differences are concerned with minutiae of vocalization and accent. Specifically, Ben Naphtali influenced the further development of the text by using the metheg far more frequently. There were occasional differences also of pronunciation. The prefixes בְּ, וְ, and לְ before a י were pronounced differently, e.g., בְּיִשְׂרָאֵל by Ben Asher, בִּישְׂרָאֵל by Ben Naphtali. Considering that the differences are limited to such minor details, we must agree with Goshen-Gottstein's judgment that both of these Masoretes represent one and the same school,[43] but that, interestingly enough, Ben Naphtali preserves the text of the older Moses ben Asher more faithfully than does his son Aaron ben Asher (cf. p. 35). This close relationship is also attested by Mishael, who mentions more than four hundred instances where Ben Asher and Ben Naphtali stand in agreement, apparently against other Masoretes.

A tenth-century discussion of the shewa mentions five members of the Ben Asher family and the names of several other Tiberian Masoretes, with an account of their differences over qames and patah, sere and seghol, shewa mobile and shewa quiescens.[44] More than this we do not know. Kahle considers it possible that their pointing was "the predecessor of the punctuation of Codex Reuchlinianus and the large number of related MSS"[45] which he edited in *Masoreten des Westens* 2 (1930): 45-68 as the biblical text of Ben Naphtali, but which are regarded today, with all their differences, as representing a system quite different from that of Ben Asher and Ben Naphtali.[46] Thus Codex Reuchlinianus (written in Italy in A.D. 1105)[47] does not distinguish between long and short vowels, writing the qames and patah, the sere and seghol indiscriminately;[48] even the daghesh does not have the same function. Rudolf Meyer says of this pointing system that "in many respects it is better and more precise, and occasionally more original than anything we have found to date in the best of the Ben Asher manuscripts. . . . Yet it remains true that the Reuchlinian pointing system

43. M. H. Goshen-Gottstein 1963: 112.

44. K. Levy 1936: 8; P. Kahle 1959: 78ff.

45. P. Kahle 1959: 79.

46. This has been rightly pointed out by many, including S. Morag 1959; M. H. Goshen-Gottstein 1963: 108ff., with further bibliography; and others.

47. Facsimile edition: A. Sperber 1956; 1969.

48. R. Meyer 1963: 55.

is based upon different principles, and that its linguistic approach is quite different from Ben Asher."[49]

The fact that such a text was not only widely used in the tenth century[50] but still enjoyed circulation at the beginning of the twelfth century shows that the text of Aaron ben Asher, the last member of his family, achieved the status of an authoritative text, supplanting all rival forms of the text, only through the course of several centuries. The esteem in which the great Jewish philosopher Maimonides (1135-1204) held it may have contributed to its acceptance as authoritative. This text, influenced by Ben Naphtali only in such matters as the insertion of the metheg which Aaron ben Asher had used sparingly, and other minor details of pointing and accent, became accepted by the fourteenth century as a kind of textus receptus and was used, for example, by Jacob ben Chayyim for his edition (cf. p. 39).

From this historical survey it appears that we may assume a fairly constant consonantal text even from the beginning of the second century A.D., but that the pointing and accents of the present text were first formulated in the course of the ninth and tenth centuries as the culmination of centuries of study, research, and experimentation.

There remains finally a question of the ***relationship between the Masoretic and the older Hebrew pronunciation.*** A number of observations have been made questioning the authenticity of the Masoretic pronunciation. More than a millennium separates the Masoretes of Tiberias from the days when Hebrew was a living national language, and it is altogether probable that the pronunciation of Hebrew had undergone some change in this interval, especially considering that it was written without vowels. In fact, Greek and Latin transliterations of the early Hebrew texts do reflect some differences from the pronunciation of the Tiberian Masoretes, as does also the Samaritan tradition. Within the tradition itself there were variations of pronunciation evidenced by differences among

49. R. Meyer 1963: 60. For further characteristics of this group of manuscripts, see below, p. 182. M. H. Goshen-Gottstein 1963: 112ff., calls this text the "Tiberian non-receptus" in contrast to the Ben Asher (and Ben Naphtali) text which he calls the "Tiberian proto-receptus" in order to express the view that this tradition was in its own way just as Masoretic as "our" Tiberian text. I believe that this describes the facts more accurately than any such terms as "pre-Masoretic" (Sperber), "post-Masoretic" (Morag), or "non-Masoretic" (Yeivin). A. Díez Macho 1963 prefers to regard these as "proto-Tiberian" manuscripts deriving from the Palestinian tradition (p. 16). For further examples of these manuscripts wrongly attributed to Ben Naphtali, see J. Prijs 1957.

50. R. Meyer 1966: 35, where he calls this school "Pseudo-Ben Naftali."

the Masoretes, as in the few texts with Palestinian pointing which do not always agree with צ‎, and also the differences between Ben Asher and Ben Naphtali noted above. It would seem necessary, then, to expect a fair number of artificial forms in the Tiberian system, related to the Masoretes' desire to produce a correct pronunciation which made them susceptible to such outside influences as Syriac and Islamic philology. For example, the almost consistent stress on the ultima derives from the Tiberian Masoretes, as does also the double pronunciation of the letters בגדכפת (a Syriac influence). But again, the Tiberian pronunciation agrees with certain forms which were regarded as very late until their antiquity was unexpectedly attested by the free use of vowel letters in the Qumran manuscripts, especially in the first discovered Isaiah scroll (1QIs^a = ℚ^a). For example, the Masoretic pronunciation of the second person singular masculine suffix as -^{e}ka is found in the Isaiah scroll, whereas the other pre-Masoretic texts have the pronunciation -āk. In other instances the Isaiah scroll's pronunciation is found among the Samaritans where the Masoretes clearly use later forms, e.g., the second and third person plural masculine pronouns and suffixes are pronounced 'attimma, lakimma, bahimma, ^{a}lehimma, etc., in the Isaiah scroll and the Samaritan, where the Masoretes have 'attem, lakem, bahem, 'alehem, etc. The Tiberian pronunciation therefore must not be regarded as absolutely authoritative. Much may be said rather for the thesis that "the Tiberian system is related historically to the early medieval period, and should never be adduced as direct evidence for Canaanite-Hebrew usage without careful examination. For between them lies that great complex, of such tremendous importance for the history of the language, which is commonly called pre-Masoretic."[51] There is no question that the Masoretes believed themselves to be preserving the early pronunciation.

Further, the introduction of pointing met with scattered opposition. In the ninth century it was still rejected by the head of a Babylonian school, Gaon Natronai II, on the ground that it did not derive from Sinai. Later its

---

51. R. Meyer 1950: 726. On the whole problem, cf. especially P. Kahle 1959: 141-188; Z. Ben-Ḥayyim 1958: 200-214; K. Beyer 1969: 33, characterizes the Tiberian system in the following way: "Reflections of Old Hebrew, all the stages of Aramaic, and false reconstructions as well are found here mingled together inseparably. And yet the Masoretic material continues to be indispensable, because on the strictest examination it still surpasses all else in its wealth of information." But cf. M. H. Goshen-Gottstein 1963: 94: "In my opinion, the work of the Masoretes . . . is to be understood as the invention and perfection of an ever more refined graphic notation for an age-old tradition."

recent origin was disputed. About A.D. 1100 the Karaite Hadassi stated that God did not create the Torah unpointed, a position revived in an adapted form by Johann Buxtorf the Elder (1564-1629). Following the above discussion no further evidence is necessary to show that the pointing does not possess the same authority as the consonantal text. While this is significant for textual criticism, it should also be remembered that when the Masoretes pointed the text they were not attempting to be original, but rather to preserve with accuracy the tradition they had received.

4. The Masora[52]

ℳ The Masoretic notes which are usually referred to as the Masora in the narrow sense are printed beside the text in BH. Among the Western Masoretes a distinction is drawn between the *marginal Masora* (Masora marginalis) written in the four margins, and the *final Masora* (Masora finalis), an alphabetical arrangement at the end of the Bible. The marginal Mp　Masora is divided into the *Masora parva* (Mp) in the side margins and the Mm　*Masora magna* (Mm) in the upper and lower margins. BHK includes only the Mp reproduced from manuscript L, its textual base. The first volume of Mm, issued as a supplement to BHS, appeared in 1971.[53]

The *Masora parva* offers observations on the literal form of the text designed to assist in preserving the form unaltered. Wherever the text is readily open to transcriptional error there is a note, e.g., when a word could easily be written plene but is written defective, and vice versa; or when the multiple occurrence of a word like את in a single verse might give rise to an omission by oversight. Singular expressions are not simply recorded as such: it is also noted if a similar form or a parallel construction is to be found elsewhere. Thus enumerations are frequent, giving the number of times a particular form occurs, or identifying hapax legomena. Thus, for example, it is noted at Gen. 1:1 that בראשית occurs five times, of which three are at the beginning of a verse, ברא אלהים occurs three times, and the collocation את השמים is found here alone; at Gen. 1:11 ויהי כן is found six times in the same pericope; at Gen. 1:12 that ותוצא occurs three times, twice plene and once defective. Occasionally certain incidental peculiarities are noted, as at Deut. 31:3, that this and two other verses begin and end with the divine name

52. G. E. Weil 1963: 266-284; I. Yeivin 1980: 64-80.
53. G. E. Weil 1971.

יהוה. Also noted in the Mp are the Sebirim, Qeres, etc. Frequently the Masoretic notes may seem strange, trivial, and of no practical value. But we must realize that these are the result of a passionate desire to protect the text, guarding it from willful or careless scribal errors, even in such matters as the use of the vowel letters ו and י, where the writing of a form plene or defective is completely fortuitous, involving neither consistency of usage nor significance for the meaning of the text. The Masora witnesses to an extremely exact revision of the text which demands our respect even though it risks the danger of losing the spirit of the text while concentrating on the letter.

With regard to the Masora in BHS, these facts should be noted: although the text of BHS reproduces manuscript L with the greatest fidelity, the editor of the Masora, Gérard E. Weil, is much freer with it. The notes of the Mp in the margin of BHS are still based on the Mp of L, but its terminology and abbreviations are made consistent in a standardized form, and its references are filled out where the manuscript itself is incomplete. In other words, when the Mp of L indicates multiple occurrences of a word or expression in the text, and a corresponding note is lacking at the parallel passages in L, the editor has supplied corresponding notes at the parallel passages in BHS. The expansion of the Mp in BHS to three times as many entries as in BHK, which reproduces only the references found in L, suggests how frequently such supplements were necessary. The larger part of the Mp in BHS, then, was supplied by the editor who completed the pattern of L where it was defective.

Where the Mp gives statistics on the frequency of a word or an expression's occurrence, the *Masora magna* provides specific lists of these instances; in the early manuscripts these lists are in the upper and lower margins, but in BHS they are given in a supplementary volume. Thus at Gen. 1:1 the Mp reads "בְּרֵאשִׁית five times: three times at the beginning and twice in the middle of a verse." The notes in BHS refer to tables 1 and 2 in Weil's edition of the Mm, where the specific instances are spelled out as in a concordance: Gen. 1:1; Jer. 26:1; 27:1; and Jer. 28:1; 48:34. *Massorah Gedolah* 1 contains a total of 4,282 such lists (including the 11 lists added while the volume was at press). For further information cf. BHS, Foreword II, pp. xiii-xviii.

In the *Masora finalis* the Masoretic material is arranged alphabetically. As the base for the final Masora in his famous Rabbinic Bible, Rabbi Jacob ben Chayyim used a medieval collection entitled *Okhla w^eOkhla*   Okhl (Okhl [Ochla]). This begins with an alphabetical list of words which occur only twice in the Holy Scriptures, once without and once with ו at the

beginning. The collection derives its name from its first entry, which is אכלה (1 Sam. 1:9) ואכלה (Gen. 27:19). It was edited by S. Frensdorff from a Paris manuscript in 1864 (reprint: New York, 1972), and by Fernando Diaz Esteban from a manuscript at Halle in 1975.

The Masoretic material was transmitted orally at first, but as it continued to grow it was progressively entered in manuscripts themselves.

The language of the Masora is primarily Aramaic, but with some Hebrew as well. Obviously the Masora must be adapted to the particular form of the text for which it is intended. There was accordingly an independent Babylonian Masora[54] which differed from the Palestinian in terminology and to some extent in order. The Masora is concise in style and replete with abbreviations, requiring a considerable amount of knowledge for their full understanding. It was quite natural that a later generation of scribes would no longer understand the notes of the Masoretes and would consider them unimportant; by the late medieval period they were reduced to mere ornamentation of the manuscripts. It was Jacob ben Chayyim who restored clarity and order to them (cf. p. 39).

G   **Christian D. Ginsburg** made a survey of the manuscript materials known in his day in an unfinished work of four volumes entitled *The Massorah compiled from manuscripts alphabetically and lexically arranged* (1: 1880; 2: 1883; 3: Appendices, 1885; 4/1: Supplement, 1905; repr. New York, 1968, with a prolegomenon by A. Dotan).

5. Manuscripts

In view of the purpose of this book the present chronological survey includes only those manuscripts, of the large number that exist, which are used in BH or which deserve mention because of their special importance, such as the Nash Papyrus and the Ben Asher Codex of Aleppo.

We may note that Hebrew manuscripts of the Bible from the tenth and eleventh centuries are very rare. The overwhelming majority of manuscripts are from a later period. The most comprehensive collection of Hebrew manuscripts, and the most valuable because of its wealth in early manuscripts, is the State Public Library in St. Petersburg. Two collections were brought there in 1863 and 1876 by the Russian Karaite Abraham Firkowitsch (1785-1874), who had shown an unparalleled zeal in assem-

---

54. G. E. Weil 1962, 1963a, 1963b, 1968.

bling them, mainly from Karaite synagogues of the East.[55] Firkowitsch was
also a notorious forger, frequently adding new colophons or altering the
dates in early manuscripts in order to prove the antiquity of Karaite
Judaism, which was for him the only true Judaism. Yet the manuscripts
which he assembled are of very great importance. The biblical part alone
of the second Firkowitsch collection comprises 1,582 items on parchment
and 725 on paper. Another collection in the same library includes about
1,200 fragments, probably derived from the Cairo Geniza, which were
assembled by Antonin, a Russian archimandrite in Jerusalem.

The most important event in the recent history of the Old Testament
text is the successive discoveries of manuscripts at **Qumran** (ℚ) by the   ℚ
Dead Sea since 1947. These discoveries have put us in possession of
manuscript materials several centuries older than any we had known before,
and coming from a time and a group for which there was no single form
of the text which was regarded and transmitted as exclusively authoritative.
These texts presented us for the first time with a large number of variants.
After the chance discovery of the first cave in 1947, search parties of
archaeologists and Bedouin between 1952 and 1956 led to the discovery
of texts in ten more caves. Especially productive were Cave 4 with fragments of more than 380 manuscripts (about 120 of which have biblical
texts), and Cave 11 which contained (like Cave 1) relatively undamaged
texts. It is to be regretted that for nearly forty years the majority of these
remained unpublished. Along with the Qumran texts which may be dated
by archaeological evidence before A.D. 70,[56] the discoveries at **Murabbaʿat**
(Mur) including biblical texts from the second century A.D. deserve special   Mur

55. The first collection was described by A. Harkavy and H. L. Strack 1875; in
this some variants of the individual manuscripts are noted (cited in BHK as V^F). On
the criticisms of Firkowitsch mentioned next, cf. now S. Szyszman 1959, where the
charges of forgery are challenged; on the significant collections of Hebrew manuscripts
in the USSR, cf. A. I. Katsh 1959.

56. The dating of the texts has now been confirmed, primarily by archaeological
evidence. The jars found in the caves are from the Roman period (cf. p. 148). A piece
of linen found in Cave 1 has been dated by its radioactive carbon-14 content between
167 B.C. and A.D. 233. The results of the excavation of Khirbet Qumran since 1952
under the direction of G. L. Harding and R. de Vaux make it most probable that the
manuscripts were hidden during the first Jewish war (A.D. 66-70; cf. now R. de Vaux
1973). They must all, therefore, have been written before then. This dating is supported
by the texts from Wadi Murabbaʿat, which may be dated with certainty at the time of
the revolt of Bar Kochba (A.D. 132-135): "The script is more developed, the biblical
text is definitely that of the Masora, and it must be concluded from this that the
documents from Qumran are older, earlier than the second century" (de Vaux 1953:
267).

attention (cf. below note 60 for the edition). Also important are the remains of fourteen scrolls with biblical texts from the period before A.D. 733, discovered in 1963-1965 while excavating the rock fortress of **Masada** in the Judean desert. These agree extensively with the traditional biblical texts — only in the text of Ezekiel are there a few insignificant variants.[57]

1QGenAp The scrolls found in Cave 1 in 1947 were acquired at the time partly by the Hebrew University of Jerusalem and partly by the Syrian Monastery of St. Mark in Jerusalem. During the Israeli-Arab war the scrolls belonging to St. Mark's Monastery were taken to the United States, where they were published with the exception of the Genesis Apocryphon.[58] These scrolls were acquired for the Hebrew University for $300,000 in 1954, bringing the texts from Cave 1 together again in a single collection.[59] All the other texts were the property of the State of Jordan, preserved in the Palestine Archaeological Museum in Jerusalem. As the result of political events in 1967 they are now in Israeli possession in the renamed Rockefeller Museum.[60] The published manuscripts from Caves 2-11 have yielded fresh evidence of the great value of the Qumran texts.[61]

---

57. Y. Yadin 1976: 168-179, 187.

58. M. Burrows 1950, 1951; newly edited in J. C. Trever 1972.

59. The texts acquired by the Hebrew University in 1947 and edited by E. L. Sukenik were published under the title אוצר המגילות הגנוזות שבידי האוניברסיטה העברית (1954); in English: *The Dead Sea Scrolls of the Hebrew University* (1955). It was followed by N. Avigad and Y. Yadin, ed., *A Genesis Apocryphon* (1956).

60. The painstaking process of editing these manuscripts has been assigned since 1953/54 to an international team of scholars. They have been published in the series *Discoveries in the Judaean Desert,* edited by the Palestinian Archaeological Museum and the École Biblique et Archéologique Française. Volumes already published include: 1: *Qumrân Cave I,* edited by D. Barthélemy and J. T. Milik (1955) (includes the smaller fragments found on reinvestigating Cave 1); 2: *Les Grottes de Murab'ât,* edited by P. Benoît, J. T. Milik, and R. de Vaux (1961); 3: *Les 'Petites Grottes' de Qumrân: 2Q, 3Q, 5Q, 6Q, 7Q, à 10Q. Le Rouleau de cuivre,* edited by M. Baillet, J. T. Milik, and R. de Vaux, with an essay by H. W. Baker (1962); 4: *The Psalms Scroll of Qumrân Cave 11 (11QPs^a),* edited by J. A. Sanders (1965); 5: *Qumrân Cave 4 I (4Q158-4Q186),* edited by J. M. Allegro with the collaboration of A. A. Anderson (1968); 6: *Qumrân Grotte 4,* edited by R. de Vaux and J. T. Milik, with contributions by J. W. B. Barns and J. Carswell (1977): I: *Archéologie;* II: *Tefillin, Mezuzot et Targums* (4Q128– 4Q157); 7: *Qumrân Grotte 4.* III: (4Q482–4Q520), edited by M. Baillet (1982); 8/1: *The Greek Minor Prophets Scroll from Naḥal Ḥever (8 Ḥev XIIgr),* edited by Emanuel Tov et al. (1990); 9: *Qumrân Cave 4.* IV: *Palaeo-Hebrew and Greek Biblical Manuscripts,* edited by P. Skehan, E. Ulrich, and J. Sanderson (1992).

61. We can mention here only a few of the major manuscripts. For the material thus far published, see the valuable annotated survey by J. Hempel 1965: 290-295; cf. also the "survey of the published or announced finds of OT texts in Hebrew" in

They exhibit a total of 175 biblical manuscripts, including 70(!) with texts from the Pentateuch.

As a result of the discoveries made in 1947, the first place among all Old Testament manuscripts must be given to:

(a) The *Isaiah manuscript from Cave 1* (1QIs^a = $\mathfrak{Q}^a$; pl. 10, 11). For $\mathfrak{Q}^a$
the physical characteristics of the scroll, see p. 7. It is remarkable that two different text types are represented in the scroll, dividing the book into precisely two halves (ch. 1–33, 34–66). In the second half the plene forms are found far more frequently than in the first half. Either a single scribe was copying from two different exemplars, or there were two scribes with different characteristics working at the same time, as also happened with papyrus scrolls in Egypt. The scroll essentially supports 𝔐, but also offers a great number of variants. In a number of instances these coincide with variants found in the early versions or with emendations proposed by modern scholars. Some of the variants may be attributed to an interest in a particular interpretation of the text. Shemaryahu Talmon[62] regards 1QIs^a as a witness to Jewish exegesis, and its scribe as an exegete of considerable skill. Arie van der Kooij[63] has made a thorough study of the scroll's "interpretive variants" among other things. From his observation that the scroll's writer "related the prophecies of the Book of Isaiah to his own times," he concludes that "he was not merely a copyist, but rather a learned scholar" (p. 95), "comparable to the (first) Teacher of Righteousness" (p. 96). The third apparatus of BHK exhibited about 1,375 readings which remain after setting aside approximately 4,500 orthographic variants. A second Isaiah manuscript (1QIs^b = $\mathfrak{Q}^b$; pl. 12)[64] is fragmentary, but stands $\mathfrak{Q}^b$
much closer to the Masoretic text (cf. pp. 14, 156).

(b) The *Habakkuk Commentary from Cave 1* (1QpHab; pl. 13). This scroll comprises two sheets of leather sewn together, and only the upper (larger) part has been preserved. Sentences of varying length from the first two chapters of Habakkuk are cited and followed by the formula "this means . . ." to introduce an interpretation adapted to the period of the commentary, showing how the present national and religious scene had been foretold by the prophet Habakkuk. A group of variants in Hab. 1–2

E. Sellin-G. Fohrer 1968: 494-497 (1968a: 587f.); J. A. Sanders 1975: 401-413, lists of published texts; J. A. Fitzmyer 1990; H. P. Scanlin 1993, annotated list of biblical texts.

62. S. Talmon 1962.
63. A. van der Kooij 1981.
64. Edition: Sukenik 1954 (Hebrew), 1955 (English).

is worth serious consideration (cf. the third apparatus of BHK and the apparatus of BHS). The sacred name Yahweh is written in the Old Hebrew script (cf. p. 4).[65]

(c) The *Psalm Scroll from Cave 11* (11QPs[a]) contains forty-one canonical psalms from the last third of the Psalter and seven apocryphal psalms including one known from the LXX translation (Ps. 151), two from Syriac translations, and one from Sir. 51:13-30. The order of the Psalms differs largely from the Masoretic text, with the apocryphal psalms placed among the canonical psalms; in Ps. 145 each verse is followed by the refrain: "Praise be to Yahweh! May his name be praised always and for ever!" The evidence would indicate that this is not a proper Psalter, but a collection with a liturgical purpose.[66] Also in this scroll the name Yahweh is written in Old Hebrew script.[67]

(d) The *Nash Papyrus* (Pap. Nash; pl. 6).[68] Until 1947 the oldest known witness to the Hebrew Old Testament text was the papyrus sheet acquired in 1902 by W. L. Nash in Egypt and donated to the Cambridge University Library. The Nash Papyrus, as it is called, contains a somewhat damaged copy of the Decalogue, following mostly the text of Exod. 20:2-17, partly Deut. 5:6-21, with the Shema' from Deut. 6:4f. appended. The sequence of the text shows that it is not derived from a biblical scroll, but from a liturgical, devotional, or instructional document. The papyrus was dated in the second or first century A.D. by its first editors. On the grounds of its paleographical traits (which were not disputed at the time, and have since been confirmed by the Qumran texts), Albright assigned it to the Maccabean period,[69] while Kahle assigned it on internal grounds to the period before the destruction of the Temple.[70] The sixth and seventh commandments appear in reverse order, and the Shema' begins with a phrase found in 𝕲 but not in 𝔐.

𝕮   (e) The *Geniza Fragments* (𝕮). The origin of these has been discussed above (p. 11). The range of the treasures recovered from the Geniza is amazing. The number of fragments has been estimated at 200,000. Besides biblical texts in Hebrew and in Aramaic and Arabic translations, there are

65. Cf. the thorough study by K. Elliger 1953.
66. M. H. Goshen-Gottstein 1966.
67. Y. Yadin 1966 has published a further fragment to supplement the editions referred to in nn. 58, 59 above. Cf. also J. A. Sanders 1967.
68. First published: S. A. Cook 1903.
69. W. F. Albright 1937: 145-176.
70. P. Kahle 1951: 5f. For dating in the second half of the second century B.C., cf. N. Avigad 1958: 65.

also Midrash, Mishna, Talmud, liturgical texts, lists, letters, and much else. Of particular importance was the discovery of a nearly complete copy of the Wisdom of Jesus ben Sirach in Hebrew, previously known only in Greek; also a previously unknown writing in Hebrew was found, dating probably from the second or first century B.C., which was called the Zadokite Document, and has enjoyed a revival of interest in recent years because of its relation to the Manual of Discipline[71] discovered in 1947. The biblical fragments alone from the Geniza, the earliest of which may date from the fifth century A.D., shed new light on the development of Masoretic activity prior to the great Masoretes of Tiberias, enabling us to recognize the growth of the pointing system as we have described it above. Geniza fragments are now found in many libraries, most of them being in the Cambridge University Library and in the Bodleian Library at Oxford.[72]

(f) *Ben Asher Manuscripts.* For five or six generations, from the second half of the eighth century to the mid-tenth century, the Ben Asher family played a leading part in the Masoretic work at Tiberias. In the two surviving manuscripts that go back to the last two members of the family we find a faithful record of their scholarly achievements.

Codex Cairensis (C; pl. 20).[73] This manuscript, containing the C Former and Latter Prophets, was written and pointed by Moses ben Asher in A.D. 895. In one colophon (a note at the end of medieval manuscripts giving information about the scribe and other matters) he mentions the patron who commissioned the manuscript, and in a second colophon he names himself as the scribe. Further colophons record the fortunes of the manuscript. It was presented to the Karaite community in Jerusalem where it was seized as loot by the Crusaders in 1099. Later it was restored, coming into the possession of the Karaite community in Cairo, where it may still be today.[74] L. Lipschütz and others have demonstrated in an ingenious way that the codex is closer to the Ben Naphtali tradition than it is to the Ben Asher tradition.[75] This has led many to question its authenticity, e.g., H. Yalon, J. L. Teicher, D. S. Loewinger, Lipschütz; but contra cf. M. H. Goshen-Gottstein,[76] who insists that Ben Naphtali preserved the system of Moses ben Asher more faithfully than did his son Aaron (cf. p. 25 above).

71. Published in M. Burrows 1951.
72. For basic information on the Geniza fragments, see M. H. Goshen-Gottstein 1962: 35-44.
73. Facsimile edition: Loewinger 1971; Critical edition: F. Pérez Castro, 1979–.
74. Cf. Fernández Tejero 1983a.
75. L. Lipschütz 1964: 6.
76. M. H. Goshen-Gottstein 1963: 107.

The **Aleppo Codex** (pl. 21).[77] This manuscript contains the complete Old Testament and dates from the first half of the tenth century. According to a colophon, Aaron ben Moses ben Asher did not himself write the manuscript; he was responsible only for the pointing and the Masora. The pointing was done with special care, and it was regarded as a model codex: it was to be used liturgically only on the Feasts of Passover, Weeks, and Tabernacles, and otherwise used only for consultation by scholars to settle matters of doubt, and not for study. It was originally in Jerusalem, but came later to Cairo and finally to Aleppo. It was not available for use in BHK, as the editors explain on p. xxix. There was a report of its destruction during the anti-Jewish riots of 1947, but fortunately this proved false. It was saved, although with the loss of a quarter of its folios (i.e., Gen. 1:1–Deut. 28:26 at the beginning and from Song 3:12 to the end, including Ecclesiastes, Lamentation, Esther, Daniel, Ezra, and Nehemiah)[78] and is now in Jerusalem. As the facsimile edition was not published until 1976 (cf. n. 76), the codex was not available to the editors of BHS. Now that it has been made available for scholarly examination it will be used as the base for a critical edition of the Bible to be published by the Hebrew University, Jerusalem.[79]

L   **Codex Leningradensis** (L; pl. 24).[80] In view of the unavailability of the oldest surviving manuscript of the complete Bible deriving from the last member of the Ben Asher family, the Codex Leningradensis, reproduced in BH, is of special importance as a witness to the Ben Asher text. According to its colophon it was copied in A.D. 1008 from exemplars

77. Facsimile edition: M. H. Goshen-Gottstein 1976. Maimonides' evaluation was based on the format of the Pentateuch (its divisions into open and closed parashoth, and the arrangement of poetic lines; cf. p. 174). It is particularly significant in the Jewish perspective that the format of the manuscript observes the halakhic prescriptions (cf. M. H. Goshen-Gottstein 1979: 151f.). Cf. D. Barthélemy 1986a for a discussion of some problems in using this edition.

78. Subsequently the text of Deut. 4:38–6:3 was found in a photographic reproduction in the book *Travels through Northern Syria* by J. Segall (1910); cf. M. H. Goshen-Gottstein 1966a. In addition there are photographs of Gen. 26:37–27:30 in W. Wickes 1887; cf. M. H. Goshen-Gottstein 1960 (following p. 16). Another folio (2 Chr 35:7–36:19) was found in the Hebrew University Library (*Tarbiz* 51 [1982]).

79. Cf. the articles by I. Ben-Zvi, M. Goshen-Gottstein, D. S. Loewinger in *Textus* 1 (1960): 1-111; on the Hebrew University Bible Project, see below, p. 43. See also pl. 21 and comments, p. 174.

80. Facsimile edition by D. S. Loewinger 1970. A diplomatic edition of L has also been published by A. Dotan 1973. Recently rephotographed by the Ancient Biblical Manuscript Center in Claremont, CA.

written by Aaron ben Moses ben Asher. For a refutation of the earlier doubts of this colophon's authenticity, cf. BHK, p. xxix.[81]

(g) The *Petersburg Codex of the Prophets* (V[P]).[82] This manuscript V[P] contains Isaiah, Jeremiah, Ezekiel, and the Minor Prophets, with both the small and the large Masora. The codex was discovered by Firkowitsch in 1839, as he claims, in the synagogue of Chufutkaleh in the Crimea. Its significance derives not only from its age (dated A.D. 916), but also from the fact that its discovery finally made it possible to appreciate the nature of the Babylonian pointing system, the knowledge of which had been lost for centuries. Close examination and comparison with manuscripts discovered at the same time or later has shown, however, that while using the Eastern signs the codex actually follows the Western tradition in its consonantal text and its pointing. Thus it stands as an impressive symbol of the victory of the Western tradition over the Eastern (cf. pp. 12, 22f.). On several pages (212a, 221a) the Babylonian signs have been replaced by the Tiberian signs, and on folio 1b both systems stand side by side.

(h) The *Erfurt Codices.* Three more codices are used in BHK, known from their earlier location as Erfurtensis 1, 2, and 3. They belong to the former Prussian State Library in Berlin (Ms. Orient. 1210/11, 1212, 1213), now the National Library of Prussian Cultural Properties. They were used among others by Joh. Heinrich Michaelis for his edition in 1720 (cf. p. 40). They are noteworthy in that they (especially E3) are more or less related to the type of text earlier mistaken as the Ben Naphtali text (cf. p. 24), though they mark a stage of transition to the later textus receptus.

E1, fourteenth century, contains the Hebrew Old Testament, Targums, and the large and small Masora.

---

81. P. Kahle 1961: 77 mentions that L shows many corrections, and he conjectures that these "represent the results of its collation with other Ben Asher codices." It is the judgment of M. H. Goshen-Gottstein "that the Leningrad Codex was basically not a Ben Asher codex. It was secondarily brought into harmony with a Ben Asher *Vorlage* by endless erasures and changes" (Goshen-Gottstein 1963: 101f.); but I. Yeivin 1980: 18 disagrees, asserting that "This is the MS showing the closest tradition to A." For Goshen-Gottstein the only actually known representative of the (Aaron) Ben Asher text is the Aleppo Codex. If he is correct in this very one-sided theory, it would then necessarily follow, for example, that after the loss of nearly a quarter of the Aleppo Codex we now in fact possess no Ben Asher text for nearly the whole of the Pentateuch. Will Goshen-Gottstein go this far? On his far-reaching hypotheses, cf. B. J. Roberts 1964.

82. Published in a facsimile edition by H. L. Strack 1876; also recently under the title *The Hebrew Bible — Latter Prophets: The Babylonian Codex of Petrograd. Edited with Preface and Critical Annotations. Prolegomenon by P. Wernberg-Møller* (1971).

E2, probably thirteenth century, contains the Hebrew Old Testament, Targum Onkelos, and the large and small Masora.

E3 is the most important of these manuscripts in both age and text; it is one of the oldest German manuscripts (Kahle dates it before A.D. 1100).[83] Contents: the Hebrew Old Testament, large and small Masora, and extracts from *Okhla weOkhla* (cf. p. 29). The consonantal text is by two scribes; the pointing is by four different hands, following in part the special tradition mentioned above (p. 25), and in part showing contacts with it.

(i) *Lost codices.* Finally, in some instances there are important codices cited which no longer exist but whose peculiar readings have been preserved. A number of these codices are referred to in BH.

Sev   *Codex Severi* (Sev). A medieval list found in manuscripts in Paris and in Prague enumerates thirty-two variant readings of a Pentateuch manuscript from the Severus synagogue in Rome. This manuscript was reputedly a part of the booty brought to Rome in A.D. 70, and presented by the Emperor Severus (222-235) to a synagogue he had built. If this tradition were correct, the manuscript would have been a scroll and not a codex (cf. pp. 7, 11). Cf. BH apparatus at Gen. 18:21; 24:7; and BHK at Num. 4:3.[84]

Hill   *Codex Hillel* (Hill). Traditionally written by Rabbi Hillel ben Moshe ben Hillel about A.D. 600, this codex is said to have been very accurate and used for revision of other manuscripts. Readings of this manuscript are cited repeatedly by medieval Masoretes and grammarians. Cf. BHK apparatus at Gen. 6:3; 19:6; and BHS also at Exod. 25:19; Lev. 26:9.

The medieval Masoretes also mention among others the following codices as standard, and cite readings from them:

Codex Muga (cited in Ms. 4445, cf. n. 92 below, and in the Petersburg Codex of the Prophets); cf. BH apparatus at Lev. 26:39; also BHK at Lev. 23:13. It is not certain whether Muga is the name of a scribe (Ginsburg), or if *muga* ("corrected") indicates a corrected text.

Codex Jericho; cf. BH apparatus at Gen. 31:36; Num. 24:23; and BHK at Num. 5:28.

Codex Yerushalmi; cf. BHK at Gen. 10:19.

Nothing more is known about these codices.

---

83. E3 is probably of Italian origin according to J. Prijs 1957: 172f.

84. Cf. also M. H. Segal 1953: 45-47, where all thirty-two variants are recorded; also J. P. Siegel 1975.

6. Printed Editions

We can describe here only the most important of a large number of editions which have been printed. For a variety of reasons the most important among the earliest printed editions are the following:

(a) The *Second Rabbinic Bible* of *Jacob ben Chayyim*[85] was published by Daniel Bomberg in Venice, 1524/25, and is known as Bombergiana (ℬ). It was not the earliest,[86] yet it was the most important of ℬ its period, and it remained the standard printed text of the Hebrew Old Testament until the twentieth century. It is a Rabbinic Bible, which means that together with the Hebrew text is printed an Aramaic version (Targum) and comments by outstanding rabbis (Rashi, Ibn Ezra, Kimchi, etc.) — an extensive work of 925 leaves in four folio volumes. The special feature of the Bombergiana is that it also includes the large, the small, and the final Masora, which the editor had painstakingly assembled with tremendous labor from a number of manuscripts which were largely defective and copied without any understanding of the Masoretic material (cf. p. 30), and that on the basis of this research his text was established. Also the variant readings of manuscripts which Jacob ben Chayyim collated are recorded. This text enjoyed an almost canonical authority up to our own time. Even in 1897 Ginsburg wrote that it represented the only Masoretic recension, and that any modern editor of the Hebrew text must show conclusive evidence for introducing any deviation from it. Kittel also reprinted it in the first two editions of his *Biblia Hebraica*. But by basing his work on late medieval manuscripts or on printed editions which reproduced them, Jacob ben Chayyim himself offers only the late medieval textus receptus. Nor should we expect the methodological standards of a sixteenth-century scholar's edition to meet the requirements we would demand of a modern critical edition today, after several centuries of further scientific development. It is with full justification that from its third edition BH has replaced this text with an older one.

85. Reprint: edited by M. H. Goshen-Gottstein 1972. Jacob ben Chayyim was a Jewish refugee from Tunis who later became a Christian. He died before 1538.

86. Earlier editions included portions (all with rabbinic commentary and to some extent with Targum), e.g., Psalms, 1477 (Bologna?), Prophets, 1485/86 (Soncino), Writings, 1486/87 (Naples), Pentateuch, 1491 (Lisbon), etc.; and complete Bibles, e.g., 1488 (Soncino), 1491/93 (Naples), 1494 (Brescia). The first Rabbinic Bible was edited by Felix Pratensis and was also published by Daniel Bomberg in 1516/17, a considerable critical achievement which in large measure served as a basis for the second Rabbinic Bible of Jacob ben Chayyim (cf. P. Kahle 1947a: 32-36). For further details see p. 184.

(b) The edition of *Johann Heinrich Michaelis* (BHK: V(ar)^M),[87] a Protestant theologian and orientalist at Halle and a prominent Pietist (1668-1738), follows mainly the text of Daniel E. Jablonski's 1669 edition, with an apparatus including the most important readings of the five Erfurt manuscripts (cf. p. 37), and of a number of published editions. Many of these variants are only a matter of accents. Parallel passages are noted in the margin.

V$^{Ken\ 96}$ etc.

(c) *Benjamin Kennicott,* 1718-1783 (an Oxford theologian; librarian, 1767; and canon, 1770), published a compendious collection of variants still useful today (V^{Ken}).[88] Kennicott published the Masoretic text following the 1705 edition by E. van der Hooght, the Dutch scholar, and the Samaritan text following Brian Walton's London Polyglot of 1753-1757. The copious apparatus notes the variants from the consonantal text in more than six hundred manuscripts and fifty-two editions of the Hebrew text, and in sixteen manuscripts of the Samaritan. Kennicott was able to undertake the massive task of collating all these manuscripts only with the aid of a staff of assistants, not all of whom were competent. Further, the manuscripts collated were comparatively late. The significance of this edition is discussed below and p. 114.

(d) *G. B. de Rossi* did not publish an edition of the text, but only a collection of variants.[89] It contains a selection of the more important readings of 1,475 manuscripts and editions (p. xlv). The material surveyed is more extensive than that in Kennicott's apparatus, and also more accurately represented. De Rossi also notes only variants of the consonantal text.

The actual value of both Kennicott's and de Rossi's collections of variants for the recovery of the original text is very small. Apart from orthographic differences and simple scribal errors (such as haplography, dittography, inversion of consonants), the variants they record are concerned with the use of the plural or singular with collective nouns, the addition or omission of such words as כל or ו, the interchange of prepositions with similar meanings or of words with synonymous expressions (e.g., דבר for אמר), or of singular and plural forms (e.g., דבריך and דברך). This certainly demonstrates the lack of any absolute uniformity in the transmission of the text, such as is assumed by the theory of a single archetype. But what is lacking is variants of any real significance for the meaning of the text, such as are found in New Testament manuscripts.

---

87. J. H. Michaelis 1720.
88. B. Kennicott 1776-80.
89. G. B. de Rossi 1784-1788, with a supplement in 1798; repr. 1969-70.

These collections of variants provide scarcely any help in dealing with corrupt passages. The manuscripts they are based on have been so standardized in the Masoretic tradition that no startling results can be achieved by studying them. After our observations in discussing the history of the Masoretic text we can well understand these disappointing conclusions which in due course led to a decline in Masoretic studies.[90] The nineteenth and twentieth centuries have produced no comparable collections.

(e) *S. Baer* (BHK: Var[B]) collaborated with Franz Delitzsch from 1869 to 1895 in an attempt to produce the Masoretic text of the Old Testament (except for Exodus-Deuteronomy) in as exact a form as possible, basing their work on early editions and manuscripts.[91] "These editions contain much valuable material, but the arbitrary and unsystematic way Baer treated the Masora led him to reconstruct a text which never actually existed, so that his editions must be used with caution."[92]

(f) *Christian D. Ginsburg* (BHK: V(ar)[G]) prepared an edition for the British and Foreign Bible Society (1908ff.).[93] A new edition appeared in 1926. Ginsburg prints "substantially" the text of Jacob ben Chayyim's 1524/25 edition which he valued so highly (cf. p. 39), including in an apparatus the variant readings of more than seventy manuscripts and of nineteen editions published before 1524. These variants relate to orthography, vowel points, accents, and divisions of the text. The manuscripts he collated, mostly from the British Library, are mainly from the thirteenth century and later.[94] Although this edition has a certain importance as a collection of Masoretic material, its value is lessened by the unevenness

90. Cf. the opinion of E. F. K. Rosenmüller in discussing B. Kennicott's collection: "This whole congeries of variants, assembled at such an expense of time and money, leads only to one simple conclusion: that all the extant codices are very late in relation to the original . . . that they contain a wealth of scribal errors but a dearth of significant and useful readings, and that correspondingly little if any help may be anticipated from them for the corrupted passages in the Hebrew text"; Rosenmüller 1797: 247, cited in E. Preuschen 1889: 303. Cf. also M. H. Goshen-Gottstein 1967.

91. S. Baer and F. Delitzsch 1869-1895.

92. P. Kahle in H. Bauer and P. Leander 1922: 90; P. Kahle 1961: 11-16.

93. *The Old Testament, diligently revised according to the Massorah and the early editions with the various readings from MSS and the ancient versions* (Ginsburg 1908-26). After the death of Ginsburg in 1914 the work was continued by H. E. Holmes and A. S. Geden.

94. But they also include the Pentateuch manuscript in the British Library, Ms. Or. 4445, which Ginsburg dated about A.D. 820-850, although it should be dated about a century later. This manuscript has no scribal colophon, as it has lost both its beginning and end. The way in which Ben Asher is cited suggests that it was written during his lifetime (pl. 22).

of the material, which was gathered almost haphazardly, and the absence of any attempt to weigh or to group it. By far the majority of the variants are trivial, and do not affect the sense or interpretation of the text. Variants in the early versions are very rarely noticed. The accuracy of the collations has also received occasional criticism, but this is due to the enormous size of the task Ginsburg undertook, which necessitated reliance on a great number of assistants.[95]

(g) The British and Foreign Bible Society published a new edition in 1958, prepared by *Norman H. Snaith* (תורה, נביאים, כתובים). It is based primarily on British Library Ms. Or. 2626-2628, which was written in Lisbon in 1482.[96] Other manuscripts used include British Library Ms. Or. 2375 (a Yemenite manuscript written in 1468-1480) and the Shem Tob Bible (a Spanish manuscript dated 1312) which was earlier in the library of David Sassoon. These manuscripts represent the Ben Asher tradition, making the text closely related to the third edition of BHK.[97] Following the practice of the Bible Society, the edition is without introduction and apparatus, although a list of the Haphtaroth (cf. p. 166 below) for the liturgical year is appended in some printings.

(h) The *Biblia Hebraica* of the German Bible Society, Stuttgart (the Württemberg Bible Society until 1975, and from 1976-1980 the German Bible Foundation) has a special position among printed editions because it represents a new direction undertaken by Rudolf Kittel. In his programmatic essay "On the Necessity and Possibility of a New Edition of the Hebrew Bible: Studies and Reflections" (1902)[98] Kittel proposed that "for use in private study as well as in schools and universities there is an urgent need for a critically established edition of the Hebrew text" free of all obvious errors, scribal flaws and blemishes (pp. 2f.). He suggested two ways this could be accomplished: by printing the Masoretic textus receptus as the text and registering the necessary changes in the margin (footnotes), or by printing a "new" critically edited text with all the errors corrected and reporting the Masoretic tradition in footnotes. Kittel regarded the latter course as the "only proper" procedure, though admitting it would be far more difficult to achieve than the "basically inferior" first alternative (pp. 77f.).

With the collaboration of eight other Old Testament scholars Kittel

---

95. M. D. Cassuto 1953; cf. the critical review by P. Kahle 1954c: 109f.
96. Facsimile edition: G. Sed-Rajna 1988.
97. Cf. N. H. Snaith 1957; 1962.
98. Kittel 1902.

was able to publish in 1906 (1909[2]) a text prepared on the basis of the first procedure.[99] The text was that of Jakob ben Chayyim's 1524/25 edition.[100] The apparatus was the first to provide an edition with a copious linguistic commentary, exhibiting the most important variant readings in selected passages, together with conjectural emendations by modern textual scholars.

This *Biblia Hebraica* became the most significant tool of the century for the study of Hebrew Bible. It achieved international recognition. No scholarly work on the Old Testament, whether for research, seminars, or private study, could afford to ignore Kittel's *Biblia Hebraica* (BHK). But   BHK it should also be remembered that it was essentially a school text, and not too much could be demanded of it. R. Kittel always insisted that it give due recognition to advances in scholarly research ("dies diem docet").

His work was thoroughly revised and significantly improved in a third edition (1929-1937) by Albrecht Alt and Otto Eissfeldt. With the collaboration of P. Kahle it became possible to use the text of Ben Asher in the Leningrad manuscript B 19[A] (dated 1008; L, cf. pp. 36, 180) as a base. The apparatus was expanded substantially (in two parts: the upper with minor variants and comments; the lower with more significant variants and comments), and in 1951 the variants of the Isaiah manuscript 1QIs[a] (cf. p. 33) were added to make them conveniently available.

In the 1967-1977 revision (cf. p. 10) under the distinctive title *Biblia Hebraica Stuttgartensia* (BHS) the text was reviewed once more to reflect   BHS more precisely the last hand of Manuscript L. This is important because this manuscript is the oldest (after the Aleppo Codex) and most complete manuscript available, and a diplomatic edition of it was a desideratum. The apparatus was also completely revised, taking into full consideration the criticisms of BHK for its frequent citation of conjectures. The individual books vary considerably in their scope and quality, so that in many books the use of BHK may be recommended; it is retained in the Hebrew-German edition of 1974.

(i) The ***Hebrew University in Jerusalem*** has undertaken an edition of the Old Testament (The Hebrew University Bible Project). Publications to date include: a *Sample Edition* published in 1965 containing Isa. 2, 5,

99. Although Kittel regarded the second procedure as the only appropriate one, he did not adopt it partly because many corrupt passages could be restored only by conjecture and subjective standards. Once these "corrections" appeared in the text they could easily give the impression of a certainty they could not rightly claim. Cf. the chapters on textual criticism below, pp. 105ff.

100. Cf. p. 39.

11, and 51, and an extensive introduction, followed by two volumes of the book of Isaiah.[101] The text is an exact reproduction of the Aleppo Codex (cf. p. 36), including its large and small Masora. The special importance of this edition for scholarship lies not only in its making the text of this codex available for the first time, but also in the comprehensiveness of its critical apparatus which reflects the history of the Old Testament text: the first gives the variants of the early versions (especially 𝕲); the second gives those of the scrolls of the Judean desert and the rabbinic literature; the third, the medieval manuscripts; and the fourth apparatus records peculiarities of script, pointing, and accents (of the St. Petersburg, Cairo, and other manuscripts); in the fifth and sixth apparatuses are found critical comments, particularly on the first apparatus (in Hebrew and English). This edition is planned to provide a more comprehensive basis for the study of the Old Testament and its history than has ever before been available; its first two apparatuses in particular promise a wealth of information, especially for rabbinic literature, which has always been very difficult of access. The achievement of this undertaking will not be accomplished soon.[102]

101. M. H. Goshen-Gottstein 1965-81.
102. Cf. M. H. Goshen-Gottstein 1991: 117f.

III. The Samaritan Pentateuch (barriscript)

The separation of the Samaritans from the Jews was an important event in the history of postexilic Judaism. We do not know precisely when it was that the Samaritan community made the final break from Jerusalem. According to an earlier view it occurred in the course of the fourth century B.C. as the culmination of a long process. But more recent research based on recent archaeological studies and the Qumran texts makes it probable that the separation did not occur until the Hasmonean period, when Shechem was destroyed and the sanctuary on Mount Gerizim was ravaged by John Hyrcanus.[1] The Samaritans took the Pentateuch with them when they went into schism: thus we have the Pentateuch in a second Hebrew recension, the Samaritan. As we remarked above (p. 4), the Samaritan Pentateuch was written in a special script derived from an archaizing form of the Old Hebrew script of the Hasmonean period (pl. 27).

When the Samaritan Pentateuch (cited as barriscript in BH) first became known to the West through the discovery of a manuscript in Damascus in 1616, it aroused the most sanguine expectations. Some believed that it brought them substantially closer to the original text of the Pentateuch. Later its prestige waned, and as a result of Wilhelm Gesenius' verdict in 1815 it was long regarded by many as practically worthless for the purposes of textual criticism. Gesenius did not judge barriscript to be an independent witness to the text, but rather a revision of barriscript, adapted in both its language and matter to the views of the Samaritans. This inadequate appreciation was challenged in the nineteenth century by Abraham Geiger, and in the twentieth by Paul Kahle.[2]

1. J. D. Purvis 1968; also H. G. Kippenberg 1971; R. J. Coggins 1975; R. Pummer 1976-77; F. Dexinger and R. Pummer 1992.
2. P. Kahle 1915.

45

The problem of the Samaritan Pentateuch is that it differs from 𝔐 in some six thousand instances. While it is true that a great number of these variants are merely orthographic (especially in its more frequent use of the plene forms), and many others are trivial and do not affect the meaning of the text, yet it is significant that in about nineteen hundred instances 𝔴 agrees with 𝔊 against 𝔐.[3] Some of the variants in 𝔴 must be regarded as alterations introduced by the Samaritans in the interest of their own cult. This is true especially of the command inserted after Exod. 20:17 to build a sanctuary on Mount Gerizim, of Deut. 11:30 where מול שכם is added to מרה (𝔐 מרא), and of nineteen passages in Deuteronomy where the choice of the holy place is set in the past and the reference to Shechem is made clear (in the formula אֲשֶׁר יִבְחַם יְהוָה הַמָּ קוֹם 𝔴 reads בָּחַר for יִבְחַר).[4] But such obviously tendentious readings do not justify regarding all the other variants as intentional alterations, especially where 𝔴 agrees with 𝔊 and Qumran texts.

The peculiar textual form of the Samaritan Pentateuch is far more probably explained as a special development of the Hebrew text which is naturally not to be identified with 𝔐. Archaic forms were modernized, difficult sentence structures were simplified, and explanatory comments and expansions were derived from parallel passages.[5] Such changes were useful only as long as it was necessary to make the Hebrew text as intelligible to people as possible. They became unnecessary as soon as the next step was taken — the Hebrew text was itself translated into the popular language, Aramaic. This implies for 𝔴 a very early date and makes it impossible to regard it as dependent on 𝔐. Instead, it is a very important witness to a form of the text that once enjoyed widespread use as shown by its agreements with the Qumran texts (cf. p. 14), the Septuagint, the New Testament, and some Jewish texts that escaped revision by official Judaism. These last provide a striking example in the chronologies of Gen. 5 and 11, where 𝔴 is independent of both 𝔐 and 𝔊. For the survival of the primitive text represented by 𝔴 in medieval Masoretic manuscripts, see above (p. 19).

3. The New Testament also agrees with 𝔴 in some passages against 𝔐, as in Acts 7:4 and 7:32, and possibly also Heb. 9:3f. Presumably the New Testament depends upon a Greek Pentateuch which was similar to 𝔴 at these points.

4. It would seem probable, on the other hand, that in Deut. 27:4 (𝔐 Ebal, 𝔴 Gerizim) it was the Jewish text that was later altered. A final decision, however, is not possible; cf. the commentaries *ad loc*.

5. S. Talmon 1951.

The Samaritan pronunciation (and accenting) of the Hebrew text has hardly changed for centuries, and is independent of the Tiberian Masoretic tradition. At least in part it preserves a very early tradition which was also represented at Qumran (cf. p. 27).[6]

Manuscripts earlier than the thirteenth century are very rare. The oldest known manuscript in codex format is in the Cambridge University Library. "It contains a notice that it was sold A.H. 544 (A.D. 1149/50), and it may have been written a long time before that. It certainly gives the impression of being considerably older than the Samaritan Pentateuch MSS written since A.D. 1200, of which we know a good many."[7] The sacred scroll of the Samaritan community at Nablus (Shechem) is quite famous: it is called the Abisha Scroll after its scribe. Actually it is a compilation of many fragments. The older and more original part of the Abisha Scroll comprises the main part of Num. 35–Deut. 34, and is dated by its editor Federico Pérez Castro in the eleventh century.[8]

The Samaritan Pentateuch was first printed in the Paris and London Polyglots ($\mathfrak{m}^W$; cf. p. 226). A critical edition was edited by August von Gall 1914-1918: it offers an eclectic text based on late medieval manuscripts.[9] A new critical edition has appeared in the *Biblia Poliglota Matritensis* edited by F. Pérez Castro.[10]

For a Greek translation of the Samaritan Pentateuch, see p. 78; for the Samaritan Targum, see p. 84.[11]

6. P. Kahle 1950; 1959: 153-57, and in Appendix II, 318-335, transcriptions of texts dictated by Samaritan priests made by H. Ritter and A. Schaade and edited by A. Murtonen. These texts are cited in BHS as Samar (Gen. 1:1). The entire Pentateuch has since been transcribed by Z. Ben-Ḥayyim 1977.

7. P. Kahle, 1959: 67 n. 2.

8. P. Kahle 1953. Edition: Pérez Castro 1959; reviewed by E. Robertson 1962. Cf. also Pérez Castro 1960. A transcription of the Abisha Scroll in Samaritan script was published by A. Sadaka 1959; a transcription in Hebrew square script by A. Sadaka and R. Sadaka 1961-65 has the lacunae of the Abisha Scroll supplied from the Abu al-Barakat Scroll, and shows the text of $\mathfrak{M}$ in a parallel column with the differences distinguished typographically.

9. Cf. M. Baillet 1982a.

10. L.-F. Giron-Blanc 1976.

11. A comprehensive grammar of Samaritan Hebrew has been produced by R. Macuch 1969.

IV. Preliminary Considerations on the Versions[1]

The Hebrew text which we have today has been altered from its original form by many circumstances and undoubtedly contains many corruptions. Consequently the versions which enable us to reconstruct an older Old Testament text and to correct errors are very important. But we should also recognize that each of the versions comes with its own peculiar range of problems. For a long period the versions were approached rather naively and used directly for textual criticism on the uncritical assumption that the base from which they were translated could be readily determined. But the matter is not that simple. Anyone who translates also interprets: the translation is not simply a rendering of the underlying text but also an expression of the translator's understanding of it. And every translator is a child of a particular time and of a particular culture. Consequently every translation, and especially a translation of the Bible produced to meet the practical needs of a community, must be understood and appreciated independently in its own right.

Translations reflect the intellectual assumptions of their translators — of their age and their culture, their religious and other views which they are loyal to or respect, the concerns and prejudices which they adopt consciously or unconsciously, their education, their ability to express themselves, the conceptual range of the language they are translating into, and many other factors — and most translations of the Bible are the work of a number of anonymous translators. Therefore we must distinguish between what is derived from the original text and what is contributed by the translator. This is a formidable task to be accomplished before we can proceed to use the versions for purposes of textual criticism.

The history of most of the versions is beset by many problems which

1. For the individual versions, cf. S. P. Brock 1980 (with extensive bibliographies).

48

are yet unsolved and are perhaps insoluble, especially for the early period. In his discussion of the Syriac Peshitta, Franz Rosenthal has wisely observed that, of all the problems of literary criticism, that of the biblical versions is encumbered with such a variety of diverse factors that any hope for a scientifically conclusive solution is very slight. In almost every instance we find ourselves dealing basically not only with an unknown series of intermediate stages in the evolution of a translation, which stages have been lost to us and which we can never hope to trace with more than a bare degree of probability, but also with a wealth of oral tradition which could very well have developed for similar reasons along similar lines.[2]

The problems we have indicated make for the fascination of versional studies and provide the incentive for further research, but they also show how far we are from any final solutions.

We will consider first the primary versions, which have a prior claim in textual criticism because they are based directly on the original language, and then the remaining versions, most of which are based on the Septuagint. Jerome's version, the Latin Vulgate, claims to have been translated from the Hebrew text, but as it is strongly influenced by the Greek versions and by the Old Latin versions which preceded it, we will consider it in the third section.

2. F. Rosenthal 1939: 206.

V. The Septuagint (𝕲)

1. Introduction

In accordance with the purpose of this book 𝕲 is considered here as a witness to the text of the Old Testament, but its great significance for the history of Western thought deserves at least a brief mention. It was in 𝕲 that the Greek world first met the Old Testament revelation. "The most common attitude among Greeks who came into contact with the Old Testament was that this book and the cosmos are mutually related and must be understood together. Whatever they might think about the book, it appeared to be certain that it was a creation parallel to the world itself, equally great and comprehensive, and that both are the work of the same Creator. What other book in history has ever received a comparable verdict among thinking men?"[1]

For the early church 𝕲 was simply the standard form of the Old Testament. Augustine demanded that Jerome use this canonical form of the text and not the Hebrew original as the basis for his translation. It could well be said that the influence of the Old Testament upon the Christian world through the centuries, almost up to the present day, has been mediated linguistically and conceptually by the hellenistic forms it received in 𝕲. We must acknowledge with Victor Ehrenberg that 𝕲 is a book of such critical significance that apart from it both Christendom and the Western culture would be inconceivable.

---

1. A. von Harnack 1902: 509. An extensive bibliography of the Septuagint to 1969 has been compiled in S. P. Brock-C. T. Fritsch-S. Jellicoe 1973.

2. The Letter of Aristeas

We seem at first glance to be particularly well informed on the origins of 𝕲, since we have in the Letter of Aristeas[2] an account which purports to have been compiled by one who was himself a participant in its preparation. It tells of how one day Demetrius of Phaleron, who is erroneously identified as director of the famous library at Alexandria, reported to his royal master Ptolemy II Philadelphus (285-247 B.C.) that the Jewish Law (the Letter of Aristeas is concerned solely with the Pentateuch!) was worthy of a place in the royal library, but that it must first be translated into Greek. The king acted on this suggestion immediately. Envoys, with Aristeas among them, were sent to Eleazar the high priest in Jerusalem with the request that he provide competent individuals for the work of translating. Eleazar responded by sending seventy-two people to Alexandria, six from each of the twelve tribes, along with valuable Torah scrolls. After an impressive formal reception they provided the king with examples of Jewish wisdom in a series of profound sayings. Then they were taken to the island of Pharos, which is connected with Alexandria by a causeway, and there in quietness and seclusion they translated the Law in seventy-two days, with Demetrius writing down the text as they agreed on it. The completed translation was read first to the Jewish community (in Alexandria) who pronounced it beautiful, devout, and accurate. It was to be regarded as holy, with curses pronounced on anyone who would add anything to it, or alter it in any way. Only after receiving the approval of the community did the translation come before the king who had commissioned its production. He marvelled at the spirit of the Lawgiver, and sent the translators back to their homes laden with valuable gifts.

This is the account in the Letter of Aristeas which was accepted and given further development by others, both Jews and Christians. *Josephus* (A.D. 37/38-ca. 100) preserves it with almost literal fidelity. *Philo* (ca. 25 B.C.–A.D. 40) makes the translation an act of divine inspiration, and the translators prophets: although they worked separately they produced a single text that was literally identical throughout. The Church Fathers followed Philo, extending the account from the Law, as in the Letter of Aristeas, to the *whole* of the Old Testament. Pseudo-Justin[3] in the third

2. Text: P. Wendland 1900; H. St. J. Thackeray in H. B. Swete 1914. Translation: P. Wendland in E. Kautzsch 1900; M. Hadas 1951; R. H. Shutt 1985. Cf. also K. Müller 1978: 719-725 (bibliography).

3. *Cohortatio ad gentiles XIII* (ed. J. K. T. von Otto 1879). Cf. the statements of Philo and the Church Fathers now in R. Hanhart 1962: 146-49.

century even claims to have seen the remains of the cells where the translators did their work in strict isolation. This is obviously a pious legend witnessing to the high esteem enjoyed by 𝕲 in the Christian church.

But even what the Letter of Aristeas itself relates is incredible in many respects. It was not written by a heathen courtier as it professes, but by a Jew who praises the wisdom and the Law of his people through the lips of a heathen king. The writer did not live in the days of Ptolemy Philadelphus, but more than a century later. Further, the Jewish Law was not translated to satisfy the curiosity of a royal patron of the arts, but because the Egyptian Jews no longer understood Hebrew and were in need of just such a translation. And finally, the translators were not Palestinian Jews, but members of the Alexandrian diaspora for whom Greek was the language of everyday life.

The legendary character of the Letter of Aristeas has long been recognized.[4] And yet until quite recently it has influenced our approach to the study of 𝕲. One view holds that the letter intended to defend an early version of the Torah (the Old or Ur-Septuagint) against attacks and revision attempts, while another would understand it as an apology for a new revised version proposed as a standard text to replace earlier translations (Targums). We will discuss in more detail on p. 63 both these views and their implications for Septuagint studies.

3. The Origin and History of the Septuagint to the Second Century A.D.

We noticed that the Letter of Aristeas places the origin of the Pentateuch version in the first half of the third century B.C. In this it may very well be correct. It is also reliable in associating the version with the Jewish community in Alexandria, which was the most important in the Jewish diaspora. A Greek translation was needed there much as an Aramaic translation was

---

4. According to B. H. Stricker's (1956) interpretation of the Letter of Aristeas, the translation of the Pentateuch was ordered by Ptolemy II Philadelphus in connection with his policy of hellenizing the Jews; but contra, cf. R. Hanhart 1962: 141-43. L. Rost 1970 evaluates the data in the Letter of Aristeas in a more positive way: the translation of the Torah would provide a text guaranteed in its authenticity as an official version, authorized by the highest religious and political authority in Judaism, the high priest in Jerusalem. This would have been a necessity for political reasons if it were to secure special rights for Jews in hellenistic cities in the future and to protect these privileges. Similarly D. Barthélemy 1974.

needed in Palestine, and perhaps as with the Targums its beginnings may have been in the oral translations made for worship services. It is natural that the first part to be translated would be the most important part of the Old Testament for Jews, the Torah, and that the other books would follow in due course. The prologue to the Wisdom of Jesus ben Sirach (Ecclesiasticus, ca. 116 B.C.) refers to a Greek version of the Law and also of "the Prophets and the other books." A long period must be allowed for the translation of the entire Old Testament. This precludes the possibility that 𝕲 was the work of a single translator or group of translators. A close examination of the version's character yields the same conclusion. The translations of the individual books are not at all uniform, and the differences which occur even within single books have led Henry St. John Thackeray, as well as Johannes Herrmann and Friedrich Baumgärtel, to suspect that Isaiah, Jeremiah, and the Minor Prophets were divided between two translators, while Ezekiel was the work of three.[5] It is probable that in the Pentateuch each book was the work of a single translator (or group of translators), but no two books were by the same translator.[6] Many books are almost literal translations, while others such as Job and Daniel are quite free. And yet, when the Greek Jeremiah lacks some 2,700 words that are found in the Hebrew,[7] and the order of the text differs somewhat as well, it is evident that the difference is due not simply to the translator, but to his Hebrew exemplar, which must have differed from the Masoretic text we have today. In the texts from Qumran we find not only the longer text represented, but in a fragmentary Hebrew manuscript (4QJer[b]) we have the shorter text found hitherto only in Greek.[8]

We may say in summary that what we find in 𝕲 is not a single version but a collection of versions made by various writers who differed greatly in their translation methods, their knowledge of Hebrew, their styles, and

5. H. St. J. Thackeray 1921; J. Herrmann and F. Baumgärtel 1923. While this thesis may hold for Jeremiah and Ezekiel, it has been contested for the other books; cf. J. Ziegler 1934; cf. also p. 194. E. Tov 1976 explains the differences between Jer. 1–28 and 29–52 by the following hypothesis: the first part preserves the original Greek translation, while the second part represents the revision of a lost original Greek translation. A redactor's hand in the second part had already been suspected by J. Ziegler 1957: 128.

6. Hanhart 1984b: 7, with reference to J. W. Wevers.

7. This number is based on the calculations of H.-J. Min 1977; cf. Sonderlund 1985: 11.

8. F. M. Cross 1961: 187. On the special problems of the textual history of Jeremiah in the Septuagint and the various attempts to deal with them, cf. the survey by S. Sonderlund 1985: 47.

in other ways. This diversity which makes it necessary to consider each book of the Bible individually is a large part of the problem posed by ⅁, making it impossible to formulate the value of the version as a whole for textual criticism in any uniform way.

⅁ made it possible for Jews living in the Greek diaspora to read their Holy Scriptures in their own familiar language. But it also provided an opportunity for non-Jews to study the Old Testament (cf. Acts 8:26f.). This was very important for the early church, because it gave wide currency to ideas with which the Christian message could be related. Furthermore, ⅁ became *the* holy book of the Christians of the early centuries. This placed the Jewish community in a peculiar situation with regard to the version it had produced and held in honor. In disputes between Jews and Christians the Christians would often appeal to ⅁, as in the discussion of Isa. 7:14. The Jews claimed that this passage refers to a young woman (νεᾶνις), not to a virgin (παρθένος). The Christians could respond by pointing out that even the version the Jews themselves had produced read παρθένος. In the course of time Christian insertions crept into the text, as in ⅁ Ps. 95, Ps. 13, and elsewhere.[9] This appropriation of the Greek Old Testament by the Christian church led the Jews to disown ⅁[10] and create for themselves new forms of the text in Greek, whether by revision or by independent translation.

4. Revisions and Later Greek Versions

The earliest translations of the Scriptures in written form (the Old Septuagint) were pioneer undertakings accomplished without adequate tools (lexicons, etc.). Even before the Christian era, perhaps from the very first, comparing these translations with the Hebrew text revealed them to be inadequate and inspired efforts to bring the Greek text more into conformity with the Hebrew original. One such attempt to edit the text on the basis of specific principles is attested by a fragmentary Greek scroll of the Twelve Prophets discovered at Naḥal Ḥever in 1952 and published by Dominique Barthélemy in 1963 (cf. p. 192).[11] As one of its characteristics is the rendering of גַּם or וְגַם by καί γε (instead of simply καί), it is known as

9. On the Christian insertions (additamenta christiana), cf.A. Rahlfs 1931: 30-32.

10. Rabbis later regarded the making of a Greek version as a calamity and commemorated it with a day of fasting; cf. R. Hanhart 1962: 144.

11. D. Barthélemy 1963. Official publication by E. Tov, *et al.* 1990.

the *kaige* (or Palestinian) recension.[12] The fragment may be dated about
A.D. 50 (or fifty years earlier), and like the Papyrus Fouad 266 of a century
earlier,[13] it demonstrates that even prior to Jewish-Christian discussions
there had been a trend toward conforming the Greek to the Hebrew text.[14]
These discussions and the definition of a standard Hebrew text only served
to give it further impetus. Thus originated the translations of Aquila, of
Symmachus for the Ebionite Jewish Christian community, and the revision
of Theodotion. It is likely that these drew upon the earlier Palestinian
recension, because they share many readings with it (Barthélemy: "surre-
censeurs").

(a) *Aquila* (α′) of Sinope in Pontus was a proselyte and a disciple of   α′
Rabbi Akiba,[15] according to Jewish tradition, in whose spirit he produced
his slavishly literal translation. Although his vocabulary shows that he had
a good knowledge of Greek, he was so absurdly devoted to the principle
of literalism that the meaning of the text often suffered and his version
sounded distinctly un-Greek. But it was exactly this bold literalism combined with an almost precious precision, especially in using words of
similar sounds, that recommended Aquila's work to his Jewish contem-
poraries of about A.D. 130 and gave it considerable authority among them.[16]
As late as A.D. 533 we find that in Emperor Justinian's conciliatory Codicil
No. 146 this version is cited along with the inspired Septuagint as sanc-
tioned for use in synagogues. Our knowledge of Aquila's version is based
not only on quotations and Hexaplaric fragments (cf. pp. 57ff.), but also
on the sixth-century palimpsests from the Cairo Geniza.[17]

(b) *Symmachus* (σ′) produced another new version ca. A.D. 170   σ′

---

12. This recension may also be identified in the text of 2 Samuel 11:21–1 Kings
2:11 and 1 Kings 22–2 Kings 25. Other characteristics are listed by K. G. O'Connell
1976: 378.

13. Cf. p. 190, and R. Hanhart 1978.

14. Revised forms of the Septuagint text may be found in quotations in the New
Testament; cf. R. Hanhart 1981.

15. On Akiba's hermeneutics and his influence on Aquila, cf. D. Barthélemy
1963: 1-30.

16. For examples of Aquila's translation, cf. A. Rahlfs 1935: 1:xxiv-xxvi (editio
minor, lvii-lxi); J. Reider and N. Turner 1966; K. Hyvärinen 1977 (but note the critical
review by S. P. Brock 1978).

17. Cf. F. C. Burkitt 1897; C. F. Taylor 1900. P. Katz 1950 traces the biblical
citations in Philo's writings which depart from the Septuagint to a late recension of the
Septuagint influenced by Aquila which replaced the original Septuagint text in some
Philonic manuscripts. Cf. G. D. Kilpatrick 1951: 89. P. E. Kahle identifies these citations as fragments of an early Jewish translation.

designed not only for literal accuracy but also for good Greek idiom.[18] According to Eusebius and Jerome, Symmachus was an Ebionite; according to Epiphanius he was a Samaritan converted to Judaism.[19] His version is found in only a few Hexapla fragments.

θ′   (c) **Theodotion** (θ′) was a proselyte at the end of the second century according to early church tradition.[20] He did not produce a new version, but revised an existing Greek version following the Hebrew text. Whether the version he used was the Septuagint (as Alfred Rahlfs affirms) is disputed. The problem is posed by "Theodotionic" readings occurring in texts which are earlier than Theodotion (e.g., the New Testament, Barnabas, Clement, Hermas). Frederic G. Kenyon and Paul E. Kahle assume that Theodotion revised an earlier text which is to be distinguished from the Septuagint, and which has survived in only a few early Christian quotations although it was once widely used. It has been commonly accepted that Theodotion's version of the book of Daniel supplanted that of the Septuagint in almost all manuscripts. This assumption should now be qualified, according to Armin Schmitt's research,[21] by the recognition that the "θ" text in Daniel apparently cannot be ascribed to Theodotion.

In early manuscripts these three later versions are sometimes cited
οἱ γ′, as (οἱ) γ′ = οἱ τρεῖς (ἑρμηνευταί) or as (οἱ) λ′ = οἱ λοιποί (ἑρμηνευταί).[22]
οἱ λ′ These sigla are also used in BHS.

In Origen's scholarly magnum opus (which we will discuss next) he made use not only of these three versions, each of which has exercised a considerable influence on the transmission of the Septuagint, but also of yet other versions which are otherwise virtually unknown to us and which
ε′ he called **Quinta** (ε′),[23] **Sexta,** and **Septima.** "The availability of so many

18. Cf. B. A. van der Kooij 1988.

19. Both views are still held in the twentieth century. According to H. J. Schoeps 1950: 82-119, Symmachus was undoubtedly an Ebionite Christian (Ebionite theology, Greek education, and dependence on rabbinic exegesis). But on the other hand D. Barthélemy 1974a regards him as a recircumcised Samaritan convert to Judaism and a pupil of Rabbi Meir (probably to be identified with Sûmkhôs of the Talmud). On his translation: J. R. Busto-Saiz 1978.

20. D. Barthélemy 1963: 144f. suggests that Theodotion may be identified with Jonathan ben 'Uzziel, who lived in the first half of the first century A.D., and that the *kaige* recension may be traced to him. There were evidently two men named Theodotion who lived at different times and to whom a recension has been attributed.

21. A. Schmitt 1966.

22. J. Ziegler 1943: 72, 108.

23. D. Barthélemy 1953: 29 and 1963: 215-220, wishes to identify this with the text which is attested in the leather scroll containing the Greek text of the Minor

different Greek versions of the Bible among the Jews of that time is incontrovertible proof of their great need for contemporary Greek translations, and of the inadequacy of the older versions made centuries earlier for the demands of the time."[24]

5. Origen's Hexapla   Orig

The number of competing versions in addition to the original text was undoubtedly confusing, especially in discussions with the Jews. The Hexapla, a massive work compiled by the Alexandrian theologian Origen between A.D. 230 and 240, was an attempt to achieve some clarification. Origen stated that the chief purpose of the undertaking was to equip Christians for their discussions with Jews who made their appeal to the original text. It is not altogether certain whether he actually appreciated the textual problems of ⑤ and was restrained in his comments because of its prestige in the church, as is so often asserted. He may himself have considered ⑤ to be inspired.

Origen arranged the following texts in six parallel columns: (1) the Hebrew text (ο εβρ′); (2) the Hebrew text transliterated into Greek;[25] ο εβρ′
(3) Aquila; (4) Symmachus; (5) the Septuagint; (6) Theodotion. Eusebius reports that in the Psalms Origen added a fifth, sixth, and seventh version (see above). The Hebrew text stands in first place as the original, and the sequence of the versions corresponds to their relationship to the original, priority going to Aquila as the most literal. The primary interest of the Alexandrian scholar was to link ⑤ to the original Hebrew text with the help of the other more literal versions.[26] To this end he borrowed certain

---

Prophets. Actually he can adduce some striking examples of agreement between the Greek Minor Prophets and the readings of Quinta cited by Jerome. H. J. Venetz 1974 is in agreement and extends the characteristics of the Kaige recension. For a critical review of "pan kaige-ism" cf. A. Pietersma 1985.

24. P. E. Kahle 1954: 90.

25. On the problem of the transliterated text, which was not Origen's own creation but derived from elsewhere, cf. P. E. Kahle 1960: 113-17; S. Jellicoe 1968: 106ff. But to the contrary see J. A. Emerton 1956, 1970, 1971: the second column was designed to aid the reader in vocalizing the first column.

26. The tendency for such assimilations may be observed even much earlier; cf. above pp. 54f. Also: H. A. Sanders and C. Schmidt 1927: 25-29, 265; J. Ziegler 1943: 33f.; 1945/48 (see below, p. 194); P. Katz 1957. P. E. Kahle 1954: 88 has stressed particularly that this tendency was already present in pre-Christian times, and that Origen "continued the work of the Jews of previous centuries, applying it to the Bible

sigla designed by the great textual critic Aristarchus (217-145 B.C.) which were in use in Alexandrian philological studies: the obelos (–, ÷, ÷), the metobelos (/., /., Ɱ), and the asterisk (※). These were used as follows:

c ob (a) Words in 𝕲 which are lacking in the original text and which strictly should be deleted are placed between an obelos and a metobelos, e.g., ÷εἰς φαῦσιν τῆς γῆςⱮ Gen. 1:14.

c ast (b) Words in the original text which are lacking in 𝕲 were borrowed from another version and inserted in the 𝕲 column placed between an asterisk and a metobelos, e.g., ※καὶ ἐγένετο οὕτωςⱮ Gen. 1:7.[27] On occasion Origen seems also to have used asterisks to indicate the correction of a faulty text.[28]

But Origen also interfered with the text of 𝕲 without indicating it, so that the form of 𝕲 he gave in the fifth column is called the Hexaplaric 𝕲O recension (𝕲O). This soon began to have a profound effect on manuscripts. Jerome writes, "There is hardly a single book to be found that does not have these (Hexaplaric additions)."[29]

The *Milan Fragments* (Codex rescriptus Bybliothecae Ambrosianae O 39 sup.) discovered by Giovanni Mercati in 1895 show a clear example of the format of the Hexapla (pl. 34). It is a palimpsest: the lower text is an exegetical compilation (minuscule, ninth to eleventh century). First there is the text of a Psalm in the columnar order of the Hexapla. This is followed by the Septuagint text of the same Psalm and the catena written in continuous lines (cf. p. 62). Some 150 verses of the Hexapla Psalter are preserved in this way. The first column with the text in Hebrew is lacking, and the sixth column does not give the text of Theodotion as we might expect, but that of Quinta. The Septuagint column does not have the Aristarchan sigla (cf. n. 21). The unique material in this palimpsest is of great value not only for the study of the Greek versions, but also for the history of the Hebrew language, because the transliteration of the Hebrew text in the second column (the first column

---

text of the Christians." D. Barthélemy 1963: ix speaks of "a definite program for the translation and revision of the Greek Bible" which developed in Palestine under the influence of the Rabbinate in the first century A.D.

27. P. E. Kahle 1960: 115f. has deduced from the lack of Aristarchan signs in the Milan Hexapla fragments (see below) that the Septuagint column did not contain diacritical signs in either the Hexapla or the Tetrapla; instead, the Hexapla with its collection of significant Jewish biblical texts simply provided the basis for Origen's work in textual criticism.

28. J. W. Wevers 1952: 189.

29. "Vix enim unus aut alter invenietur liber, qui ista (i.e., additamenta hexaplaria) non habeat."

in this manuscript) reveals a pronunciation of the Hebrew that antedates the Tiberian usage by centuries.[30]

Origen produced a second work besides the Hexapla, the *Tetrapla,* which contained only the four Greek versions. It is not certain whether the Tetrapla was a later abridgment of the Hexapla (the common view) or an earlier stage of its formation.[31]

Both works were of enormous dimensions — the Hexapla comprised six thousand folios in fifty volumes — and could hardly have been copied often in their entirety. The original was in Caesarea in Palestine, and was probably destroyed in the Islamic conquest. Fortunately the Hexaplaric text of 𝕲 was often copied; Pamphilus and Eusebius promoted its circulation. Although no authentic manuscript of the Hexaplaric Septuagint has survived, there are manuscripts which represent the text of Origen more or less closely. The relationships vary greatly from book to book. Among the important witnesses are *Codex Colberto-Sarravianus* (G; pl. 35) of the fourth or fifth century, which has the Aristarchan sigla, and several minuscules.[32] The Syriac translation of 𝕲^O known as the *Syro-Hexapla* (Syh; pl. 37) is of great value. It was prepared with meticulous care by Bishop Paul of Tella in A.D. 616-617 (pl. 37), and it also preserves the Aristarchan sigla. One of the surviving witnesses to this version is the ninth-century Milan *Codex Ambrosianus Syrohexaplaris,* which contains the Prophets and the Writings.[33] Besides these manuscripts of the Hexaplaric family there are also several belonging to other textual families which are significant for reconstructing Origen's text because of the Hexaplaric readings recorded in their margins. Among the uncials are *Codex Coislinianus* (M) and *Codex Marchalianus* (Q; pl. 36). A survey of all the Hexaplaric material known in his time was compiled by *Frederick Field* 1875. An account of a recent find of Hexaplaric material for Isaiah is given by August Möhle 1934.

𝕲^O

Syh

---

30. Published by G. Mercati 1958, with an introduction followed by photographs and transcriptions of the fragments; 1965, a further volume of critical notes; a volume with fragments of other manuscripts (indirect witnesses) is promised.

31. O. Procksch 1935.

32. Cf. A. Schenker 1975.

33. Photographic edition by A. M. Ceriani 1874. Other Syro-Hexaplar texts have been published by P. A. de Lagarde 1892, and W. Baars 1968. The text of the Psalter in the Syro-Hexapla, however, is not Hexaplaric; cf. A. Rahlfs 1931: 52. In 1964 Arthur Vööbus discovered in the area of Tur Abdin (Turkey) an eleventh/twelfth-century manuscript containing the Syro-Hexaplaric version of Gen. 32:9–Deut. 32:25 (with minor lacunae; Syh^T), supplied with many Hexaplaric signs. Edition by A. Vööbus 1975.

6. Other Recensions of the Septuagint

Origen was not the only one to revise the Septuagint. Jerome mentions *three* recensions in his preface to Chronicles written about A.D. 400: "Alexandria and Egypt honor **Hesychius** as editor of the Septuagint; in Constantinople and as far as Antioch copies by the martyr **Lucian** are commended. The provinces between these two read the Palestinian codices prepared by **Origen** and promoted by Eusebius and Pamphilus. Thus the whole world is divided in competition by this threefold variety."[34] According to this statement the different provinces of the early church each had its own biblical text. But we should not infer from Jerome's statement that these three were the only recensions, or that Hesychius and Lucian were regarded anywhere as absolutely authoritative.[35]

Lucian, a presbyter from Antioch, died a martyr in A.D. 312. Hesychius is perhaps to be identified with the bishop who was killed in the persecutions of Diocletian. While the Lucianic recension $\mathfrak{G}^L$) is mentioned elsewhere, that of Hesychius is not. Our information about it is too vague to permit either description or dating.[36] There is no single principle which characterized the Lucianic recension. Joseph Ziegler describes it for Isaiah and the Minor Prophets in this way: "Lucian produced it from the Hexaplaric recension, but with no attempt to parallel the text of $\mathfrak{M}$ with any precision. The corrections based on $\mathfrak{M}$ (through the Hexaplaric recension, especially the later versions) are few in number and of little significance. More important for Lucian are the laws of Greek grammar and style, and it is in this area that most of his improvements are found."[37] Lucian's text is witnessed in the biblical quotations of Chrysostom and Theodoret of Cyrrhus, as well as in numerous minuscules.[38] Beside the main body of

---

34. Alexandria et Aegyptus in Septuaginta suis *Hesychium* laudat auctorem; Constantinopolis usque Antiochiam *Luciani* martyris exemplaria probat. Mediae inter has provinciae Palaestinos codices legunt, quos ab *Origene* elaboratos Eusebius et Pamphilus vulgaverunt; totusque orbis hac inter se trifaria varietate compugnat.

35. H. Dörrie 1940: 69.

36. J. Ziegler 1939: 23; R. Hanhart 1966: 98f. For discussion of the Hesychian recension, cf. S. Jellicoe 1968: 146-156, and J. W. Wevers 1968: 37f., who refers to "this shadowy figure" and "this phantasy."

37. J. Ziegler 1943: 89.

38. P. E. Kahle 1954: 83-86, has indicated several older texts which contain Lucianic readings (e.g., John Rylands Papyrus Greek 458, Justin Martyr, Philo, Josephus), and reaches the conclusion: "Textual forms of the Greek Bible such as Lucian used for his revision must therefore have been widespread in the early centuries of our era" (col. 85). Indeed, the John Rylands Papyrus Greek 458 and the leather scroll

Lucianic witnesses ($\mathfrak{G}^L$), two subgroups designated $\mathfrak{G}^{II}$ and $\mathfrak{G}^{III}$ may be $\mathfrak{G}^{II}, \mathfrak{G}^{III}$
identified in some manuscripts.[39]

The recensions mentioned above do not mark the final stage of the
history of the Greek text. It continued to develop. The revised texts tended
to mingle and influence one another, resulting in more or less mixed texts
in all the surviving manuscripts. Because manuscripts could be copied from
different exemplars, a single manuscript might follow different revisions
in its different parts, and on occasion this has misled Septuagint scholarship.
When Paul A. de Lagarde edited the Septuagint text of Genesis to Ruth in
1883 (in BHK: $\mathfrak{G}^L$),[40] he relied on manuscripts 19 and 108 on the assumption that because they are clearly Lucianic after 1 Samuel, they must also
be Lucianic in the earlier books. Rahlfs was later able to prove that these
manuscripts are not Lucianic from Genesis to Ruth 4:10, but represent here
another text type. "Thus even Lagarde's supposedly Lucianic text is not
Lucianic at all from Genesis to Ruth 4:10; only the last twelve verses of
Ruth (4:11-22) are actually Lucianic in manuscripts 19 and 108, and consequently also in Lagarde's edition, because of a shift in the text type of
the exemplar they followed."[41]

7. Lagarde's Program

From what we have said it is evident that the history of the transmission
of the Septuagint is quite complex. None of the various surviving forms
of the text has preserved the original form of the version. Is it possible to
reach beyond the variety of the textual forms which exist today and find
a hypothetical unity underlying them — the original Septuagint? *Paul de
Lagarde* (1827-1891), who did so much for Septuagint research during the
last century, operated with a clearly defined program: "It has been my
intention through the years to reconstruct the three original recensions of
the Septuagint attested by Jerome, to have them printed in parallel columns,

---

found in 1952 containing the Greek text of the Minor Prophets "prove with certainty
the existence of textual forms akin to Lucian . . . in the pre-Christian era" (col. 86).
On the history of the Lucianic text which seems "to become ever more complex," cf.
also J. W. Wevers 1954: 98-100. D. Barthélemy 1963: 127 is critical of the existence
of a "Lucianic recension": it is rather the "Antiochene text," or essentially "the old
Septuagint, more or less corrupted."

39. Cf. J. Ziegler 1939: 74ff.; 1943: 74ff.; 1952: 45f.
40. P. A. de Lagarde 1883.
41. A. Rahlfs 1928: 77.

and to draw further conclusions from a comparison of these three texts."[42] Thus Lagarde proposed the classification of Septuagint manuscripts, assigning them to the individual recensions with the help of patristic quotations and other criteria. After achieving this vantage the next step could be taken toward the original text, which he assumed would be the form farthest from the Masoretic text.

A great deal has been done to solve this problem, especially by the Septuagint Project of the Göttinger Gesellschaft der Wissenschaften (cf. p. 77). But the goal proposed by Lagarde could not be attained. As we have noted, the Hesychian recension cannot be recovered. And in other respects as well the material itself demanded a modification of Lagarde's principles. The problems in each book are different, as the two following examples show.

(a) In Rahlfs's edition of Genesis[43] he has distinguished between two larger groups (Origen and the Catena text[44]), six smaller groups, and a minuscule manuscript with a Lucianic text. Further, seven uncial manuscripts and several minuscules refused to conform to any group. Wevers[45] distinguished ten different groups (none identified with the Lucianic text) and the O-recension.

(b) In Ziegler's edition of Isaiah[46] the evidence is divided into four groups: (1) the Alexandrian text, represented by Alexandrinus, Marchalianus, minuscule manuscripts, Cyril of Alexandria,[47] and others. This group has best preserved the text of $\mathfrak{G}$, but has itself been influenced by secondary material, especially by the recensions (by $\mathfrak{G}^O$ in particular); (2) the Hexaplaric recension, attested by Vaticanus, Venetus, the Syro-Hexaplar, some minuscules, and the Church Fathers Eusebius of Caesarea, Basil the Great, and Jerome; (3) the recension of Lucian, found in a main group of five minuscules and several subgroups, and in the commentaries of Theodoret and of (Pseudo-) Chrysostom, who defends the Lucianic text vigorously and explicitly against Palestinian attacks; and (4) the Catena group.

---

42. P. A. de Lagarde 1891: 3.

43. A. Rahlfs 1926.

$\mathfrak{G}^c$

44. Catena is the name given to "chain commentaries" made up of exegetical comments from various Church Fathers, in use from the sixth century (cf. pl. 38). The Catena manuscripts offer their own special late recension of the text, which is also taken over in other manuscripts with the omission of the catena itself.

45. J. W. Wevers 1974a.

46. J. Ziegler 1939.

Cyr

47. Cyril, Patriarch of Alexandria (412-444), through his commentaries on a number of Old Testament books (cited as Cyr [$\mathfrak{G}^{Cyr}$]), is an important witness to the text used in Alexandria.

From these two examples it is apparent that the surviving evidence is much more varied than was suspected in Lagarde's program. Yet it is possible to distinguish certain groupings (although in Genesis even this requires further qualification), and while these groupings cannot be identified with the three classical recensions, yet their comparison can lead us back to an earlier form of the text. To this extent it may be said that Lagarde's proposals have been proven correct in their essentials, even though requiring some modification.[48]

8. Kahle's Thesis

But does the view of the origin and development of the Septuagint held by Lagarde and his followers actually correspond to the facts? Do they not attempt to treat a translation, where different principles apply, on the analogy of an original text? This question has been posed repeatedly, especially by P. Kahle in the Schweich Lectures for 1941, where he challenged Lagarde's thesis vigorously, with great thoroughness, marshalling a wealth of evidence.[49] His statements there should be reviewed with careful attention, for they touch on a central problem of Septuagintal research.

Kahle begins with a fresh interpretation of the Letter of Aristeas. He regards it, of course, as legendary, but the question remains as to why it was written. It is concerned with a translation of the Torah which was regarded as authoritative by the Jewish community in Alexandria. There cannot be any doubt that the letter was written as propaganda for this standard translation.[50] The letter itself recognizes that this was not the first translation, for it mentions earlier unreliable ones (par. 314-16). Greek translations were as necessary for Jews living in the Greek-speaking diaspora as the Aramaic Targums were for their fellow Jews in Palestine (cf. pp. 79ff.). The first attempts may have been made as early as 300 B.C., and as they could hardly have been very satisfactory they were constantly subject to revision. This led to the desire and the need for a reliable standard Greek text, and one was produced by a commission on behalf of the Jewish

---

48. Cf. H. Dörrie 1940, and P. Katz 1949, 1956.

49. P. E. Kahle 1959: 209-264; a summary of the conclusions drawn there was published by Kahle 1947. The basic hypothesis had already been stated in Kahle 1915: 410-12.

50. P. E. Kahle 1959: 211.

community in Alexandria.[51] It is this *revised* version with which the letter of Aristeas is concerned.[52] As the letter was written about 100 B.C., or perhaps a little earlier according to the modern view, it is this period to which the origins of the standard version (of the Torah alone!) must be assigned.

The standard text did not meet with immediate and exclusive acceptance any more than we should expect from parallel examples in the history of Bible translating. Other translations continued in use. We find traces of them in the Old Testament quotations of Philo, Josephus, the New Testament,[53] and in other texts, although the original form has sometimes been obscured by later corrections to agree with 𝕲. And even in the book of Judges, where Codex Alexandrinus and Codex Vaticanus differ so greatly that even Lagarde spoke of two different versions, the explanation is that we have here two forms of an Old Testament Targum.

Judaism made no attempt to produce a standard text beyond the Torah, as far as we know. And even this standard text, the Septuagint, was completely abandoned in the second century for new versions (cf. pp. 54ff.) which adhered closely to the officially established Hebrew text. This Hebrew text was the final standard of authority for Judaism.

The Christian church, however, soon needed an authoritative *Greek* text of the Bible. This was achieved only after a transitional period in which different versions borrowed from the Jews were used side by side. Only one of these competitors survived while the others fell into disuse. To this text of the *entire* Old Testament, itself a collection of different versions lacking any marks of overall unity, the name "Septuagint" with all its attendant prestige was transferred in the second century. "The manuscripts handed down in the church lead us at best to a standard text used in the church — a text which was only gradually established, and did not itself stand at the beginning of the tradition."[54]

Thus in brief, Kahle may be said to view 𝕲 on the analogy of the Aramaic Targums. The unity of the Targums was not in their origins, but something achieved over the centuries through the efforts of anonymous groups, and it was the same with 𝕲, the Greek Targum. This is where Kahle's program of Septuagint studies differs essentially from that of

51. It seems probable that this commission met on the island of Pharos. Philo tells us (*de Vita Mosis* 2.5-7) that an annual festival was held there to commemorate the completion of the Septuagint.

52. P. E. Kahle 1959: 214.

53. Particularly at variance with the text of 𝕲 is the quotation of Isa. 42:1-4 in Matt. 12:20.

54. P. E. Kahle 1947: 177.

Lagarde and his followers: "The task set for scholarship here is not to reconstruct or even attempt a hypothetical reconstruction of the original text of the version, but to assemble and examine with the greatest care all the fragments and traces of the earliest forms of the Greek Bible we can discover. Only in this way will we be in a position to gain a realistic view of the Greek version of the Old Testament."[55]

The view of the development of the Septuagint sketched by Kahle has not been supported by new discoveries which have given us our first glimpse of the Greek text in the pre-Christian period. While Kahle appealed to the text of the Greek Minor Prophets scroll of the mid-first century A.D. for his thesis,[56] the majority of scholars who have examined it have not been convinced. Thus John W. Wevers has demonstrated for the text of Hab. 2:6, which has survived almost complete: "It is clear that the text represents a revision based upon the Hebrew text, because the changes tend toward a more literal translation . . . but it is equally clear that the reviser began from a Septuagint base."[57] His conclusion is that: "Our text should bury Kahle's theory of 'multiple versions' once for all. This is an obviously Jewish text which is equally obviously a revision of the reputedly 'Christian' Septuagint text."[58] In theory there is much to be said for Kahle's admonition: "The editor of a Platonic *Dialogue* must attempt to produce the original text of Plato's autograph as nearly as possible. Can we speak, though, of such an original text for a version of the Bible?"[59] Yet his thesis has not been substantiated by the early texts that have thus far been found.

The Targum hypothesis, however, is certainly valid for certain aspects of the early and later history of the Septuagint:

(a) It should not be supposed that the "original Septuagint" represents the first translation made of the Hebrew text, particularly of the Pentateuch. The need for a text that would be understood by Greek-speaking Jews, for use in public worship, study, education, and private devotion, gave occasion from early times for ad hoc translations. Even the Letter of Aristeas acknowledges this in referring to "earlier inadequate versions of the Law."[60]

---

55. *Ibid.*, 180.

56. P. E. Kahle 1954: 89f.

57. J. W. Wevers 1968: 68.

58. *Ibid.*, 67f. Cf. also R. Hanhart's observation (1979b: 294) that "the few texts of the Greek Bible of pre-Christian Jewish origin . . . witness without exception to the unrevised form of the text transmitted in Christian manuscripts of the Septuagint."

59. P. E. Kahle 1947: 162.

60. Aristeas 314.

Those who were responsible (whether individuals or groups of translators) for the various books of the Septuagint would have made use of just such translations[61] while editing them for "stylistic consistency."[62]

(b) But the version that was produced in this way did not enjoy the security of an original literary production — precisely because it was a translation. It was subject not only to scribal errors but also to such widespread editing (cf. pp. 54f.) that it could give the impression of multiple translations (targums). From such a perspective on the growth of the Septuagint, the contrast between the "original Septuagint" theory and the Targum theory becomes a relative matter (Robert Hanhart).

9. The Septuagint and the Hebrew Text

No other version has received as much attention for textual criticism as 𝕲. Not only was it valued highly in antiquity, but in the nineteenth century many scholars practically preferred it over the Masoretic text. They believed that because of its pre-Christian origins it could assist in the recovery of an earlier, pre-Masoretic text that would be closer to the original than 𝔐. But today we recognize that 𝕲 neither was nor was intended to be a precise scholarly translation. Many other factors and interests played a part in its formation. An uncritical use of it which ignores these factors can only lead to false conclusions. In the following paragraphs a few basic considerations are noted, with the reminder that 𝕲 differs so greatly from book to book that no generalization can be made without reservations.

(a) If we are tempted to prefer 𝕲 to 𝔐 as an older witness to the text, we should recall the unevenness of its own textual tradition. Whereas the consonantal text of 𝔐 has remained remarkably constant since the second century A.D., the Septuagint manuscripts even centuries later have widely divergent texts. Lagarde was quite justified when he insisted from his own standpoint on establishing a consistent "original text" of 𝕲 before using the version for textual criticism.

Even if an "original text" such as the Göttingen Septuagint seeks to establish were available, should it be preferred unquestioningly over 𝔐 simply because of its age? This raises the question of the Hebrew text underlying 𝕲. Is it necessarily better than 𝔐 because it is older? We have

---

61. Thus J. Ziegler 1934a: 42 believes that Greek texts of the passages of Isaiah read liturgically in the synagogue were available to the translator.
62. R. Hanhart 1984b: 6.

already noted that in hundreds of instances 𝕲 agrees with the Samaritan Pentateuch (cf. p. 46). This and other observations suggest that the Hebrew text underlying 𝕲 was far inferior to 𝔐. Whereas 𝔐 offers a careful recension, 𝕲 and 𝕾 are derived from early popular recensions in use among the Jews of the Diaspora.[63] Today even after the discovery of Qumran texts in agreement with 𝕲 caution is observed. Thus, for example, Emanuel Tov concludes that the great mass of variants from 𝔐 found in 𝕲 — more than are found in all other witnesses put together — cannot be subsumed under any common denominator, such as shorter, expansive, better, older, popular, etc. All the variants deserve individual consideration and are not susceptible to generalized judgments: this is true not only of the significant examples in 1-2 Samuel, where 𝔐 is frequently corrupt, but also in Joshua, Ezekiel 40–48, Jeremiah, and Esther.[64]

A word should be added here about the form of *script* used in the translation base of the Septuagint, because this is closely related to the concerns of textual criticism and has already led to far-reaching practical consequences. The question received considerable attention following 1923, when F. X. Wutz first proposed in an essay the thesis he later developed in more extensive studies:[65] that the translators of the Septuagint worked from a Hebrew text transliterated into Greek letters. This transliterated text was supposedly corrupted by scribal and other errors, or misconstrued by the translators. Working from these assumptions Wutz believed he could recover the original Hebrew text. The fact that transliterated Hebrew texts existed cannot be denied, but so many factors argue against the assumption that 𝕲 was translated solely from such a text that Wutz's thesis has not found acceptance. In a few instances it might well apply, but on the whole the Septuagint was apparently based on texts written in the new Aramaic script which in many forms already anticipated the square script.[66]

(b) How should 𝕲 be assessed as a translation? What presuppositions did the translators bring to their work, what motives influenced them, and how accurately does their work reflect the original?[67] The answers to these questions are important for deciding how and to what extent 𝕲 may serve as a useful witness in textual criticism. Here we can only indicate a few specific examples of characteristic features.

---

63. H. S. Nyberg 1934: 254.
64. E. Tov 1981: 272.
65. F. X. Wutz 1923, 1937, etc. Cf. P. E. Kahle 1961: 31-41.
66. Cf. the various works of J. Fischer, e.g., 1930, etc.
67. Cf. C. Rabin 1968.

(i) The *language* of Ⅎ is *Koine* Greek, the common Greek of the hellenistic period. Naturally in a Jewish translation from Hebrew there is no lack of Hebraisms and Aramaisms, but these are fewer than was imagined before the discoveries of Koine Greek papyri since the end of the nineteenth century.

Even where the translators tried to depart from the original text as little as possible, some degree of change was inevitable due to the nature of the Greek language. One example is the Greek preference for subordinate constructions over coordinate clauses, e.g., Gen. 24:28 𝔐 ותרץ הנער ותגד לבית אמה, Ⅎ καὶ δραμοῦσα ἡ παῖς ἀπήγγειλεν εἰς τὸν οἶκον τῆς μητρός.

For a Hebrew word with as broad a range of meanings as דבר (ῥῆμα, λόγος, etc.) the translators could not always use the same Greek equivalent; they would have to find expressions appropriate to the context from the view of Greek idiom and thought. Thus for דבר we find Exod. 1:18 πρᾶγμα; 12:35 συντάσσειν; 18:16 ἀντιλογία; 18:22 κρίμα; 24:14 κρίσις; 8:8 ὁρισμός; 4:10 ἱκανός; 5:13, 19 καθῆκον; 16:4 τό (τῆς ἡμέρας); 18:11, 14 τοῦτο; 29:1 ταῦτα; 5:11 οὐδείς (with negative).[68] In these passages it would be unrealistic to imagine that the translators were dealing with different Hebrew words.

Often the Hebrew text demanded more lexical and grammatical knowledge on the part of the early translators than they possessed. They were apparently unaware of the precise meaning of such a common word as דֶּבֶר ("pestilence"), for they rendered it either in the general meaning of θάνατος, or read it as דָּבָר (Hos. 13:14 δίκη; Hab. 3:5; Ps. 90:3 λόγος; Ps. 90:6 πρᾶγμα).[69] Ziegler's verdict on the translator of Isaiah is that "he was not scrupulously concerned to translate his original precisely, word for word. He does not hesitate to omit difficult or rare words if it does not disturb the meaning of a sentence, or to reconstrue the parts of a sentence if he has difficulty understanding the original. Sometimes he seems dominated by a particular idea which he permits to influence his translation of a passage. Thus in Isaiah we find a great number of examples of what we must strictly call 'free' translations."[70]

(ii) The differences between the Jews of the Greek diaspora and the

---

68. G. Bertram 1938: 153, where further examples may be found.
69. *Ibid.*, 155f.
70. J. Ziegler 1934a: 7f. E. Tov 1984 considers the possibility that the number of Septuagint readings based upon sheer conjecture is greater than has hitherto been suspected.

people who wrote the Hebrew Old Testament were not restricted to matters of their language alone. They lived in a world of different social conditions, with different ways of thinking, and not least with differences of belief. Their environment affected them, "hellenized" them. They spoke more abstractly and philosophically about God than the "Hebrews," and they avoided the anthropomorphic and anthropopathic expressions which are so characteristic of the Hebrew Old Testament: Exod. 19:3, Moses does not ascend to God, but to the *mountain* of God; Exod. 24:10, the elders do not see God, but the place where God stands; Josh. 4:24, יד יהוה is translated δύναμις τοῦ κυρίου. The statement that "God repented" is avoided by circumlocution.[71]

Of particular significance is the expansion of the concept of God implied by the consistent translation of the divine name יהוה by κύριος: "The Bible whose God is Yahweh is a national Bible; the Bible whose God is κύριος is a universal Bible."[72]

In other instances the translators eliminated possible theological misunderstandings by avoiding literal translations. For example, they did not adopt the common Old Testament image of God as "the Rock" (צור), but substituted other expressions. Hellenistic religions saw in rocks and stones the symbols, abodes, and representations of divinity, so that "the use of this image in the Greek Old Testament, the Septuagint, which in contrast to the Hebrew text was always directed toward missionary, propaganda and apologetic purposes, could have led to serious misunderstandings, as though a rock were worshipped as the God of the Old Testament. So the image is sacrificed to the meaning. The Septuagint gives a new form to the text of the Old Testament, and in so doing preserves the spirit of the Old Testament revelation of God."[73]

(iii) The efforts of the translators to make the Old Testament intelligible to their compatriots in Egypt led them to use terms native to their Egyptian and Alexandrian environment which were not the exact equivalents of Hebrew expressions. Thus the נגשים ("slave drivers") of Exod.

---

71. E. Stauffer 1965: 109, where further examples may be found. Cf. especially C. T. Fritsch 1943, and the review by T. W. Manson 1945: 78f.; for a discussion of the problem, cf. J. W. Wevers 1954: 174-76. B. M. Zlotowitz 1981 disputes with H. M. Orlinsky (Introduction) that the translator avoided anthropomorphisms.

72. A. Deissmann 1903: 174. More recently it has been disputed whether the early translators transcribed Yahweh with κύριος or the tetragrammaton (cf. p. 190 on Pap. Fouad 266); cf. also A. Pietersma 1984. On its significance for religious history cf. R. Hanhart 1967: 57ff.

73. G. Bertram 1939: 101.

5:6, 10, 13 became the ἐργοδιῶκται ("overseers, foremen") familiar to us from the papyri of hellenistic Egypt.[74] For the particularly difficult list of fashion novelties in Isa. 31:18-24 which were strange to the translator, he simply supplied a list of comparable items from his own age and environment. "We cannot call his work here 'translation'; most of the expressions are substitutes rather than equivalents. Thus the Greek translation often refers to completely different objects, and is useless for determining the meaning of the Hebrew word."[75]

Finally we should note the attempt to make ancient words relevant to contemporary circumstances in Egyptian life. In Deut. 23:18 we read: "There shall be no cult prostitute (קְדֵשָׁה, Greek πόρνη) of the daughters of Israel, neither shall there be a cult prostitute (קָדֵשׁ, Greek πορνεύων) of the sons of Israel." The choice of the terms πόρνη and πορνεύων for קָדֵשׁ instead of ἱερόδουλος already alters the meaning of the passage. But even more significant is the addition: οὐκ ἔσται τελεσφόρος ἀπὸ θυγατέρων Ισραηλ, καὶ οὐκ ἔσται τελισκόμενος ἀπὸ υἱῶν Ισραηλ. The terms τελεσφόρος and τελισκόμενος refer to participation in the Mysteries. As cultic prostitution was a temptation to be resisted in ancient Israel, so the Mysteries were a temptation in hellenistic Egypt.[76] The Egyptian translators felt as justified as the Targumists in relating the text to their own times.

The influence of Jewish tradition as formulated in the Talmud and Midrash may also be observed in 𝕲. Thus behind a tradition in 𝕲 which departs from 𝔐 there may stand an interpretation which has its parallels in Jewish literature.[77]

In summary, the language and content of 𝕲 must be understood against the background of the particular doctrinal and religious situation which produced it and which it was intended to serve. This complicates its usefulness for textual criticism. Undoubtedly it is a most important and even indispensable witness to the text, assisting in the emendation of many corrupted passages. But it can be useful for textual criticism only after a careful appreciation of its nature, its various translation techniques, and its history. We must beware of attempting to reach the underlying Hebrew text through a simple and direct back-translation of the Greek text into Hebrew. Georg Bertram's conclusion is sound: "The Septuagint belongs to the history of Old Testament interpretation rather than to the history of the Old

74. Cf. I. L. Seeligmann 1990.
75. J. Ziegler 1934a: 208.
76. Cf. Seeligmann 1990: 390d.
77. Cf. H. M. Orlinsky 1946: 24, and L. Prijs 1948; D. J. Halperin 1982.

Testament text. It can be used as a textual witness only after its own understanding of the Old Testament text has been made clear."[78]

10. Manuscripts

The manuscript tradition of ⑥ is very extensive. Robert Holmes and James Parsons collated a total of 311 (actually 297) codices, including 21 uncials, for their edition (cf. p. 76). Rahlfs enumerated over 1,500 complete and fragmentary manuscripts (up to and including the sixteenth century) in his 1914 index of Greek manuscripts of the Old Testament,[79] which has been continued in the Göttingen Septuagint Project. Roman upper case letters are used for selected uncial manuscripts, while minuscules are designated by arabic numerals in this list, and cited in BHS as ⑥[22.26.etc.]. In addition ⑥[22.26.etc.] to these there are indirect witnesses, which include patristic quotations and versions in other languages which are based on ⑥. Recent decades have also brought a valuable enrichment of evidence in the discovery of papyri which are earlier than any materials hitherto available.

(a) *Papyri*

(i) *Papyrus Greek 458 of the John Rylands Library* in Manchester dates from the middle of the second century B.C. and offers the *earliest* surviving text of the Greek Bible (pl. 28).[80] These six fragments retrieved from the wrapping of a mummy, together with *Papyrus Fouad 266* (pl. 29) and a *leather scroll with the Greek text of the Minor Prophets* (pl. 30), constitute the few surviving fragments of the Greek Bible from the pre-Christian period whose Jewish origins are probable or certain.[81] They contain parts of Deut. 23:24–24:3; 25:1-3; 26:12, 17-19; 28:31-33, comprising a total of some fifteen verses and including a number of readings which are either peculiar to these fragments or find support in a very few other witnesses.[82]

(ii) The *Chester Beatty Papyri* (BHK: ⑥[Beatty]; pl. 31) are the most important of the papyri because of their extent and age. When they were

---

78. G. Bertram 1936: 109; cf. also 1957. Pertinent to the whole problem is the thorough work by E. Tov 1981.

79. A. Rahlfs 1914. Today *ca.* 2050 manuscripts are known, apart from lectionaries.

80. C. H. Roberts 1936.

81. Several fragments of the Greek Bible were also found at Qumran in Cave 4 (cf. P. W. Skehan 1957: 155-58, and also P. E. Kahle 1959: 223-26) and in Cave 7 (cf. p. 32).

82. Cf. the thorough study by J. Hempel 1937: 115-127.

discovered they were described as the most important event for textual criticism since the discovery of Codex Sinaiticus. They comprise the remains of eleven codices, containing parts of nine Old Testament and fifteen New Testament books, the book of Enoch, and a homily by the Church Father Melito of Sardis. They date from the second to the fourth century A.D., and are probably the remains of a Christian library in the Fayyum. The greater part of these manuscripts was acquired by the Englishman Chester Beatty in 1929 from the local people who had found them; other parts came into the possession of the University of Michigan and the American John H. Scheide; smaller fragments are in Vienna, in Italy, and in private collections,[83] and further extensive fragments of manuscript 967 are in papyrus collections of Cologne (Ezekiel, Daniel, Esther) and Madrid (Ezekiel).[84] The Old Testament is represented in the Beatty papyri by considerable portions of Genesis, Numbers, Deuteronomy, and fragments of Isaiah and Jeremiah, parts of Ezekiel, Daniel, and Esther, and fragments of Sirach. The text of Daniel is especially noteworthy, because in Daniel another version had replaced that of $\mathfrak{G}$ in the manuscript tradition (cf. p. 56), so that until now the text of $\mathfrak{G}$ was known from only *one* eleventh-century manuscript.

(iii) The ***Berlin fragments*** of a Genesis manuscript (late third century, containing Gen. 1:16–35:8; pl. 32) should also be mentioned. These were published together with a late third-century codex of the Minor Prophets in 1927,[85] and the Papyrus Bodmer XXIV, containing Ps. 17–118 and also from the third century A.D.[86] From the fourth century there is the Antinoopolis papyrus, edited by C. H. Roberts in 1950, containing fragments of Proverbs. The papyrus book of the British Library ($\mathfrak{G}^U$) is relatively late, from the seventh century; it was the first biblical papyrus to be discovered and has been in the British Library since 1836 (Papyrus 37). It comprises thirty-two folios of a Psalm codex containing the text of Ps. 10:2–18:6; 20:14–34:6, and represents the so-called Upper Egyptian text.

$\mathfrak{G}^U$

(b) ***Manuscripts.*** Among Greek manuscripts a distinction is observed between uncials or majuscules (in capital letters) and minuscules (in small letters). In antiquity for literature only the capital letters were used, written in sequence but separately and without ligatures, although for common use (as in private correspondence) the letters were joined together in a cursive

$\mathfrak{G}^{maj}$,
$\mathfrak{G}^{min}$

---

83. Publications: F. G. Kenyon 1933-37; 1958; A. C. Johnson, H. S. Gehman, E. H. Kase 1938.
84. A. Geissen 1968; W. Hamm 1969; M. Fernandez-Galliano 1971.
85. H. A. Sanders and C. Schmidt 1927.
86. R. Kasser and M. Testuz 1967.

hand. From this cursive form the minuscule hand of the medieval period developed. Until the eighth century there were only uncials, in the ninth and tenth centuries uncials and minuscules were used side by side, and from the eleventh century only minuscules. Even though the minuscule manuscripts are later, they may be valuable as textual witnesses if they were copied from lost uncials containing a good text. For textual criticism it is important to recognize that until the eighth century texts were written with their letters in continuous sequence, without word division, accents, breathings, or punctuation.

As *sigla* to distinguish individual manuscripts Holmes and Parsons used roman numerals for the uncials (e.g., $\mathfrak{G}^{XI}$) and arabic numerals for the minuscules (e.g., $\mathfrak{G}^{62.147}$). Later Lagarde introduced capital Latin letters $\mathfrak{G}^{Ms(s)}$ for the uncials, many of which have been widely adopted and are used also in BH (cf. also p. 71). The following list of manuscripts cited in BH is in chronological order.[87]

α) *Codex Vaticanus* (B). Fourth century. Vatican Library. Old Testa- $\mathfrak{G}^B$ ment complete, but Gen. 1–46:28; Ps. 105:27–137:6 added in the fifteenth century. This manuscript enjoys very great authority. Rahlfs ascribed it to Lower Egypt on the basis of its content and text.

β) *Codex Sinaiticus* (S; BHK: א; pl. 33). Fourth century. Discovered $\mathfrak{G}^S$ by Constantin von Tischendorf at St. Catherine's Monastery, Mt. Sinai, in 1844 and 1859. The main body of the manuscript is in the British Library, London (since 1933, previously in St. Petersburg), but a small part is in Leipzig (Codex Frederico-Augustanus); place of origin possibly Palestine. Recent research attributes the manuscript to three scribes, two of whom were also correctors. Later correctors have also been identified and designated in BHS as $\mathfrak{G}^{S1.2.3}$, and in BHK as $\mathfrak{G}^{\aleph\ c.a,c.b,c.c}$. The Old Testament text survives $\mathfrak{G}^{S1.2.3}$, for Gen. 23:19–24:46; Num. 5:26–7:20 (both with lacunae); 1 Chr. 9:27–19:17; Ezra-Nehemiah (from Ezra 9:9), Esther, Tobit, Judith, 1 and 4 Maccabees, Isaiah, Jeremiah (to Lam. 2:20), Joel-Malachi (Greek order), Psalms, Proverbs, Ecclesiastes, Song of Solomon, Wisdom, Sirach, and Job.

γ) *Codex Alexandrinus* (A). Fifth century. British Library, London. $\mathfrak{G}^A$ Gift to King Charles I of England in 1627, previously in the Patriarchal Library at Alexandria (hence its name). Old Testament lacks 1 Sam. 12:17–14:9; Ps. 49:20–79:11.

δ) *Codex Colberto-Sarravianus* (G; BHK: $\mathfrak{G}^G$; pl. 35). Fourth/fifth

---

87. It is not possible here to go into questions of the textual characteristics and importance of the surviving papyri and manuscripts. For this see the introductions to the volumes of the Göttingen Septuagint.

century. Main body of manuscript in Leiden, a smaller part in Paris, one folio in Leningrad. Contains Gen. 31:5–Judg. 21:12 in the Hexaplaric recension with Aristarchan sigla (cf. pp. 57, 202).

𝔊F ε) *Codex Ambrosianus* (F). Fifth century. Biblioteca Ambrosiana, Milan. Contains Gen. 31:15–Josh. 12:12 (with lacunae).

ζ) *Codex Freer* (Θ; BHK: 𝔊Θ). Fifth century. Acquired by Freer at Gizeh in 1906, now in the Smithsonian Institution, Washington, D.C. Contains Deuteronomy (except 5:16–16:18) and Joshua (except 3:3–4:10).

𝔊C η) *Codex Ephraemi Syri rescriptus* (C). Bibliothèque Nationale, Paris. A palimpsest, named for its upper writing, a thirteenth-century copy of the works of Ephraem Syrus. The lower writing is from the fifth century, containing fragments of Job, Proverbs, Ecclesiastes, Song of Solomon, Wisdom, Sirach, and the New Testament.

θ) *Codex Cottonianus* (D; BHK: 𝔊D). Fifth/sixth century. British Library, London. 150 fragments of a manuscript destroyed by a fire in Ashburnham House in 1731; there is an old collation made before the fire. Contains only Genesis.[88]

𝔊Q ι) *Codex Marchalianus* (Q; pl. 36). Sixth century. Vatican Library. Contains Isaiah, Jeremiah, Ezekiel, Daniel, Minor Prophets. Hexaplaric notes in the margin enhance the value of this manuscript (cf. p. 58).

𝔊M κ) *Codex Coislinianus* (M). Seventh century. Bibliothèque Nationale, Paris. Contains Genesis–1 Kgs. 8:40 (with lacunae), with scholia and Hexaplaric notes (cf. p. 58).

λ) *Codex Lipsiensis* (K; BHK: 𝔊K). Seventh/eighth century. University Library, Leipzig; previously St. Saba Monastery, Jerusalem, acquired by Tischendorf in 1844. A palimpsest with upper writing in Arabic, A.D. 885-886; lower writing contains brief portions of Numbers-Judges. Also belonging to this manuscript are six folios in Leningrad containing fragments of Numbers-Judges.

𝔊N μ) *Codex Basiliano-Vaticanus* (N). Eighth century. Vatican Library; previously belonged to the Basilians in Rome. Belongs with 𝔊V together with which it contains large sections of the Old Testament apart from the Psalms; lacking are Gen.–Lev. 13:59, and other parts.

𝔊V ν) *Codex Venetus* (V). The second part of the above.

ξ) *Codex rescriptus Cryptoferratensis* (Γ; BHK: 𝔊Γ). Grottaferrata in the Albian Hills. Palimpsest, lower writing eighth century, upper writing thirteenth century. The lower writing contains fragments from several of the Minor Prophets, from Isaiah, Jeremiah, Ezekiel, and Daniel.

88. Cf. K. Weitzmann and H. L. Kessler 1986.

o) *Codex Bodleianus Geneseos* (E; BHK: $\mathfrak{G}^E$). Ninth/tenth century. Bodleian Library, Oxford. Contains Gen. 1–42:18 (with lacunae) written in uncials. To the same manuscript also belong folios containing Gen. 42:18–1 Kgs. 16:28 in a minuscule hand found in Cambridge (1f.), Leningrad (146ff.), and London (16ff.). The manuscript was discovered by Tischendorf and presumably came from the monastery on Mt. Sinai.

π) *Codex Atheniensis* (W; BHK: $\mathfrak{G}^W$). Thirteenth century. National Library, Athens. Contains the historical books, Esther, Judith, and Tobit.

BHS also cites:

ρ) *Codex Veronensis* (R). Sixth century. A Greek-Old Latin Psalter $\mathfrak{G}^R$ in the Biblioteca Capitolare, Verona. The Septuagint text here represents the Western text according to Rahlfs. Cf. $\mathfrak{L}^R$, p. 93.

σ) *A Codex fragment* (W). Fourth century. Contains 1 Sam. 18:8-25. $\mathfrak{G}^W$

11. Editions

Theoretically there are two editorial methods possible in publishing an ancient text which has been preserved in a variety of forms in different manuscripts. (a) The text of a single manuscript can be printed, with the variant readings of the other manuscripts indicated in an apparatus. The use of such an edition requires working through all the assembled evidence and making one's own judgments. (b) A text can be reconstructed by selecting from the various available readings those which appear to be the earliest. Such an eclectic procedure produces a critical recension of the text which can be verified by the evidence provided in the apparatus. The first method has been followed in all the great scholarly editions of the past; the second is being tried for the first time in the Göttingen Septuagint. The method best suited to the Septuagint is still a matter of discussion. The principal editions are the following.

(a) The *Complutensian Polyglot* (1514-1517; BHK: $\mathfrak{G}^{C(om)pl}$). The manuscripts on which this was based are now lost. Joseph Ziegler has shown that for the Minor Prophets it agrees frequently with the Lucianic text type,[89] with the third-century papyrus codex edited by H. A. Sanders (cf. p. 72), with the marginal notes of minuscule 86, and with the Coptic and Old Latin versions. From this we may infer that the Complutensian Greek text "was based on a text transmitting quite early readings which

89. J. Ziegler 1944b.

are not found in manuscripts known today."[90] Its text is therefore of particular value (pl. 47).

(b) The *Aldine* edition (Venice, 1518; BHK: $\mathfrak{G}^{Vn}$) offers a late text of little value. Ziegler has shown that for the Minor Prophets the Aldine text is based on a manuscript now lost, the larger part of which was derived from minuscule 68, and the remainder from minuscule 97.[91] "It is unfortunate that the editor of the Aldine edition relied on a manuscript transmitting a late text derived from the heavily Hexaplaric and Lucianic Catena group such as we find in minuscules 68 and 97."[92]

(c) The *Sixtine* edition (Rome, 1587) was an officially sponsored edition commissioned by Pope Sixtus V. The text is essentially that of $\mathfrak{G}^B$, with its lacunae supplied from several Vatican manuscripts, and with a wealth of variants appended. The use of $\mathfrak{G}^B$ marks significant progress, although this is marred by dependence on the Aldine edition.[93] The Sixtine has served as normative for many editions into the nineteenth century, e.g., the London Polyglot (1654-1657), Holmes and Parsons (1798ff.), Leander van Ess (1824 and later), the polyglot of Ewald Rudolf Stier and Karl Gottfried Theile (1847-1855), Tischendorf (1850 and later), the Clarendon Press edition (1875) on which the concordance by Edwin Hatch and Henry Redpath (1897ff.) is based.

(d) *Holmes and Parsons, Vetus Testamentum Graecum cum variis lectionibus* (1798-1827). The text is based on the Sixtine edition, with the addition of variants derived from three hundred manuscripts collated for this edition from patristic quotations and from daughter versions. These five large folio volumes contain a wealth of material that remains unsurpassed today. It is among the resources of BHK ($\mathfrak{G}^{MSS(Holmes-)Parsons}$ = manuscripts according to Holmes-Parsons).

(e) *Henry Barclay Swete, The Old Testament in Greek* (3 vols., 1887-91, and several later editions). A convenient popular edition which prints the text of $\mathfrak{G}^B$ (with lacunae supplied from A and S [ℵ], with an apparatus of readings from several important uncials.

(f) *Brooke-McLean-Thackeray, The Old Testament in Greek according to the Text of Codex Vaticanus, Supplemented from Other Uncial Manuscripts, with a Critical Apparatus Containing the Variants of the Chief*

90. *Ibid.*, 309.

91. J. Ziegler 1945.

92. *Ibid.*, 51.

93. According to Lagarde and Rahlfs, with whom Ziegler agrees, the Sixtine represents an Aldine edition corrected from $\mathfrak{G}^B$ (and other manuscripts); cf. J. Ziegler 1945: 49f.

Ancient Authorities for the Text of the Septuagint (Cambridge, 1906ff.). The editors considered the time not yet ripe for preparing a critical edition, and offered the evidence quite objectively. The text is that of $\mathfrak{G}^B$,[94] with the correction of obvious errors and with lacunae supplied from A and S [א]. In the apparatus are noted all the uncials, some thirty selected minuscules, the daughter versions, Philo, Josephus, and early Christian writings. Published volumes include Genesis (1906) to Tobit (1940); no further volumes are planned.

(g) The alternative of presenting the text in a critical edition has been realized for the first time in the **Göttingen Septuagint:** *Septuaginta: Vetus Testamentum Graecum auctoritate Societatis Litterarum Göttingensis editum.*[95] The text printed here is not that of a particular manuscript. At each point the reading is chosen which appears best in the light of the manuscript tradition as a whole, and with due reference to the Hebrew text. The apparatus, which offers a wealth of manuscript evidence arranged by textual groups (recensions), makes it possible for the reader to form a judgment of the textual tradition independently of the editor. The goal is the best attainable text, which involves no claim that the original form has been recovered in every instance. The editions are furnished with valuable introductions. For the plan of this undertaking, which derives ultimately from Lagarde, and for criticism of it, see above (pp. 61f.). Already published are: 1/1:*Genesis* (1974), 2/1: *Exodus* (1991), 2/2: *Leviticus* (1986), 3/1: *Numbers* (1982), 3/2: *Deuteronomy* (1977), edited by **John W. Wevers** (3/1 in collaboration with **Udo Quast**); 8/1: *Esdrae liber I* (1974, [2]1991), 8/3: *Esther* (1966, [2]1983), 8/4: *Judith* (1979), 8/5: *Tobit* (1983), edited by **Robert Hanhart**; 9/1: *Maccabaeorum liber I* (1936, [3]1990), edited by **Werner Kappler**; 9/2: *Maccabaeorum liber II* (1959, [2]1976), 9/3: *Maccabaeorum liber III* (1960, [2]1980), edited by **Hanhart**; 10: *Psalmi cum Odis* (1931, [3]1979), edited by **Alfred Rahlfs**; 11/4: *Iob* (1982), 12/1: *Sapientia Salomonis* (1962, [2]1980), 12/2: *Sapientia Iesu Filii Sirach* (1965, [2]1980), 13: *Duodecim Prophetae* (1943, [3]1984), 14: *Isaias* (1943, [3]1983), 15: *Ieremias, Baruch, Threni, Epistula Ieremiae* (1957, [2]1976), 16/1: *Ezechiel* (1952, [2]1978), 16/2: *Susanna, Daniel, Bel et Draco* (1954), edited by **Joseph Ziegler**. In the supplementary series *Mitteilungen des Septuaginta-Unternehmens* the following were also published: by **Hanhart**: *Text und Textgeschichte des 1. Esrabuches* (1974); *Text und Textgeschichte des*

94. From Exodus onward the text of the corrector of B (instead of the first hand) is adopted where it agrees with the main line of tradition.
95. For its history and method, cf. R. Hanhart and J. W. Wevers 1977.

Buches Judith (1979), *Text und Textgeschichte des Buches Tobit* (1984); by **Wevers**: *Text History of the Greek Genesis* (1974), *Text History of the Greek Deuteronomy* (1978), *Text History of the Greek Numbers* (1982), *Text History of the Greek Leviticus* (1986); by **Ziegler**: *Beiträge zum griechischen Iob* (1985).

In a smaller format Rahlfs also published the book of *Ruth* in 1922 and *Genesis* in 1926.

Max L. Margolis, *The Book of Joshua in Greek* (1931-1938), is modeled on the same principles as the Göttingen Septuagint. The last fascicle (part 5) was never published and was thought to be lost. However, it was recently discovered and published with a preface by Emanuel Tov, (1992).

(h) A critical manual edition of the entire Septuagint, designed for the use of students and ministers and at a modest price, was produced by **Rahlfs** in 1935 at the Württemberg Bible Society (now the German Bible Society). It is based mainly on the three major manuscripts B, S [‫א‬], and A, and provides "the basis for all subsequent major editions of the text because of its critical textual value and because of its extensive use of all the revisional elements of the Christian revisions recognized at the time."[96]

As an indispensable tool for research on ⅏ we should mention *Hatch and Redpath*, *A Concordance to the Septuagint*, 2 vols. (1897), *Supplement* (1906); reprinted Graz (1954), Oxford (1975), and Grand Rapids (1983).

12. The Samariticon

The Samaritan Pentateuch was also translated into Greek. Origen often cites this translation as the **Samariticon**. Fragments have been identified in a manuscript from the fourth century A.D.;[97] but this probably represents a Samaritan revision of the ⅏ text.[98] An inscription with the Greek text of the Blessing of Aaron (Num. 6:22-27), found in a Samaritan synagogue built in Thessalonica in the fourth century A.D., has been published by B. Lifshitz and J. Schiby.[99]

96. *Ibid.*, 7f.
97. Cf. P. Glaue and A. Rahlfs 1911.
98. E. Tov 1971.
99. Cf. B. Lifshitz and J. Schiby 1968.

VI. The Aramaic Targums (𝕿)[1]

1. Origin and Character

It is known that in postexilic Judaism Hebrew ceased to be spoken as the common language and was replaced by Aramaic, which had become the official written language of the western Persian Empire. Hebrew was of course still understood and used in intellectual circles, especially among theologians. But for the larger part of the Jewish community it became necessary to combine the usual Scripture lessons, which were read in Hebrew in the synagogue, with a translation into Aramaic. The translating was called *targem,* the translator *turgeman(a)* or *meturgeman(a),* and the translation *targum.* Since the need was felt at an early date, the custom must be old and certainly pre-Christian. The Jewish tradition associating it with Ezra (cf. Neh. 8:8) may well be correct.

In the worship service the translation could be made only orally, not read from a scroll; this was presumably to preserve its distinction from the truly sacred text which was in Hebrew. The writing down of Aramaic translations was not forbidden, and the existence of written Targums (for study and for the training of translators) by the beginning of the Christian era at the latest is no longer in question. It is told of Rabbi Gamaliel, the teacher of Paul, that when a Targum of Job was placed before him he

1. On the problem of the Targums, cf. R. le Déaut 1966, with full bibliographies; also J. Bowker 1969; M. McNamara 1966; E. Levine 1982a and comprehensively 1988; P. Schäfer 1980. Bibliography: B. Grossfeld 1972-78.

2. Thus a Targum of the book of Job was found at Qumran in Cave 11; editions: J. P. M. van der Ploeg and A. S. van der Woude 1971; M. Sokoloff 1974; J. Gray 1974. Otherwise to date only the remains of a literal Aramaic version of Leviticus and another fragment of a Targum to Job in Cave 4 have been found. The so-called Genesis Apocryphon is an early midrash. Cf. G. Vermès 1973: 96ff.

spurned it and had it buried in a wall. Targums were in use even at Qumran.[2] But with their development from oral translations it is only natural that the precise wording of the Targums should differ from place to place. While the Hebrew text and its normally accepted interpretation in Judaism remained authoritative, there remained the possibility of individual characteristics appearing in the form of words, extent of paraphrase, interpretation, representation, etc. Thus there was not at first a single original standard and authoritative Targum text, but rather a whole series of different Aramaic versions.

These different versions share in varying degrees certain characteristics which reflect their common practical purpose. The community was to be taught and edified; it was necessary to spell out clearly for them the message of the text. Consequently in no other versions of the Bible is the interpretive element as pronounced as in the Targums. They paraphrase, they add explanatory phrases, they reinterpret the text (sometimes quite boldly) according to the theological temper of their time, they relate the text to contemporary life and political circumstances, and so on. In particular they attempt to avoid anthropomorphic and anthropopathic statements about God. This approach to the text of the Targums, which occasionally almost ignores the meaning of the Hebrew text, reduces their value as textual witnesses, but makes them important documents for the history of Old Testament exegesis.[3]

2. The Various Targums

Of the varied profusion of the Aramaic versions that once existed only a small fraction has survived. Two basically different forms should be distinguished: those texts which represent the early Palestinian Targum, and those which were revised in Babylon — Onkelos for the Pentateuch and Jonathan for the Prophets. Most of the surviving Targums contain material from very different periods. Determining and dating the various strata is possible only with careful investigation — a process which is in many respects now only in its beginning stages.[4]

3. A particularly bold reinterpretation was necessitated in Isa. 52:13–53:12 under the influence of anti-Christian polemics. The translation is now conveniently available in J. Jeremias 1967: 693f.

4. On the problem of dating the Targumic traditions: P. Wernberg-Møller 1962: 312-330; cf. also Vermès 1973.

(a) The *Palestinian Targum* was never edited officially, and consequently it has never had a single authoritative form of text. All the manuscripts differ from each other to a greater or lesser extent. The characteristic traits of the older Targums just mentioned are especially pronounced in them.

Thanks to several fortunate discoveries in recent decades which have also advanced our knowledge of long-familiar texts, we are now able to see the Palestinian Targum in a clearer perspective. To begin with, Paul Kahle recognized and edited the remains of an old Palestinian Pentateuch Targum which had survived in fragments of seven manuscripts from the Cairo Geniza, dating from the seventh to the ninth century (cited in BH as $\mathbb{C}^P$ = Targum Palestinense).[5] These texts are not simple and literal translations of the Hebrew. Instead they have extensive explanatory insertions of a midrashic and homiletical nature. When the same passage has survived in several fragments, the differences between them are so great that there can be no question of a standard text. Further fragments have since been discovered, but most significant has been the discovery by Alejandro Díez Macho in 1957 of a complete manuscript of the Palestinian Targum in *Ms. Neofiti I* of the Vatican Library comprising 450 parchment folios.[6] This manuscript was apparently written in Italy in the early sixteenth century,[7] although its contents are obviously much earlier. It is of the greatest importance for our knowledge of the Palestinian Targum and its related problems, especially in view of the fragmentary nature of the materials hitherto available. It has been published by Díez Macho (1968-1979) in six volumes, containing an introduction and the Aramaic text together with a critical apparatus and translations in Spanish, French (by Roger J. le Déaut), and English (by Martin McNamara and Michael Maher).

These discoveries have made it possible to achieve a fresh historical understanding of long known and published Targums, and to prove their relationship to the Palestinian Targum. This is true of the so-called Fragment Targum and Targum Pseudo-Jonathan. The *Fragment Targum*, also known as *Targum Jerusalem II* and cited in BH as $\mathbb{C}^{J\,II}$, is called a "fragment" because it contains only the midrashic comments on individual verses, omitting the continuous translation of the text itself. Kahle regards

$\mathbb{C}^P$

$\mathbb{C}^{J\,II}$

---

5. P. Kahle 1927-30: II.

6. A. Díez Macho 1960 discusses some of the major problems of the Palestinian Targum, and includes a survey of the texts presently known (pp. 236f.). On Codex Neofiti I, cf. A. Díez Macho 1956: 446f.; 1962: 19-25; and M. Black 1957: 662-64. On the complex character of Neofiti I, now cf. S. Lund and J. Foster 1977.

7. M. F. Martin 1963.

it "as a collection of midrashic material from the Palestinian Pentateuch Targum which was considered too valuable to ignore when Targum Onkelos was introduced as the standard Targum for Palestine as well."[8] It was published by Moses Ginsburger in 1899.[9] A new edition has been published by Michael L. Klein.[10]

Targum Pseudo-Jonathan of the Pentateuch, also called *Targum Jerusalem I*,[11] is peculiar in combining with the text of the official Targum   𝔗ᴶ Onkelos (see below) midrashic material which was usually omitted from it. Earlier it was thought that the midrashic material had been introduced into Targum Onkelos only after it was accepted as standard in Palestine — the people were accustomed to it and missed it in the new Targum. But recently Díez Macho has advocated an explanation to the contrary with ample evidence that Pseudo-Jonathan represents a Palestinian Targum more or less thoroughly revised from the Onkelos text.[12] Possibly both were derived from an earlier Palestinian Targum (Géza Vermès, P. Schäfer).

The foundations of the Palestinian Targum apparently go back to pre-Christian times, and thus it contributes significantly to our understanding of Judaism in the period of Christian beginnings. Its language is the Aramaic spoken in Palestine, so that we can find here valuable material for the study of Aramaic as it was spoken in the Palestine of Jesus' time. These important texts have been published: A. Díez Macho, *Targum Palestinense in Pentateuchum. Additur Targum Pseudojonatan eiusque Hispanica Versio*, vol. 4. *Numeri* (1977); vol. 2. *Exodus*, 3. *Leviticus*, vol. 5. *Deuteronomium* (1980);[13] a French translation of Neofiti I and Pseudo-Jonathan edited by R. J. le Déaut and J. Robert, *Targum du Pentateuque*, in 5 volumes (1978-1982).[14]

(b) *Targum Onkelos* and *Targum Jonathan*. Targum Onkelos (BHK: 𝔗ᴼ) for the Pentateuch and Targum Jonathan for the Prophets are the best known of the Targums, and are authoritative for Judaism. These are quite distinct from the Palestinian Targums with their differing forms. These are

---

8. P. Kahle 1958: 110.

9. M. Ginsburger 1899.

10. M. L. Klein (1980): four different Targum fragments with English translation, based on manuscripts in Paris, the Vatican, Nuremberg, and Leipzig; cf. also his 1986 edition, with plates.

11. Edited by M. Ginsburger (1903) from the British Library Ms. Add. 27031,   𝔗ᴶ and cited in BH as 𝔗ᴶ; newly edited by D. Reider 1974.

12. A. Díez Macho 1960: 239.

13. A. Díez Macho 1977, 1980.

14. R. J. le Déaut 1978-82.

official Targums whose definitive wording was evidently established in Babylon in the fifth century after a long history of development. They are based on older material that probably derives ultimately from Palestine. Their names are probably derived (erroneously) from the Greek translators Aquila (Onkelos) and Theodotion (Jonathan in Hebrew), who were known for their literal versions of the Bible, faithful to Jewish exegesis. Actually these two Targums can hardly have been the work of single individuals. They were more probably produced by commissions appointed to replace the various forms of the text then in circulation with an official version conforming to orthodox Jewish interpretation, revised according to the Hebrew text, and largely purged of midrashic elaborations. Thus they mark a definitive point in the history of the Targums, and only later came to establish themselves firmly in Palestine. Both Targums attempt to reproduce the Hebrew text quite literally, so that as in the earlier Greek versions of Aquila the language (a literary form of Aramaic understood in all Aramaic-speaking lands) had to suffer. And yet they also contain numerous subtle interpretative differences from 𝔐.

Of these two Targum Onkelos of the Pentateuch was naturally accorded the greater authority, and like the original Hebrew text it was also supplied with a Masora. The text was edited by Abraham Berliner (1884-1886) following the Editio Sabioneta of 1557.[15]

Targum Jonathan, which contains more haggadic material and in part goes back to pre-Christian times, was edited by Paul A. de Lagarde (1872) from Codex Reuchlinianus; cited in BHS as 𝕮ᶠ.[16] BHS also cites the editio princeps of Targum Jonathan, published in Leiria (Portugal) in 1494.

The Targum for Joshua and Judges in the Yemenite tradition was edited by Franz Praetorius in 1899 and 1900 (cited in BHK as 𝕮ᴾʳ).[17]

A new edition of the Targum has been published by Alexander Sperber: *The Bible in Aramaic*, 1, *The Pentateuch according to Targum Onkelos* (1959); 2, *The Former Prophets according to Targum Jonathan* (1959); 3, *The Latter Prophets according to Targum Jonathan* (1962); 4-A, *The Hagiographa: Transition from Translation to Midrash* (1968); 4-B, *The Targum and the Hebrew Bible* (1973). In BHS volumes 1-3 are cited and for the Hagiographa Lagarde's edition is cited (see below) as 𝕮.

---

15. The Masora was edited by A. Berliner 1877, and by S. Landauer 1896. For a description of Targum Onkelos, cf. M. Aberbach and B. Grossfeld 1982; I. Drazin 1982.

16. L. Smolar, M. Aberbach, P. Churgin 1983.

17. F. Praetorius 1899; 1900.

(c) Besides the editions already mentioned, BH also refers to: the Targum to the *Writings* edited by **Lagarde** in 1873 (*Hagiographa Chaldaice,* cited in BHK as $\mathfrak{C}^L$); a selection of Targum texts edited in 1888 by **Adalbert Merx** with notes and a glossary, based on old manuscripts and printed editions (*Chrestomathia Targumica,* cited in BHK as $\mathfrak{C}^M$); the Targums of **Jacob ben Chayyim's** Rabbinic Bible of 1524/25 (cited in BHK as $\mathfrak{C}^B$); the Targums of **Johannes the Elder Buxtorf's** edition of Basel,

$\mathfrak{C}^{Buxt}$ 1618-1619 ($\mathfrak{C}^{Buxt}$); and a wealth of material in **Brian Walton's** London Polyglot of 1654-57 (cited in BHK as $\mathfrak{C}^W$).

$\mathfrak{w}^T$

3. The Samaritan Targum (cited in BH as $\mathfrak{w}^T$)

Among the Samaritans also the sacred text, the Pentateuch, was translated into Aramaic, but there was never an official recension of it. Consequently almost every surviving manuscript has its own text. "We have here an excellent example of a Targum in an earlier phase through which translations of the Bible usually pass before they reach their final text."[18]

Editions: The Paris (1645) and London Polyglots (1657); Julius Heinrich Petermann and Carl Vollers, *Pentateuchus Samaritanus* (1872-1891; uncritical methodology). Kahle has edited fragments with comments in *Zeitschrift für Assyriologie* 16 (1901) and 17 (1902). A new edition of the Samaritan Targum has been published by Abraham Tal (Rosenthal) of Tel Aviv University.[19]

18. P. Kahle 1959: 52.

19. A. Tal 1980-83 (3 vols; vol. 3 is the Introduction), a diplomatic edition of the British Library Ms. Or. 7562 [J] with the text of Shechem Synagogue Ms. 3 in parallel, and two apparatuses with critical notes and the readings of other manuscripts.

VII. The Syriac Version (Peshitta, S)[1] ܣ

1. Name and Literary Problem

At a rather late date the Syriac church designated the version of the Old Testament in common use as the Peshitta (Jacobite pronunciation: Peshitto), i.e., "the simple or plain (version)." It is not certain in what sense this was intended, whether to indicate it as the common (vulgaris) version, or one lacking in paraphrase, or perhaps to distinguish it as "simple" in contrast to the annotated Syro-Hexaplar text derived from the Hexapla (cf. p. 59).

The literary problem of the Peshitta is rather complex[2] and suffers from the lack of a critical edition describing the manuscript tradition. Syriac information on the origin of the Peshitta is largely of a legendary nature and of little value, e.g., one tradition dates the version in the reign of King Solomon, while another ascribes it to Christian sources.

The Peshitta has had a most varied history as revealed in its manuscript tradition and the differences from the standard text to be found in patristic quotations from the Bible. These relationships have been studied most thoroughly in the Pentateuch, but even here there is no consensus on the most important problem: the origin of the version. While Leo Haefeli regarded these books as a rather faithful translation of the Hebrew text, others support the thesis that in the Pentateuch the Peshitta was derived from an eastern Aramaic (Syriac) recasting of a western Aramaic Targum. Such is the view

---

1. Cf. P. A. H. de Boer 1981 for a good historical survey of research and editing. Cf. also C. van der Puyvelde 1960, and P. B. Dirksen 1989.

2. Cf. the opinion of P. B. Dirksen, a member of the Peshitta Institute in Leiden (1985: 468): "There is . . . no certain answer to the question where and when this translation came into being, whether originally it was a Jewish or a Christian translation, what the relation is between the text of the Peshitta and the Targumic tradition, and even what was the exact meaning of the name."

of Anton Baumstark, Paul E. Kahle, and Curt Peters among others, and especially of Arthur Vööbus. The latter demonstrated by a thorough examination of both the manuscript tradition and the patristic literature that in the Pentateuch there was an early stage so closely related to the Targums that the inference of direct dependence on an early Palestinian Targum is inescapable.[3] On the basis of his examination of the text of Exodus in a large number of manuscripts from the fifth to the nineteenth century, M. D. Koster has come to the conclusion that the present text of the Peshitta has developed through three stages, the oldest of which is witnessed by British Museum Ms. Add. 14,425 (cf. pl. 39), and reveals a close connection with the Hebrew text.[4] "This makes it plausible for the Pentateuch at least that [the Peshitta], as we know and use it, emerged from a faithful translation of the Hebrew original" (p. 197). Yeshayahu Maori[5] acknowledges the influence of Jewish exegesis as a characteristic of the Peshitta in the Pentateuch, but he also denies any direct dependence on an existing Targum. Thus it now appears probable that the Peshitta is of Jewish origin and was translated from the Hebrew text. Jewish origins are historically easy to imagine. During the first century the ruling house and leading circles of Adiabene (east of the Tigris) were won over to the Jewish faith for several decades (*ca.* A.D. 40-70). They needed a version of the Old Testament, especially of the Pentateuch, in their own language — Syriac. This places the beginnings of the Syriac version of the Old Testament in the middle of the first century A.D.[6]

The arguments made earlier for Christian or Jewish Christian origins of the Pentateuch based on a certain laxness in the rendering of the Levitical Law have been refuted by J. A. Emerton.[7]

The Peshitta text for Isaiah, which Lienhard Delekat ascribed to Targumic origins,[8] has now been shown by Arie van der Kooij[9] to be a translation of a proto-Masoretic text made by a Jewish Christian who was "very familiar" with the text of ᵹ (p. 287), and "somewhat less familiar" with Targums to Isaiah and the Prophets (p. 290). Date: no earlier than A.D. second century (p. 292).

The later history of the text is as complicated as its origins — clarification awaits the appearance of the forthcoming critical edition (cf. p. 89).

3. A. Vööbus 1958; cf. however the critical review by J. Ziegler 1962b: 304ff.
4. M. D. Koster 1977.
5. Y. Maori 1975.
6. Cf. P. Kahle 1959: 270-73, which still supports Targumic origins.
7. J. A. Emerton 1962.
8. L. Delekat 1957: 21-54; 1957a: 185-199, 321-335.
9. A. van der Kooij 1981.

Koster's observations have led him to the conclusion that in the Pentateuch the version has gradually moved farther away from the Hebrew text by internal development, by adding explanatory or harmonizing words and phrases.[10] But van der Kooij has not found this true for Isaiah.[11]

Scribes were generally not meticulous copyists, but enjoyed considerable freedom in their choice of words and grammatical details.[12] Further, the fact that scribal centers were widely scattered tended to promote the development of local traditions. No attempt seems to have been made to revise or standardize the text. But in the ninth/tenth century there was a turning point, for manuscripts of the fifth to the ninth century show a certain degree of variation in their textual consistency, and manuscripts after the ninth/tenth century seem to derive from a single exemplar, an archetype. This striking turn in the textual tradition is explained by P. B. Dirksen by the fact that about this time a great number of manuscripts were taken to the monastery of Der es-Suryan in Egypt, where the Abbot Moses of Nisibis recorded the accession of 250 copies in the year 932 alone. The vacuum this created in Syria was filled by copies made from a ninth century manuscript which chanced to remain in Syria. "And so, on the basis of this MS, a new text tradition came up which gradually branched out in various geographical and textual directions."[13] These events explain why nearly all the earlier manuscripts in London and Rome came from Egypt, and why the later manuscripts have little significance for research in the history of the Peshitta text.

Further research on the Peshitta is necessary to establish its history and textual importance for *all* the books of the Old Testament. But already it may be affirmed that as a version in a language closely related to Hebrew the Peshitta is important among the early witnesses to the Old Testament text, and must certainly be taken into account by the textual critic.

---

10. M. D. Koster 1977: 528f. Koster has presented an exhaustive study of the Peshitta text in the book of Exodus and concludes that there was a single translation of the basic Hebrew text which then developed independently: "This development is characterized by a gradual extension of the text through the addition of complementary words and even a few explanatory sentences, which clearly mark the transition between the different stages. In as far as one can speak of a 'Targumisches Profil' in P, this is therefore to be found not at the beginning but at the end of the development of its text" (p. 212). Koster's important conclusions argue against the Targum and recension hypothesis: the extent of their relevance for the *whole* of the Old Testament remains to be demonstrated by further research.

11. A. van der Kooij 1981: 297.

12. P. B. Dirksen 1985: 476f.

13. *Ibid.,* 484.

2. Manuscripts and Editions

S^{Mss} In the fifth century the Syriac church became divided into Nestorians and Jacobites, and accordingly the Nestorian (East Syriac) and Jacobite (West Syriac) traditions are to be distinguished.[14] There is a group of early Peshitta manuscripts[15] beginning in the fifth century A.D., such as the British Museum Ms. Add. 14,425 from the year 464 containing Genesis, Exodus, Numbers, and Deuteronomy. The most important of these is the West Syriac *Codex Ambrosianus* in Milan, from the sixth or seventh century, containing the entire Old Testament; a photolithographic edition was published by Antonius Maria Ceriani, *Translatio Pescitto Veteris Testamenti*, 1876 (S^A). The new edition of the Peshitta (cf. p. 89) is based on this manuscript.

Also of importance are the biblical quotations of the Syriac Church Fathers, such as Ephraem Syrus (d. 373) and Aphraates, who lived in the period before the division of the church. In BHK the readings of Aphraates, whose twenty-three treatises from the years 337-345 are the earliest surviving writings in the Syriac language, are cited as S^Aphr.[16]

There has been to date no edition of the Peshitta that is completely satisfactory for critical purposes. The Paris Polyglot of 1645 became the standard text on which later editions were based, but it was itself dependent on a poor manuscript from the seventeenth century as its principal source. Although the deficiencies of this edition were recognized, it was reprinted in an even worse form by Brian Walton in the London Polyglot of 1657 (S^W), with the readings of a few Syriac manuscripts appended in the sixth volume. All later editions were prepared for practical (missionary) pur-

---

14. According to Dirksen 1985 this division had no significance for the history of the Peshitta text.

15. Cf. *List of Old Testament Peshiṭta Manuscripts,* edited by the Peshitta Institute, University of Leiden (1961); and supplements, "Peshiṭta Institute Communications," *VT* 12 (1962): 127f., 237f., 351; 18 (1968): 128-143; 27 (1977): 508-511; 31 (1981): 358; 35 (1985): 466f.

16. In 1-2 Sam. BHS also cites the following manuscripts: codex British Library Add. 14,431 (S^B), 6th century (with lacunae); codex Leningrad Public Library No. 2 (S^C), 5th century (with lacunae); codex British Library Add. 14,442, and codex Wadi Natrun (S^D), 6th/7th century (both fragmentary). Patristic quotations: the readings of Bishop Jacob of Edessa (633-708), who revised the Peshitta from the Syro-Hexaplar, following M. H. Goshen-Gottstein 1956, S^Jac edess; the readings of Bishop Bar Hebraeus (1225-1308) following M. Sprengling and W. C. Graham 1931, S^Bar Hebr

poses, for the use of the surviving Syriac communities in the mountains of Kurdistan, around Lake Urmia, and in northern Iran. Their textual value is slight. The edition of Samuel Lee (1823, reprinted 1979; cited in BH as S^L) is based mainly on the London Polyglot together with a few other S^L manuscripts. The edition of Urmia (1852, reprinted 1854; cited as S^U) by S^U J. Perkins for the American Board of Commissioners for Foreign Missions, and that of the Dominicans of Mosul in 1887-91 (edited by C. Joseph David and G. Ebed-Jesus Khayyath; reprinted 1951; cited in BHS as S^M) differ S^M from the editions mentioned above by representing the East Syriac tradition.

Editions of individual books were prepared by William Emery Barnes and others. In 1904 there appeared *The Peshitta Psalter according to the West Syrian Text edited with an Apparatus Criticus*, and in 1914 the *Pentateuchus Syriace post Samuelum Lee*, revised by G. E. Barnes with C. W. Mitchell and I. Pinkerton, intended for practical use but drawing also upon manuscript studies.

A new edition of the Peshitta is in preparation under the direction of P. A. H. de Boer and his successor Martin Jan Mulder at the Peshitta Institute of the University of Leiden, sponsored by the International Organization for the Study of the Old Testament. It is based on Codex Ambrosianus following the facsimile edition of Ceriani (cf. p. 88). Obvious errors in Ambrosianus and readings which lack the support of at least two manuscripts earlier than the eleventh century are corrected, and listed in the first apparatus. A second apparatus records variant readings from the period before the eleventh century.

A preliminary volume, *The Old Testament in Syriac according to the Peshitta Version, Sample Edition: Song of Songs, Tobit, 4 Ezra* (edited by J. A. Emerton, J. C. H. Lebram, and R. J. Bidawid), appeared in 1966, followed by a "General Preface to the Complete Work" by P. A. H. de Boer and W. Baars in 1972. Since then the following volumes have been published: 1/1: *Preface* (de Boer), *Genesis* (T. Jansma/Peshitta Institute), *Exodus* (Koster), 1977; 1/2: *Leviticus* (D. J. Lane), *Numbers* (A. P. Hayman), *Deuteronomy* (W. M. van Vliet), 1991; 2/1a: *Job* (Lars G. Rignell), 1982; 2/1b: *Joshua* (Lane, *et al.*), 1990; 2/2: *Judges* (Dirksen), *Samuel* (de Boer), 1978; 2/3: *Psalms* (D. M. Walter), 1980; 2/4: *Kings* (Hans Gottlieb in collaboration with Erling Hammershaimb), 1976; 2/5: *Proverbs* (Alexander A. di Lella), *Wisdom of Solomon* (Emerton and Lane), *Qoheleth* (Lane), *Song of Songs* (Emerton and Lane), 1979; 3/1: *Isaiah* (Sebastian P. Brock), 1986; 3/3: *Ezekiel* (Martin Jan Mulder), 1985; 3/4: *Dodekapropheton* (A. Gelston), *Daniel-Bel-Draco* (based on T. Sprey), 1980; 4/3: *Apoc-*

alypse of Baruch, 4 Esdras (S. Dedering/R. J. Bidawid), 1973; 4/6: *Canticles or Odes* (Heinrich Schneider), *Prayer of Manasseh* (Baars and Schneider), *Apocryphal Psalms* (Baars), *Psalms of Solomon* (Baars), *Tobit* (Lebram), *I (3) Esdras* (Baars and Lebram), 1972.

VIII. The Old Latin (𝕷)

𝔏

1. Origin and Problems

In Rome itself Greek supplanted Latin as the language of religion and philosophy until the third century A.D., when Latin again became dominant; meanwhile in Southern Gaul and in North Africa Latin always held its ground, and it is in these areas that we first find Latin biblical texts around A.D. 150. *Tertullian* (b. in Carthage *ca.* 160) apparently used a written version of the Scriptures in a Latin quite different from his own. The Latin version, like others, was produced to meet the practical needs of public worship and private devotion. Presumably at first the Lessons read in the worship service were translated orally for those who were unacquainted with Greek. Then these translations were written down and extended to include all the books of the Bible. It is certain that *Cyprian* (d. 258) was dependent on the Old Latin text for his Bible quotations.

Tert

The *Old Latin* version, as distinct from the later version by Jerome, was translated from the Septuagint, the text customarily used in the Christian communities: it has been called "the Septuagint in Latin clothing."[1] The Old Latin is a particularly important witness to the Septuagint text because it goes back to the period before the Septuagint recensions. But there are great preliminary difficulties in the way of its use for textual criticism, and these can only be overcome by research based on critical editions of the manuscript tradition. The basic problem of Old Latin research is the question whether there was originally a single version from which the known forms were derived or whether there were several independent versions. Statements by the Church Fathers suggest a plurality of versions, as when Augustine distinguishes between Itala and several other

1. J. Ziegler 1960: 5.

Latin versions. The problem is only made more difficult by the fact that if there was an original version it was regarded as neither official nor inviolate: independent alterations to improve its popular Latin idiom and bring it closer to its Greek base could well have produced such different forms of the text that their common origin would hardly be suspected. At all events an African text can now be distinguished from a European text which itself comprises several different subtypes. Thus Old Latin must be taken as a collective term rather than as designating a particular text. Considering the variety of the tradition which attests to continuous work on the texts, we cannot expect more than a fraction of the surviving manuscripts to have escaped the influence of the Septuagint recensions.

2. Editions and Manuscripts

As the Old Latin was superseded by the Vulgate in the early medieval period, interest in its manuscript tradition waned. Thus it has not survived in complete manuscripts in the way 𝔊 has. Instead, it has to be assembled from fragmentary manuscripts, liturgical books, and patristic quotations in commentaries, sermons, letters, etc. The Benedictine *Pierre Sabatier* (1682-1742) edited a collection of the material then known in *Bibliorum* 𝔏 *sacrorum latinae versiones antiquae* (1739-1749; cited as 𝔏). Sabatier prints in one column the fullest continuous text he could find for a passage, and beside it the Vulgate, together with variants from other Old Latin sources in an apparatus. There are naturally many lacunae in the 𝔏 text.

Samuel Berger[2] has brought together a series of unpublished Old Latin texts of the Old Testament [BHK: 𝔏(Berger)].

A new edition following modern scholarly methods and including evidence discovered since Sabatier was undertaken in 1949: *Vetus Latina: Die Reste der altlateinischen Bibel nach Petrus Sabatier neu gesammelt und herausgegeben von der Erzabtei Beuron* (edited by Bonifatius Fischer). This large edition will include (1) all manuscripts and fragments of the Old Latin Bible, (2) all quotations in the writings of the Church Fathers to the period of Isidore of Seville (*ca.* 560-636), and of the more important later writers to the Carolingian period. Already published: 1. *Sigla* (1949); 2. *Genesis* (1951-1954); cited in BHS as 𝔏.

Besides the collections of Sabatier and Berger, BHK also refers to the following manuscripts.

2. S. Berger 1893: 119-152.

(a) The *Constance Old Latin fragments of the Prophets,* edited by Alban Dold (1923), with glosses together with the corresponding texts of the Prophets from Zürich and St. Gall (pl. 40; BHK: $\mathfrak{L}^D$). This is a comprehensive edition and study of the fragments from a manuscript of the Prophets once in Constance which was probably written in northern Italy in the fifth century, and fragments of which have been discovered since 1856 in the bindings of twenty-six parchment manuscripts. It includes fragments of Hosea, Amos, Micah, Joel, Jonah, Nahum, Ezekiel, and Daniel.

(b) The *Würzburg palimpsest codex* published by Ernst Ranke (1871; BHK: $\mathfrak{L}^h$). The lower writing is from the fifth century (probably from central eastern France) and contains fragments of the Pentateuch and the Prophets.

(c) *Codex Lugdunensis* (pl. 41), in the Municipal Library of Lyons (BHK: $\mathfrak{L}^L$). Edition: Ulysse Robert 1881, 1900. An uncial of the seventh century, probably written in Lyons; now mutilated, the manuscript contains parts of Gen. 16:9–Judg. 20:31.

(d) *Codex Gothicus Legionensis* ($\mathfrak{L}^{91 3}$), Léon, S. Isidoro. A Vulgate text from A.D. 960 with many Old Latin readings noted in the margin by the same hand ($\mathfrak{L}^{Lg}$) for the Heptateuch and the books of Samuel, Kings, and Chronicles in the Old Testament. $\quad\mathfrak{L}^{91}, \mathfrak{L}^{93}$ $\quad\mathfrak{L}^{Lg}$

(e) *Palimpsestus Vindobonensis* (BHK: $\mathfrak{L}^{Vind}$), in the Biblioteca Nazionale of Naples since 1919. The lower writing is from the fifth century, probably Italian. Contains parts of Genesis, Exodus, and Leviticus. The edition by Johannes E. Belsheim (1885) is faulty (Dold, Fischer).

In BHS the following are also referred to.

(f) *Codex Parisinus Latinus bibliothecae nationalis 11947* ($\mathfrak{L}^G$). An Old Latin Psalter of the fifth to sixth century, probably from the Benedictine Abbey of Corbie (France), now in the Bibliothèque Nationale, Paris. $\quad\mathfrak{L}^G$

(g) *Codex Veronensis* ($\mathfrak{L}^R$). A Greek-Old Latin Psalter in the Biblioteca Capitolare, Verona, from the sixth century. The following canticles are added to the Psalms: Exod. 15:1-21; Deut. 32:1-44 + 31:30; 1 Sam. 2:1-10; Isa. 5:1-9; Jonah 2:3-10; Hab. 3:2-19; Luke 1:46-55; Dan. 3:51-90 (cf. $\mathfrak{G}^R$, p. 75). $\quad\mathfrak{L}^R$

(h) *Fragmenta Sangallensia Prophetarum* ($\mathfrak{L}^S$). These are derived from a manuscript of the ninth to tenth century "whose leaves were found in the binding of manuscripts bound at St. Gall" (Dold). Edited and published by Dold (1940). Included are fragments of Ezekiel, Daniel, Hosea, $\quad\mathfrak{L}^S$

3. Arabic numerals for Old Latin manuscripts following B. Fischer 1949.

Amos, Habakkuk, and Zephaniah; cf. (a) above for the publication of other fragments from the same source.

𝔏⁹⁴   (i) Escorial, Biblioteca de S. Lorenzo 54 (𝔏⁹⁴). Glosses from a lost tenth(?)-century manuscript inscribed in 1577 by a Dominican in the margin of the Vulgate *editio princeps* Escorial, Biblioteca de S. Lorenzo, Incunabulum 54 (Venice, 1478).

𝔏¹¹⁵   (k) Naples, Biblioteca Nazionale, Latin 1 (𝔏¹¹⁵; earlier Vindob. 17). Fragments of 1 Samuel–2 Kings from a fifth-century manuscript.

𝔏¹¹⁶   (l) ***Fragmenta Quedlinburgensia et Magdeburgensia*** (𝔏¹¹⁶). Fragments of a fifth-century manuscript in the Preussische Staatsbibliothek, Berlin, and the Archiv St. Servatii, Quedlinberg, containing 1 Samuel–2 Kings.

𝔏¹¹⁷   (m) ***Fragmenta Vindobonensia*** (𝔏¹¹⁷). Endsheets from a seventh/eighth century manuscript in the binding of a codex, containing fragments of 2 Samuel.

Ambr Often Old Latin biblical quotations are preserved in the writings of
𝔏ᶜʸ, Tert, Church Fathers, e.g., ***Ambrose,*** bishop of Milan (d. 397), who is cited in
Eus BHS as Ambr, Cyprian as 𝔏ᶜʸ, Tertullian as Tert,[4] Eusebius as Eus, and
Tyc the North African reformed Donatist Tyconius (d. *ca.* 400) as Tyc.

𝔏ᵀᴱ   4. But also Tertullian's *Adversus Marcionem* (E. Kroymann, ed., 1906) as 𝔏ᵀᴱ.

IX. The Vulgate (𝔙)

1. Jerome's Version

We have seen that the text of the Bible circulated in a wide variety of forms in the Latin-speaking church. A uniform and reliable text was badly needed for theological discussion and liturgical use. Pope Damasus I (366-384) was accordingly moved to commission Jerome, a scholar eminently qual-   Hier ified by his knowledge of Latin, Greek, and Hebrew, to produce such a text. Jerome was born between 340 and 350 in Dalmatia, studied grammar and logic in Rome, and then dedicated himself to an ascetic life and theological studies, living at various places in the western and eastern parts of the empire. As a hermit in the desert of Chalcis he had learned Hebrew from a Jewish Christian, and later as a priest he had studied under Apollinarius of Laodicea and Gregory of Nazianzus. He was recalled to Rome in 382 and commissioned to work on the Latin Bible, which he began in Rome and continued as head of a monastery near Bethlehem from the autumn of 386. His work there went far beyond the original plans. We can discuss only his work on the Old Testament here.

Various stages are to be distinguished:

(a) At first Jerome made a rapid *(cursim)* and partial revision of the Psalter according to the Septuagint, which enjoyed canonical authority at the time. This revision was introduced into the liturgy of the city of Rome, whence it received the name ***Psalterium Romanum.*** It is still in use today in the Office at St. Peter's and in the Psalm texts of the Old Roman Mass.[1]

(b) Jerome undertook a second revision of the Psalter in Palestine,

---

1. Edition: R. Weber 1953. D. de Bruyne's theory (1930) that the Psalterium Romanum has nothing to do with this revision by Jerome has not been generally accepted.

based on the Hexapla of Origen found at Caesarea in Palestine. This Psalter, which was first used liturgically in Gaul and is hence called the ***Psalterium*** Ga ***Gallicanum*** (Ga), was soon adopted elsewhere and is still today a part of the official Roman edition of the Vulgate.[2] It is essentially a revision of the Old Latin according to the fifth column of the Hexapla. Apparently Jerome made similar revisions of the entire Old Testament, but only the texts of Job and fragments of Proverbs, Song of Solomon, and Ecclesiastes have survived.

(c) The work which represents the real achievement of Jerome, establishing his significance for the history of the text and exercising the broadest influence for the history of Western culture, is his ***translation of the Old Testament from the Hebrew text*** which he accomplished in the years 390-405. He alone among the Christians in the West was capable of making this translation from the original text, because of his knowledge of Hebrew. Quite apart from the flood of criticism from those who regarded him as a forger *(falsarius)*, we can appreciate how unprecedented, how inconceivable his undertaking was if we consider that even Augustine himself was disquieted at Jerome's setting aside the inspired, canonical Septuagint to go back to a text which no one in the church but himself could understand. Augustine feared that this would lead to a division between the Greek and Latin churches, and he never relinquished his misgivings over the church's use of this version based on the Hebrew text. This difference between Jerome and Augustine reflects different appreciations of the Septuagint. Augustine regarded it as inspired ("Spiritus enim, qui in prophetis erat, quando illa dixerunt, idem ipse erat etiam in septuaginta uiris, quando illa interpretati sunt," *De Civitate Dei* 18.43), while Jerome contested the inspiration of the Septuagint ("Aliud est enim vatem, aliud esse interpretem: ibi Spiritus ventura praedicit, hic eruditio et verborum copia ea quae intelligit transfert").[3]

Jerome, however, was no iconoclast, and the independence of his version should not be exaggerated, even though recent studies credit him with a deeper knowledge of Hebrew than was earlier recognized.[4] As there

2. Published as vol. 10 of the large Benedictine edition of the Vulgate: *Liber Psalmorum ex recensione Sancti Hieronymi* (1953). It includes the *Epistula ad Sunniam et Fretelam,* in which Jerome comments on particular passages in the Psalms and on the method he has observed. Cf. also J. Ziegler 1960.

3. *Praefatio in Pentateuchum, Biblia Sacra iuxta Latinam Vulgatam Versionem* 1 (1926): 67; R. Weber 1969: 3. Cf. also W. Schwarz 1955: 26-30.

4. Cf. B. Kedar-Kopfstein 1968: 50ff.; J. Barr 1966/1967; but cf. the odd view of P. Nautin 1986: 311 "that he hardly knew this language."

were no dictionaries or grammars in his day, his most important aids were the Greek versions of the Septuagint, Aquila, Symmachus, and Theodotion, and any information he could obtain from Jewish sources. As a result Jerome kept very much along traditional lines, and the influences of the resources mentioned above are clearly observable in his work.[5] The distrust of his work shown by the majority of the theologians, as well as his own churchmanship, urged him to consider carefully the current Latin text.[6] Jerome reinterpreted some passages in a quite Christian sense. On the other hand, the version does not hide the Greco-Roman education of its author, even if many particular traits may be attributed to later revisers. Thus the Rome edition of the Vulgate now in preparation (cf. p. 99) states that "the 'Ciceronisms' of the Vulgate are largely from Alcuin. It is true that in many passages Jerome approaches classical Latin usage, yet he also retained more (real or supposed) 'vulgarisms' than the traditionally accepted text suggested."[7]

The work of Jerome thus presents a very complex image from the very beginning, and its later developments, which we can sketch only briefly in the next section, further increased this complexity. This seriously affects its value for textual criticism, for it is difficult to determine from the version without careful research precisely what Hebrew text Jerome had before him. In Friedrich Stummer's words, "When Jerome agrees with the Septuagint or with the later translations against our present Masoretic text, I believe he should usually be disregarded. For at most it proves that in his day or at some later time this was the reading of the Septuagint; it cannot prove without further evidence that Jerome's Hebrew text differed from our own."[8]

2. The History of the Vulgate[9]

It was only over a period of centuries that Jerome's version attained the general recognition that has been associated with the name "Vulgate"

---

5. The extent of Jerome's debt to the later Greek translators, especially Aquila and Symmachus, is shown by a wealth of evidence in the study by J. Ziegler 1943/1944.

6. G. Q. A. Meershoek 1966: 244, speaks of a "fidelité à la consuetudo." Meershoek suggests that as in the Gospels, so also in many books of the Old Testament Jerome's version deserves to be called a revision rather than a translation.

7. F. Stummer 1940/41: 258.

8. F. Stummer 1928: 123.

9. Cf. R. Loewe 1969.

since the sixteenth century.[10] At the beginning of the seventh century it was on a par with the Old Latin in the esteem and usage of the church, but in the eighth and ninth centuries it won the lead. It was inevitable that when these two texts of the Latin Bible remained in use side by side they should influence one another. A revision of great importance was made by *Alcuin* (730/735-804), who was close to Charlemagne and from 796 was the Abbot of St. Martin in Tours. He made stylistic alterations in Jerome's version, as we have indicated. Through the scriptorium at Tours the text edited by Alcuin became "the standard text of France, (thus) bringing to its conclusion a process of development which finally assured, through centuries of struggles and vicissitudes, the sole and uncontested authority to the Vulgate text of St. Jerome."[11] About the year 1100 Abbot *Stephen Harding* produced an important scholarly edition for the Cistercian monasteries. In the later Middle Ages a newly revised standard text called the Paris Bible[12] became widely influential. It was in this recension that a division of the text into chapters devised by Stephen Langton, a teacher at Paris and later Archbishop of Canterbury (d. 1228), achieved general acceptance.

The decree of the Council of Trent on April 8, 1546, was of epoch-making significance for the later history of the Vulgate: it declared the Vulgate, in contrast to the burgeoning variety of new versions, to be the authentic Bible of the Catholic Church, "i.e., authoritative in matters of faith and morals, without any implication of rejecting or forbidding either the Septuagint or the original Hebrew text, or in the New Testament the Greek text."[13]

The special recognition of the Vulgate necessitated an official edition of its text, but it was nearly a half-century before one was available. After a variety of attempts, a hastily prepared edition revised by Sixtus V himself (the *Sixtine* edition) appeared in 1589. This was withdrawn after his death and replaced by the edition of Clement VIII (the *Clementine* edition of 1592; the second and third editions of 1593 and 1598 included some improvements). Although even this edition cannot claim to have restored the text of Jerome, it remained the official text until the publication of the

10. On the history of the name "Vulgate," cf. E. F. Sutcliffe 1948; A. Allgeier 1948.

11. B. Fischer 1957: 19.

12. The text which achieved wide distribution through the first Gutenberg Bible of 1452/55 and its successors in the fifteenth century was a very slightly revised form of this Paris Bible; cf. H. Schneider 1954.

13. F. Stummer 1928: 172.

Nova Vulgata in 1979.[14] Worthy of note among the many modern editions of the Clementine text is the 1959 edition by the Benedictine Monastery of St. Jerome, Rome. The apparatus compares the critical editions thus far published of Rome (Old Testament, see below) and Oxford (New Testament). The Psalms are printed in parallel columns representing the *Psalterium Gallicum*, the *Psalterium iuxta Hebraeos* (following the critical edition by Dom H. de Sainte Marie, see below), and the *nova versio* prepared by the Pontifical Biblical Institute in 1945.

The Benedictine Order has been commissioned since 1907 with the preparation of a comprehensive edition, taking full account of the wealth of manuscript evidence (about eight thousand manuscripts), and designed to give a complete picture of the textual tradition. After exhaustive preliminary studies it began to appear in 1926. The Old Testament was completed in 1986.[15]

A manual edition of the Vulgate has been published by the German Bible Society, edited by Robert Weber with the assistance of Bonifatius Fischer OSB, Johannes Gribomont OSB, H. F. D. Sparks, and Walter Thiele (1969, [3]1983). "Our text is a new text, established from the evidence of the manuscripts with the help of the two big modern editions" (p. xxii), i.e., for the Old Testament, the Benedictine edition mentioned above. Its text has been accepted in this manual edition subject to careful verification and correction where necessary. For the Minor Prophets, which were not available in the Benedictine edition in 1983, a provisional text was printed (see the Foreword of the edition for a statement of its editorial principles). In the Psalter the *Psalmi iuxta Septuaginta emendati* (the Gallican Psalter) and the *Psalmi iuxta Hebraicum translati* are printed on facing pages. Concordance: B. Fischer 1977.

A critical edition of Jerome's version of the Psalter from the Hebrew, which was not included in the Vulgate, has been produced by Henri de Sainte Marie (1954).

14. *Nova Vulgata Bibliorum Sacrorum editio, sacros. oecum. concilii Vaticani II ratione habita iussu Pauli PP. VI recognita auctoritate Ioannis Pauli PP. II promulgata.* The *Nova Vulgata* of 1979 does not represent a reconstruction of Jerome's historical text, but rather a revision of it based on the original languages of Hebrew, Aramaic, and Greek. It should not be confused with the critical edition being produced by the Benedictine Order.

15. It must be added that several books contained in the Vulgate were not revised by Jerome because he did not regard them as canonical: Baruch (with the Letter of Jeremiah), Wisdom, Sirach, 1 and 2 Maccabees. These books appear, therefore, in the Old Latin version.

X. The Coptic Versions (Ⲕ)

Coptic is the language of the native Egyptian Christians, and is written in an alphabet mainly derived from Greek (pl. 44). The Greek language was widely spoken in Egypt, but not among the native peasant population. As Christianity spread to these circles at an early date it had to use Coptic, the popular language, enriched by Greek loanwords. There are several dialects of Coptic, so that there are many quite different versions grouped together in BH under the term Coptic (Ⲕ). The earliest was undoubtedly

Sa the *Sahidic* version of Upper Egypt,[1] translated from the Greek about the middle of the third century A.D., and probably undertaken at the official request of the church. This was followed by *Akhmimic,* which was based

Bo upon the Sahidic, and later in the fourth century by the *Bohairic* (Lower Egyptian), which was translated from the Greek independently of the Sahidic.[2]

For textual criticism, especially for Septuagintal research, these versions are valuable for their antiquity. A great many complete and fragmentary manuscripts written before the end of the fifth century have survived, not a few of which date from the third or fourth century. On the basis of evidence presented by Willem Grossouw and Joseph Ziegler for the Minor Prophets,[3] Paul E. Kahle has suggested "that the basis for the Sahidic version was the Septuagint text as established by Origen for the fifth column of his Hexapla." "It is very probable that in the Sahidic version of the Minor Prophets we have evidence for the Septuagint text of Origen which

1. According to P. E. Kahle, Jr., 1954 Sahidic was the official dialect of the native population of Egypt and the official language of Alexandria long before the spread of Christianity.

2. On the history of the Coptic dialects and the Coptic versions of the Bible, cf. R. Kasser 1965.

3. W. Grossouw 1938; J. Ziegler 1944a.

was translated either within Origen's lifetime or at any rate very soon after his death, and which as early as the fourth century is supported by MS evidence (Jonah in Budge 1912), evidence almost 400 years older than the Syro-Hexaplaric version translated by Paul of Tella in the years 616 to 617, which up to now has been accepted as the main source for the Septuagint of Origen."[4] Ziegler himself is more cautious. He sees indications in this and related evidence "that even before Origen various passages had been corrected from the Hebrew text: we must beware of attributing agreements with 𝔐 too readily to Hexaplaric influence."[5]

Recent editions: W. Kosack 1973 (Proverbs); M. K. H. Peters 1983 (Deuteronomy), 1985 (Genesis), 1986 (Exodus).[6]

4. P. Kahle 1954: 94; 1959: 261. Cf. pl. 44.
5. J. Ziegler 1943: 34.
6. Cf. also M. K. H. Peters 1979.

XI. The Ethiopic Version (ℷ)

About the middle of the fourth century the king of Aksum in Ethiopia and his people were won over to Christianity. A translation of the Bible from the Greek[1] was probably begun shortly afterward, but the completion of the version took a long while, possibly several centuries. Consequently the quality of the individual books varies. The Old Ethiopian version is represented in only some of the surviving manuscripts, the earliest of which is from the thirteenth century (pl. 45). It may be inferred from the various manuscripts that it was revised from an Arabic Bible (a "popular" recension), from Greek manuscripts, and corrected from the Hebrew (an "academic" recension).[2] Only the Old Ethiopic is of significance as a witness to the Septuagint text. Joseph Ziegler has found that the Ethiopic version in the Minor Prophets is often associated with the Alexandrian group of Septuagint witnesses. "The Ethiopic frequently has a very free rendering. This is at times because the translator was not familiar with the Greek vocabulary, but at times due to his efforts to achieve a fluency of style and to render the difficult Greek original more readably."[3] (Cf. also p. 222.)

---

1. According to E. Ullendorff 1968 it appears that Hebrew, Aramaic, and Syriac exemplars may have been used at times. He suggests a "team of translators" (p. 56). He writes: "Work on one single linguistic *Vorlage* was, perhaps, the exception rather than the rule in the peculiar circumstances that obtained in the Aksumite kingdom of the fourth-sixth centuries." Cf. E. Ullendorff 1980.

2. J. Ziegler 1957: 30.

3. J. Ziegler 1943: 25.

XII. The Armenian Version (Arm)

At the beginning of the fifth century, after a period in which the national Armenian church used Greek and Syriac for both literature and liturgy, the Armenian priest Mesrob (*ca.* 361-439) invented the Armenian alphabet and laid the basis for a national Armenian literature. At this time the Bible was translated. According to Armenian tradition this first version of the Bible (*ca.* A.D. 414) was based on the Syriac Peshitta, but nothing further is known about it.[1] The final official version which has come down to us was based on the Septuagint, with perhaps some influence from the Peshitta. It has been suspected that this official version was actually a revision of the first version which was made, at least in some books, with the aid of the Septuagint. In his thorough research of Deuteronomy Claude E. Cox concluded that influence from the Peshitta or an earlier Armenian version cannot be proved.[2] Since the Armenian follows the Hexaplaric recension extensively and Hexaplaric signs are frequently found in the manuscripts (cf. p. 58), this version is an important witness for the fifth column of Origen's Hexapla.[3]

1. L. Leloir 1960.
2. C. E. Cox 1981: 326f.: "That there has been no influence from P upon Arm is impossible to prove. That the translator of Arm may have known P is quite possible. However, the small number of minor agreements with P do not prove that there is any sort of textual relationship. If there existed, before the translation from Greek, an Armenian translation of Deuteronomy based on the Peshitta, its existence cannot be proven by examining the Armenian text now extant. The Armenian as we know it, if actually a revised Armenian translation, was so thoroughly done as to constitute a translation in its own right with little or no remains of what hypothetically was an earlier translation."
3. C. E. Cox 1986. The influence of Hexaplaric manuscripts in the Armenian version was also noted by B. Johnson 1968.

XIII. The Arabic Versions (ר)

With the victory of Islam the use of Arabic spread widely, and for Jews and Christians in the conquered lands it became the language of daily life. This gave rise to the need for Arabic versions of the Bible, which need was met by a number of versions, mainly independent and concerned primarily for interpretation (pl. 46). The version by Saadia Gaon[1] (of Egypt, and from 928 the head of the Jewish academy at Sura in Babylonia), of which only a part has survived, was based on the Hebrew text. It was also accepted by the Samaritans at first, but later subjected continually to alterations, as is evident from the manuscripts. The textus receptus of the Arabic version used today among the Samaritans is attributed to Abu Saʿid, who lived in the mid-thirteenth century.[2]

The value of the Arabic versions for textual criticism is slight. But they make a contribution to the history of interpretation, and by shedding light on the development of earlier versions they offer suggestions toward the solution of their problems.[3]

Translations into Arabic were also made from the Septuagint, from the Peshitta, and from other versions. The manuscripts and editions (especially the polyglots) contain for the most part translations of very diverse origins. Thus it is in no sense a unified Arabic version that is represented in BH by the sign ר.

1. R. Ecker 1962.
2. P. Kahle 1959: 53f.; H. Shehadeh 1978.
3. Cf. R. Edelmann 1953: 75.

XIV. The Aims of Textual Criticism[1]

The history of the text shows clearly that all our witnesses as they stand are far removed from the original text both by time and by the processes of transmission. Many generations of scribes and translators have played a role in transmitting the text of the Old Testament. They contain, therefore, a great variety of scribal errors, such as occur inevitably in any form of manuscript transmission, caused by errors of reading, errors of hearing, orthographical slips, and defective exemplars. It should also be recognized that they contain textual changes due to other causes as well, some deliberate and some accidental (e.g., translations reflecting inadequate comprehension). Textual criticism is the skill by which Old Testament scholarship deals with such problems. It attempts to ferret out all the errors and alterations (variants) that have occurred, and to achieve on the basis of scholarly principles a Hebrew text providing a solid foundation on which higher criticism, exegesis, etc., can build. The task of textual criticism was long defined as establishing the textual form of the Old Testament books when they attained their present shape and content and gained canonical status, i.e., in the fourth century B.C. or later, depending on the book. There are two basic considerations that should be mentioned with regard to this definition. First, the canonization of the Old Testament books did not involve or imply a standardized form of their text in our sense of the term. Prior to canonization, which may be dated about A.D. 100, their text was still fluid. This was because the scribes, who were theologically educated and interested, would often write the texts from memory (a practice that was later forbidden) and did not regard their work as restricted to mechanical transcription. They were permitted to make certain changes in the

---

1. Among the works on textual criticism the following deserve special attention: J. Barr 1968; S. Talmon 1975; M. Greenberg 1977; E. Tov 1981, 1982a, 1992.

wording if they did not distort the sense of the text — as they understood it. Thus a fixed and unalterable text is conceivable only after the second century A.D. Second, the Masoretic text as it now exists exhibits corruptions that must have occurred very early, i.e., in the period before canonization; their correction, sometimes possible only by conjecture, is the task of textual criticism.

For these reasons the goal of textual criticism is not to establish the text of a particular time in history. It should be seen rather as editing a text which has the greatest degree of probable authenticity or originality based on the review of the textual witnesses and the scholarly principles of textual criticism (cf. pp. 107ff.). Such a text would explain most plausibly the emergence of variant and corrupt readings and conform best to its context in both the strict and broader senses.

The apparatus of Biblia Hebraica, while its scope may vary in individual books, is a useful tool for critical research. It records significant variants, calling attention to problem passages, citing conjectural emendations suggested in the past as well as new hints[2] for the restoration of the text.

The prehistory of our present Old Testament books lies beyond the province of textual criticism. Reconstructing the ipsissima verba of the prophets in their presumably original form, separating the various strands of the Pentateuch, investigating questions of literary integrity, and the like, are among the tasks properly entrusted to higher criticism, literary criticism, and exegesis. Although textual criticism, literary criticism, and exegesis frequently come into close contact and occasionally overlap in their practical application, yet in the interest of methodological clarity it is necessary to preserve in principle the distinction between these areas of research.

l, dl   2. Hints in the sense that abbreviations such as l = lege(ndum) "read," dl = dele(ndum) "delete," etc., are to be understood as working suggestions. Special introductions to the terminology of the apparatus include H. P. Rüger 1983; R. Wonneberger 1990.

XV. Causes of Textual Corruption

1. General Remarks

If the goal of textual criticism consists in removing textual errors and restoring the original readings, the textual critic must have a clear idea of the kinds of errors to expect. Errors can occur in every conceivable way when copying out a text, as we well know from our own experience: sometimes we find it difficult to explain to ourselves later just how we came to make some particular error in writing down or transcribing a sentence. We can hardly expect at the outset to be able to correct and explain all the errors which eluded the attention of the early scribes, perhaps through sheer fatigue. A reading that appears doubtful or corrupt today may well have been caused by a lacuna in the copyist's exemplar due to a damaged writing surface, or a word or group of words that had become illegible. One error could easily give rise to several others and leave us no clue to how it happened. In many instances the assumption of a textual corruption which cannot be explained may be justified. But obviously such an assumption should be made as rarely as possible.

Besides those instances of textual corruption which cannot be explained because they depend on mere chance, there is a whole series of errors which recur constantly whenever texts are copied out by hand. Where we can verify these typical errors we are on relatively safe grounds for restoring the text. A sound diagnosis is the first step toward a cure. Two major groups of typical errors may be distinguished: errors which are due to an unintentional, mechanical lapse on the part of copyists (errors of reading and writing), and alterations which result from deliberation, leading to a departure from the copyist's exemplar (intentional alterations).

2. Errors of Reading and Writing[1]

These include all textual errors which arise from scribal misreading and miswriting (or even mishearing if transcribing from dictation). In order to prove that these errors are not the invention of modern textual critics but have actually occurred in manuscripts and can be expected in any manuscript, the following examples are taken primarily from a comparison of 𝔐 with the Isaiah scroll from Qumran (1QIs[a]). Because we are concerned here only with indicating a possible range of errors, the variants are simply listed without discussion.[2]

(a) *Confusion of similar letters* is the most frequent cause of errors in reading and writing. In the Hebrew square script the following are the most frequent confusions:

   (i) ב and כ: Isa. 28:20 𝔐 כהתכנס, 1QIs[a] בהתכנס; Isa. 28:21 𝔐 כהר, בעמק, 1QIs[a] בהר כעמק.

   (ii) ד and ר: Isa. 9:8 𝔐 וידעו, 1QIs[a] וירעו; Isa. 14:4 𝔐 מדהבה, 1QIs[a] correctly מרהבה; Isa. 47:10 𝔐 ברעתך, 1QIs[a] בדעתך; Isa. 33:8 𝔐 ערים, 1QIs[a] correctly עדים.

   (iii) ה and ח: Isa. 30:33 𝔐 תפתה, 1QIs[a] תפתח; Isa. 42:16 𝔐 מחשך, 1QIs[a] מהשוכים; Isa. 47:13 𝔐 (K) הברו, 1QIs[a] חוברי, note also י for ו as in 𝔐 (Q); Isa. 51:9 𝔐 רהב, 1QIs[a] רחוב.

   (iv) ה and ת: Isa. 42:25 𝔐 חמה אפו, 1QIs[a] correctly חמת אפו; Judg. 7:8 read צדת העם for צדה העם.

   (v) ו and י: Isa. 5:29 𝔐 ושאג, 1QIs[a] ישאג as also 𝔐 (Q); Isa. 11:6 𝔐 ומריא, 1QIs[a] ימרו; Isa. 33:13 𝔐 ודעו, 1QIs[a] ידעו.

   (vi) ע and צ: 2 Kgs. 20:4 𝔐 העיר, many manuscripts, Q, versions חצר (also confusion of ה and ח).

   (vii) כ and נ: Isa. 33:1 𝔐 כנלתך, 1QIs[a] ככלותך.

For a large part of the Old Testament we must also consider the possibility of confusion occurring in the Old Hebrew script. Thus in Ps. 19:5 בהם may be derived from בים through a confusion of י with ה, which was quite similar in form. As the Lachish ostraca indicate, the letters א and ת,[3] כ

---

1. F. Delitzsch 1920 provides a wealth of material; cf. also J. Kennedy 1928.
2. Numerous examples of scribal errors are given in J. Hempel 1959: 220-234.
3. S. Talmon 1981 discusses numerous variant readings apparently due to a confusion of *aleph* and *taw* in the Old Hebrew script; in 1985 he examines possible confusions between the letters *tsadhe* and *yod*.

and ג, and ע and ד were quite similar in the Old Hebrew script, as were also ב and ר, ה and ח, and מ and נ (cf. pl. 48).

For assessing the readings of 𝕲 it is often important to remember the possible confusions of Greek uncial letters such as occur in the textual transmission of the New Testament.

(b) *Transposition of letters* can occur most easily in an unpointed text, and it does occur frequently; Isa. 9:18 𝔐 נעתם 1QIsᵃ נתעם; Isa. 32:19 𝔐 העיר, 1QIsᵃ היער; Isa. 28:1, 4 𝔐 גיא, 1QIsᵃ גאי (as also proposed by L. Rost 1935).

(c) *Haplography* (hpgr; "single writing") occurs when two identical or similar letters, groups of letters, or words are found together in an immediate sequence, and one of them is omitted by error.

(i) *Omission of a single letter:* Isa. 5:8 𝔐 בית בבית, 1QIsᵃ בית בית; Isa. 8:11 𝔐 בחזקת היד, 1QIsᵃ כחזקת יד; Isa. 8:19 𝔐 בעד החיים, 1QIsᵃ בעד חיים. In the Lachish ostraca (3.9) the form חיהוה (= חי יהוה) is found; this suggests that two identical letters occurring together could sometimes be written once, even though they belonged to different words. The reader had no difficulty in reading it correctly. It is tempting to view the many haplographies in the Old Testament in this light.[4]

(ii) *Omission of one in a pair of identical or similar words:* Isa. 26:3f. 𝔐 בך בטוח בטחו, 1QIsᵃ בך בטחו; Isa. 38:11 𝔐 יה יה יה, 1QIsᵃ יה.

(d) *Dittography* (dttg) is the accidental repetition of a letter, a group of letters, a word, or a group of words: Isa. 30:30 𝔐 והשמיע, 1QIsᵃ השמיע השמיע; in Isa. 38:20 1QIsᵃ repeats the whole of the preceding verse almost verbatim.

(e) *Omission by homoioteleuton* (homtel; "similar ending") occurs when two words which are identical, are similar in form, or have identical endings are found close to each other, and the eye of the copyist moves from the first to the second, omitting the words that lie between them, e.g., Isa. 4:5f.: ברא יהוה .... ענן [יומם ועשן ונגה אש להבה לילה כי על כל כבוד חפה וסכה תהיה לצל] יומם מחרב. The words in brackets are lacking in 1QIsᵃ; the scribe's eye passed from יומם in v. 5 to יומם in v. 6. For further examples in 1QIsᵃ see Isa. 16:8f.; 23:15; 37:29; and perhaps also 40:7f. where the omitted words have been inserted. Omissions due to similarities in the beginnings of words are rarer (*homoioarcton*, homark).

hpgr

dttg

homtel

homark

---

4. On the principle of the double value of letters (whether single letters or groups of letters) which may be observed from the sixth century B.C. to the first century A.D., cf. now I. O. Lehman 1967.

(f) *Errors of joining and dividing words.* By contrast with Greek, which was written well into the medieval period without spacing or dividing signs between words *(scriptio continua),* there is no real proof of scriptio continua in Hebrew. A dividing sign is found regularly in the Siloam inscription and the Samaritan ostraca, and frequently in the Lachish ostraca. As the recently discovered manuscripts show, a space is found regularly between words in the square script, although it is admittedly so small at times that it may be doubtful where one word ends and another begins. In such instances two words could be construed erroneously as one. The Lachish ostraca show examples of a scribe writing two words without an intervening space in order to fit the words into the space available (4.9; 5.10). And again, a single word could be divided between two lines. Both examples could easily lead to misunderstanding and a wrong construction of words and their divisions.

Erroneous joining of words is evident in Amos 6:12, where the generally adopted reading בבקר ים instead of בבקרים restores both parallelism and sense.

Erroneous word division is found in 𝔐 in Isa. 2:20 לחפר פרות, 1QIs^a correctly לחפרפרים. In Jer. 2:21 the text has been made unintelligible by a wrong word division לי סורי הגפן; Bernard Duhm and many others read לסוריה גפן ("into a rotten vine").

(g) *Errors due to vowel letters.* Consonants were used as vowel signs at an early period, and as the recently discovered manuscripts show, they were used quite freely for a time. If a vowel letter were later misconstrued as a consonant it would naturally lead to an error in the text. Thus from 1QIs^a it appears that א was used as a vowel sign for *a* (e.g., Isa. 1:17, 23 יאתום for יתום, 1:4 עאון for עון, etc.). In Amos 2:7 a similar א is misconstrued as part of the root: read השפים for השאפים.

(h) G. R. Driver has demonstrated that *abbreviations* played a considerable role in the Hebrew text before the Septuagint, and that their misunderstanding led to garbled texts.[5] Shemaryahu Talmon has also shown how many *double readings* have resulted from the insertion of synonymous expressions, etc.[6] Many obscure or corrupt passages can be restored when these sources of textual corruption are recognized.

5. G. R. Driver 1960, 1964; cf. M. Fishbane 1976.
6. S. Talmon 1960; 1964; also 1961.

3. Deliberate Alterations

Before the text of the Old Testament was officially established it was not regarded as unalterable. Accordingly we should expect to find that those who were concerned with the transmission of the text would occasionally make deliberate, fully intentional alterations in the text. In evaluating these alterations we must avoid thinking of them as "corruptions." They were made in good faith, with no intention of introducing a foreign element into the text, but rather with the aim of restoring the true text and (from the copyist's view) preventing misunderstandings. They must have originated in a period when the letter of the text could still be changed in order to express its message more effectively for its readership and audience.

Many of these alterations can be recognized only with great difficulty if at all because the manuscripts tradition of 𝔐 has preserved only a very few variant readings. Others are properly the province of higher criticism, whose borders are rather fluid at this point. Some examples should be given here.

There are certain small, common words which were easily inserted in the text, such as לאמר, שם, אשר, עתה, אחד, כל, ו. We have mentioned these in discussing the characteristics of the non-Masoretic texts, but this tendency is also represented in the manuscript tradition of 𝔐. "These words are almost always inserted to support an interpretation which is in itself quite possible. But it becomes significantly dangerous when they render obligatory an interpretation which would otherwise be no more than one possibility among others, especially when they have a bearing on the construction of whole sentences, determining their broader relationships."[7]

It is quite natural that a text which was not simply the object of scholarly study but intended to be read constantly by the whole of the Jewish community would be adapted to the linguistic needs of the community. Thus a rare word, or one used in an unusual sense, would give place to a more common word; e.g., in Isa. 39:1 𝔐 reads חזק in the sense of "get well, recuperate." The usual word for this is חיה, and 1QIs^a actually replaces חזק with חיה in this passage. Other examples of adaptation to colloquial usage have been mentioned above (see p. 15). The lack of early material for comparison makes it impossible to demonstrate these alterations in 𝔐 on a larger scale. But the parallel texts show that even 𝔐 was not immune to them. As a general rule, when the tradition offers variant readings with the alternatives lying between rare and common words, or

7. J. Wellhausen 1871: 26.

involved and simple constructions, in each instance the former may be considered the original (lectio difficilior probabilior; but cf. p. 119).

Since the wording of the text was subject to variation before it was officially established, it was also possible to substitute acceptable expressions for ones which were morally or religiously offensive. The treatment of the divine name בעל has been noted above (see p. 17). Another example is found in Job 1:5, 11; 2:5, 9 where we now read ברך "to bless" (with God as object), and should expect קלל "to curse." The scribes replaced the offensive expression "to curse God" with a euphemism.[8]

gl   *Additions and glosses*[9] to the text should also be included among deliberate alterations. Thus in 1 Kgs. 18:19 there are 400 prophets of Astarte mentioned together with 450 prophets of Baal. They are absent, however, from vv. 22 and 40, where they should have been included if they had been a part of the original story. They are probably a later addition, the result of a scholarly surmise. Occasionally an expression was given a further explanation in the margin or between the lines, and this gloss then found its way into the text. Beside the early expression דביר הבית in 1 Kgs 8:6 we find the later and more usual expression קדש הקדשים. Such glosses can often be recognized because they have not been inserted at the right place in the text, and are awkward in the context; e.g., in Gen. 10:14 the marginal note "from whom the Philistines are descended" is found before its antecedent "the men of Caphtor" instead of after it, where it should be if it were original.

The editorial activity which we glimpse in these deliberate alterations was in many respects official, and may be traced to an early period.[10] This is a wide field which unfortunately has not yet been examined as systematically as it deserves.

8. Cf. A. Geiger 1857: 267ff., which contains a great deal of material relevant to this subject.

9. For textual criticism "glosses" are "extraneous intrusions" in the text (H. Gunkel 1928: 1230); cf. G. Fohrer 1951, an instructive essay on glosses in Ezekiel.

10. P. Volz 1936: 103f.

XVI. The Methods
of Textual Criticism[1]

1. General Remarks

Textual criticism, like any other science, cannot achieve convincing results without a methodology which is appropriate to its subject matter and defined by it. An arbitrary procedure which hastily and unnecessarily dismisses the traditional text to rely on private conjecture can lead only to a subjective form of the text which is uncertain historically and without any claim to theological relevance. It is also likely to arouse a basic distrust of textual criticism itself, even where it is justifiable and necessary.

There is no precisely defined method for Old Testament textual criticism. Further, it is questionable whether one is possible, because the tradition is so varied that an effective procedure for one problem would not be appropriate for another. But there are certain fundamental principles which are widely recognized, at least in theory if not in practice, and which are designed to keep textual criticism on a sound basis, avoiding the excesses of arbitrariness and subjectivity. These principles are not specifically theological, but have developed from the application of the standard procedures of the science of textual criticism to the specific conditions of the Old Testament. Even beginners should be familiar with them because they will not only provide some criteria for assessing the results of the critical work of others that they will constantly encounter in their exegetical work, but also provide guidance for their own further thought and practical applications. We will therefore outline them briefly here.

1. P. Maas 1958, and A. Jepsen 1963.

2. Establishing the Traditional Text

The starting point for any textual study must be the textual tradition itself. Therefore it must first be decided which text is to be regarded as the traditional text. The various witnesses to the text should be examined, beginning with 𝕸, and continuing with the rest in roughly the order of their significance for textual criticism, e.g., 𝖜, 𝖰, 𝕲, α', σ', θ', 𝕾, 𝕮, 𝕯, 𝕷, Sa, 𝕶, 𝖀, 𝖀, and Arm (for the justification of this order, see the discussion of the textual history of each of these witnesses). In this way the whole of the available manuscript evidence should be reviewed.[2] Thus 𝕸 becomes the starting point: any differences are designated as variants — but without implying any evaluation.

A relatively simple picture can be given on the whole for 𝕸, whose manuscript variants are found in Kennicott, de Rossi, and Ginsburg, because real variants are rare. Historically from the beginning of the second century A.D. the text transmitted was exclusively of a single type; consequently the information to be gleaned for textual criticism from medieval Hebrew manuscripts is quite sparse, and in no way comparable to the variety found among the Greek manuscripts of the Old and New Testaments. Moshe Goshen-Gottstein has been led to a very negative conclusion by the researches of Johannes Hempel,[3] Hartmut Gese,[4] and himself: "Among all the MSS and fragments known so far there is not even one the deviations of which can be significantly connected with any non-Massoretic tradition. We possess no medieval manuscript which, on the strength of its readings, may be termed 'valuable' or be worthy of our attention more than any other."[5]

The relationships among the manuscripts from Qumran present a radical contrast. The examples cited from 1QIs[a] (pp. 108ff. above) give a hint of the variety to be found there. There are some agreements with readings found in 𝕲. Some fragments have the shorter text of Jeremiah, and others the longer text of Samuel. The readings attested at Qumran suggest that extensive freedom was observed in transcribing manuscripts. Thus each variant must also be tested for possible traces of intentional change.[6]

---

2. This means, of course, that for work in textual criticism the apparatus of BH is not adequate by itself. A manual edition designed for students cannot possibly represent the full range of variants; it must be supplemented by the use of critical editions.

3. J. Hempel 1930; 1934.

4. H. Gese 1957.

5. M. H. Goshen-Gottstein 1967: 277.

6. Cf. B. A. van der Kooij 1981: 85f. on Isa. 8:11; 28:10.

For the *versions,* especially for ๕, the manuscript tradition is much more complex. This must first be clarified before inferences may be drawn about the Hebrew text underlying it. For ๕, the editions of the Göttingen Septuagint provide a valuable guide through the mass of variants when used with discretion. Here also a preliminary sifting of the evidence should be made as it is collected. Variants within the ๕ tradition may be recognized and set aside immediately, e.g., corruptions of the Greek text (confusions of letters, etc.), or deliberate alterations (for a more idiomatic Greek usage). When assessing the variants in the manuscript tradition of any particular version, it should also be remembered that in many versions the text has been assimilated to ๓; thus if one reading agrees with ๓ while another reading differs, the former may be suspected of being a late assimilation to ๓. Since the versions, and in particular ๕, are characterized in contrast with ๓ by differences in the manuscript traditions, it is important when evaluating them to consider the provenance and general character of the individual manuscripts: *"manuscripta ponderantur, non numerantur"* ("manuscripts should be weighed, not simply counted"). No less a scholar than Paul A. de Lagarde has observed that "no manuscript of the Septuagint is so good that it does not have a share of poor readings, or so poor that it does not have its good readings."[7]

Obviously versions which are based upon or influenced by a particular version (usually ๕) may be accounted independent witnesses to the text only under certain conditions, such as when they appear likely or certain to have preserved an original reading of the version which has since been altered, perhaps by assimilation to ๓. Thus a reading which is attested by ๕ and ๕ is really attested only once, because ๕ is a daughter version of ๕.

3. Examination of the Traditional Text

After deciding which text is to be regarded as the traditional text — a task which we have seen is not merely a mechanical process of collecting the evidence but also involves a critical sifting of it — the real examination of the tradition can begin. For convenience we may divide this between the two aspects of linguistic form and subject matter. Our main interest focuses first on ๓. In every instance it deserves special attention because it is based

---

7. P. A. de Lagarde 1863: 3, n. 1. It has often been noted with criticism that in the apparatus of BHK the versions, and ๕ in particular, are cited far too extensively, uncritically, and indiscriminately. BHS has done well in exercising a far greater discretion in this regard.

on direct transmission in the original language, and it has been handed down with great care. The earlier tendency to undervalue 𝔐 in favor of the Greek version or even of modern conjectures has now been almost entirely abandoned, because 𝔐 has repeatedly been demonstrated to be the best witness to the text. Any deviation from it therefore requires justification. But this does not mean that we should cling to 𝔐 under all circumstances, as it has become popular to do in some circles, because it also has its undeniable faults which can be corrected to some extent with the help of other witnesses. It is clear from the history of the text that the vocalization of 𝔐 does not have the same significance as the consonantal text, and that alterations in the pointing do not qualify properly as emendations (cf. pp. 21ff.).

As a general rule 𝔐 is to be preferred over all other traditions whenever it cannot be faulted either linguistically or for its material content, unless in particular instances there is good reason for favoring another tradition. The question whether 𝔐 can be faulted either linguistically or materially is to be decided at times only after intensive investigations. Specifically, if a reading of 𝔐 is rejected, every possible interpretation of it must first have been fully examined. It is unscholarly to oppose a reading of 𝔐 merely for its lack of agreement with an interpreter's viewpoint. When such a conflict arises, it is the theory that should defer to the textual tradition, and not the reverse.

The *linguistic* examination is concerned first with grammatical and lexical possibilities. Research in these fields is still continuing, so that we must often look for new interpretations which have not yet been incorporated in the standard grammars and lexicons. The possible range of meanings for a word can often be detected only by using a concordance[8] and checking all the occurrences of a word in the Old Testament. Not infrequently such an "internal interpretation" suggests a possible construction of a text that has not been noted before and which makes good sense of the traditional Hebrew text. Especially useful are instances of *parallelismus membrorum.* This approach has shown many widely accepted emendations to be unnecessary. Another useful tool for linguistic interpretation is the study of *related Semitic languages.* These often shed a

---

8. Useful tools include the concordances of S. Mandelkern 1937[2] (repr. 1955), and G. Lisowsky 1990[3]. The references in the lexicons of W. Gesenius-F. Buhl 1915[17] (latest repr. 1962), L. Köhler and W. Baumgartner 1958[2], 1969[3], and F. Brown, S. R. Driver, and C. A. Briggs 1907 (corrected ed. 1952) take the place of a concordance for many words. Revised editions of both works are in preparation (cf. Appendix).

new light on words whose meaning in the Old Testament is still obscure. In addition to Arabic, which has long been in use, we are now indebted also to Akkadian, Old South Arabic, and Ugaritic among others, as well as to Egyptian, a mixed Semitic-Hamitic language which is important for loanwords in the Old Testament. This is a rapidly developing field, with excavations constantly increasing our resources (cf. recently the texts from Ugarit and Mari). Many useful results may be expected.[9] As an example may be cited Hab. 3:6b-7a, where the unintelligible phrase לו תחת און is the Ugaritic word תחתאון "destruction" with the preposition ל.[10]

Finally in this connection it should be noticed whether or not a text appears genuine on the basis of stylistic, material, form critical, or other grounds. Irregularities detected in this way often lead to the recognition of insertions, glosses, displacements, and other disturbances in the original text. As our knowledge in many of these fields (e.g., meter) is still quite limited and open to discussion, and subjective judgments are particularly easy to make, a greater degree of critical reserve than is commonly observed is in order.

In examining the *subject matter* we are concerned with determining whether or not a topic, an idea, or an expression is an original part of the text in the light of what is known from other parts of the Old Testament world. This approach leads to the recognition of later alterations and the elimination of later insertions. Textual criticism comes into close contact at this point with literary criticism and exegesis. Therefore for methodological integrity it is very important to be quite clear whether a text is contested on the grounds of textual criticism, literary criticism, or exegesis. The limits of textual criticism as defined above (p. 106) should be recalled explicitly in this context. Finally, in examining the subject matter we should remember how fragmentary our knowledge of the Old Testament world remains. We should recognize the possibility that we may not understand a particular text because our knowledge is limited. As it grows — and it does grow with every excavation — we have greater grounds for confidence that we may yet learn the meaning of passages that are still obscure. It is essential for the Old Testament scholar to follow closely every new discovery in the world of the Old Testament, and be prepared to reconsider earlier solutions in the light of new knowledge.

9. Cf. G. R. Driver 1950. J. Barr 1968: 320-337 discusses in detail the problems of linguistic comparisons, with 344 examples of textual emendations proposed by various Old Testament scholars.

10. Cf. K. Elliger, *Das Buch der zwölf kleinen Propheten II. Das Alte Testament Deutsch* 25, *ad loc.;* the suggestion goes back to W. F. Albright.

Not only 𝔐, but the versions also must be subjected to intensive examination, for it is conceivable that even when 𝔐 reads an acceptable or possible text, a version which differs from it may preserve the original text. When evaluating an early version for textual criticism it is particularly important that it not be treated piecemeal, i.e., considering only isolated readings without regard for the whole character of the version, its translation method, its bias, its intellectual background, etc. The information in the apparatus of BH should be regarded only as suggestions to be followed up by intensive research in the versions themselves. Only those variant readings which cannot be construed as translational errors, oversights, or due to language, spirit, bias, or translation method of the version should be (back-translated[11] and) placed beside 𝔐 as genuine variants.

4. The Decision

After the evidence of the tradition has been collected and examined, the decision must be made as to which text is to be regarded as the original or the nearest approximation to it. When the various textual witnesses are reviewed the following patterns are generally found.

(a) 𝔐 and all other witnesses offer a text which is unobjectionable, which makes sense, and has been preserved without a variant. Here we may naturally assume that the original text has been preserved by the tradition, and that it should be accepted implicitly. It may seem strange that this point requires statement here, because it seems so obvious. But anyone acquainted with the history of Old Testament scholarship will not consider it unnecessary.

(b) When 𝔐 and all or some of the other witnesses are found on careful examination to differ from each other so that there are real variants, the following possibilities may occur.

(i) 𝔐 preserves a reading which is either probably or certainly original, while the variants supported by the other witnesses are secondary (misreadings, misunderstandings, intentional or unconscious corrections); here 𝔐 is to be followed.

---

11. The problems and practice of back-translating from 𝔊 are discussed in detail by E. Tov 1981. Back-translating can be exceedingly difficult, and most often there remains an element of doubt. "What seems self-evident to one scholar may look like a house of cards to his fellow" (M. H. Goshen-Gottstein 1963a: 132). It is all the more welcome, therefore, that when BHS cites a Hebrew back-translation from a version it frequently also provides a control by showing the text of the version itself.

(ii) 𝔐 and the other witnesses support different but apparently equally possible or plausible readings, none of which is clearly or even probably secondary. Generally 𝔐 would be given preference here as a matter of basic principle, but other factors must also be considered. The rule may apply of preferring the reading which is more difficult from the viewpoint of language and subject matter *(lectio difficilior)* — or the alternate rule that of two readings the one which best explains the development of the other is to be preferred. Often in such instances the verdict *non liquet* ("unsolved") must be given, and both readings must be recognized.

(iii) The text of 𝔐 is doubtful or impossible on linguistic or contextual grounds, while other witnesses offer a satisfactory reading. If evidence for the originality of the latter is available, and especially if the reading of 𝔐 is demonstrably a corruption of it, then the text of 𝔐 should certainly be corrected by it. The objection that 𝔐 offers the lectio difficilior in this instance is not valid because the contrast is not between an easier and a harder reading but between a satisfactory reading and one that is meaningless or corrupt, and the rule of lectio difficilior should not be used to "justify even the crassest of scribal errors."[12] But again, if the satisfactory reading in a version seems to be a translator's attempt to cope with a Hebrew text which was already corrupt, then the version offers nothing more than a very early conjecture, and the verdict must be that the original text of the tradition has not been preserved.

(c) In such an instance, and similarly when 𝔐 and the other witnesses fail to provide a reading that is linguistically or contextually probable or even possible, an emendation may be attempted by conjecture or the problem may be regarded as beyond solution *(crux interpretum)*. A conjecture may be justified if textual corruption has entered the tradition so early that it antedates the earliest versions. But if a text is to be emended by conjecture, this should be done with as close a dependence as possible on the existing textual tradition, and with due regard for the causes of textual corruption sketched above in chapter XV (cf., for example, the conjecture at Jer. 2:21, p. 110). And further, the tentativeness of any text established in this way should also be acknowledged.

5. Psychological Considerations

Finally, we should underscore once again the importance of giving due attention to the psychological aspect present in all textual critical work.

12. Cf. R. Borger 1987: 8; also B. Albrektson 1981.

Namely, whenever an error is suspected, the conditions that could have given rise to such an error should be considered. The various possible causes of textual corruption listed in chapter XV may be useful as suggestions, but they are by no means exhaustive. If the cause of an error can be discovered, the first step has been taken toward recovering the original text with some degree of certainty. It is precisely the careful consideration of this psychological aspect that assures to textual criticism the certainty it needs, that makes proposed emendations more convincing, and provides a proper finish to the work. If it does no more than place a restraint on too drastic a treatment of the text, this is no small achievement.[13]

13. A committee of six Old Testament scholars under the direction of D. Barthélemy and sponsored by the United Bible Societies has undertaken a comprehensive text-critical study; two (of five) volumes have been published: Barthélemy 1982; 1986. This expands the 5-volume *Preliminary and Interim Report on the Hebrew Old Testament Text Project* (Barthélemy 1976-1980). The discussion of about five thousand problem passages is oriented to the need of translators into modern languages. While useful for details of early (including medieval Jewish) and modern interpretations of the text, it is of limited value for textual criticism because of its partiality to 𝔐 as the canonical and sacred text, its rejection of conjectures almost on principle, and its extreme expansion of the rule lectio difficilior probabilior. Cf. among others B. Albrektson 1981; J. Barr 1986.

XVII. The Theological Significance of Textual Criticism and the History of the Text

No book in the literature of the world has been so often copied, printed, translated, read, and studied as the Bible. It stands uniquely as the object of so much effort devoted to preserving it faithfully, to understanding it, and to making it understandable to others. We may remember the scribes and Masoretes with their strict regulations and subtle studies, the translators, the medieval monks tracing the text out letter by letter in their quiet cells, the exegetes, and especially Martin Luther, who devoted the greater part of his exegetical work to the Old Testament.

What was the real motive for all this concern about the Bible? Certainly not merely an interest in a venerable relic which deserved preservation because of its antiquity. Literatures as old or older than the Old and New Testaments have disappeared, leaving only some scant allusions and an occasional fortunate discovery of fragmentary remains to remind us that they once existed. It is something else that has made people devote themselves to the Bible and ensure its preservation for their own and later generations: the recognition of its meaning for all generations, the knowledge that here flows the fountain of life, because God himself speaks in it.

It is this same motivation which inspires our work on the Bible today. It would be wrong to regard the present account of the vicissitudes of the Old Testament text in its transmission as though it were written solely as a matter of academic interest in things past, or even as an attempt to expose the imperfections of the text incurred in its transmission by human beings. Even this has its serious theological significance if we think of the servant form of the Word of God as finding expression also in the transmission of the text. Yet we are not so much concerned with discovering imperfections and errors as with overcoming them. We are concerned primarily with the original form of the Old Testament record, as we are concerned with the message of the Bible as a whole, because we want to be confronted with

this original Word itself, and not with an interpretation made of it by fallible scribes in the course of its transmission. The history of the text, as well as the textual criticism which is based on it, is inseparably a part of any Old Testament scholarship that is consciously theological. "Without textual criticism there can be no real understanding of Old Testament religion, no real Old Testament theology. Anyone who penetrates more deeply into textual criticism knows that theology and textual criticism are not two separate fields, but that at this deepest level they are interdependent."[1]

But does concentration on the letter of the text, many people tend to ask, actually lead to confrontation with the message of the Bible? Is this not precisely the wrong approach? This attitude probably appeals to such statements of Luther as: "No one can understand even one iota of the Scriptures unless he has the Spirit of God."[2] But this reveals a misunderstanding, for we must remember that it was the same Luther who insisted so strongly on the "Word" in opposition to the "Spirit" of the religious enthusiasts, and who repeatedly pointed out that God "never gives anyone the Spirit or faith without the outward sign or word in which he has enshrined it."[3] What Luther means by these apparently contradictory statements is that "God has linked his Spirit to the written and spoken word; but he controls the working of his Spirit in the Word by his own unlimited sovereign will."[4] "Literal understanding and spiritual understanding are therefore not to be separated. We cannot acquire the one without also having the other."[5] Because this is so, the concern for the letter of the text which this book seeks to promote has genuine theological significance.

1. P. Volz 1936: 113.
2. *De servo arbitrio,* Weimar ed. (1883ff.) 18, 609.
3. *Idem,* 136.
4. H. Bornkamm 1933: 12.
5. K. Holl 1948: 558.

Appendix:
Resources for Textual Research

Research on the text of the Old Testament depends, in part, on the use of the best tools. This brief survey offers guidance in several major categories. Traditional printed resources are now supplemented with texts in electronic form and a variety of computer programs. These electronic tools are becoming increasingly important since most researchers now have ready access to computers with enough power and storage capacity to facilitate electronic-based research. This is a rapidly developing field, so any list of resources will soon be outdated. Computer programs described here were considered to be among the most useful at the time of this writing, but one should also check for the newest versions of existing programs and newer programs as well. A number of academic journals in the field of biblical studies now review computer software.

1. Text

The complexities of any Masoretic manuscript, including B 19[A], as well as the terminology of the apparatus in BHS can be daunting. Several useful guides are available to supplement the Preface in BHS. Reinhard Wonneberger's *Understanding BHS: A Manual for the Users of Biblia Hebraica Stuttgartensia* (1990) has already been mentioned (see p. 106). Another useful guide has been prepared by William R. Scott, *A Simplified Guide to BHS* (1990). Scott provides a concise guide to the system of Masoretic notation, an English guide to the symbols and abbreviations used in the *Masora parva,* and includes the *English Key* prepared by Hans Peter Rüger (1983), which is especially useful when using the critical apparatus. The *Data for the Sigla of the BHS* (1983), prepared by R. I. Vasholz, is a concise eight page guide. The beginning student can benefit from the judicious use

123

of an interlinear text. The only interlinear edition based on BHS was prepared by John R. Kohlenberger, *The NIV Interlinear Hebrew-English Old Testament* (1987).

2. Concordances

The first of the concordances of the Hebrew Bible in the modern era was compiled by Solomon Mandelkern and first published in 1896. It has been reprinted many times. The entries are arranged by Hebrew roots, with every related form arranged in sub-entries. Forms with or without the *waw* prefix are even listed separately. Because of this arrangement Mandelkern's concordance is quite helpful for grammatical analysis. Each lemma is fully vocalized. For further information on Mandelkern and the history of Hebrew Bible concordances the reader may consult Hans H. Wellisch 1985-1986.

Gerhard Lisowsky published a concordance of the Hebrew Bible, based on BHK^3 (1958). The arrangement of the Lisowsky concordance simply by words, without distinguishing inflectional subgroupings, makes it handier to use, especially for quick reference. A special feature of Lisowsky's concordance is semantic information through the use of superscript letters. The book was reproduced from Lisowsky's handwritten manuscript, which is quite legible. A third edition, with an appendix of nearly three hundred corrections, appeared in 1990, and in reduced format in 1993.

The most recent concordance of the Hebrew Bible was compiled by Abraham Even-Shoshan and first published in 1977-1980. It was based on the Hebrew text as found in the Koren (Jerusalem) edition. The use of the earlier editions was somewhat difficult for students unfamiliar with Hebrew names of the biblical books as well as the use of Hebrew letters for numerals. The second edition, *A New Concordance of the Old Testament: Using the Hebrew and Aramaic Text* (1989), provides English book names and arabic numerals, as well as an English introduction and guide for use, prepared by John H. Sailhamer. The arrangement of entries allows the same kind of analysis provided by Mandelkern, with each root entry being subdivided according to extant forms found in the Hebrew Bible. At the head of each entry some semantic analysis is also provided.

A Topical Concordance of the Old Testament: Using the Hebrew and Aramaic Text, compiled by Eliezer Katz (1992), like the Even-Shoshan concordance, was originally published with Hebrew book names and Hebrew chapter and verse numbers, but now gives references in

English. Biblical references are arranged within fifty-six topics, with many sub-topics.

When working with fragmentary manuscripts one will frequently encounter places where the beginning of a word is lost. An index which lists the vocabulary of the Hebrew Bible in the reverse sequence of their letters can show immediately all possible beginnings of words known in Biblical Hebrew. The *Rücklaufiges Hebräisches Wörterbuch,* compiled by Karl Georg Kuhn (1958), provides such a tool. In addition to the vocabulary of the Hebrew Bible, Kuhn added the main nonbiblical manuscripts from Qumran Cave 1, the extant Hebrew portions of Sirach, and several major ancient Hebrew inscriptions.

For the Septuagint and the other ancient Greek versions the nineteenth-century concordance prepared by Edwin Hatch and Henry A. Redpath is indispensable. It has been reprinted twice, in 1954 and 1983. The complete range of presumed Hebrew equivalents is given at the head of each entry and the citation lines of all occurrences are keyed to this list of Hebrew equivalents. Emanuel Tov 1981 discusses "The use of concordances in the Reconstruction of the *Vorlage* of the LXX."[1] The lack of a complete Hebrew index in Hatch and Redpath has been remedied by Elmar Camilo dos Santos in *An Expanded Hebrew Index for the Hatch-Redpath Concordance to the Septuagint* (1973).

One of the most valuable uses of the computer is concordance searches. The value of the electronic concordance goes beyond convenient lookup of individual words. Combination searches can be carried out as well, using the AND, OR, and NOT searches known as Boolean operators. Additional search criteria such as proximity and sequence can enable the researcher to formulate complex searches. Some data bases also are "tagged" with grammatical information, providing full morphological analysis. More advanced analyses above the morphological level are currently under development as well. These data bases will enable the user to add elements of syntax and semantics to a search.

The text of the Hebrew Old Testament, as well as the ancient Greek and Latin versions, is available from the Center for the Computer Analysis of Texts (CCAT) at the University of Pennsylvania, Philadelphia. This Hebrew Bible text in electronic form, sometimes called the Michigan-Claremont text for the two academic institutions who did the original work of encoding the text in electronic form, represents *BHS.* The work was

---

1. Excursus I to Hatch and Redpath 1983, a revised version of an article which first appeared in *CBQ* 40 (1978): 29-36.

originally based on the first edition of *BHS,* but has been upgraded to represent the latest edition of *BHS.* The work of revision has been carried out by Westminster Theological Seminary, Philadelphia, under the direction of J. Alan Groves, and Hebrew University, Jerusalem, under the direction of Emanuel Tov. In the course of their work they checked the Michigan-Claremont against other electronic texts such as that prepared by the Centre 'Informatique et Bible' in Maredsous, Belgium. The electronic texts were also compared with available photographs of B 19^A and the edition of B 19^A published by Aron Dotan. Differences found were carefully recorded and resulted in improvements introduced into the fourth edition of *BHS.* Due to the poor quality of the photographs of B 19^A available at the time, a number of uncertainties still remain. Now that the manuscript has been skillfully rephotographed in color by the Ancient Biblical Manuscript Center in Claremont, CA, numerous readings can be determined with a much higher degree of certainty and will eventually be incorporated into subsequent printings of *BHS.* Groves 1989 gives a full description of their checking process. Additional information on this and other data bases can be found in Eep Talstra 1989.

The electronic text of the Hebrew Bible tagged with grammatical information and combined with a search program called *QUEST* was produced as a joint effort by the Dutch Bible Society, the Vrije University (Amsterdam), Westminster Theological Seminary (Philadelphia), Kirchliche Hochschule Bethel (Bielefeld, Germany), and AND Software, Inc. (Rotterdam). The morphological encoding encompasses the entire Hebrew Bible, and several selected books also have phrase and clause markers to enable higher levels of grammatical searching. The morphologically tagged database can also be used with Lbase, by Silver Mountain Software, Dallas, and with AnyText, a Macintosh program from Linguists Software, Inc., Edmonds, WA.

The Computer Assisted Tools for Septuagint Studies (CATSS), University of Pennsylvania, has produced a computerized database for Septuagint studies. The database includes morphological tagging for the entire Septuagint and a parallel alignment of the Hebrew and Greek texts of some books, arranged in such a way as to facilitate comparison of textual base and translation technique. For these books the textual variants recorded in the Göttingen Septuagint or the Cambridge Septuagint are also included in the database. Emanuel Tov 1986 provides a general introduction to the features of the parallel alignment and guides the researcher in its proper use.

The text of the Latin Vulgate, Weber edition, is also available in electronic form, including textual variants recorded in that edition.

3. Dictionaries

The foundations of modern Hebrew lexicography go back to the work of Wilhelm Gesenius (1786-1842), culminating in his magnum opus, *Thesaurus philologicus criticus linguae hebraeae et chaldaeae Veteris Testamenti* (1829-58), completed by Ernst Roediger after Gesenius' death. A number of English translations of Gesenius' *Hebräisches und aramäisches Handwörterbuch* appeared in the nineteenth and early twentieth centuries. The most famous of these is by Francis Brown, Samuel Rolles Driver, and Charles A. Briggs, first published in 1907. Bearing tribute to its enduring value, it remains in print today. Though now outdated by great advances in linguistic study and the discovery of many ancient documents both in Hebrew and related Northwest Semitic languages, it was never revised, despite several concerted efforts to do so. Recently James Barr, who headed up the revision team, announced that plans to revise BDB were being abandoned. The revision committee felt that Hebrew lexicography had advanced too far in the twentieth century to make a revision practical. But the German edition of the Gesenius-Buhl *Hebräisches und aramäisches Handwörterbuch über das Alte Testament* (17th edition 1921) is being revised under the editorship of Rudolf Meyer and Herbert Donner. The first of a projected six fascicles appeared in 1987. It continues the arrangement of entries by root.

The *Lexicon in Veteris Testamenti Libros* of Ludwig Köhler and Walter Baumgartner, though valuable, has not fully replaced Brown-Driver-Briggs, although it considers in some detail linguistic evidence from cognate languages which has come to light in the past eighty years. The Hebrew section of the thoroughly revised third edition has now been published (1990), and the Aramaic section is forthcoming. The publisher has announced the publication of an English edition, beginning with a first fascicle in 1994. The earlier editions contained entries in both German and English.

The student still awaits a lexicon that takes advantage of recent work in lexicography. Accordingly the time is ripe for the appearance of entirely new lexicons. No less than six Hebrew lexicons are scheduled to appear shortly. Each is an independently produced work. Three of them are described in some detail by their editors.

David J. A. Clines 1989 claims that the most characteristic feature of *The Dictionary of Classical Hebrew* (DCH) is "its general orientation to the principles of modern linguistics" (p. 73). This project is sponsored by the (British) Society for Old Testament Study, with publication by the Sheffield Academic Press. Volume one of eight, containing entries for

aleph, appeared in 1993. DCH, like the other contemporary projects, includes the entire vocabulary of the Hebrew Bible as well as other texts and inscriptions in Classical Hebrew. DCB, correctly in my opinion, includes the Hebrew of the Dead Sea Scrolls and Ben Sira. These texts show a greater affinity to late Biblical Hebrew than the Hebrew of the Mishnah, which is excluded in DCH. This is not to say that Mishnaic Hebrew (MH) is without value in the study of Classical Hebrew lexicography, but the entire corpus need not be included in such a lexicon.

According to Clines, lexical analysis is both syntagmatic and paradigmatic. While earlier lexicons certainly cited contexts, especially when dealing with fixed phrases, DCH has made a special effort to deal with syntagmatic relations in a systematic way. DCH is certainly an improvement over earlier lexicons, but the entries are still organized in such way as to find a common etymological thread wherever possible. The entries are enhanced by using English glosses for all cited occurrences of a word, including collocations and syntagmatic relations. For those who are familiar with the use of the terms "meaning" and "gloss" in the Johannes P. Louw-Eugene A. Nida *Greek-English Lexicon of the New Testament,* "gloss" is used in a different sense in DCH, where glosses refer to head entries. DCH has made a serious effort to deal with paradigmatic relationships, but feels that a full analysis awaits a "complete description of the semantic fields in Hebrew." Clines reminds us that the Classical Hebrew corpus presents a special challenge because the vast majority of evidence comes from only one source, the Hebrew Bible. The new DCH, with its limited application of modern linguistic theory, is a promising replacement for BDB. One editorial judgment which is linguistically logical but will be disappointing to the Old Testament student is the decision not to include Biblical Aramaic.

Philippe Reymond 1989 provides a much briefer description of the work being done in preparation of *Le Dictionnaire d'Hebreu et d'Arameen bibliques* (DHAB) (1992–). This project appears to be more modest in scope, but will provide French readers with a very useful lexicon that has benefitted from recent lexicographic studies. Several sample entries are given in Reymond's article.

J. J. M. Roberts 1989 reports on the progress of the Princeton Classical Hebrew Dictionary Project sponsored by the Society of Biblical Literature. Choon-Leong Seow and Richard E. Whitaker join Roberts as associate editors. Although not described in this report, the Princeton Project represents the confluence of several different efforts to develop a new Hebrew lexicon. For example, this project will benefit from a great deal

of computer-based work which has been done on the morphology and lexicon of the Hebrew Bible. The corpus generally corresponds to that of DCH. The entries will follow the alphabetic arrangement of Köhler-Baumgartner, which was the first major lexicon to break from the Gesenius-BDB approach of organization by Hebrew roots. But the Princeton Project will guide the user to roots and cognates, with an essay "to facilitate the proper use of cognates . . ." (p. 89). From the sample entries given, the Princeton Project lexicon will probably stand somewhere between the new Gesenius 18th edition and the DCH. A useful feature of the Princeton Project is the inclusion of many references to relevant discussions in commentaries, as well as to grammars and other literature.

The first two fascicles of a Hebrew-Spanish lexicon under the directorship of Luis Alonso-Schökel appeared in 1990: the *Diccionario Bíblico Hebreo-Español*. Bible translators, especially in the Spanish-speaking world, are familiar with Alonso-Schökel's writings on Bible translation theory and Hebrew poetics. We can expect a departure from the lexicography model of BDB and other lexicons with their undue emphasis on etymology and a traditional approach to semantics. The first sample entries from the new Alonso-Schökel lexicon indicate that far more attention will be paid to semantic relationships, with a discussion of synonyms and antonyms as well.

4. Grammars

As in the case of lexicons, the standard grammars go back to the days of Gesenius. The standard edition today is still *Gesenius' Hebrew Grammar as edited and enlarged by the late E. Kautzsch, Second English edition revised by A. E. Cowley,* first published in 1910 and reprinted many times. The index of passages was revised and greatly enlarged in the 1980 printing. Perhaps the most important comprehensive grammar published in the twentieth century is by Paul Joüon 1923, which has been translated into English, with additions and revisions by Takemitsu Muraoka 1991. An important treatment of syntax, based on modern linguistic principles, may be found in *An Introduction to Biblical Hebrew Syntax,* by Bruce Waltke and Michael P. O'Connor 1990. Their chapter 3, "Basic Concepts," as well as the glossary and bibliography, forms a useful guide for orientation into the modern study of Hebrew grammar. Nahum M. Waldman 1989 has produced an even more extensive bibliography, dealing with all stages of the Hebrew language, and with extensive treatment of works written in Modern

Hebrew, entitled *The Recent Study of Hebrew: A Survey of the Literature with a Selected Bibliography*. The "selected" bibliography is 182 pages long, which suggests how extensive the literature is. Chapter 3, "The Masoretes," is particularly useful for the study of textual criticism.

5. Synopses

Primus Vannutelli, *Libri synoptici Veteris Testamenti seu librorum Regum et Chronicorum loci paralleli* (2 vols., 1931-34), contains parallels from the Hebrew text and the Vulgate on the lefthand page. The righthand page presents the corresponding parallels from the Septuagint, with a full critical apparatus. Parallels from Josephus, where available, are placed at the foot of the pages. For the Hebrew text alone the synopsis of Abba Ben-David 1972 highlights textual differences in red ink. In addition to the Samuel-Kings and Chronicles parallels, Ben-David presents a selection of other parallel passages such as Isa. 2:1-4, with parallels in Micah and Joel.

6. Inscriptions

The corpus of all known Hebrew inscriptions, datable on archaeological or palaeographic grounds down to 200 B.C., is presented in transliterated form, with a complete concordance, in *Ancient Hebrew Inscriptions*, by Graham I. Davies, *et al.* 1991. There are several published collections of Hebrew inscriptions, which include discussions of the content and features of the texts: J. C. L. Gibson 1971-1982, Herbert Donner and W. Röllig 1971-1976. A useful guide to further research is Robert W. Suder 1984. *Zeitschrift für Althebraistik* regularly includes a bibliographic survey of recent studies in Hebrew lexicography and inscriptions.

7. Special Literature

Bleddyn J. Roberts, *The Old Testament Text and Versions* (1951), provides a detailed discussion of matters treated only briefly in this volume. Naturally, Roberts was only able to incorporate evidence from the earliest Qumran finds. He uses the name first given to these scrolls, "The Jerusalem Scrolls." Over forty years later, the impact of the Qumran evidence is still being debated. But it is fair to say that the history of the Old Testament

text is being completely rewritten in light of the Dead Sea Scrolls. Emanuel Tov, now the editor-in-chief of the official Dead Sea Scroll Manuscript Project, published in 1989 *The Textual Criticism of the Bible: An Introduction* in Hebrew (English edition 1992). Ferdinand E. Deist, *Witnesses to the Old Testament: Introducing Old Testament Textual Criticism* (1988), also offers a useful introduction and emphasizes the relationship of textual transmission and text forms to canonical studies. The volume *Mikra,* edited by Martin Jan Mulder (1988), contains a number of valuable essays on the text of the Old Testament, including Mulder on the transmission of the biblical text, Tov on the Septuagint, Abraham Tal on the Samaritan Targum of the Pentateuch, Philip S. Alexander on Aramaic translations, Peter B. Dirksen on the Peshitta, and Benjamin Kedar-Kopfstein on the Latin translations.

Two collections of reprinted essays deserve mention: *The Canon and Masorah of the Hebrew Bible: An Introductory Reader,* compiled by Sid Z. Leiman (1974), and *Studies in the Septuagint: Origins, Recensions, and Interpretations,* edited by Sidney Jellicoe (1974). Each volume includes an introductory essay by the editor to bring the discussion up to date.

8. International Organizations

Several academic organizations are devoted to specialized studies in the field of Old Testament textual criticism. Many presentations made at their regular meetings are published, providing a significant source for information on current perspectives.

The *International Organization for Masoretic Studies (IOMS)* was founded in 1972 and meets annually either at the time of the annual meeting of the Society of Biblical Literature or at the triennial meeting of the International Organization for the Study of the Old Testament (IOSOT). Proceedings are frequently published in their Masoretic Studies series, beginning with 1972-1973 (Missoula, Montana: Scholars Press, 1974). Proceedings of the fifth congress were published in *Estudios Masoreticos* (Emilia Fernández Tejero 1983). The proceedings of the *VIII International Congress of the International Organization for Masoretic Studies* were edited by Ernest John Revell 1990.

The *International Organization for Septuagint and Cognate Studies (IOSCS)* follows the same schedule as IOMS for its annual meetings. IOSCS publishes an annual *Bulletin,* and the proceedings of their recent international congresses have also been published:

1980 *The Hebrew and Greek Texts of Samuel: 1980 Proceedings IOSCS — Vienna.* (Jerusalem: Academon, 1980).

1983 *La Septuaginta en la investigacion contemporanea (V Congreso de la IOSCS)* (Madrid: Instituto "Arias Montano," 1985).

1986 *VI Congress of the International Organization for Septuagint and Cognate Studies: Jerusalem 1986* (Atlanta: Scholars Press, 1987).

1989 *VII Congress of the International Organization for Septuagint and Cognate Studies: Leuven 1989* (Atlanta: Scholars Press, 1991).

Plates

1. AN INSCRIBED BOWL FROM LACHISH

Cf. p. 3. Illustration from O. Tufnell, *et al.* 1958.

The bowl found in 1935 is now ascribed by David Diringer (1962: 240) to the thirteenth century B.C.; earlier (1958a: 129) Diringer proposed the second quarter of the fourteenth century. The inscription is an example of proto-Canaanite writing, written with a brush dipped in white chalk. Seven of the eleven signs are well preserved. The inscription should be read from right to left.

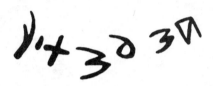

Most scholars identify the first five signs with the letters *b š l š t,* i.e., a form of the number "three" with the prepositional prefix *b*. Other readings have been proposed for the first letter; the inscription has also been considered to read from left to right (cf. Diringer's review of various suggestions, 1958a: 129).

The sixth sign is probably a division mark, and the seventh the beginning of another word now illegible.

2. THE STELE OF MESHA, KING OF MOAB (*ca.* **840 B.C.**)

Cf. p. 2. Illustration from F. G. Kenyon 1949.

In 1868 F. A. Klein, a missionary, discovered this victory inscription on black basalt in Dhiban (the ancient Dibon, capital of Mesha), north of the river Arnon (Wâdī el-Môjib) in Jordan. The stone was later broken up by Bedouin, but a paper squeeze made earlier enabled the text to be reassembled and restored. The monument is 1 m. high, 0.6 m. across, and is now at the Louvre in Paris.

Of the thirty-four lines in Phoenician-Old Hebrew script (cf. pp. 2, 229), twenty-seven are preserved entirely. They celebrate the victory of Moab over Israel after a period of Moabite submission (cf. 2 Kgs. 3:4-27) and record Mesha's program of building cities.

"This stele of Mesha' king of Moab is of great importance as the sole historical monument of the Moabite kingdom and a record of historical relations between Moab and Israel which are glossed over or omitted from the Old Testament. It further reveals Moabite as a Semitic dialect almost identical with Hebrew and proves the advanced stage of writing in a petty kingdom lying off the main historical routes in the 9th century B.C." (G. R. Driver 1954: 109).

The script is remarkably developed, with a tendency toward cursive and simplified forms. It is noteworthy that both words and sentences are divided, the words by dots and the sentences by strokes.

Text with translation and commentary: H. Donner and W. Röllig 1971-76 no. 181; J. C. L. Gibson 1971: 71-84.

Translation: H. Gressmann 1926-27: 440-42; W. F. Albright 1969: 320f.; E. Ullendorf 1961: 195-99; K. Galling 1968: 51-53.

3. THE SILOAM INSCRIPTION FROM JERUSALEM (*ca.* 700 B.C.)

Cf. p. 2. Illustration from David Diringer 1968.

In 1880 an inscription in Old Hebrew letters was found on the rock facing at the opening of a rock tunnel leading from the Gihon spring (now Mary's Well) to the Pool of Siloam (cf. p. 2). It records the successful completion of the tunnel. The original was later removed and is now at the Museum of the Ancient Orient in Istanbul.

Although the account gives neither names nor date, it most probably refers to the cutting of a tunnel by Hezekiah (725-697 B.C.; cf. 2 Kgs. 20:20; 2 Chr. 32:30), which suggests a date around 700 B.C. This is confirmed by palaeographical evidence. "The writing may fairly be assigned to the same general stage of development as that represented by the Moabite Stone but is lighter and more flowing, while some of the letters have considerably altered their shape" (G. R. Driver 1954: 119).

The text of six lines is 38 cm. high and 72 cm. wide. An area of about 70 cm. square was prepared and the inscription occupies the lower half. Was the upper half intended for a pictorial representation (Hugo Gressmann), or has the first half of the inscription been lost (William F. Albright)?

Text with translation and commentary: H. Donner and W. Röllig 1971-76 no. 189; J. C. L. Gibson 1971: 71-84.

Translations: H. Gressmann 1926-27: 445; W. F. Albright 1969: 321 (with bibliography); N. H. Snaith 1961: 209-211; K. Galling 1968: 59.

4. LACHISH LETTER NO. 4

Cf. p. 2. Illustration from H. Torczyner, *et al.* 1938.

During the excavation of a room under the city gate-tower of Tell ed-Duweir, the site of the biblical Lachish, eighteen ostraca inscribed in the Old Hebrew script were found in 1935, and another three in 1938 (cf. p. 5). They were found in a burned stratum, apparently from the destruction of the city by the Babylonians when the kingdom of Judah was defeated in 588-587 B.C.; thus they represent the last days of the southern kingdom. Their contents comprise mostly a military correspondence revealing the distressed state of Judah during the Babylonian invasion.

"As in other countries where potsherds were used for messages, the writer begins his letter on the outside of the sherd and continues only when necessary on the less smooth inner surface. The scribes of the Lachish Letters used a reed pen, and wrote in an iron-carbide ink, as the chemical analysis has shown" (Torczyner, *et al.* 1938: 204).

The hand is a beautiful cursive, the product of a literary tradition centuries old. The use of word dividers is irregular: for the writing of יהוה in 3.9, cf. p. 109. The language is Biblical Hebrew, especially reminiscent of Jeremiah and Deuteronomy. It confirms the fact that the language of the biblical books preserved in 𝔐 is predominantly that of preexilic Judah. The ostraca are of great philological, palaeographical, and historical value as the only known group of documents in classical Hebrew. They are now in Jerusalem and London.

Transliteration in square character (selections): K. Galling 1950: 63-65.

Translations: J. Hempel 1938: 126-139; W. F. Albright 1969: 321f.; D. W. Thomas 1961: 216f.

Complete edition: H. Torczyner, *et al.* 1940.

140

5. THE ELEPHANTINE PAPYRUS

Cf. p. 1. Illustration from E. Sachau 1911, pl. 1. Contents: Letter to Bagoas, lines 1-17.

Numerous papyri in the Aramaic language and script were among the documents discovered by the Berlin Papyrus Commission during excavations undertaken in 1907 and 1908 on the island of Elephantine in the Nile opposite Aswan. These papyri date from the fifth century B.C. and include letters, legal documents, parts of the Story of Ahikar, fragments of the Darius inscription of Behistun in an Aramaic translation, and other items. From these we have learned about the existence of a "Jewish military colony" in Elephantine[1] with a temple in which Yahu (Yahweh) was worshipped together with a goddess Anathbethel and another god (אשמביתאל, pronunciation unknown; cf. M. Noth 1963: 266f.).

These papyri attest how widely the Aramaic language and script were used in the Persian Empire (cf. p. 2). After the Phoenician-Old Hebrew script, the Aramaic script represents a second branch of the North Semitic alphabet from which developed not only the square script, but the Nabatean, Palmyrene, and Syrian (Estrangela) scripts as well. Its earliest examples are ninth-century B.C. inscriptions from the area of Aleppo. "The Aramaic script gradually assumed a distinctive character which is marked by the following main tendencies: (1) The opening of the tops and sides of a few letters (the *beth,* the *daleth* and *resh,* and *'ayin*) is a prominent feature. (2) The endeavour to reduce the number of separate strokes, in the *kheth* and *teth,* for instance, is also noticeable. (3) Angles become rounded and ligatures develop. These tendencies were completed during the Persian period. By the fifth century B.C. the transformation is complete, as we can gather . . . especially from the cursive Aramaic writing on papyrus used in Egypt between 500 and 200 B.C." (D. Diringer 1968: 1:200).

Cf. A. E. Cowley 1919, 1923; H. H. Rowley 1961: 260-65. Also E. G. Kraeling 1953.

---

1. On the military colony of Elephantine cf. E. G. Kraeling 1958: 415-18 (with bibliography); B. Porten 1968.

6. THE NASH PAPYRUS

Cf. p. 34. Illustration enlarged from the infrared photograph in W. F. Albright 1949a. The words in parentheses are supplemented from Exod. 20 and Deut. 5.

(אנכי י)הוה אלהיך אשר (הוצא)תיך מארץ מ(צרים)

(לוא יהיה ל)ך אלהים אחרים (על־פנ)י לוא תעשה (לך פסל)

(וכל תמונה) אשר בשמים ממעל ואשר בארץ (מתחת)

(ואשר במים) מתחת לארץ לוא תשתחוה להם (ולוא)

(תעבדם כי) אנכי יהוה אלהיך אל קנוא פק(ד עון אבות)   5

(על בני)ם על שלשים ועל רבעים לשנאי (ועשה חסד)

(לאלפים) לאהבי ולשמרי מצותי לוא ת(שא את שם)

(יהוה א)להיך לשוא כי לוא ינקה יהוה (את אשר)

(ישא את ש)מה לשוא זכור את יום השבת ל(קדשו)

(ששת ימים) תעבוד ועשית כל מלאבתך וביום (השביעי)   10

(שבת ליהוה) אלהיך לוא תעשה בה כל מלאב(ה אתה)

(ובנך ובתך) עבדך ואמתך שורך וחמרך וכל ב(המתך)

(וגרך אשר) בשעריך כי ששת י(מי)ם עשה י(הוה)

(את השמי)ם ואת הארץ את הים ואת כל א(שר בם)

(וינח ביום) השביעי עלכן ברך יהוה את (יום)   15

השביעי ויקד־שיו כבד את אביך ואת אמ(ך למען)

ייטב לך ולמען יאריכון ימיך על האדמה (אשר)

יהוה אלהיך נתן לך לוא תנאף לוא תרצח לו(א)

(תג)נב לוא תענה ברעך עד שוא לוא תחמוד (את)

(אשת רעך לו)א תתאוה את ב(י)ת רעך שד(הו ועבדו)   20

(ואמתו וש)ורו וחמרו וכל אשר לרעך

(ואלה החק)ים והמשפטים אשר צוה משה את (בני)

(ישראל) במדבר בצאתם מארץ מצרים שמ(ע)

(ישרא)ל יהוה אלהינו יהוה אחד הוא וא(הבת)

144

7. THE ENTRANCE TO QUMRAN CAVE 1

Cf. p. 11. Illustration from E. L. Sukenik 1954.

In the spring of 1947 in Jerusalem the now famous manuscripts found in a cave near the Dead Sea first came to light. The war in Palestine prevented searching for the cave itself until the beginning of 1949, when it was examined under the direction of G. Lankester Harding and Roland de Vaux, but no further texts of any considerable extent were discovered. The cave is in a particularly dry area of Palestine, 12 km. south of Jericho, 1 km. north of Khirbet Qumran, 150 m. up a precipice difficult to scale. It was discovered accidentally by a herder searching for a lost goat. Later investigation revealed about thirty caves in the area which showed traces of use in antiquity. In ten of them further manuscripts were found hidden, some of which were of considerable length (Caves 2-11).

All of these caves are very closely associated with the ancient settlement of Khirbet Qumran. From the excavations carried out from 1951 to 1956 we learn that Qumran was founded under John Hyrcanus (135-104 B.C.) or Alexander Jannaeus (103-76 B.C.).[1] It was "the administrative center, the place of assembly, and the burial ground of a community that lived scattered about the area" (Roland de Vaux), until it was destroyed by Roman troops in A.D. 68 during the First Jewish War (A.D. 66-70). Most probably the scrolls found since 1947 were hidden in the caves because of these military events. Later, Qumran appears to have served as a Roman military post, and finally as a stronghold for the Jewish rebels of the Second Jewish War.[2]

The evidence of the excavations and many details in the writings discovered argue for the identification of Qumran with the site in the Judean desert "above En-gedi" described by Pliny the Elder as the center of a community of pious Jews who lived in solitude as celibates — the Essenes.[3]

---

1. A first settlement in the later Jewish monarchy (eighth to seventh/sixth century B.C.), apparently to be identified with 'Ir-hammelach (City of Salt, Josh. 15:62), ended in complete destruction.

2. On the excavations of Khirbet Qumran, cf. R. de Vaux 1973.

3. Objections to this identification have been raised by K. H. Rengstorf 1960, who prefers to identify the library with a library of the Jerusalem temple.

8. TWO JARS FROM CAVE 1

Cf. p. 7. Illustration from E. L. Sukenik 1950.

The undamaged jars illustrated here were taken by the Bedouin when they first discovered the cave, and later bought by Professor Eleazar L. Sukenik of Jerusalem. Their height (without lids) is 65.7 cm. and 47.5 cm., and their width is 25 cm. and 26.5 cm., respectively. They were designed to protect the scrolls from damage.

Fragments of about fifty more jars of the same or similar pattern were found in an archaeological examination of the cave. If each contained three or more scrolls, Cave 1 could once have accommodated a library of 150 to 200 scrolls. But "the only solid evidence for the possible quantity is the number of different books which can be identified, and these amount to about seventy-five. How or when so many of these documents were removed or damaged is a question which is at present unanswerable."[1] As for the possible removal of manuscripts centuries ago, we may remember a letter from the Nestorian Patriarch Timothy I of Seleucia (727-823), which tells of an Arab hunter who was led by his dog to a cave where he found a large number of books. "The hunter went to Jerusalem and reported it to the Jews. They came in crowds and found the books of the Old (Testament) and others in Hebrew script."[2] But nothing definite can be asserted about this.

Jars of the same or similar patterns have also been found in nearby caves and in Khirbet Qumran itself. These are very important for establishing dates. "All this pottery belongs to the Hellenistic and Roman period, and there is nothing from later periods. When we reflect that the manuscripts are numerous and the pottery plentiful, that the manuscripts constitute a homogeneous group, and that the pottery belongs to a single period, it is difficult to resist the conclusion that the manuscripts were deposited or abandoned in the caves at the same time as the pottery."[3]

1. Barthélemy and Milik 1955: 3.
2. The letter was reported by O. Eissfeldt 1949a: 597f.
3. R. de Vaux 1973: 102.

9a. A SAMUEL FRAGMENT FROM CAVE 4 (4QSam[b])

Illustrations 9a and 9b from J. T. Milik 1959. Text: 1 Sam. 23:9-13.

The fragments of 4QSam[b] are among the oldest biblical texts from Qumran, and are ascribed by Frank M. Cross (1955: 147-172) to the period about 200 B.C. or somewhat earlier.

9b. A FRAGMENT OF THE SONG OF MOSES (4QDtn 32)

The fragments of the Song of Moses written in stichs, of which Patrick W. Skehan 1954 published Deut. 32:8, 37-43, are of particular importance for preserving (with 𝕲) a text more original than 𝔐, which reads a shortened and "demythologized" version.[1] V. 43 is illustrated here:

4Q	𝔐
הרנינו שמים עמו	הרנינו גוים עמו
והשתחוו לו כל אלהים	
כי דם בניו יקום	כי דם־עבדיו יקום
ונקם ישיב לצריו	ונקם ישיב לצריו
ולמשנאיו ישלם	
ויכפר אדמת עמו	וכפר אדמתו עמו

Rejoice, you heavens, with him;	Praise, O nations, his people;
And bow before him, all you gods.	
For he avenges the blood of his sons	For he avenges the blood of his servants
And takes vengeance upon his adversaries.	And takes vengeance upon his adversaries.
He repays those who hate him	
And atones for the land of his people.	And atones for his land, his people.

1. According to R. Meyer 1961, who has reviewed the fragment at length.

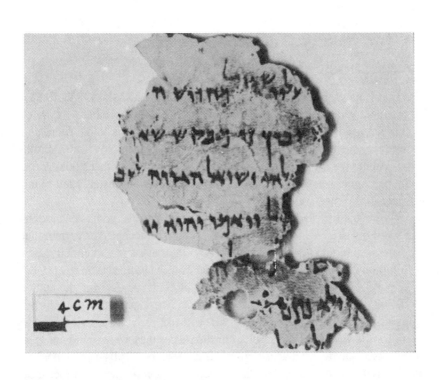

10. THE FIRST ISAIAH SCROLL (1QIs^a = $\mathbb{Q}^a$)

Cf. pp. 7, 33. Illustration from E. L. Sukenik 1950.

The first Isaiah scroll is shown opened to col. 32 and 33 (Isa. 38:8–40:28). It can clearly be seen that the scroll is composed of separate sheets of leather. Its use is also clear: the beginning of the scroll is to the right, and the end is to the left. For convenience in using and preserving Torah scrolls a rod (roller) was attached at each end to roll it on; for other books a rod at the beginning was adequate. At the end one sheet was usually left blank to serve as a protective covering for the scroll.

Now that the place where the scrolls were discovered has been identified and investigated (cf. pp. 146, 148), it may be accepted as certain that they are ancient and genuine. Doubts about their age and authenticity such as Solomon Zeitlin raised repeatedly in the *Jewish Quarterly Review* (1949-50) can be regarded as settled on the basis of evidence. Even in the matter of dating there has been definite progress. The destruction of Khirbet Qumran, which occurred in A.D. 68 (cf. p. 146), provides a terminus ante quem for the writing of the scrolls, for the places they were found are very closely associated with that settlement. But when the scrolls were deposited in the cave they could already have been considerably aged; in fact they show unmistakable signs of long and heavy use (cf. the back of the scroll in the illustration). Now it is significant that the wealth of documents from the caves in the Judean desert has given a fresh impetus to the study of Hebrew palaeography. The researches of William F. Albright, Eleazar L. Sukenik, John C. Trever, Solomon A. Birnbaum, Frank M. Cross, and others have made it possible to trace the development of the script from the third century B.C. to the second century A.D.,[1] and to determine the place of individual documents in this sequence. This does not mean, of course, that a specific year can be assigned to each document. The first Isaiah scroll is in the script of the earliest scrolls from Cave 1, and can be dated in the second century B.C.; it lacks final forms for kaph, pe, and tsade.

---

1. Cf. the progress report on the research by N. Avigad 1958: 56ff., and especially F. M. Cross 1961a.

11. THE FIRST ISAIAH SCROLL (1QIsᵃ = 𝕼ᵃ)

Cf. p. 33. Illustration (Isa. 40:6-20; slightly enlarged) from the edition by M. Burrows 1950, cf. p. 32.

The illustration shows that the original text of the Isaiah scroll in vv. 7f. lacked the words

כי רוח יהוה נשבה בו אכן חציר העם יבש חציר נבל ציץ

which are present in 𝔐. A later hand has added them in an awkward script between the lines and down the left margin. It is obvious that the omission could have been caused by homoioteleuton. The scribe's eye skipped from נבל ציץ in v. 7 to the identical words in v. 8. But it is striking that the same omission is found in 𝕲, and that the words are marked with an asterisk by Origen (cf. p. 58). It is conceivable that the agreement between the original text of the Isaiah scroll and 𝕲 is sheer coincidence: the omission in both instances could have been due to homoioteleuton. But it is also possible that the text of 𝔐 is the result of a later expansion which was lacking in the exemplar of 𝕲 and the Isaiah scroll. The phrase

אכן חציר העם

has frequently aroused suspicions.

In the added phrase the name of God is represented by four dots. Did the scribe stand in such awe of the divine name that he dared not write it? It is more probable that the space was reserved in this way for the addition of the name later — in a different script. In other texts the name Yahweh is frequently written in Old Hebrew script (cf. pp. 4, 158).

In v. 7 (𝔐 v. 8) the word ודבר has a dot under each letter, probably to indicate that this word would be deleted.

In 40:14-16 (from the second וילמדהו to the end of the verse) the hand is different from that of the surrounding text. But there is no suggestion that an original omission in the manuscript is being supplied. "Either another scribe has spelled his colleague for a brief moment, or the scribe has simply sharpened his pen or changed to different pen" (M. Burrows 1949: 32).

Two of the many variants in the excerpt are of special importance: in 40:6 ואומרה (𝔐 ואמר) confirms the commonly proposed emendation wa'omar (𝕲), and in 40:17 וכאפס (𝔐 מאפס) supports the conjecture כאפס (cf. BHK second apparatus and BHS apparatus).

154

12. THE SECOND ISAIAH SCROLL (1QIs^b = 𝒬^b)

Cf. p. 33. Illustration from E. L. Sukenik 1950.

The second Isaiah scroll, as the illustration shows (col. 1, Isa. 48:17–49:7; col. 2, Isa. 50:7–51:8), is in poor condition. The leather has disintegrated in part, with lacunae in each column. Opening the scroll was particularly difficult because in many places the leather had become glued together. The surviving portions are from 2 Isaiah, with only fragments remaining from 1 Isaiah.

The script is relatively small, but it is neat and clear. In comparison with the first Isaiah scroll the agreement of the second Isaiah scroll with 𝔐 is striking. To an extent the vowel letters are used even more sparingly than in 𝔐: שלמך 𝔐) שלומך (48:18; צר (צור) 48:21; כלתי (כליתי) 49:4. But it also uses vowel letters where they are lacking in 𝔐: יצרי יוצרי) 49:5; גואל (גאל) and קדוש קדש (49:7.

Variants from 𝔐: 48:17 מדרכיך (מדריכך); 49:4 אך (אכן); 49:6 הנקל (נקל) and ארץ (הארץ); 49:7 with the first Isaiah scroll אדני יהוה (אדני); 50:11 ומאזרי (מאזרי). (וקמו) יקומו. The second Isaiah scroll exhibits significantly fewer variants from 𝔐 than the first, and these do not go beyond the range of variants observed in medieval manuscripts. This fact led Paul E. Kahle to infer that 1QIs^b had been assimilated to the standard consonantal text, and therefore could not have been written before this standard text was available.[1] But since the scroll cannot be dated later than the 60s of the first century A.D. on archaeological grounds, and on the basis of palaeographical evidence it should apparently be assigned several decades earlier and could itself very well transmit the text of an even earlier exemplar, it has been taken by some as evidence for the existence of the type of text we identify as Masoretic long before the Masoretic period.[2] Although the text of this scroll presents very few problems in itself, it poses for us the basic and still unsolved problem of the age of the Masoretic text.

1. Kahle 1951: 81.
2. Cf. especially B. J. Roberts 1959/60: 144, who refers to the "likely existence of a pre-Massoretic 'Massoretic' text"; cf. also p. 14.

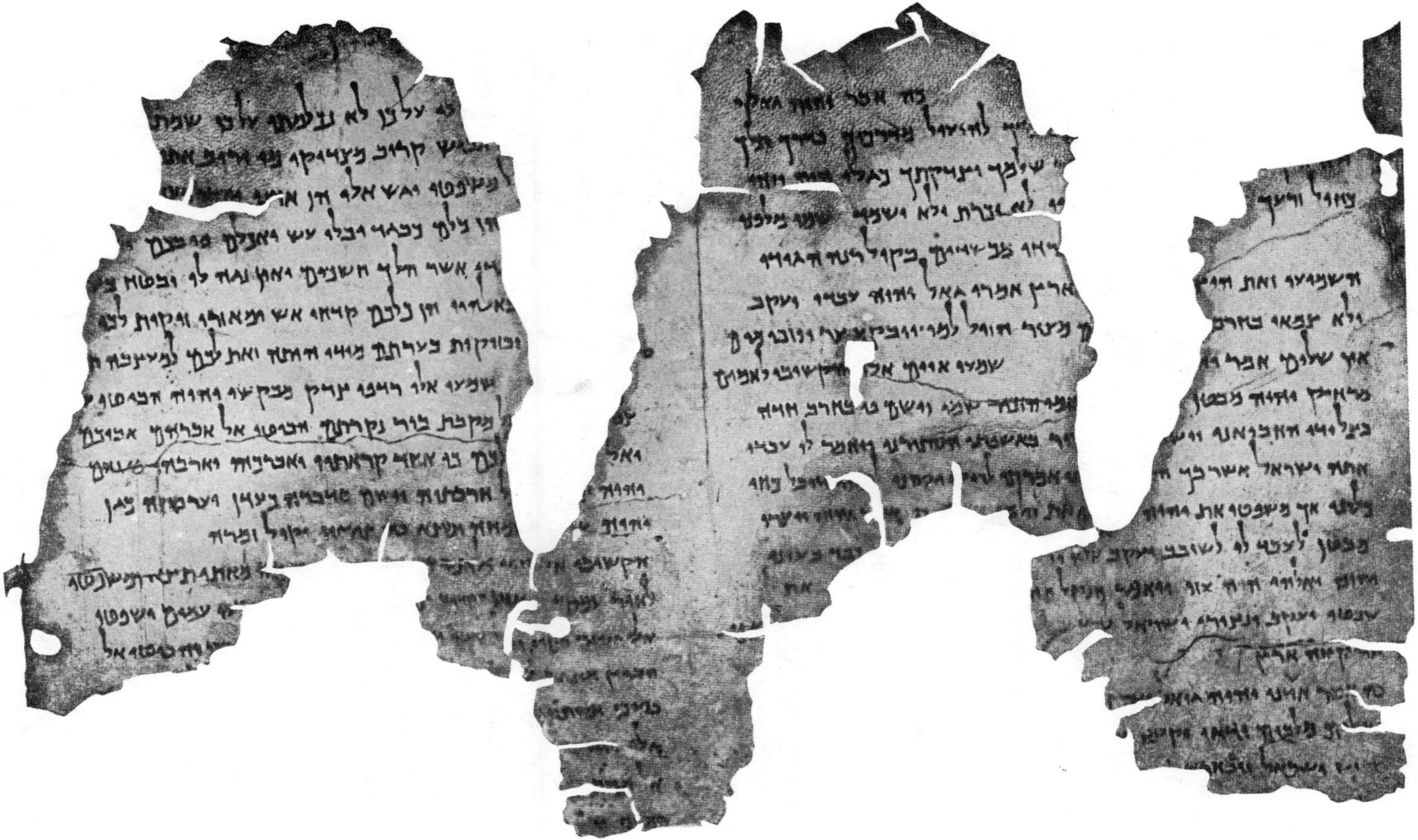

13. THE HABAKKUK COMMENTARY

Cf. p. 33. Illustration (col. 9 and 10, Hab. 2:7-14) from M. Burrows, 1950, pl. lix.

This scroll is of special religious and historical significance because, like the Manual of Discipline and other Qumran texts, it is a new source of information about a religious movement in pre-Christian Judaism. It is important for the history and criticism of the Old Testament text because the prophetic words of Hab. 1 and 2 are cited and commented upon sentence by sentence. The text cited in the scroll differs from that of 𝕸 in a way reminiscent of the first Isaiah scroll. Some sixty examples of its deviations from 𝕸 which are more than purely orthographical (e.g., scriptio plena) are cited in the third apparatus of BHK. In some instances the lemma and the comment on it exhibit discrepancies in their citation of the text of Habakkuk (cf. 1:8, 11; 2:16).

It is particularly noteworthy that the divine name Yahweh is written in Old Hebrew script (cf. col. 10, lines 7 and 14). In other scrolls the words אל and אלי are treated similarly. This peculiar writing of the divine name is referred to by Origen and also a Jewish tradition. And again, among the fragments found in the Cairo Geniza are some examples of the Aquila version in which the divine name written in Old Hebrew script occurs in the Greek text. This would imply that such a practice was once very common. In the text of the commentary itself the tetragrammaton is avoided and אל is used in its place. In the period of these manuscripts it is evident that 'adonai was read for the tetragrammaton because the first Isaiah scroll, for example, reads אדני where 𝕸 has יהוה (3:17), and conversely (6:11; 7:14; 9:7; 21:16; 28:2). Whether written in Old Hebrew or in the square script, יהוה served merely as an ideogram for אדני.[1]

The illustration shows clearly the horizontal lines from which the letters are suspended, and the vertical lines which mark off the columns of the text. Scholars of the third century A.D. regarded these lines as essential components of the book format. They traced the lining of texts back to Adam, regarding the practice as of extreme antiquity.[2]

1. Cf. Eissfeldt 1949: 225; also Kahle 1951: 63ff.
2. L. Blau 1902: 142ff.

14. FRAGMENTS OF LEVITICUS IN OLD HEBREW SCRIPT

Cf. p. 3. Illustration with transcription from E. L. Sukenik 1950.

The texts illustrated contain parts of Lev. 19:31-34; 20:20-23; 21:24–22:3; 22:4, 5. They were brought to light during the investigation of Cave 1 directed by Roland de Vaux and G. Lankester Harding in February 1949. These fragments are the earliest examples of the Old Hebrew script written on leather. A dot is also used here as a word divider. One variant from מ is found in 20:21: היא replaces the Masoretic הוא with Qere perpetuum.

The conjecture that the fragment is of Samaritan origin derives its probability from the known Samaritan practice of using the Old Hebrew script for the Torah. But Paul E. Kahle has pointed out that the fragment follows the Jewish text where the Jewish and Samaritan traditions differ in Lev. 20:22. Dating the fragment posed great difficulties at first because comparable material was lacking; suggestions ranged from the fifth to the first century B.C. The use of the Old Hebrew script has in itself little bearing on the age of the document because there were still scrolls written in this script in the first Christian centuries (cf. p. 3). Qumran experts are agreed today that the texts in the Old Hebrew script come from the same period as the texts in the square script. It is possible that this script which was preserved from the preexilic period enjoyed a renaissance in the Maccabean period with its surge of nationalism (cf. F. M. Cross 1961: 34). Just as the Samaritan text found its parallels in Qumran, so did the script which the Samaritans preserved and used.

אלהיכם . מפנ[י]ן

מאלהיך . אני . יהו[ה]

את[ו] כאזרח . מכם

ישאו

[א]חיו . נדה . היא . [ער]ות

[ושמרת]ם . את . כל . חקתי . ואת . כל

אתכם . הארץ . אשר . אני .

תלכו

אל[ה]

ישראל

. בניו .

. אשר .

[לדרתיכ]ם . כל . איש . אשר .

[א]שר . י[קדישו] . בני .

[מלפ]ני . [א]נ[י]

נפ[ש]

בכל . ש[ר]ץ[

15a. A FRAGMENT WITH PARTS OF DEUT. 29:14-18 AND 30:20–31:5

Illustration from G. L. Harding 1949, pl. 20.

The fragment was acquired from "outside sources" (Harding 1949), and has been published as fragment 13 of 1QDeut[b] (= 1Q5). Its text of Deut. 31:1 is sensational! The verse reads:

𝔐	וילך משה וידבר את[1] הדברים
Fragment	ויכל משה לדבר את כל
𝔊	καὶ συνετέλεσεν Μωυσῆς λαλῶν πάντας τοὺς λόγους τούτους.

𝔊 and the fragment are in agreement against 𝔐. "Thus for the first time in the history of the Bible we are confronted with a Hebrew scroll of Deuteronomy which actually supports the Septuagint text of an entire verse."[2] This confirms the conjecture that in this passage 𝔊 is based on a Hebrew exemplar that differed from 𝔐. Alfred Bertholet, Karl Marti, and Carl Steuernagel had already emended 𝔐 on the basis of 𝔊, while Eduard König defended the originality of 𝔐 (cf. the commentaries). The variants arose because of a transposition of the letters in the first word. The defense of the reading in 𝔐 rests on its being the lectio difficilior, but against it is the fact that its idiom is strained. The latter argument weighs so heavily that in my opinion the reading of 𝔐 must be rejected.

15b. PART OF AN UNOPENED SCROLL

From the 1949 excavations. Illustration from G. L. Harding 1949, pl. 21.

1. Twenty-eight Hebrew manuscripts add כל.
2. J. Leveen 1949: 323.

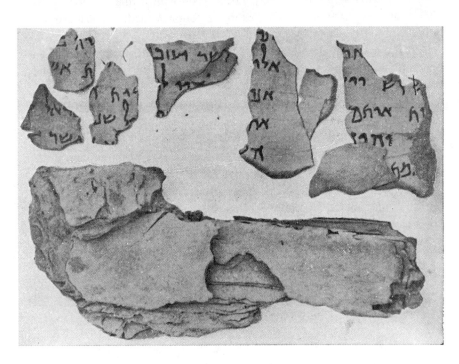

16. THE MINOR PROPHETS SCROLL (Murabba'at 88)

Illustration (Amos 8:11–9:15) from P. Benoit, J. T. Milik, R. de Vaux 1961.

In the fall of 1951 four caves were discovered by Bedouin in the deep recesses of Wadi Murabba'at in the Judean desert, 17 km. to the south of Qumran and quite unrelated to it. In the spring of 1952 they were investigated carefully by G. Lankester Harding and Roland de Vaux. It was evident from the objects discovered that the caves had been inhabited repeatedly from 4000 B.C. to the Arabian period. A papyrus palimpsest in the Old Hebrew script, the oldest manuscript from Palestine, is from the eighth-century B.C. settlement (cf. p. 6). A great number of documents including two letters from Simon ben Kosiba (Bar Kochba) attest that these caves served during the Second Jewish revolt (A.D. 132-135) as a refuge for a group of Jewish insurgents.

The Minor Prophets scroll (col. 8 is shown here) was found by Bedouin in 1955 in a fifth cave which was used as a grave. It dates from the second century A.D. The scribal hand is more developed and exhibits a greater consistency in the Murabba'at texts than in the Qumran texts. There are even striking similarities to the script of medieval manuscripts (J. T. Milik 1959: 71).

The text is in almost complete agreement with 𝔐, suggesting that an authoritative standard text already existed in the first half of the second century A.D. (cf. pp. 13f.).

Note in the illustration: Amos 8:11 (line 1) the three words והשלחתי רעב בארץ have been added above the line; 9:5 has ואבל כל יושב instead of the plural in 𝔐; 9:8 (line 22) a י has been added to השמיד.

To mark the end of the book of Amos a space of three lines at the end of the column and of two lines at the beginning of the next column has been left blank. Single blank lines indicate the end of a paragraph (lines 6, 18, 22); cf. the use of ס after 8:14 and פ after 9:12 in BH. The beginning of a new paragraph after 9:6 is not observed in 𝔐.

17. A PAGE WITH BABYLONIAN POINTING

Cf. p. 22. Illustration (Job 37:17–38:15; Berlin Ms. or. qu. 680 = Ec 1) from P. E. Kahle 1913.

The ninety-four parchment folios now in Berlin are the remains of a once complete manuscript of the Writings; seven more folios are in the Glaser collection in New York. Originally the pointing was purely Babylonian. This was later revised by a Yemenite hand. "In the reproduction the original pointing is often very difficult to read, while the revised pointing stands out clearly" (Kahle). The Masora parva has been written for the most part in the text and over the word it refers to. The Masora magna is in the lower margin; it cannot be seen in the illustration because it has been destroyed by mildew. For a detailed discussion see P. E. Kahle 1902, and also 1913: 140.

18. A HAPHTARAH FRAGMENT WITH BABYLONIAN POINTING

Cf. p. 22. Illustration (Isa. 62:8f., and Hos. 14:2f., with Targum; Cambridge B 15^1 = Kb 7,1) from P. E. Kahle 1913.

Selections from the Prophets were read in the Jewish worship service immediately after the Law. Such a selection was called a Haphtarah (plural Haphtaroth). The name (from Hebrew הפטיר "to conclude") is evidently to be explained from the fact that the reading from the Prophets concluded the reading of the Scriptures (Ismar Elbogen 1962: 174-184). From an early time the Haphtaroth were collected in special scrolls or books.

The page illustrated contains verses from the Haphtarah for the Sabbath before the New Year celebration and from the Haphtarah for the Sabbath after the New Year. According to Kahle it derives from a sumptuous manuscript like the Petersburg Codex of the Prophets, and is an example of the most developed form of the eastern system of pointing.

As was customary, each Hebrew verse is followed by its Targum. In the margin Isa. 63:7-16 has been written by a later hand, also with each verse followed by its Targum.

אשר בצריך וחלים · בהשקט אלץ מורם
הדלקוע עלמו לשחקים · חזקים שמאו מוצקין
הודיעני מה נגאמר לו · לא נערך מפני חשך
היספר לו כי אדבר · אם אמר איש כי יבלע
ועתה לא ראו אור בהיר הוא בשחקים · ורוח עברה ותטהרם
מצפון זהב יאתה · על אלוה נורא הוד
שדי לא מצאנהו · שגיא כח
ומשפט ורב צדקה · לא יענה
לכן יראוהו אנשים · לא יראה כל חכמי לב

ויען יהוה את איוב מן הסערה ויאמר ׃

מי זה מחשיך עצה במלין · בלי דעת
אזר נא כגבר חלציך · ואשאלך והודיעני
איפה היית ביסדי ארץ · הגד אם ידעת בינה
מי שם ממדיה כי תדע · או מי נטה עליה קו
על מה אדניה הטבעו · או מי ירה אבן פנתה
ברן יחד כוכבי בקר · ויריעו כל בני אלהים
ויסך בדלתים ים · בגיחו מרחם יצא
בשומי ענן לבשו · וערפל חתלתו
ואשבר עליו חקי · ואשים בריח ודלתים
ואמר עד פה תבוא ולא תסיף · ופא ישית בגאון גליך
המימיך צוית בקר · ידעת השחר מקמו
לאחז בכנפות הארץ · וינערו רשעים ממנה
תתהפך כחמר חותם · ויתיצבו כמו לבוש

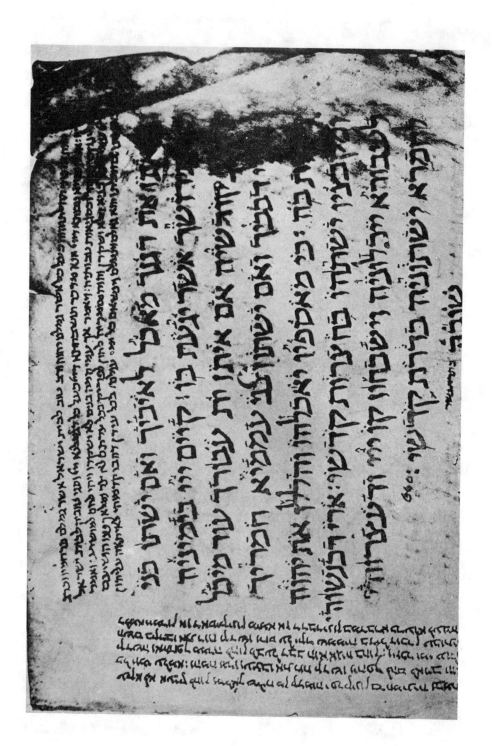

שובה ישראל עד יהוה אלהיך כי כשלת בעונך
תוב ישראל לדחלתא דייי אלהך ארי
איתקילתא בחובך: קחו עמכם דברים
ושובו אל יהוה אמרו אליו כל תשא עון וקח
טוב ונשלמה פרים שפתינו: קריבו
עמכון פיתגמין [illegible]

19. A FRAGMENT WITH PALESTINIAN POINTING

Cf. p. 23. Illustration (Isa. 7:11–9:8) from P. Kahle 1927-30, II.

The rediscovery of the Palestinian system of pointing at the end of the last century was due to this fragment (Oxford Ms. Heb e 30, fol. 48b) and a few other folios which together comprise the remains of a manuscript of the Prophets (cf. P. E. Kahle 1901).

This manuscript is also remarkable for presenting the Hebrew text in an *abbreviated* form. Only the first word of each verse is written in full, and each of the following words is represented by a single (not always the first) letter together with vowel point and accent. These abbreviated forms are already referred to in the Talmud by the term סירוגין. They were probably designed as memory aids for synagogue lectors and school students.

Whereas words are abbreviated consistently in this text, biblical manuscripts had long made occasional use of abbreviations for certain words that occur frequently. When these abbreviations were not recognized in copying, they would naturally lead to textual corruption. Felix Perles in particular has sought to prove that abbreviations were the cause of corruption in numerous passages in the pre-Masoretic text of the Bible.[1]

1. Perles 1895; cf. now also G. R. Driver 1960, 1964.

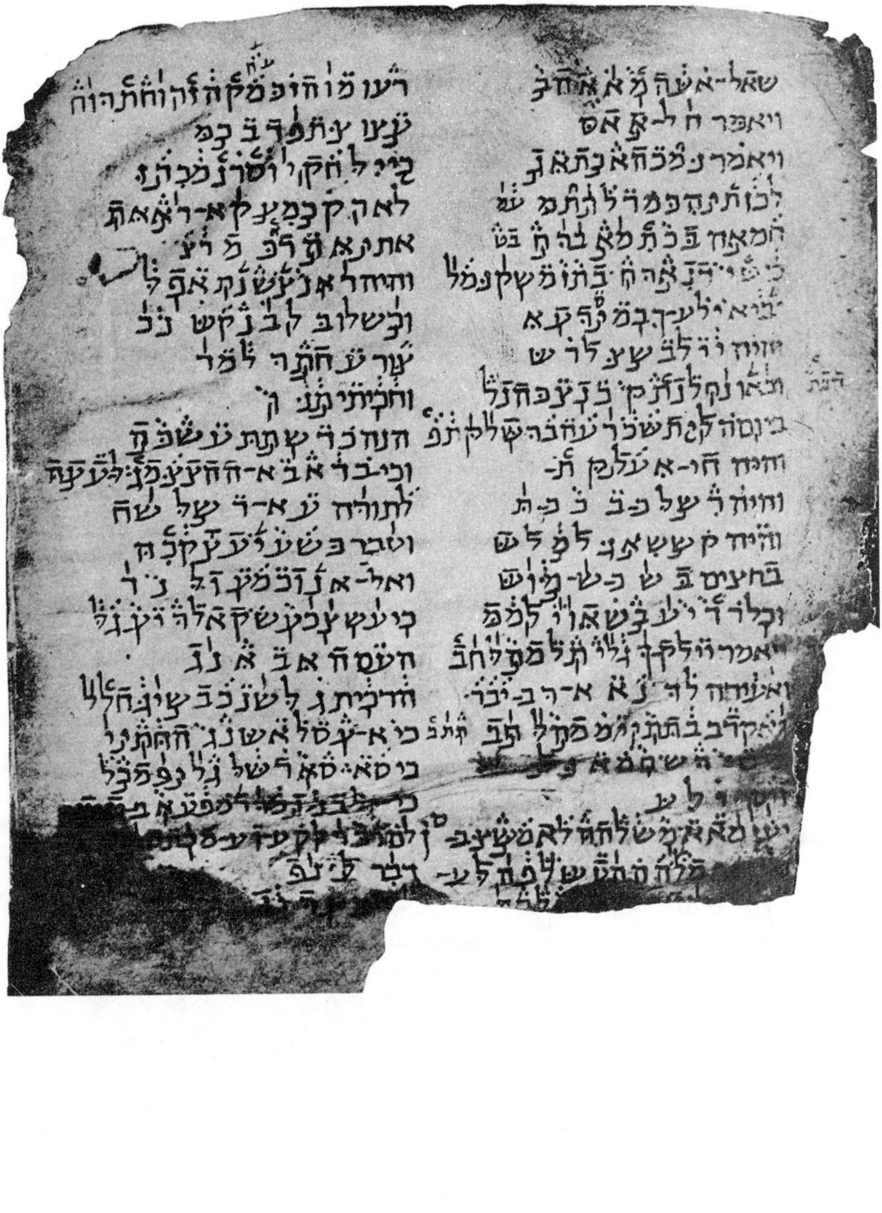

20. CODEX CAIRENSIS

Cf. p. 35. Illustration (Jer. 2:16-33) from a photograph kindly provided by P. E. Kahle.

An excerpt from the second colophon at the end of the manuscript:

> I, Moshe ben Asher have written this Codex *(maḥzor)* of the Scripture according to my judgment 'as the good hand of my God was upon me' (Neh. ii,8), 'very clearly' (Deut. xxvii,8), in the city of Ma'azya-Ṭabarīya, 'the renowned city' (Ezek. xxvi,17) . . .
>
> It was written in the year 827 after the destruction of the Second Temple [= A.D. 895] . . .
>
> [by another hand] Whoever alters a word of this Maḥzor or this writing or erases one letter or tears off one leaf — unless he understands and knows that there is a word in it in which we have erred in the writing or in the punctuation or in the Masora, or in defective or in plene — may he have neither pardon nor forgiveness, neither 'let him behold the beauty of the Lord' (Ps xxvii,4) nor let him see the good that is reserved for those who fear Him (Jer. xxix,32). He shall be like a woman in impurity and like a leprous man who has to be locked up so that his limbs may be crushed, the pride of his power be broken, his flesh be consumed away that it cannot be seen and his bones that were covered made bare (Job xxxiii,21). Amen!
>
> Whoever reads shall hear; whoever hears shall understand; whoever sees shall perceive. Peace! (P. E. Kahle 1959: 96).

For the complete text of the colophons with English translation see Kahle 1959: 92-97; German translation in Kahle 1927-30: I, 15f.

‏מסר ג כל וסמך אחד וסמפתאה וכסמברי חר אכל אריה גריי • עאם ז פרפטח כל ארית וסתפכרי סגלה אמרי • וחד תסאמ לפני יהלי•‏

עמוד א (ימין)

‏קדקד יהל ואת אתב‏
‏תעשה לך עכל את‏
‏חזק זאת לדיך כעת מ‏
‏מדקן כידיך ועתה‏
‏מה לד לדרך מצרים‏
‏לשתות מי שחור וכסרד‏
‏לדיך אשור לשתות‏
‏מינהר תנסכי דרעז‏
‏ומשבותיך תוכחך‏
‏ודעי וראי כי רעומר‏
‏עזבך את יהוה אלהך‏
‏ולא פחדתי אליך נאם‏
‏אדני יהוה צבאות כי‏
‏מעולם שברתי עלך‏
‏נתקתי מוסרותיך‏
‏ותאמרי לא אעבוד‏
‏כי על כל גבעה גבהה‏
‏ותחת כל עץ רענן‏
‏את צעה יחן ואנכי‏
‏נטעתיך שורק כלה‏
‏זרע אמת ואיך נהפכ‏
‏לי סורי הגפן נכריה‏
‏כי אם תכבסי בנתר‏

עמוד ב (אמצע)

‏ותרבי לך כיתם נכתם‏
‏עונך לפני נאם אדני‏
‏יהוה איך תאמרי לא‏
‏נטמאתי אחרי הבעלים‏
‏לא הלכתי ראי דרכך‏
‏בגיא דעי מה עשית‏
‏בכרה קלה משרכת‏
‏דרכיה פרה למד‏
‏מדבר באות נפשו‏
‏שאפה רוח תאנתה‏
‏מי ישיבנה כל מבקשיה‏
‏לא ייעפו בחרשה‏
‏ימצאונה מנעי רגלך‏
‏מיחף וגרונך מצמאה‏
‏ותאמרי נואש לואף‏
‏אהבתי זרים ואחריהם‏
‏אלך כבשת גנב כי‏
‏ימצא כן הבישו בית‏
‏ישראל המה מלכיהם‏
‏שריהם וכהניהם ונביאיהם‏
‏אמרים לעץ אבי אתה‏
‏אבן את ילדתנו ולא באו‏
‏וידהפכו פנו אלי ואף‏

עמוד ג (שמאל)

‏ולא פנים ובעת רעתם‏
‏יאמרו קומה והושיענו‏
‏ואיה אלהיך אשר‏
‏עשית לך יקומו אם‏
‏יושיעוך בעת רעתך‏
‏כי מספר עריך היו‏
‏אלהיך יהודה‏
‏למה תריבו אלי‏
‏כלכם פשעתם בי נאם‏
‏יהוה לשוא הכיתי‏
‏את בניכם מוסר לא‏
‏לקחו אכלה חרבכם‏
‏נביאיכם כאריה משחית‏
‏הדור אתם ראו דבר‏
‏יהוה המדבר הייתי‏
‏לישראל אם ארץ‏
‏מאפליה מדוע אמרו‏
‏עמי רדנו לוא נבוא‏
‏עוד אליך התשכח‏
‏בתולה עדיה כלה‏
‏קשריה ועמי שיחוני‏
‏ימים אין מספר מה‏
‏תיטבי דרכך לבקש‏

‏נלוע ז וכו לחו וסיכן סא ביח • ואוד ג אל של ומלן וסיכתן צל חוך • וסמחרך בי לא חלחאואות תיסדיך‏
‏עסאמל ואלא וקמיזי • לקן נ.ז.כמתין חיואכרי כי יחנעי כי חתו כלו רטח • אתסרי ז כ.כפרק י ומריך • ואל אד א. הל ז.חתי•‏

21. THE ALEPPO CODEX

Cf. p. 36. Illustration (Deut. 31:28–32:14) with the kind permission of the Hebrew University Bible Project.

The Aleppo Codex (A), which has probably been in Aleppo since the end of the fourteenth century and has been kept in Israel for the past several years, is described in a dedication inscription as written by Shelomo ben Buya'a, the scribe of the manuscript dated A.D. 930 and shown in pl. 23, and provided with pointing and Masora by Aaron ben Asher. Recent research has proved the Aleppo Codex to be a particularly valuable witness to the Ben Asher tradition. A report (apparently accurate) that can be traced back to the fifteenth century identifies it with the "model codex" of Maimonides, who wrote: ". . . and the book we rely on in these matters (scil. the correct transcription of the open and closed parashoth of the Torah, and the format of the Psalms) is the book recognized in Old Cairo (מצרים) which contains all twenty-four books and was earlier in Jerusalem where it was employed for the correction of other books. Everyone has relied upon this book because Ben Asher corrected it (לפי שהגיהו) and established the details of its text (ודקדק בו) over a period of many years, correcting it many times as it has been transmitted; I have relied upon it in the Torah book which I have transcribed in accordance with his prescriptions" (translation in P. E. Kahle 1927-30: I, 11f.; on its identification cf. now the exhaustive study by M. H. Goshen-Gottstein 1960: 17-58, and 1963/64: 149-156).[1]

The page illustrated departs from the usual format of the codex (of three columns a page) in accordance with the Masoretic rules for the Song of Moses which are mentioned by Maimonides. The six lines before the Song are to begin with particular words; signs resembling letters are used to fill out the lines as necessary. According to Maimonides the Song itself should be written in sixty-seven lines, the precise number in A (others stipulate seventy lines). There were also rules for the five lines following the Song.

1. A. Dotan 1964/65: 136-155 (cf. *IZBG* 13 [1966/67]: 1) considers the grounds proposed by Goshen-Gottstein for identification to be inadequate. In spite of the colophon he insists that the pointing of the manuscript cannot be ascribed to Aaron ben Asher.

נמסר ד' רב אשיעד יענאשרש בדוזה ג' מל ירבסיו יחולבכתך וירד הרך ·
לֹ אורייגא חֲלֵקַם בֹּר חֹ א ידיגב לֹ ירעוני וכל קרייול ולדוכוד
בר גם חד דיעו יחזיחזו ואמד עשר שלשה הַזאת חפמ ב·

וְאָעִ֣ידָה בָּ֗ם אֶת־הַשָּׁמַ֙יִם֙ וְאֶת־הָאָ֔רֶץ כִּֽי יָדַ֔עְתִּי
אַחֲרֵ֣י מוֹתִ֔י כִּֽי־הַשְׁחֵ֤ת תַּשְׁחִתוּן֙ וְסַרְתֶּ֣ם מִן־
הַדֶּ֔רֶךְ אֲשֶׁ֥ר צִוִּ֖יתִי אֶתְכֶ֑ם וְקָרָ֤את אֶתְכֶם֙ הָֽרָעָ֔ה
בְּאַחֲרִ֣ית הַיָּמִ֔ים כִּֽי־תַעֲשׂ֤וּ אֶת־הָרַע֙ בְּעֵינֵ֣י יְ֔הֹוָה
לְהַכְעִיס֖וֹ בְּמַעֲשֵׂ֥ה יְדֵיכֶֽם׃ וַיְדַבֵּ֣ר מֹשֶׁ֗ה בְּאׇזְנֵ֞י כׇּל־
קְהַ֤ל יִשְׂרָאֵל֙ אֶת־דִּבְרֵ֞י הַשִּׁירָ֧ה הַזֹּ֛את עַ֖ד תֻּמָּֽם׃

וְתִשְׁמַ֥ע הָאָ֖רֶץ אִמְרֵי־פִֽי׃	הַאֲזִ֥ינוּ הַשָּׁמַ֖יִם וַאֲדַבֵּ֑רָה
תִּזַּ֤ל כַּטַּל֙ אִמְרָתִ֔י	יַעֲרֹ֤ף כַּמָּטָר֙ לִקְחִ֔י
וְכִרְבִיבִ֖ים עֲלֵי־עֵֽשֶׂב׃	כִּשְׂעִירִ֥ם עֲלֵי־דֶ֖שֶׁא
הָב֥וּ גֹ֖דֶל לֵאלֹהֵֽינוּ׃	כִּ֛י שֵׁ֥ם יְהֹוָ֖ה אֶקְרָ֑א
כִּ֥י כׇל־דְּרָכָ֖יו מִשְׁפָּ֑ט	הַצּוּר֙ תָּמִ֣ים פׇּעֳל֔וֹ
צַדִּ֥יק וְיָשָׁ֖ר הֽוּא׃	אֵ֤ל אֱמוּנָה֙ וְאֵ֣ין עָ֔וֶל
דּ֥וֹר עִקֵּ֖שׁ וּפְתַלְתֹּֽל׃	שִׁחֵ֣ת ל֗וֹ לֹ֚א בָּנָ֣יו מוּמָ֔ם
עַ֥ם נָבָ֖ל וְלֹ֣א חָכָ֑ם	הֲלַיְהֹוָה֙ תִּגְמְלוּ־זֹ֔את
שְׁאַ֤ל אָבִ֙יךָ֙ וְיַגֵּ֔דְךָ זְקֵנֶ֖יךָ וְיֹ֥אמְרוּ לָֽךְ׃	זְכֹר֙ יְמ֣וֹת עוֹלָ֔ם בִּ֖ינוּ שְׁנ֣וֹת דּוֹר־וָדֹ֑ר
בְּהַפְרִיד֖וֹ בְּנֵ֣י אָדָ֑ם	בְּהַנְחֵ֤ל עֶלְיוֹן֙ גּוֹיִ֔ם
לְמִסְפַּ֖ר בְּנֵ֥י יִשְׂרָאֵֽל׃	יַצֵּב֙ גְּבֻלֹ֣ת עַמִּ֔ים
יַעֲקֹ֖ב חֶ֥בֶל נַחֲלָתֽוֹ׃	כִּ֛י חֵ֥לֶק יְהֹוָ֖ה עַמּ֑וֹ
וּבְתֹ֖הוּ יְלֵ֣ל יְשִׁמֹ֑ן	יִמְצָאֵ֙הוּ֙ בְּאֶ֣רֶץ מִדְבָּ֔ר
יִצְּרֶ֖נְהוּ כְּאִישׁ֥וֹן עֵינֽוֹ׃	יְסֹבְבֶ֙נְהוּ֙ יְב֣וֹנְנֵ֔הוּ
יִפְרֹ֤שׂ כְּנָפָיו֙ יִקָּחֵ֔הוּ יִשָּׂאֵ֖הוּ עַל־אֶבְרָתֽוֹ׃	כְּנֶ֙שֶׁר֙ יָעִ֣יר קִנּ֔וֹ עַל־גּוֹזָלָ֖יו יְרַחֵ֑ף
וְאֵ֥ין עִמּ֖וֹ אֵ֥ל נֵכָֽר׃	יְהֹוָ֖ה בָּדָ֣ד יַנְחֶ֑נּוּ
וַיֹּאכַ֖ל תְּנוּבֹ֣ת שָׂדָ֑י	יַרְכִּבֵ֙הוּ֙ עַל־[בָּ֣מ]וֹתֵי אָ֔רֶץ
וְשֶׁ֖מֶן מֵֽחַלְמִ֥ישׁ צֽוּר׃	וַיֵּנִקֵ֤הֽוּ דְבַשׁ֙ מִסֶּ֔לַע
עִם־חֵ֥לֶב כָּרִ֖ים וְאֵילִ֑ים	חֶמְאַ֨ת בָּקָ֜ר וַחֲלֵ֣ב צֹ֗אן
עִם־חֵ֖לֶב כִּלְי֥וֹת חִטָּ֑ה	בְּנֵֽי־בָשָׁ֣ן וְעַתּוּדִ֔ים

עייג יל' קורל ועוקשואול זימבְּמחה עמבאוחבריתועובל רעורעו ואושב חשך ירושלם·וזו·תמעו יהודיעורימאתב בהרבעבם לבלליעווד· וחוב נבלוֹל ירֵיחל
מה יה ד' היל' עלשל עריל יתיד ·ואוער לֹ רב יף·תֹנבדול יעלךֹ ליֹ חללֹ אמוילֹו וחבל·והול בלֹ יעמ·אתול עגיריל ועליד ועורור לֹ חונו ·
ועֵי· ח נעשר שעוֹל ירייריח ב גו למדר אלֹאע לרוֹימ כי עעֹר את ללוריד·

22. BRITISH LIBRARY CODEX OR. 4445

Cf. p. 41. Illustration in reduced size (Num. 26:12-27) with the kind permission of the British Library.

This manuscript of the Pentateuch is pointed and accented: the defective portions at the beginning (Gen. 1–39:19) and end (from Deut. 1:34 on), as well as Num. 7:46-73 and 9:12–10:18, are lacking or have been supplied by a later hand. The manuscript is written in a good, clear hand with three columns to a page, the Masora parva in the side margins, and the Masora magna in the upper and lower margins. Christian D. Ginsburg 1897: 469-474 recognized this as the oldest manuscript and dated the consonantal text and its pointing about A.D. 820-850; he thought the masora was added about a century later by a Nakdan (cf. p. 13) who also revised the text. It may be assumed that the Masora was written while Ben Asher was still alive, because he is mentioned without the form of blessing usual for one who has died. Paul E. Kahle, however, places the origin of the entire manuscript within the lifetime of Ben Asher: "[that] Ben Asher was obviously the great authority for the copyist, and that he really copied a Ben Asher text, is confirmed by the book of Mishael b. ʿUzziel" (Kahle 1951a: 167; cf. also 1927: I, 17f.; on Mishael ben ʿUzziel cf. p. 24 above and BHK, xxixf.).

כל דיבור עמל יוֹקֵד רגלֵך בני מ‌ מ‌ רפאים וסימנהתו חנודר ויולד עזרד קרדבר מטפח ואל עזד וכיש וביש ערזקיוד וסמבר
יברחתו משרפל ריח מרלא מאלה אלכת לי ל חונורל קי יברין אוכח יחו מלך אל ביל חרבמסרשו רבו הוקף ל רבתחון·

מִשְׁפַּחַת הַנְּמוּאֵלִי	מִשְׁפַּחַת בְּנֵגֶךְ ·	בְּנֵי יִשָּׂשכָר לְמִשְׁפַּחֹתָם
לְיָמִין מִשְׁפַּחַת	לִפְקֻרֵיהֶם אַרְבָּעִם	תּוֹלָע מִשְׁפַּחַת
הַיָּמִינִי לְיָכִין מִשְׁפַּחַת	אֶלֶף וַחֲמֵשׁ מֵאוֹת	הַתּוֹלָעִי לְפֻ
הַיָּכִינִי לְזֶרַח מִשְׁפַּחַת	בְּנֵי יְהוּדָה	מִשְׁפַּחַת הַפּוּנִי
הַזַּרְחִי לְשָׁאוּל מִשְׁפַּחַת	עֵר וְאוֹנָן וַיָּמָת עֵר	לְיָשׁוּב מִשְׁפַּחַת
הַשָּׁאוּלִי · אֵלֶּה	וְאוֹנָב אֶרֶץ כְּנָעַן	הַיָּשֻׁבִי לְשִׁמְרֹן
מִשְׁפַּחַת שִׁמְעֹנִי	וַיִּהְיוּ בְנֵי יְהוּדָן	מִשְׁפַּחַת הַשִּׁמְרֹנִי
שְׁנַיִם וְעֶשְׂרִים אָלֶף	לְמִשְׁפַּחֹתָם לְשֵׁלָה	אֵלֶּה מִשְׁפַּחֹת
וּמָאתָיִם בְּנֵי	מִשְׁפַּחַת הַחֶצְלָם	יִשָּׂשכָר לִפְקֻרֵיהֶם
גָּד לְמִשְׁפַּחֹתָם ·	לְפֶרֶץ מִשְׁפַּחַת	אַרְבָּעָה וְשִׁשִּׁים
לִצְפוֹן מִשְׁפַּחַת	הַפַּרְצִי לְזֶרַח ·	אֶלֶף וּשְׁלֹשׁ מֵאוֹת
הַצְּפוֹנִי לְחַגִּי ·	מִשְׁפַּחַת הַזַּרְחִי	בְּנֵי זְבוּלֻן לְמִשְׁפַּחֹתָם
מִשְׁפַּחַת הַחַגִּי	וַיִּהְיוּ בְנֵי פֶרֶץ	לְסֶרֶד מִשְׁפַּחַת
לְשׁוּנִי מִשְׁפַּחַת	לְחֶצְרֹן מִשְׁפַּחַת	הַסַּרְדִּי לְאֵלוֹן
הַשּׁוּנִי · לְאָזְנִי	הַחֶצְרֹנִי לְחָמוּל	מִשְׁפַּחַת הָאֵלֹנִי
מִשְׁפַּחַת הָאָזְנִי	מִשְׁפַּחַת הֶחָמוּלִי	לְנַחְלְאֵל מִשְׁפַּחַת
לְעֵרִי מִשְׁפַּחַת	אֵלֶּה מִשְׁפַּחֹת	הַנַּחְלְאֵלִי · אֵלֶּה
הָעֵרִי · לַאֲרוֹד ·	יְהוּדָה לִפְקֻרֵיהֶם	מִשְׁפַּחַת הַזְּבוּלֹנִי
מִשְׁפַּחַת הָאֲרוֹדִי	שִׁשָּׁה וְשִׁבְעִים	לִפְקֻרֵיהֶם שִׁשִּׁים
לְאַרְאֵלִי מִשְׁפַּחַת	אֶלֶף וַחֲמֵשׁ מֵאוֹת	אֶלֶף וַחֲמֵשׁ מֵאוֹת
הָאַרְאֵלִי · אֵלֶּה	פ	

נ בטועם בני פרוני בעיונֵך · וסימנהתן ושששכר נפתי ל דן ם חבוליך ג · וכל כל· וסימנהתו אלה משפחת חזבולם אילֵן
חדבוליה וחביא·רום מן רוֹתִי : בטֵע בעינֵעל גד יהורח שמעון ובויל אשֵד אפרים בניאגן נ א גד רבת ס סואקוועוֹעֵסה
בן חפרי · ולי גולפחתר בן חפר גו ער מחלה וענֵע חנֵלה גלכח ותר יעֵד מלחֹאֹן · ותקוֹרבוֹה מֹנֹחֹן זתהויֵעד מרֹוֹוֹן ⸻

23. A TORAH MANUSCRIPT FROM THE YEAR A.D. 930

Codex 17 of the second Firkowitz collection (cf. p. 30). Illustration (Deut. 9:15-23) from P. E. Kahle 1927-30: I.

At the end of the codex, which comprises 241 folios with three columns of text per page, the scribe and the Masorete of the codex, two brothers, give separate accounts of their activities.

The scribal colophon:

I, Shelomo ha-Levi, son of Buya'a,[1] pupil of Sa'id the son of Fargai also called Balquq, have written this book of the Torah of Moses, as the good hand of my God is upon me, for our lord Barhon and for our lord Salich, the sons of our lord Maimun. . . .

The Masorete writes:

I, Ephraim, son of Rabbi Buya'a, have completed this Torah, pointing it, providing the Masora, and verifying it as the good hand of my God is upon me, and if there is a fault in it, may God not count it against me as a sin. I completed it on Friday, the eighth day of Kislev in the year 1241 of the [Seleucid] era for our lord Abraham and our lord Salich, the sons of our lord Maimun. May this Torah be for them, as well as for us and for all Israel, a good sign, a sign of blessing for salvation and for help, for the coming of the Messiah and the building of Jerusalem and for the gathering of the captivity of Israel, as it is promised to us by our Creator, the Builder of Jerusalem. Yahweh will gather the scattered of Israel, and raise up a banner for the nations and gather the scattered of Israel and the destroyed of Judah he will gather from the four corners of the earth (Isa. 11:12).[2]

1. Shelomo ben Buya'a also wrote the Ben Asher codex in Aleppo (cf. p. 174)
2. Text from P. E. Kahle 1927-30: I, 58f. The Hebrew text (in S. Baer and H. L. Strack 1879) was not available to me.

...נור וזהב
בערבאש ושן
לוהתהברית על
שתימידי וארא
והנה חטאתם י
ליהוה אלהיכם
עשיתם לכם י
עגל מסכה יי
סרתם מהרמו
הדרך אשר צוה
ויהוה אתכם יי
ואתפש בשנן
הלחתואשלכם
מעל שתי ידי
ואשברם לעיניכם
ואתנפל לפני
יהוה כראשנה
ארבעים יום י
וארבעים לילה

מסלא אבלתי
מים לא שתיתי
על כל חטאתכם
אשר חטאתם
לעשות הרע יי
מעני יהוה לא
לה כעסו כי יי
וגרתי מפני האף
והחמה אשר
קצף יהוה עליכם
להשמיד אתכם
וישמע יהוה יי
אלי גם בפעם
ההוא ובאהרן
התאנף יהוה
מאד להשמידו
ואתפלל גם בעד
אהרן בעת ההוא
ואת חטאתכם
אשר עשיתי

אתעה עגל
לקחתי ואשרף
אתו באש ואכת
אתו טחון חיטב
עד אשר דק
לעפר ואשלך
את עפרו אל
הנחל הירד מן
ההר ובתבערה
ובמסה ובקברת
התאוה מקצפם
חייתם את יהוה
וכשלח יהוה
אתכם מקדש
ברנע לאמר
עלו ורשו את
הארץ אשר
נתתי לכם ותמרו
את פי יהוה
אלהיכם ולא

24. CODEX LENINGRADENSIS

Cf. p. 36. Illustration (Gen. 28:18–29:22) from a photograph kindly provided by P. E. Kahle.

The date of the manuscript is described in the following colophon:[1]

> This codex, the whole of the Holy Scriptures, was written and completed with pointing and Masora and carefully corrected in the Metropolis of Egypt [Cairo]. It was completed (a) in the month of Siwan of the year 4770 of the Creation of the world. (b) This is the year 1444 of the Exile of King Jehoiakin. (c) This is the year (1)319 of the Greek Reign, according to the reckoning of the Seleucid era and the Cessation of Prophecy. (d) This is the year 940 after the destruction of the Second Temple. (e) This is the year 399 of the Reign of the Small Horn [cf. Dan. 8:9; Islam is intended]. It was acquired by Meborach ben Nathaniel, known as Ben Osdad, priest. . . .

The dating indicates the following years: (a) A.D. 1010, (c) 1008, (d) 1009, (e) 1008. The date (b) falls wide of this period and probably derives from erroneous assumptions. The date (e) A.D. 1008 is probably the most trustworthy because the writer lived in an Islamic country.

The following colophon refers to Ben Asher:

> Samuel ben Jacob wrote and pointed and provided with Masora this codex of the Holy Scriptures from the corrected and annotated books prepared by Aaron ben Moses ben Asher the teacher, may he rest in the Garden of Eden! It has been corrected and properly annotated.

Its dependence on the Ben Asher tradition, which has been questioned on occasion, has been confirmed by recent research (cf. BHK, xxix-xxxiii).

---

1. The text of the colophon is printed and translated in part by A. Harkavy and H. L. Strack 1875: 265ff.

קלין יו דחיר ומראהאמפין ס' שטיע ש ויהי בשטע אלם לא תישאקטעלגישי ומלכן שגבו מפיכת שבא
כאשר שמרגי ותקיא כאשע חורלי אישר
כשטאקוס

וישומצטי מלרשעעוער אלט את אצטסיוח וישאטטו מלא קירכן שטן קרחר ימכריכ בלע בשטי

וַיֹּאמֶר מֶחָן אֲמֶן		עָלִי אֹשֶׁה וַיְקְבֹּא אֶת
וַיֹּאמֶר לְהֶסַתְחַיְעֶתֶםאֶת		שֶׁ חֻמַּקָּ קוֹקָ הַהוּא בֵּיתִי
לְבָזוֹנָ חָרוְיָאמְרֹהְיִבָּ עֶנּוּ		אָר וְאוּלְ לוֹ שֶׁהֶ סָ עֵיר
וְיֹּאמֶר לְהֶסָ הַשָּׁלוֹס לְוֹ		לֹא אֵשַׁ עֵיוְ וִיהֵיר וְיַעֲקֹב
וְיֹּאמְרֹו שָׁלוֹס וְהֵוּ רַחֵל		נֶרְךָ לָאמֹר אֶסַ יְחְיֶל
בְּתּוֹ בָּאָה עֹסַ הַצֹּאן יֶל		אֱלֹהִים עֲמָדִי וַשֶׁעַלְעָמִי
וַיֹּאמֶר הֶן עֹוד מַזֹּסְעֶל		בָּקְהַרָ חַדְחָאֲשֶׁרְ אֹתֶן ש
לֹא אָעֵתֶה אֶסֶף חָמָקְנֶה ש		חוֹלֹ לְלַבֶּשׁ שֶׁנַטְכַשְׁמִי
חַשְׁקוֹ הֵרֻצֹאון וּלְכֹר רְעֹוּ		וּכְנַר לְלֹבְּשִׁ שֶׁבֶרֹכַשָׁה
וַיֹּאמְרֹו לֹא נֻכֹל עָד אֲשֶׁר		אֶרְבֵּית אָבִי וּמִפְּחְ יַחְנָּחְלֵי
וַאֲסָפֹו כָל עֶדְרִים וְגָלְלֹו		לַאְלֹהֵים וְהֹאֲמֶרְ מֻזֹּאת
אֶת הָאֶכֶם עֶל פִּי הַבְּאֵר		אֲשֶׁר שֻׁמַתֵי וָקְעַבְּדֹי יְדֻשַׁ
וְהַשְׁקֹיּוּם צֹאן וְעֹדְנֹם		מֵיתֶ אַהַס הַסְכֵּל אֲשֶׁרֶיתֵּם
מִדַּבֵּר עָמֶס וְכָחֵל בָּאָה		לֹא עֶשֶׂר אֲשֶׁר קְצֵידֶשׁ
עֹסַ הַצֹּאן אֲשֶׁר לְאֲבִיהָ		וְשֶׁאֲנֹעֶקֶל רִבֶּנֹו עֹזֶרֶל
כִּיְרֹעָה הֹוֹא וַיְהִוְיׄ פַּאֲשֶׁר		צֹרֶצֶם בְּגֵרְסֹו רֹוֹ הֹאֹחֶן
רָאֹה יַעֲקֹב אֶת רָחֵל כַּת		בָּאֹרְבֵּשֶׁ רֹוֹחֻפֹּשֶׁ אֶל
לָבֶן אֲחֵי אִמֹו וְאֶת צֹאן לָבֶן		שֶׁ קֹשַׁח עֶבְּרֵ שָׁאֹר רֶל עֹס
הַבֶּן אֲחֵי אִמֹו וַיְגַּשׁ יַעֲקֹב		עֶ שָׁם כֵּרוֹ מֵיס הַפֵּרִי מַחֹוָא
וַיֵּגַל אֶת הֹאֶבֶן מֶעֶל פִּי		מֶשְׁקֹ הְעֶל מֶשְׁ מֹאֶב
הַבְּאֵר וְשֻׁקְ אֶת צֹאן לָבֶן		גַּחְיֹ עֹד חֹבֹנֹאֶ אֶ
אֲחֵי אִמֹסֹ וְיַשֶׁק יַעֲקֹב		וְנֹאַסְפֻ הֹאֲמֶחֹ דֶי הֹאֲבֶס
לְרָחֶל וַיִּשָׁא אֶת קֹלֹוְוְ		וְגָלֹר אֶת הֹאֶבֶן מֵצֵעֶרֶף
וַגֵּר מֵעֲצֹב וַיַּגֵּד לְרֹחֵל		מֵבָּאֵר וְהִשְׁקֹ אֶת דֹ בֹּא
אְפֹוחֹ אֲחֵי אֹבִיהָ הֹוֹא		וְדֹשֶׁקֹ צֹאן לֹקֹחֵר בֹּא אֲבֵי
הֹוֹא אֹטֶף וַעֶלֶד לֹאֲבֶיהָ		תֹקֹשֶׁר מָ לֹקֵח וֹבֹא אֲמֵרֹי
וֹתֹל פָּשֶׁמֹעַ עֹבֹן אֶת שֵׁמִ		לֹ הֹסֹע גֹיֹקֹב אֶחֹשֶׁ מֹאֹ אֹתֶ

25. A MANUSCRIPT WITH DISTINCTIVE POINTING

(Oxford, Bodleian Library) Cf. p. 25. Illustration (Ps. 112:2–114:3) from
P. E. Kahle 1927-30: II.

The folio illustrated, one of the six surviving folios of a Psalter manuscript,
exhibits certain peculiarities that are characteristic of a particular group of
manuscripts. This group of manuscripts differs clearly from the Ben Asher
manuscripts, and was earlier associated by Paul E. Kahle (1927-30: II,
57*f.) with Ben Naphtali. Recent research has shown, however, that it is
not related to Ben Naphtali, but represents a separate group with a distinctive pointing (cf. p. 25 above).

In the text illustrated the following peculiarities may be observed in
contrast with the Ben Asher text:

1. When the א is pronounced as a consonant it has a dot in its center:
   בארץ Ps. 112:2; אור 112:4; איש 112:5; יראה 112:8; תאות 112:10;
   את 113:1; אם 113:9. When it is not pronounced a stroke is placed
   above it: לא 112:6, 7, 8.
2. The mappiq in the final ה which indicates its consonantal value is
   placed *under* the ה: הללויה 113:1, 9.
3. When a final ו is pronounced as a consonant it has a shewa placed
   within the letter: בצריו 112:8.
4. The ח and ע have a shewa when in final position: בטוח 112:7; רשע
   112:10.
5. The pathah furtive is lacking where we would expect it: בטוח 112:7.
6. The shewa of the composite shewa with ה and ח is found over and
   not beside the vowel sign: יחרק 112:10.
7. The relative pronoun אשר is not pointed: 112:8. Proper nouns of
   frequent occurrence are similarly left unpointed or only partially
   pointed: ישראל 114:2.

The manuscript illustrated was further worked over by a second hand
which added mainly the accents of the textus receptus (Kahle 1927-30:
52*).

גִּבּוֹר בָּאָרֶץ יִהְיֶה זַרְעוֹ
הוֹן וָעֹשֶׁר בְּבֵיתוֹ
זָרַח בַּחֹשֶׁךְ אוֹר לַיְשָׁרִים
טוֹב אִישׁ חוֹנֵן וּמַלְוֶה
כִּי לְעוֹלָם לֹא יִמּוֹט
מִשְּׁמוּעָה רָעָה לֹא יִירָא
נָכוֹן לִבּוֹ לֹא יִירָא
פִּזַּר נָתַן לָאֶבְיוֹנִים צִדְקָתוֹ עֹמֶדֶת לָעַד
רָשָׁע יִרְאֶה וְכָעָס שִׁנָּיו יַחֲרֹק וְנָמָס
הַלְלוּיָהּ

דּוֹר יְשָׁרִים יְבֹרָךְ
וְצִדְקָתוֹ עֹמֶדֶת לָעַד
חַנּוּן וְרַחוּם וְצַדִּיק
יְכַלְכֵּל דְּבָרָיו בְּמִשְׁפָּט
לְזֵכֶר עוֹלָם יִהְיֶה צַדִּיק
נָכוֹן לִבּוֹ בָּטֻחַ בַּיהוה
עַד אֲשֶׁר יִרְאֶה בְצָרָיו
קֶרֶן תָּרוּם בְּכָבוֹד
תַּאֲוַת רְשָׁעִים תֹּאבֵד

הַלְלוּ עַבְדֵי יהוה
יְהִי שֵׁם יהוה מְבֹרָךְ
מִמִּזְרַח שֶׁמֶשׁ עַד מְבוֹאוֹ
רָם עַל כָּל גּוֹיִם יהוה
מִי כַּיהוה אֱלֹהֵינוּ
הַמַּשְׁפִּילִי לִרְאוֹת
מְקִימִי מֵעָפָר דָּל
לְהוֹשִׁיבִי עִם נְדִיבִים
מוֹשִׁיבִי עֲקֶרֶת הַבַּיִת

הַלְלוּ אֶת שֵׁם יהוה
מֵעַתָּה וְעַד עוֹלָם
מְהֻלָּל שֵׁם יהוה
עַל הַשָּׁמַיִם כְּבוֹדוֹ
הַמַּגְבִּיהִי לָשָׁבֶת
בַּשָּׁמַיִם וּבָאָרֶץ
מֵאַשְׁפֹּת יָרִים אֶבְיוֹן
עִם נְדִיבֵי עַמּוֹ
אֵם הַבָּנִים שְׂמֵחָה הַלְלוּיָהּ

בְּצֵאת יִשְׂרָאֵל מִמִּצְרַיִם
הָיְתָה יְהוּדָה לְקָדְשׁוֹ
הַיָּם רָאָה וַיָּנֹס

בֵּית יַעֲקֹב מֵעַם לֹעֵז
יִשְׂרָאֵל מַמְשְׁלוֹתָיו
הַיַּרְדֵּן יִסֹּב לְאָחוֹר

26. THE SECOND RABBINIC BIBLE OF JACOB BEN CHAYYIM

Cf. p. 39. Illustration (Gen. 21:33b–22:4a) from a copy at the Bodleian Library, Oxford, by the kind permission of the Bodleian Library.

Rabbinic Bibles (מקראות גדולות) are printed copies of the Old Testament produced from the sixteenth century onward in which the Hebrew text, Targum, Masora, and Rabbinic commentaries are brought together. The illustration shows the arrangement: in the center is the Hebrew text (with Masora) and the Targum, and around it are the commentaries (here of Ibn Ezra and Rashi).

The first Rabbinic Bible, as yet without Masora, was published by Felix Pratensis of the Order of Augustinian Hermits in 1516/17 at the Bomberg press in Venice. As the son of a rabbi, Felix was familiar with Hebrew studies from his youth. After his conversion to Christianity (*ca.* 1506) he became familiar with the scientific methods of classical philology. He applied these to the text of the Hebrew Bible — just as the editors of the Complutensian Polyglot were doing at about the same time (cf. p. 226). He attempted to prepare a correct text on the basis of his study of manuscripts — "an extremely difficult task, and for this reason one which had never been attempted by others."[1] In his dedication to the pope Felix explains with pride that he has restored to the Hebrew text its true and original splendor, in contrast to the many defective manuscripts in circulation at the time (probably these were actually manuscripts of a different Masoretic school; cf. p. 25). He was the first to indicate in a printed Bible the Kethib and the Qere, to introduce the *puncta extraordinaria,* and to observe the Masoretic rules about the special forms of particular letters, such as the *literae majusculae, suspensae, inversae,* etc., as well as to record variant readings from the manuscripts he used.

The work of Felix Pratensis exercised a far-reaching influence because his critical edition provided in large measure the groundwork for the second Rabbinic Bible here illustrated, the work of Jacob ben Chayyim, who may have been less significant as a scholar, but whose work became in turn the standard basis for many later editions (cf. p. 39 above).[2]

Further Rabbinic Bibles were published in Venice (1546/48, 1568, 1617/19), Basel (1618/19, edited by Johannes Buxtorf the Elder), Amsterdam (1724/25), and Warsaw (1860/66, with thirty-two commentaries).[3]

1. "Rem equidem perdifficilem nec ob id ab aliis hactenus tentatem."
2. P. E. Kahle 1947a: 32-36; 1954a: 50-74.
3. *Encyclopaedia Judaica* 4 (1929): 547f.

אבן עזרא

ויקרא שם בשם יהוה אל עולם: ויגר אברהם בארץ פלשתים ימים רבים:

ויהי אחד הדברים האלה והאלהים נסה את אברהם ויאמר אליו אברהם ויאמר הנני: ויאמר קח נא את בנך את יחידך אשר אהבת את יצחק ולך לך אל ארץ המריה והעלהו שם לעלה על אחד ההרים אשר אמר אליך: וישכם אברהם בבקר ויחבש את חמרו ויקח את שני נעריו אתו ואת יצחק בנו ויבקע עצי עלה ויקם וילך אל המקום אשר אמר לו האלהים: ביום השלישי וישא אברהם את עיניו וירא את המקום מרחק: ויאמר אברהם אל נעריו שבו לכם פה עם החמור ואני והנער נלכה עד כה ונשתחוה ונשובה אליכם: ויקח אברהם את עצי העלה וישם על יצחק בנו ויקח בידו את האש ואת המאכלת וילכו שניהם יחדו: ויאמר יצחק אל אברהם אביו ויאמר אבי ויאמר הנני בני ויאמר הנה האש והעצים ואיה השה לעלה: ויאמר אברהם אלהים יראה לו השה לעלה בני וילכו שניהם יחדו: ויבאו אל המקום אשר אמר לו האלהים ויבן שם אברהם את המזבח ויערך את העצים

27. THE SAMARITAN TRIGLOT

Cf. pp. 45f. Illustration (Deut. 31:15-19) from P. E. Kahle 1951.

The illustration shows a folio acquired by Paul E. Kahle from a valuable triglot in Nablus (Shechem), the Torah Finchasiye, which was written in the year 601 of the Mohammedan era, i.e., A.D. 1204/5. The Hebrew, Aramaic, and Arabic texts are all written in Samaritan script from right to left in three columns. This script was developed from the Old Hebrew script. Comparing this folio with the fragment of Leviticus in Old Hebrew script found by Roland de Vaux (cf. pl. 14), Kahle comments: "Of course the forms of the letters are somewhat more developed, and certain principles in the method of transcribing biblical manuscripts show signs of evolution through the years. But with it all, it is simply amazing how constant the Old Hebrew script has remained over a period of 1000 to 1500 years" (Kahle 1951: 19f.).

Note the following characteristics in the manuscript: the individual words are separated by dots. The first letter and the last two letters of each line in the Hebrew and Aramaic columns are written precisely under each other. There is also a tendency to write similar letters in successive lines directly under each other (cf. lines 7 and 8, 11 and 12). As a rule, manuscripts of the Samaritan Pentateuch are written without vowel points.

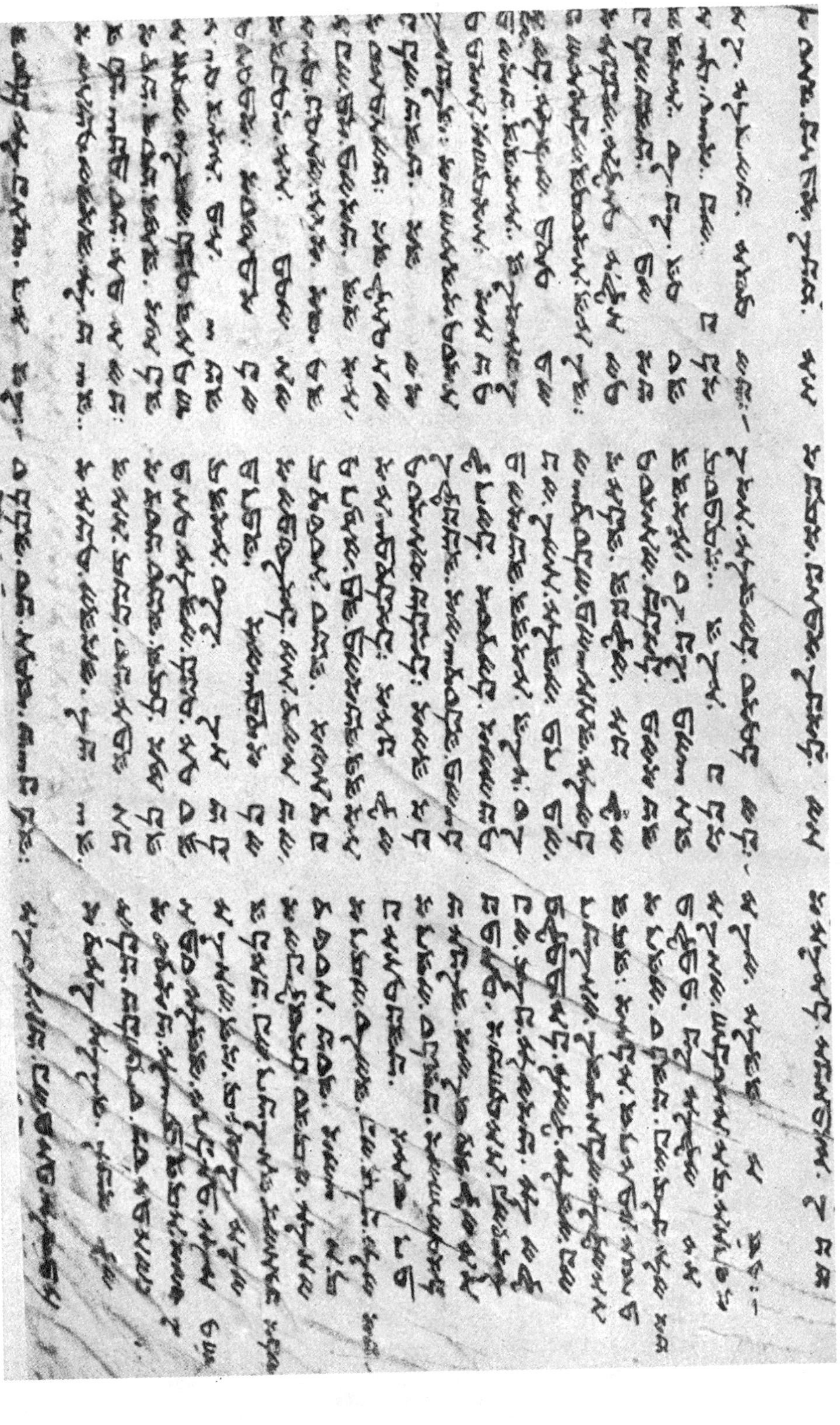

28. THE RYLANDS GREEK PAPYRUS 458

Cf. p. 71. Illustration from a photograph kindly provided by the John Rylands Library, Manchester.

Contents: (a) Deut. 23:24(26)–24:3. (b) Deut. 25:1-3. (c) Deut. 26:12. (d) Deut. 26:17-19. (e) Deut. 28:31-33. (f) Deut. 27:15(?). (g) Deut. 28:2(?). (h). ?

These fragments were found in the wrappings of a mummy acquired by J. Rendel Harris for the John Rylands Library in 1917. They presumably came from the Fayyum where we know there were two Jewish synagogues. Date: mid-second century B.C. The reverse of the Deuteronomy scroll from which the fragments are derived was later used for accounts or notes.

Of special interest is the system of spacing which is quite rare: "As can be seen from the photograph of fragment (b) the writer regularly leaves a space not only at the end of a verse or sentence, but at the end of a κῶλον or group of words. At the end of a verse (cf. frag. (a), line 14, after αυτου in the illustration) a wider space is left and a high point added; otherwise the writer's principle seems to be to leave a fairly large space at the end of a sentence or clause (cf. frag. (b)), and a smaller one at the end of a group of words" (C. H. Roberts 1936: 25). Is this division of the text related to its use in public reading, or does it reflect Aramaic influence? Otherwise the papyrus is like all other Greek manuscripts in ignoring word division.

In some readings of the papyrus Alberto Vaccari found agreements with later Lucianic manuscripts.[1] Yet it belongs among the early Septuagint witnesses.[2]

1. A. Vaccari 1936: 501-4.
2. A. Pietersma 1985: 301.

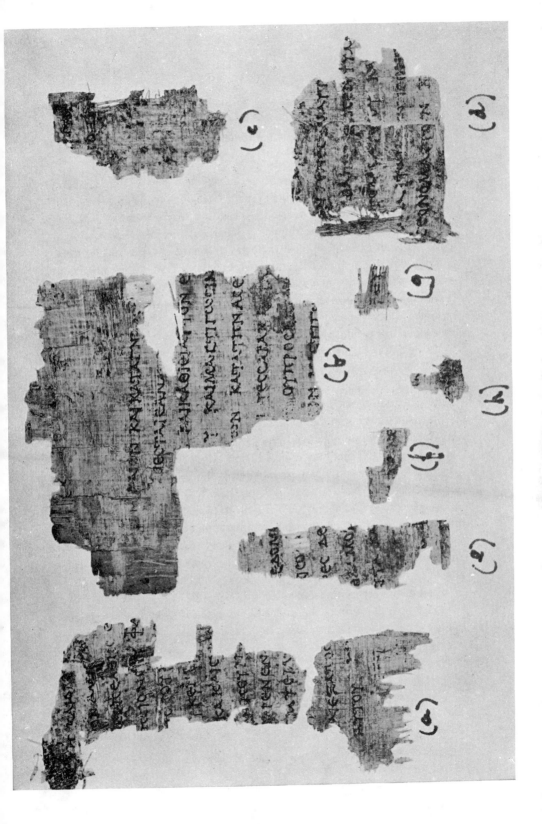

29. PAPYRUS FOUAD 266

Cf. p. 71. Société Royale de Papyrologie, Cairo; first published by W. G. Waddell 1944: 158-161. Republished with additional fragments and plates by Z. Aly and L. Koenen 1980. Illustration (Deut. 31:28–32:6) from P. E. Kahle 1951.

This papyrus is probably from the first or even the second century B.C., and is therefore the second oldest witness to the Greek text of the Old Testament after the Rylands Greek Papyrus 458.[1] It was obviously written by a Jew. The treatment of the divine name Yahweh is of particular interest. Jerome reports in the *Prologus Galeatus* on the writing of this name in Greek manuscripts: "Even today we find the tetragrammaton name of God written in archaic letters in some Greek manuscripts."[2] And in *Epistula 25 ad Marcellam*: "(The name of God is) a tetragram which they considered *anekphōnēton* (i.e., unpronounceable) and wrote the letters *yodh, he, waw, he*. Those who did not understand this would pronounce them PIPI when they read them in Greek books, because of their similarity to the Greek letters."[3]

Thus Jerome was aware of the custom of writing Yahweh in Hebrew letters in Greek manuscripts. The papyrus shown here is evidence for this in pre-Christian times: in col. 2, lines 7 and 15, Yahweh is written in the Hebrew square script in the middle of the Greek text. In fact, the scribe of the Greek text left a space, and the Hebrew letters added by the second scribe are so small that they do not fill the allotted space.

From the use of the tetragrammaton in this and in other early Greek manuscripts some have concluded that originally the Greek translation did not render the divine name YHWH with κύριος, but used the tetragrammaton instead. Yet others regard the tetragrammaton in this manuscript as evidence "that this manuscript represents a secondary stage in reaction to the earliest textual tradition of the Septuagint which it presupposes."[4] Thus the tetragrammaton appears to have been an archaizing and hebraizing revision of the earlier translation κύριος.

Cf. also the form of the divine name in the Habakkuk Commentary (pl. 13) and the related discussion on p. 158.

1. Publication: F. Dunand 1966.
2. "Nomen Domini tetragrammaton in quibusdam Graecis voluminibus usque hodie antiquis expressum litteris invenimur" (J. P. Migne 1844-64, 28: 594f.).
3. "(Dei nomen est) tetragrammum quod ἀνεκφώνητον, id est ineffabile, putaverunt et his litteris scribitur: iod, he, vau, he. Quod quidam non intelligentes propter elementorum similitudinem, cum in Graecis libris reppererint, ΠΙΠΙ legere consueverunt" (CSEL 54: 219).
4. R. Hanhart 1978: 42; in agreement is A. Pietersma 1984: 90, 99f.

ΠΡΟCΕΧΕ ΟΥ ΡΑ
ΚΑΓΑΚΟΥΕΤΩ.
ΠΡΟCΔΟΚΕΙCΘΩ
ΚΑΙΚΑΤΑΒΗΤ.
ωCΕΙΟΜΒΡΟCΕ
.ΚΟC.ΝΙΟ.
.ΙΟΝΟΜΑ...
.ΤΕΜΕΓΑΚω.
.CΑΛΗΘΙΝΑΤ
..ΠΑCΑΙΑΙΟΔΟ.
.CΠΙCΤΟCΚΑ
.Α.ΟC....
..ΤΟCΑΝΟ.
.ΕΑCΚΟ.ΛΑ.
.ΓΑ....ΑΙ.
.ΕΤωCΛΛΟCΜω.
.ΟΚΚΑΥΤΟCΟ.Τ
.ΕΙCΤΗCΑΤ.
.Μ.

.ΛΙΤΥ.
.ΑΙΤΗΝΠ
.Υ.ΚCΜΟΥ
.ΕΚΚΛΙΝΕΤΕ
.ΥΜΙΝΚΑΙ
.ΛΕCΧΑΤω.
.ΙΟΠΟΝΗΡω.
.CΤΟΝΕΝΤΟΙC
..ΛΝΑ.ΕΝ

.ΟΥ.
.ΙCΙC
ΝΑΔΙΚΙ.

30. A GREEK SCROLL OF THE MINOR PROPHETS

Cf. pp. 54, 71. Illustration (Hab. 1:14–2:5 and 2:13-15) from D. Barthélemy 1953.

This scroll, which we have referred to often, was found by the Taamire Bedouin in August 1952 in the Judean desert in a cave that was not at first identified; in 1952 and 1953 it was acquired by the Palestinian Archaeological Museum in Jerusalem. Israeli excavators were later successful in identifying the cave in Naḥal Ḥever, and in finding nine more small fragments.[1] The surviving parts of the scroll, which were published by Dominique Barthélemy 1963, are from the books of Jonah, Micah, Nahum, Habakkuk, Zephaniah, and Zechariah. In his first report Barthélemy 1953 dated the scroll toward the end of the first century A.D., while Colin H. Roberts assigned it to the century between 50 B.C. and A.D. 50 — a position essentially supported by Wilhelm Schubart (cf. P. E. Kahle 1959: 226). In his edition of the text Barthélemy now indicates the mid-first century A.D. as most probable. The scroll therefore represents a Greek biblical text written by Jews and for Jews. From the plentiful archaeological evidence (including coins) found together with the fragments by the Bedouin and Israeli excavators in Naḥal Ḥever, it is clear that the scroll was placed in the cave during the Bar Kochba rebellion (A.D. 132-135), and at that time it was already well worn.

The discussion, which has continued unabated since this amazing discovery, is evidence of the great significance of this scroll (cf. p. 65).

1. B. Lifshitz 1962: 201-7, and E. Tov 1990.

ΙϹΘΑΛ

ΛΗΓΟΥΜΕΝΟΝ

ΛΕϹΠΑϹΕΝ ΚΑΙ ΕΥΡΕΝ

ΕΙΒΛΗΘΡΩ ΑΥΤΟΥ ΚΑΙ ϹΥΝΗΓΑ

ϹΑΓΗΝΗ ΑΥΤΟΥ ΔΙΑ ΤΟΥΤΟ ΕΖ

ΚΑΙ ΧΑΡΕΙΖΙΛ ΔΙΑΓΟ ΓϹΘΑΧϹΓ

ΓΡ ΩΑΥΤΟΥ ΚΑΙ ΘΥΜΙΑϹΕΙ ΤΗ ϹΑ

ΙΩ ΕΝ ΑΥΤΟΙϹ ΕΛΙ ΠΑΝ ΘΗΛΑΡΤΟϹ

ΤΟ ΜΜΑΛΛ ΑΥΤΟΥ ΕΤΕΡΕΘΝ ΕΙΔΙΑ ΤΟϹ

ΙϹΘΛΛΛΑ ΧΑΙΓΑ ΑΥΤΟΥ ΚΑΙ ΔΙΑ ΔΙΑΠΑΝ

ΗΗ ΡΥΦΗϹΕΤΑΙ

ΛΟΥϹ ΤΗϹ

ΛϹ ΚΑΙ ΑΠΟϹΚ

ΜΕΛΛΟΙ ΚΑ ΤΙ

ΚΑΙ ΑϹΙ ΕΚΡΙϹΗ

ΙΟΡΑϹΙΝ ΚΑΙ ΕΚ ΦΛ

ΗΑΠΑΓΓΕΙ ΝΩϹ ΚΩΝ

ΑΙΡΟΝ ΚΑΙ ΕΠΙ ΦΑΝΗϹΕ

ΑΖΕΥϹΕΤΑΙ ΕΑΝ ϹΤΕΑϹ

ΤΟΝ ΟΤΙ ΕΡΧΟΜΕΝΟϹ

ΚΟΤΙ ΛΟ ΕϹΚΕΥΘΕΙΛ Ι ΑΥΤΟΙ

ΛΙΟϹ ΕΝΠΙΟϹ ΙΛΥΤΟΥ ΖΗϹϹ

ΟϹ ΑΠΙΙΡΑΛΑ ΥΩΗ ΚΑΙ ΟΥΙ

ΛΑϹ ϹΩΛΔΙϹΥΧΗ

ΟϹΟϹ ΚΕΝΠΙΠΛΛ

ΟΝ ΠΑΝ ΓΑΤΑΓΘΗΗ ΚΑΙ

ΓΗ

ΚΕΜΟΝ

ΘΗϹΕΤΑΙ

ΗϹΤΙ ΩϹ

ΘΑΛΛϹ

31. CHESTER BEATTY PAPYRUS 967

Cf. p. 71. Illustration (Ezek. 16:57–17:1) from the edition by F. G. Kenyon 1933-37, 1958 (cf. p. 72).

After a thorough examination of the Chester Beatty-Scheide Papyrus 967 (34 leaves = 68 pages of a codex of Ezekiel from the first half of the third century), Joseph Ziegler comes to the following conclusions which we cite here because of their importance for the problems of 𝔊:

1. Papyrus 967 supports the oldest, pre-Hexaplaric, original readings hitherto attested by Codex B alone. . . . Further, these readings of 967 and B are usually found also in the Old Latin, and frequently in the Coptic text. Therefore the tradition represented by 967 B La (𝔏) Co (𝔎) provides the earliest attainable form of the Greek text of Ezekiel.

2. In some instances 967 *alone* has preserved the original reading. . . .

3. Papyrus 967 is important chiefly for demonstrating that in the pre-Hexaplaric period (perhaps even in the first century A.D.) the Septuagint text of Ezekiel was being corrected toward the Hebrew text. Its agreements with 𝔐 do coincide frequently with the Hexaplaric readings which have been corrected from 𝔐, and consequently also with the renderings of the later Greek translators Aquila, Symmachus, and Theodotion, but this does not indicate dependence upon them. They do not reflect a process of thorough-going revision, but rather merely occasional corrections.[1]

4. The vocabulary of Papyrus 967 shows that the revision of the text of Ezekiel occurred at such an early date that it has affected the entire manuscript tradition, and is consequently difficult to detect. The translator was far more consistent in his rendering of the Hebrew exemplar than has long been suspected. . . . Even his rendering of the divine name as κύριος seems to have been consistent. This makes it less likely that several (three) translators shared in its preparation.

5. The occasional agreement of Papyrus 967 with readings of Alexandrian manuscripts (A and related minuscules), the Lucianic recension (L), and the Catena group (C) shows that these witnesses frequently drew upon early pre-Hexaplaric sources, and that their value should not be underestimated.[2]

1. Cf. p. 57, n. 26. P. E. Kahle, who traces the process of assimilation back to the pre-Christian era, considers it certain "that a text of Ezekiel which had been revised by Jews must have been the basis for the emendations in this valuable papyrus of Ezekiel to the extent that they represent assimilation to the Hebrew original and to the Jewish parallel versions which Ziegler has noted" (Kahle 1954: 89).

2. J. Ziegler 1945/48: 93f.

ΟΠΗΝ ΝΥΝ ΟΝΕΙΔ
ΡΩΝ ΟΥΡΙΑΟ ΚΑΙ ΠΩΝ
ΗΝ ΚΥΚΛΩ ΑΥΤΗΟ ΘΥΓΑΤΕ
ΡΩΝ ΑΛΛΟΦΥΛΩΝ ΤΩΝ ΠΕΡΙΕ
ΧΟΝΤΩΝ ΟΕ ΚΥΚΛΩ ΤΑΟ ΑΟΕΒΕΙ
ΑΟ ΟΟΥ ΚΑΙ ΤΑΟ ΑΝΟΜΑΟ ΟΟΥ ΟΥ
ΚΕΚΟΜΙΟΑΙ ΑΥΤΑΟ ΛΕΓΕΙ ΚΟ
ΚΑΙ ΠΟ· ΗΟ ΩΟ ΕΝ ΟΟΙ ΚΑΘΩΟ ΕΠΟΙΗ
ΟΑ ΟΩΟ ΗΤΙΜΩΟΑΟ ΤΑΥΤΑ ΤΟΥ
ΠΑΡΑΒΗΝΑΙ ΤΗΝ ΔΙΑΘΗΚΗΝ ΜΟΥ
ΚΑΙ ΜΝΗΟΘΗΟΟΜΑΙ ΕΓΩ ΤΗΟ ΔΙ
ΑΘΗΚΗΟ ΜΟΥ ΤΗΟ ΜΕΤΑ ΟΟΥ ΕΝ
ΗΜΕΡΑΝ ΝΗΠΙΟΤΗΤΟΟ ΟΟΥ ΚΑΝΑ
ΝΑΟΤΗΟΩ ΟΟΙ ΔΙΑΘΗΚΗΝ ΑΙΩΝΙ
ΟΝ ΚΑΙ ΜΝΗΟΘΗΟΗ ΤΗΝ ΟΔΟΝ ΟΟΥ
ΚΑΙ ΕΞΑΤΙΜΩΘΗΟΗ ΕΝ ΤΩ ΑΝΑ
ΛΑΒΕΙΝ ΜΕ ΤΑΟ ΑΔΕΛΦΑΟ ΟΟΥ ΤΑΟ
ΠΡΕΟΒΥΤΕΡΑΟ ΟΟΥ ΟΥΝ ΤΑΙΟ ΝΕ
ΩΤΕΡΑΙΟ ΟΟΥ ΚΑΙ ΔΩΟΩ ΑΥΤΑΟ
ΟΟΙ ΕΙΟ ΟΙΚΟΔΟΜΗΝ ΚΑΙ ΟΥ ΚΕΚ
ΔΙΑΘΗΚΗΟ ΟΟΥ ΚΑΙ ΑΝΑΟΤΗΟΩ
ΕΓΩ ΤΗΝ ΔΙΑΘΗΚΗΝ ΜΟΥ ΜΕ
ΤΑ ΟΟΥ ΚΑΙ ΕΠΙΓΝΩΟΗ ΟΤΙ ΕΓΩ
ΚΟ ΟΕΟ ΟΠΩΟ ΜΝΗΟΘΗΟ ΚΑΙ
ΧΥΝΘΗΟ ΚΑΙ ΜΗ Η ΟΟΙ ΕΤΙ ΑΝΟΙ
ΞΑΙ ΤΟ ΟΤΟΜΑ ΟΟΥ ΑΠΟ ΠΡΟΟΩ
ΠΟΥ ΤΗΟ ΑΤΙΜΙΑΟ ΟΟΥ ΕΝ ΤΩ ΕΞ
ΞΕΙΛΑΟ-ΟΘΑΙ ΜΕ ΟΟΙ ΚΑΤΑ ΠΑΝ
ΤΑ ΟΟΑ ΕΠΟΙΗΟΑΟ ΛΕΓΕΙ ΚΟ· ΚΝ
ΓΕΝΕΤΟ ΛΟΓΟΟ ΚΥ ΠΡΟΟ ΜΕ ΛΕ

32. THE BERLIN GENESIS

Cf. p. 72. Illustration (Gen. 34:11-25) from H. A. Sanders and C. Schmidt 1927.

This papyrus codex was bought by Carl Schmidt in 1906 at Akhmim in Upper Egypt and donated to the Prussian State Library in Berlin. The well-known papyrologist Hugo Ibscher applied his skill to opening the codex, which had suffered severely from its long burial in the ground, and to preparing it for study. A variety of circumstances delayed its publication until 1927, when it appeared together with the related papyrus codex of the Minor Prophets in the Freer Collection.

The manuscript is in codex form, comprising sixteen sheets folded once to make a single quire of thirty-two folios: the outer sheet has been lost. The script is an early cursive, revealing a variety of stylistic traits, yet from a single hand. Fitting the text within the limits of the available number of pages proved rather constrictive: the scribe's hand became a little cramped toward the end (cf. illustration). Judging from the general impression and the forms of particular letters, the hand "may be safely dated toward the end of the third century A.D." (Sanders and Schmidt 1927: 238).

Sanders observed a number of assimilations to the Hebrew text which occurred in the period before Origen: "Origen did not start this form of corruption in the text, though he doubtless increased it" (Sanders and Schmidt 1927: 265).

33. CODEX SINAITICUS

Cf. p. 73. Illustration (1 Macc. 9:12f.; 9:20-22; Jer. 9:2f.; 9:9f.; Tob. 6:5-7; 6:11f.) from H. J. M. Milne and T. C. Skeat 1938.

The illustration shows samples of the writing of three scribes who wrote this codex, according to the study mentioned above. As we noted on p. 73, many correctors worked on this manuscript. In this connection a sixth- or seventh-century note at the end of Ezra and of Esther is particularly interesting. It states that the codex had been collated with a very old manuscript which had itself been corrected by the martyr Pamphilus from a manuscript of the Hexapla which Origen himself had corrected.

The discovery of this important manuscript, the last of the great Greek codices to be found, may be described briefly. In 1844, on the first of his research journeys to libraries in the east, Constantin von Tischendorf visited the monastery of St. Catherine on Sinai. When he was in the library there he saw 129 leaves of an ancient manuscript in a waste basket, put there by the ignorant monks to be burned. He was given 43 of the leaves (later known as Codex Frederico-Augustanus) before the monks realized their value and refused to part with more. In 1853 Tischendorf visited the monastery again, hoping to obtain or make copies of the remaining leaves, but he was unsuccessful. The monks themselves had forgotten about them and could not find them. In 1859 Tischendorf went once more in quest of them, this time as an envoy of the Russian Tsar, the protector of Orthodox Christendom. Again all Tischendorf's efforts seemed in vain until the eve of his departure, when the steward of the monastery, whom he had told about his search, showed him a codex in his cell. It contained not only the 86 leaves he had seen in 1844, but 112 further leaves of the Old Testament. It also contained the complete New Testament and two early Christian writings which had been lost for centuries: the Letter of Barnabas and the Shepherd of Hermas. After lengthy negotiations the codex was placed in the Imperial Library at Petersburg, and in 1933 it was acquired by the British Museum from the Russian government for the amount of £100,000.

CΑΛΠΙΓΞΙΝΚΑΙΕCΑΛ
ΠΙCΑΝΟΙΠΑΡΑ·Υ
ΔΑΚΑΙΑΥΤΟΙCΑΛ·ΠΙ
ΠΙΞΙΝΚΑΙΕCΑΛ·Τ
ΘΗΗΓΗΑΙΤΟΤΗCΦΩ
ΝΗCΤΩΝΠΑΡΕΜΚ·
ΛΩΝΚΑΙΕΓΕΝΕΤΟ
ΟΠΟΛΕΜΟCCΥΝΗΜ
ΜΕΝΟCΑΠΟΠΡΩΪ
ΘΕΝΜΕΧΡΙΕCΠΕΡΑC

ΠΟΛΛΑCΚΑΙΕΠΙΝ
ΠΙΩCΕΠΕCΕΝΔΥΝΑ
ΤΟCCΩΖΩΝΤΟΝΙΧ
ΚΑΙΤΑΠΕΡΙCCΙΑΓ
ΛΟΓΩΝΙΟΥΔΑΚΑΙ
ΤΩΝΠΟΛΕΜΩΝΚ
ΤΩΝΑΝΔΡΑΓΑΘΙΩΝ
ΩΝΕΠΟΙΗCΕΝΚΑΙ
ΤΗCΜΕΓΑΛΩCΥΝΗ
ΑΥΤΟΥΟΥΚΑΤΕΓΡΑ

ΣΟΝΤΕΓΥΛΟCΚΑΙΟΥ
ΠΙC ΠΙCΕΝΙCΧΥCΕΝ
ΕΠΙΠΗCΙΓΗCΟΠΕΚ
ΚΑΚΩΝΕΙCΚΑΚΛΕ
ΣΗΛΘΟCΑΝ·ΚΑΙΕ
ΜΕΟΥΚΕΤΙΝΩCΑΝ·
ΕΚΑCΤΟCΑΠΟΤΟΥ
ΠΛΗCΙΟΝΑΥΤΟΥ
ΦΥΛΑΞΕCΘΙΚΑΙ
ΕΠΑΔΕΛΦΟΙCΑΥΤ

ΓΑCΤΡΙΚΟΥCΤΗCΕ
ΡΗΜΟΥΘΡΗΝΟΝΟ
ΤΙΕΞΕΧΘΠΙΟΝΠΑΡΑ
ΤΟΜΗΕΙΝΘΑΝΟΥ
ΟΥΚΗΚΟΥCΑΝΦ
ΝΗΗΝΥΠΑΡΞΕΩC
ΑΠΟΠΕΤΙΝΩΝΤ
ΟΥΡΑΝΟΥΚΑΙΕΩ
ΚΤΗΝΩΝΕΞΕCΤΗ
CΑΝΩΧΟΝΤΟΚΝ

ΚΑΙΤΟΠΠΙΑΡΚΑΙΩ
ΠΓΤΗCΕΝΤΟΥΪΧΟΥ
ΟCΚΑΙΕΦΑΙΕΝΚΑΙ
ΑΦΗΚΕΝΕCΑΥΤΟΥ
ΗΑΙCΜΕΝΟΝΚΑΙΕ
ΠΟΡΕΥΘΗCΑΝΑΜ
ΦΟΤΕΡΟΙΚΟΙΝΩC
ΕΩΔΟΗΓΓΙCΑΝΕΙC
ΜΗΛΙΑΝ
ΚΑΙΤΟΓΕΠΡΩΤΗCΕ
ΠΟΠΑΙΛΑΡΙΟΝΓΟΝ

ΜΑCΑΥΛΙCΟΗΝΑΙ
ΚΑΙΟΑΝΘΡΩΠΟC
CΥΓΓΕΝΗCCΟΥΕ
CΤΙΝΚΑΙΕCΤΙΝΑΥ
ΓΩΟΥΓΑΤΗΡΗΟΝΟ
ΜΑCΑΡΡΑΚΑΙΥΙΟC
ΑΡCΗΝΟΥΛΕΘΥΙΑΠ
ΥΠΑΡΧΕΙΑΥΓΙΩΠΛΗ
CΑΡΡΑCΜΟΝΗCΚΑΙ
CΥΕΠΠΙCΓΑΥΓΗC
ΕΙΠΑΡΑΠΑΝΓΑC

34. THE HEXAPLA FRAGMENTS OF MILAN

Illustration and transcription (Ps. 28(27):6f.) from G. Mercati 1958, with the Hebrew column added from 𝔐.

𝔐	Transliteration	Aquila	Symmachus	Septuagint	Quinta
יְהוָה	יהוה	יהוה	יהוה	יהוה κ̅ς̅	יהוה
כִּי	χι	ὅτι	ὁ	ὅτι	ὅτι
שָׁמַע	σμας	ἤκουσε	ἐπακούσας	εἰσήκουσε	εἰσήκουσε
קוֹל	κωλ	φωνῆς	τῆς φωνῆς	τῆς φωνῆς	τῆς φωνῆς
תַּחֲנוּנָי	θανουναι	δεήσεώς μου.	τῆς ἱκεσίας μου	τῆς δεήσεός μου.	τῆς δεήσεός μου.
עֻזִּי	δξει	יהוה	יהוה	יהוה κ̅ς̅	יהוה
וּמָגִנִּי	ουμαγεννι	κράτος μου	ἰσχύς μου	βοηθός μου	βοηθός μου
		(καὶ) θυρεός μου·	καὶ ὑπερασπιστής μου·	καὶ ὑπερασπιστής μου·	καὶ ὑπερασπιστής μου·
בּוֹ	βω·	ἐν αὐτῶι	αὐτῶι	ἐν αὐτῶι	ἐν αὐτῶι
בָטַח	βατε	ἐπεποίθησεν	ἐπεποίθησεν	ἤλπισεν	ἤλπισεν
לִבִּי	λεββι	καρδία μου,	ἡ καρδία μου,	ἡ καρδία μου,	καρδία μου,
וְנֶעֱזָרְתִּי	ου · ναζερθι	(καὶ) ἐβοηθήθην,	καὶ ἐβοηθήθην,	καὶ ἐβοηθήθην,	(καὶ) ἐβοηθήθην,
וַיַּעֲלֹז	ουαϊαλες	καὶ ἠγαυριάσατο	(καὶ) ἱλαρύνθ(η)	καὶ ἀνέθαλεν	καὶ ἐκραταιώθ(η)
לִבִּי	λεββι	καρδία μου·	ἡ καρδία μου·	ἡ σάρξ μου·	ἡ καρδία μου·
וּמִשִּׁירִי	ουμεσοσιρι	(καὶ) ἀπὸ αἴσματό(ς) μου	καὶ ἐν ᾠδαῖς μου	καὶ ἐκ θελήματό(ς) μου	(καὶ) ἀπὸ τοῦ ᾄσματός μου
אֲהוֹדֶנּוּ	αοθωσεννου	ἐξομολογήσωμ(αι) αὐτ(ῷ.)	ὑμνήσω αὐτόν.	ἐξομολογήσομαι αὐτ(ῷ.)	ἐξομολογήσομαι(αι)οσομαι(αι) αὐτ(ῷ.)
יְהוָה	יהוה	יהוה	יהוה	יהוה κ̅ς̅	יהוה
עֻזִּי	δξει	κράτος μου	ἰσχύς μου	βοηθός μου	βοηθός μου
וּמָגִנִּי	ουμαγιννι	καὶ θυρεός μου	καὶ ὑπερασπιστής μου·	καὶ ὑπερασπιστής μου·	καὶ ὑπερασπιστής μου·
בּוֹ	βω	ἐν αὐτῶι	αὐτῶι	ἐν αὐτῶι	ἐν αὐτῷ

200

35. CODEX COLBERTO-SARRAVIANUS

Cf. p. 73. Illustration (Josh. 10:12-19) from G. M. Perrella 1949.

The illustration shows the beauty of the manuscript, which has two columns to each page. It probably dates from the fifth century A.D., although some scholars assign it to the fourth century. It is distinctive among the uncials for preserving the Hexaplaric text with many of the Hexaplaric signs. On the page shown an obelos marks the words (left column, lines 1-5): ηνικα συνετριψεν αυτους εν γαβαων και συνετρειβησαν απο προσωπου ἰηλ (ισραηλ). This indicates that Origen found these words in ⷠ, but that they are not in the Hebrew text.

Several passages in the illustration are marked with an asterisk: this indicates that Origen did not find them in ⷠ and supplied them from other Greek versions. When such a passage extends over several lines the Aristarchan sign is repeated before each line: cf. for example v. 15, which is lacking in ⷠ and is given here with an asterisk (lower left to upper right column): και επεστρεψεν ἰς (ιησους) και πας ἰηλ μετ αυτου εις την παρεμβολην εις γαλγαλαν.

The codex contains the Octateuch and comprises 153 folios (130 in the University of Leiden, 22 in the Paris Bibliothèque Nationale, and 1 in the Leningrad Public Library). Earlier owners mentioned in the manuscript are Jean Baptiste Colbert, minister of finance for Louis XIV, and Claude Sarrave, who donated the first part to the University of Leiden.

ΗΛ · ΗΝΙΚΑ CΥΝΕΤΡΙ
ΒΕΝ ΑΥΤΟΥC ΕΝ ΓΑΒΑ
ΩΝ · ΚΑΙ CΥΝΕΤΡΕΙΒ
CΑΝ ΑΠΟ ΠΡΟCωΠΟΥ
ΙΗΛ · ΚΑΙ ΕΠΤΕΝ ΙCΟΗΝ
ΟC ΚΑΤΑ ΓΑΒΑΩC ΝΕΤΙ
ΤΩ ΚΑΙ ΗCCΑΛΗΝΗ ΚΑ
ΤΑ ΦΑΡΑΓΓΑ ΑΙΛΩΝ
ΚΑΙ ΕCΤΗ Ο ΗΛΙΟC ΚΑΙ Η
CΕΛΗΝΗ ΕΝ CΤΑCΕΙC
ωC ΗΜΥΝΑΤΟ Ο ΘC ΤΟΥ
ΕΧΘΡΟΥC ΑΥΤΩΝ · ΟΥ
ΧΙ ΤΟΥΤΟ ΓΕΓΡΑΜΜΕ
ΝΟΝ ΕΠΙ ΒΙΒΛΙΟΥ ΤΟΥ
ΕΥΘΟΟΥC · ΚΑΙ ΕCΤΗ Ο
ΗΛΙΟC ΚΑΤΑ ΜΕCΟΝ ΤΥ
ΟΥΡΑΝΟΥ ΟΥ ΠΡΟCΕ
ΠΟΡΕΥΕΤΟ ΕΙC ΔΥCΜΑC
ΕΙC ΤΕΛΟC ΗΜΕΡΑC ΜΙ
ΑC · ΚΑΙ ΟΥΚ ΕΓΕΝΕΤΟ
ΗΜΕΡΑ ΤΟΙΑΥΤΗ ΟΥΔΑ
ΤΟ ΠΡΟΤΕΡΟΝ ΟΥΔΕ
ΤΟ ΕCΧΑΤΟΝ ωCΤΕ ΕC
ΠΑΚΟΥCΑΙ ΟΝ ΘΝ ΦΩ
ΝΗC · ΑΝΟΥ ΟΤΙ ΚC CΥ
ΝΕΠΟΛΕΜΗCΕΝ ΤΩ
ΙΗΛ · ΚΑΙ ΕΠΕCΤΡΕΦΕ
ΙCΚΑΙ ΠΑCΙ ΗΛ ΜΕΤ ΑΥ

ΤΟΥ ΕΙC ΤΗΝ ΠΑΡΕΜΒ
ΛΗΝ ΕΙC ΤΑ ΑΛΓΑΛΑΝ ·
ΚΑΙ ΕΦΥΓΟΝ ΟΙ ΠΕΝΤΕ
ΒΑCΙΛΕΙC ΟΥΤΟΙ ΚΑΙ ΚΑΤΕ
ΚΡΥΒΗCΑΝ ΕΙC ΤΟ CΠΗ
ΛΑΙΟΝ ΤΟ ΕΝ ΜΑΚΗΔΑ
ΚΑΙ ΑΠΗΓΓΕΛΗ ΤΩ ΙΥ
ΛΕΓΟΝΤΕC ΕΥΡΗΝΤΑΙ
ΟΙ Ε ΒΑCΙΛΕΙC ΚΕΚΡΥ
ΜΕΝΟΙ ΕΝ ΤΩ CΠΗ
ΛΑΙΩ ΤΩ ΕΝ ΜΑΚΗΔΑ
ΚΑΙ ΕΙΠΕΝ ΙC ΚΥΛΙCΑΤΕ
ΛΙΘΟΥC ΜΕΓΑΛΟΥC ·
ΕΠΙ ΤΟ CΤΟΜΑ ΤΟΥ CΠΗ
ΛΑΙΟΥ ΚΑΙ ΚΑΤΑCΤΗ
CΑΤΕ ΕΠ ΑΥΤΟΥC ΑΝΔΡΑ
ΤΟΥC ΦΥΛΑCCΕΙΝ ΕΠΑΝ
ΤΟΥC ΥΜΕΙC ΔΕ ΜΗ ΕCΤΗ
ΚΑΤΕ ΚΑΤΑΔΙΩ
ΚΟΝΤΕC ΟΠΙCω ΤΩΝ
ΕΧΘΡΩΝ ΥΜΩΝ ΚΑΙ
ΚΑΤΑΛΑΒΕΤΕ ΤΗΝ ΟΥ
ΡΑΓΙΑΝ ΑΥΤΩΝ · ΚΑΙ ΜΗ
ΑΦΗΤΕ ΑΥΤΟΥC ΕΙCΕΛ
ΘΕΙΝ ΕΙC ΤΑC ΠΟΛΕΙC
ΑΥΤΩΝ ΠΑΡΑΔΕΔΩ
ΚΕΝ ΓΑΡ ΑΥΤΟΥC ΚC Ο ΘC
ΘΕΗ ΜΩΝ ΕΙC ΤΑC ΧΙ

36. CODEX MARCHALIANUS (Vat. Gr. 2125)

Cf. p. 74. Illustration (Jer. 24:11-19 [𝔐 35:11-19]) from P. Franchi de' Cavalieri and H. Lietzmann 1929.

The illustration gives a clear example of the peculiar features of this manuscript: a corrector has supplied in the margin the Hexaplaric readings which assimilate 𝕲 to 𝔐 together with their Hexaplaric signs. It demonstrates how frequently Origen had to supplement the Greek text of Jeremiah which is so much shorter than the Hebrew text. In Codex Marchalianus the source of these additions is sometimes given: the words εως της ημερας ταυτης οτι ηκουσαν της εντολης του πατρος αυτῶ are from Aquila (α') and Theodotion (θ'), while the phrase which 𝕲 lacks in v. 17 has been supplied from Theodotion's version.

Joseph Ziegler 1952: 34f. has demonstrated in his edition of Ezekiel that there are two stages of Hexaplaric influence in Codex Marchalianus: "The first was present in the exemplar copied by Q, whose scribe accepted the Hexaplaric additions without marking them as such; the second was the work of a corrector who identified the Hexaplaric elements already in the text with an asterisk and added missing ones in the margin of Q from another source which was also used by 88-Sy[h] (BHS: Syh)."[1] The original form of Q in Isaiah and the Minor Prophets, however, represents the Alexandrian group.

Note also in the illustration the omission of vv. 16–18 due to homoioteleuton (the omitted passage has been added in the lower margin), the corrections in the text (lines 14, 19, 24), and the abbreviation of frequently occurring words. The readings of Codex Marchalianus are noted in the Hexapla apparatus of Ziegler's edition of the Septuagint; cf. also his edition of Jeremiah (Ziegler 1957: 98ff.).

1. Ziegler 1952: 34f.

ＥＣＩＩＥΘΛΕ·ＣＩΕΡΟＹＣΑΛＨＬ·ＬＴΤ·ΠＰΟＣＥＷ
ΠΟＹＴＷＮΧΛＡΛＩＷＮ·ΚΛΙΕΤΤ·ΠΡΟＥＷ
ΠΟＹＴＨＣΔＹΝΛＵΕΩΙＴＷＮΛＥＣＹΡΙＷ
ΚΑΙΟ·ΙＫΗＣＷＵＥΝΕＫΕΙ·ΚΑＩΕΓΙΝΕＴΟ
ΛΟΓΟＣＫＹΠΡΟＣＵＥΛΓＷＮΟＹＴＷΕΛΠ
ＫＥΤΤΟΡΕＹΟＹΚΑΙΕΤΤΟΝΑＮＷΙΟＹΔＡ
ΚΑΙΤΟΙＣΚΑＴΟΙＫΟＹＣＩΝΙΛＨＬΟＹΠＨ
ΛＢΗΤΕΤΤＡＩΔＥΙＡΝ·ΑＫΟＹΕΙＮΤΟＹΕΛΟ
ΓΟＹＵΟＹ·ＥＣΤＨＣΑΝΡＨＵΑＹＩΟΙＩＷＮＡ
ΔＡＢＹΙΟＹΡＨΧΑＢＯ·ΕΝΕＴＥΙΛΑＴΟＴΟΙＣＥＰ
ＫＮΟＩＣΑＹＴΟＹＴＴΡΟＣΤΟＬＨΤΤＩΕＩＮΟＩＮΟ
ΚΑΙΟＹΚΕΤΤΙΟΝ·ΚΑＩΕΓＷΕΛΑΛＨＣΑΠΡΟ
ＹＵＡＣΟΡΘΡΟＹ·ΚΑΙΕΛΑΛＨＣΑΚΛΙΟＹΚＨΚＹ
ＣΑＴΕ·ΚΑＩΕＣΤＥΙΛΑΤΤΡΟＣＹＵＡＣΤΟＹＣ
ΔΟＹΛΟＹＣＵΟＹΤΟＹＣΤΤΡΟΦＨＴＡＣΛΕΓＷ
ΙΤΤΟＣΤΡΑΦＨＴＥＫΑＣΤＯＣΑΤΤΟＴΗＣΟΔΙＹ
ΑＹΤΟＹΤＨＣΤΤΟΝΗΡＡＣ·ΚＡＩΒΕΛΤΙΟΝＡ
ΤΤΟΙΗＣΑＴΕ·ＴΑΕΤΤΙΤΗΔＥＹＵΑＴＡＹＵＷＮ
ΚΑＩΟＹΤΤΟΡΕＹＥＣΘＥΕΤΤＩＣＷΘΕＩＷΝΕＴΕΡＷ
ＴＹΔΟＹΛΕＹＥΙＮＡＹΤΟΙＣ·ΚΑΙΟＩΚΗＣΕＴＥ
ΕＴΤΙΤＨＣΓＨＣＨＣΕΔＷΚΑΥＭΙΝ·ΚＡΙΤΟΙＣ
ΤΤΑＴΡΑＣＩΝＹＵＷΝ·ΚΑΙΟＹΚＥΚＬＩΝΑＴＥ
ΤΑＷΤＡＹＵＷΝ·ΚΑΙΟＹΚＨΚΟＹＣΑＴＥ
ＫΑＩΕＣΤＨＣΑΝΟＩΥＩΟＩΙＷΝΑΔＡＢＹΙΟＹΡＨΧΑＢ·
ΤＨＮＥΝΤΟΛＨΝΤΟＹΤΤＰＣＡＹΤＷΝＮＴＴΟΙＥＩ
ＫΑΦΟΤＩΕΝΕΤＥΙΛΑΤＯＡＹΤΟＩＣΟΤΤＨΡΑＹ
ΤＷΝΟＹΛＵＨＥΚＡΙΤΤＨΑΝＨΡΤＷΝＹＩＷ
ΙＷΝＡΔＡＢＹΙΟＹΡＨΧΑＢΤΤΑＰΕＣΤＨΚＷＣ
ＫΑＴΑΤΤΡΟＣＷΤΤΟＮＬＵΟＹΤΤΑＣΑＣΤΑＣＨＵΕΡＡＣ

ＯΔＥΛΛΟＣΟＹＴΕＣＯＹＫＨΚΟＹＣＡＮＬＵΟＹΔΙＡＴΟＹＴΟΟＹＴＷＣΕＩΠＥ
ＫＣΙΔΟＹΕΓＷΦΕΡＷΕΤＴΙΟＹΔＡＮ·ΚＡＩΕΤＴΙΤΟＹＣＫΑＴΟΙ
ΚΟＹΝＴＡＣΙΑＨＬＵΤΤΑΝＴΑＴＡΚΙΚＩ·ΕＬΑΛＨＣΑΕΤΤＡＹＴΟＹＣ
ΔΙＡＴΟＹΤΟΟＹΤＷＣＥＩΤΤΕΝＫＣΕΤΤＥΛＨＭＫΟＹＣＡＮΤΙΟＩＩＷ
ΝΛΑΛＢΥΙΟＹΡＨΧΑＢΤＨＮＥΝΤΟＬＨＮΤΟＹΤΤＡΤΡΟＣΕＩＳΤΩ

37. A SYRO-HEXAPLAR MANUSCRIPT OF A.D. 697

Cf. p. 57. Illustration (Exod. 27:10-15) from E. Tisserant 1914.

This manuscript (British Museum Ms. Add. 12134), like the one shown in pl. 39, is one of the hundreds of manuscripts brought to the British Museum in the years following 1839 from the monastery of St. Maria Deipara in the Nitrian desert of Lower Egypt. From the beginnings of Christian monasticism there has been a colony of monks in the Nitrian desert; toward the end of the fourth century they numbered into the thousands, and at times they exhibited a very lively intellectual life. The Syrian monastery of St. Maria Deipara in particular had a fine library which was considerably increased in the tenth century through the efforts of Abbot Moses of Nisibis. Later the monastery declined, and the books lay unused and largely neglected although they were zealously guarded by the few remaining uneducated monks until 1839, when an Englishman named Henry Tattam, and later others, acquired hundreds of manuscripts to take to England. An immediate result was a significant increase in Syriac studies.

The manuscript contains the book of Exodus, and according to its colophon it was written by a scribe named Lazarus in the year 1008 of the Seleucid era (i.e., A.D. 697); this is fairly close in time to the translation by Bishop Paul of Tella (616/617). As the illustration shows, the Hexaplaric signs are preserved in the text (obelos in lines 7, 13, 14f., 20; asterisk in line 12). The versions of Aquila, Symmachus, and Theodotion are noted in the margin. The long marginal note following line 2 gives an explanation of ψαλιδος (Syriac: *psalidis*); και ψαλιδος is written in the upper margin in red ink.

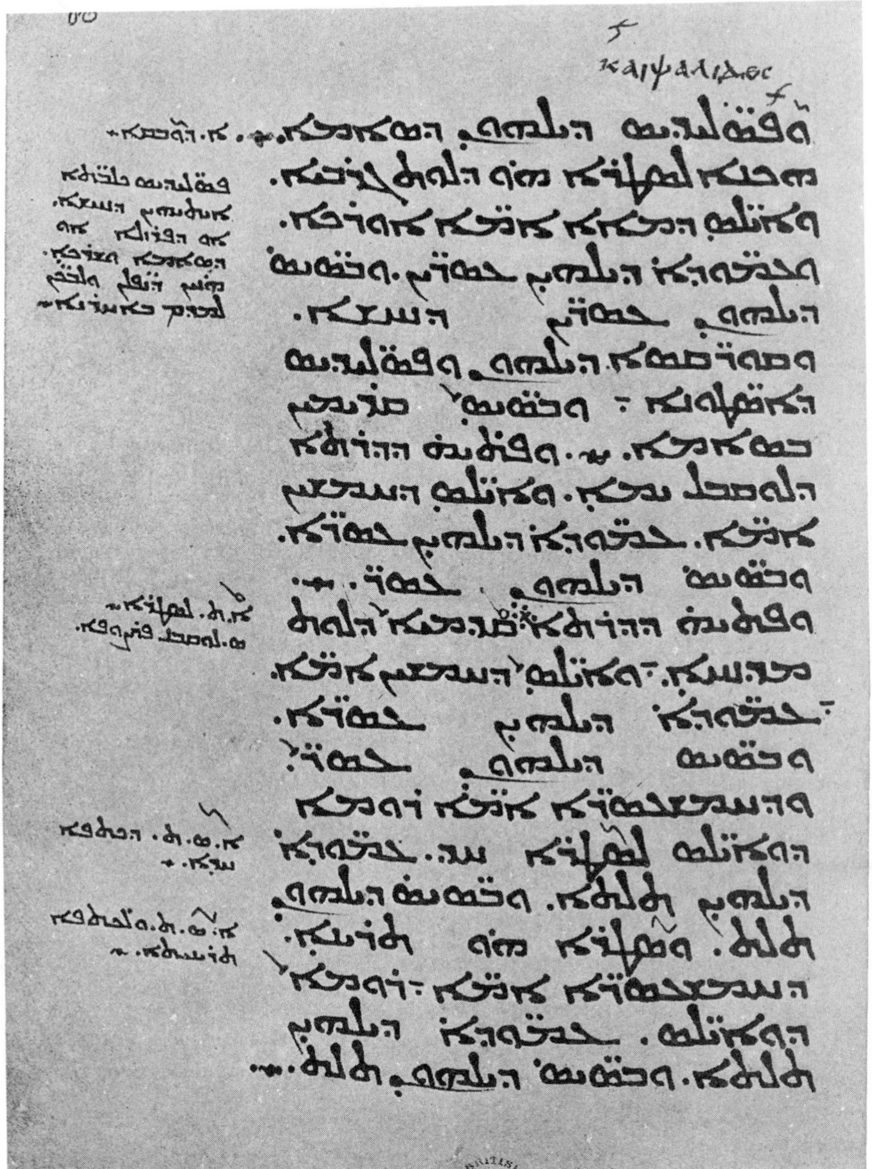

38. A CATENA MANUSCRIPT (Ninth Century A.D.)

Cf. p. 62. Illustration (Job 6:5) from P. Franchi de' Cavalieri and H. Lietz-mann 1929.

"In contrast to the more general term florilegium, catena refers to a compilation where exegetical excerpts from various authors are placed in a connected sequence like links in a chain to provide a commentary on a biblical book. This format enables the reader to formulate his own thoughts after a rapid survey of the views of the most important exegetes of the Church."[1] The Catenae are important for patristic as well as for textual studies: they preserve for the patristic scholar fragments of patristic writings that would otherwise be completely lost, and for the textual scholar they provide material relevant to the history of the text. Alfred Rahlfs has demonstrated that there was a special Catena recension of the Septuagint (cf. p. 62).

Marginal catenae and text catenae are distinguished by their formats. "The most elegant and perhaps the oldest form of the catena commentary is that of the marginal catena: the scribe wrote the sacred text in a closely confined space in the center of the page, leaving margins far wider than the space devoted to the text, in which the commentary was added in closely written lines"[2] (cf. illustration). "In the second principal form of catena commentary the Scripture verses were followed by their corresponding commentary so that while text and commentary alternated in sequence, they were written in the same area of the page."[3]

In the page illustrated the headings (lemmata) of the individual excerpts stand out because they are written in red ink (e.g., line 30 Διδύμου; line 33 καὶ μετ' ὀλίγα).[4]

1. H. Lietzmann 1897: 1.
2. *Ibid.,* 9.
3. *Ibid.,* 11.
4. G. Karo and H. Lietzmann 1902: 322.

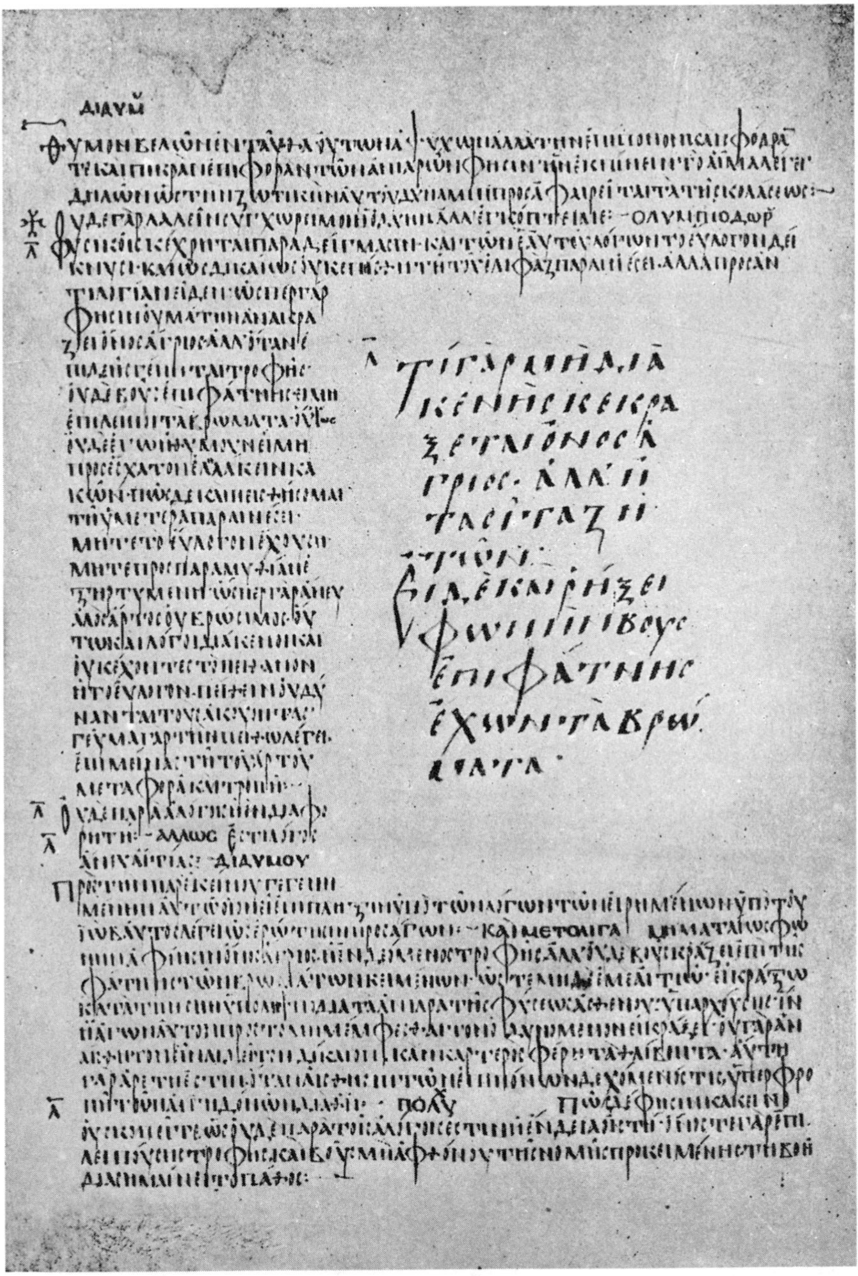
ΤΙΓΑΡΜΗΝΔΙΑ
ΚΕΝΗΣΚΕΚΡΑ
ΞΕΤΑΙΟΝΟΣΚΑ
ΓΡΙΟΣ· ΑΛΛΗ
ΤΑΣΙΤΑΖΗ
ΤΩΝ·
ΕΙΔΕΚΑΙΡΗΞΕΙ
ΦΩΝΗΝΒΟΥΣ
ΕΠΙΦΑΤΝΗΣ
ΕΧΩΝΤΑΒΡΩ
ΜΑΤΑ·

39. A PESHITTA MANUSCRIPT OF THE YEAR A.D. 464

Cf. p. 85. Illustration (Exod. 13:8-17) from W. Wright 1875-1883.

This West Syriac manuscript on parchment (British Museum Ms. Add. 14425) is one of the manuscripts from the Nitrian desert (cf. p. 206), and contains the books of Genesis, Exodus, Numbers, and Deuteronomy written in an early Estrangela script. The first two books were written in Amida (Diyarbekr) in the year 775 of the Seleucid era (i.e., A.D. 464) by a certain John. The other two books are probably from the same period but were written by a different scribe. This is one of the oldest known biblical manuscripts to contain a dated colophon. It is approximately the same age as the Greek Codex Alexandrinus. For its bearing on the problem of the Peshitta, cf. p. 85.

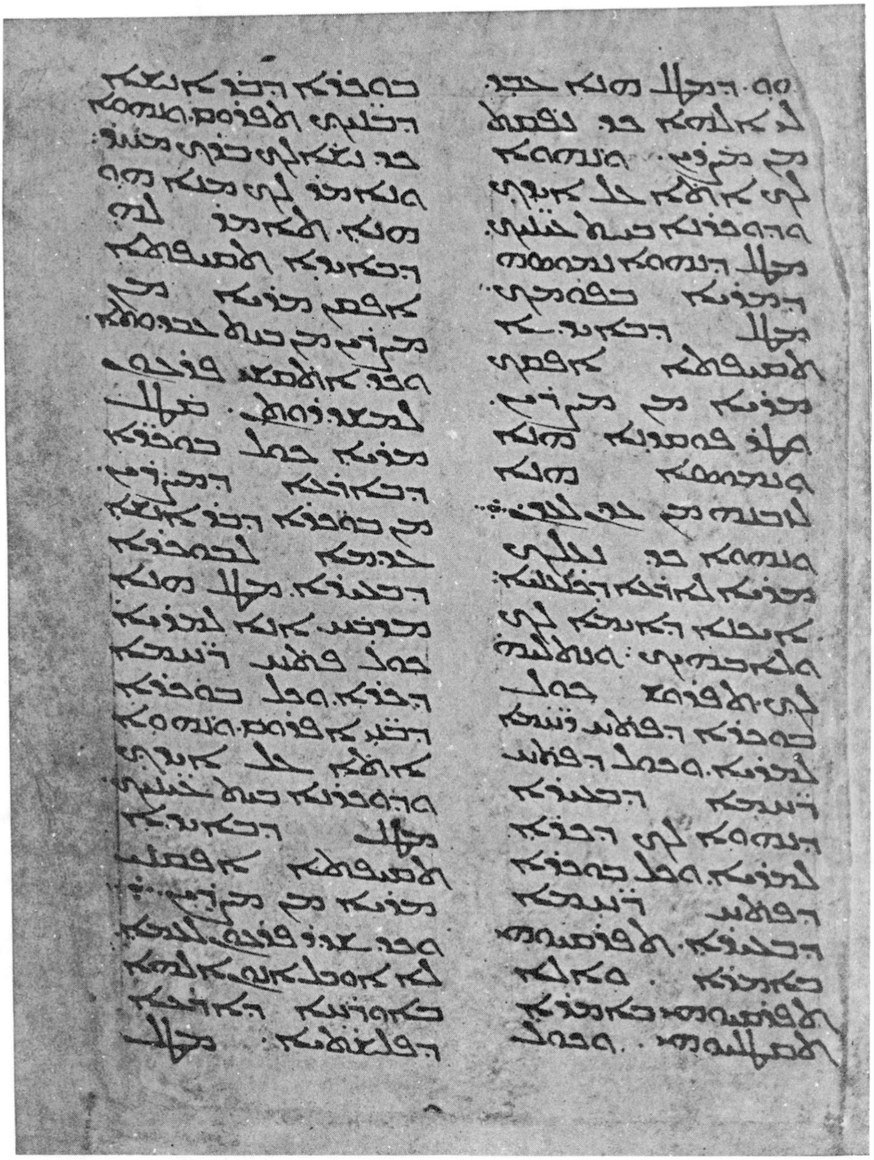

40. THE CONSTANCE FRAGMENTS
OF THE OLD LATIN PROPHETS

Cf. p. 93. Illustration (Ezek. 20:43-47 ひ) with the kind permission of Alban Dold.

Illustrated is a fragment of a sumptuous manuscript of the Prophets in Old Latin found by Alban Dold in the binding of Codex 191 of the Court Library of Fürstenberg at Donaueschingen. This manuscript of the Prophets, which was probably written in northern Italy in the fifth century, came into the Cathedral Library of Constance where it was taken apart (probably around 1450) and used in the binding of various parchment manuscripts. Fragments of this manuscript have been found in the bindings of twenty-six different manuscripts in Fulda, Darmstadt, Stuttgart, Donaueschingen, and the Benedictine monastery of St. Paul at Kärnten. In view of the scarcity of surviving Old Latin texts these fragments are of great importance: before their discovery the only known examples of the Latin Prophets before Jerome from *Bible* manuscripts were the fragments of the Würzberg palimpsest (cf. p. 93). Dold has published further fragments of the Old Latin Prophets from St. Gall (Ezekiel, Daniel, Minor Prophets) in the appendix of the book mentioned on p. 93.

Note the marginal glosses in a later hand (sixth century), which include Greek readings and other material.

MINUELLIS
UESTRIS·II
DIAUESTRA
QUIBUSCO·QUI
NABAMIN·N
EIS ETCED·
FACIES UE·
INDONINIB·S
MALINISUESTRIS
ETCOGNOSCE
TISQUIACCESUM
DMS·DUM IX
FACIOUOB·UN
NOMENMEU·
NONIFF·
TUR SECUN·
UNSUESTRA
MIALASE·

·MINABOE
·INEXSICON
·LIXA QUINERTHI
·NSICE
·KI ET
IMNABEC
·CESSALU
·BEC
·DICITDMS
·ECCAXEEN
·NIEIENEM
·OMEDAIN
·ANIUMUI
·M ETOM
·ICURUNA
·MELON

41. CODEX LUGDUNENSIS

Cf. p. 93. Illustration (Gen. 27:46–28:11) from a photograph kindly provided by A. Dold.

Codex Lugdunensis contains an Old Latin text, and is among the Old Latin evidence which has been discovered since Pierre Sabatier. It has had a checkered history. Originally in the Chapter Library of the Canon Counts of Lyons, it was later in the Municipal Library of Lyons. At some time it was divided into two parts, and the second part (now Ms. 1964) was removed from Lyons but recovered in 1895 and returned to Lyons. From the first part (now Ms. 403) seventy-nine leaves were stolen in 1847 by Count Libri[1] and sold to Lord Ashburnham, whose son learned of these circumstances in 1880 and generously returned them to the Library.

According to Ulysse Robert 1881 the manuscript was written by three different scribes. It "was used for liturgical reading, hence the variety of marginal notes in various hands from various periods, yet all probably native to Lyons. Two whole readings have been inserted: 1 Kgs. 21 for the Traditio Symboli, and 1 Pet. 2 for the Cathedra Petri; these follow the Vulgate text. Similarly the numerous corrections in the individual sections made by later hands (partly in Tironian notes, a form of Latin shorthand) are largely assimilations to the Vulgate" (B. Fischer 1951: 6). These assimilations are significant for the history of the Old Latin, which was eventually supplanted by the Vulgate.

---

1. The notorious Count Guglielmo Libri Carrucci della Sommaia (b. Florence, 1803, d. Fiesole, 1869, a naturalized Frenchman) amassed a considerable personal collection while commissioned to make an inventory of manuscripts in the public libraries of France. Cf. M. B. Stern and L. Rostenberg 1982.

DIXITAUTEMREBECCA	ERISINECCLESIISCEN	CHANNANEORUMEO
ADISAACDESTINAUIANI	TIUMETDETTIBIBE	QUODAUDIERITIACOB
MONICOPROPIERFI	NEDICTIONEMPATRIS	PATREMSUUMETMA
LIASFILIORUMCHEI	MEHABRAHAEETSE	TREMSUAMETABIE
STACCEPERITIACOB	MINITUOPOSTTE	RITINMESOPOTAMIA
UXOREMAFILIABUS	HEREDITARETERRA	ETTUNCPOSTQUAM
TERRACHINUSUIQUO	HABITATIONISTUAE	UIDITESAUQUIAMA
MIHIUIUERE	QUAMDEONDSAT	LIGNASUNTFILIAE
UOCAUITAUTEMISAC	RAHAE	CHANNANEORUM
IACOBADSEETBENE	ETDIMISITISACIACOB	ANTEISACPATREM
DIXITCUMEIPRAECE	ETABIITINMESOPO	SUUMABIITADISMA
PITCIDICENSNON	TAMIAMADLABAN	HELETACCEPITUXORE
ACCIPIESUXOREM	FILIUMBATHUELIS	FILIAMISMAELFILII
AFILIABUSCHANNA	SYRIFRATREMREBEC	ABRAHAESOROREM
NEORUMSEDSURCE	CAEMATRISIACOB	NABCOTHADUXORE
ETUADCINMESOPO	ETESAU	RESSUASSIBIUXORE
TAMIAMMNDOMU	UIDITAUTEMESAUQUIA	LCTEXIITIACOBAPUTEO
BATHUELISPATRIS	BENEDIXITISACIACOB	IURAMENTIUTIRET
MATRISTUAEETACCI	ETQUIAABIITINMESO	INCHARRAMETPER
PEINDETIBIUXORE	POTAMIAMSYRIAE	UENITINQUENDAM
EXFILIAB LABEFPATRIS	ACCIPERESIBIINDE	LOCUMETMANSIBI
MATRISTUAEETAC	UXOREMNEOQUOD	OCCEDERATENIM
CIPETIBIINDEUXORE	BENEDIXERITEUM	ACCEPITLAPIDEM
DSAUTEMMEUSBE	ETPRAECEPERITEI	EXLAPIDIBUSLOCI
NEDICATTEETAUGAT	DICENSNONACCIPIES	ETPOSUITADCAPUT
TEETREPLEATTECI	UXOREMAFILIABUS	SUUMETDORMIUIT

42. A VULGATE PALIMPSEST
FROM THE FIFTH CENTURY A.D.

Cf. pp. 95ff. Illustration (Judg. 5:15-18) from a photograph kindly provided by Alban Dold, with the permission of the Herzog August Library, Wolfenbüttel.

Among the books once treasured by the monastery of Bobbio in northern Italy there were two eighth-century manuscripts of Isidore, one of which found its way into the Vatican Library and the other into the Herzog August Library at Wolfenbüttel. These manuscripts were written on the parchment leaves of an older manuscript whose texts had been erased, one of which was a fifth-century Bible in uncial script, and another a sixth-century Bible in half-uncials. These older manuscripts followed the Vulgate text; Alban Dold published their texts after deciphering them with the aid of photographic techniques developed for the study of palimpsests at the Abbey of Beuron.[1]

The illustration shows a page of the old uncial manuscript, "probably one of the finest manuscripts of the Bible, or more precisely of a part of the Bible, remaining from antiquity" (Dold). The greater part of Judges and thirteen verses of Ruth have survived. The manuscript may have contained only these books. It was most likely written in Italy. A comparison of this earliest known text of Jerome's version with the official Vulgate (Vg) and with Codex Amiatinus (A) yields the following results: "In about 600 passages our manuscript agrees with (A) in a difference from the Vulgate about 200 times, it agrees with the (Vg) where (A) differs about 180 times, and in 220 passages it differs from both (Vg) and (A) with a reading of its own which differs distinctly although admittedly only slightly."[2]

The uncial and the above-mentioned half-uncial manuscript (Job 1:1–15:24) are of great importance for the recovery of the earliest form of Jerome's text. "These two manuscripts of such great age provide us with a most valuable link between the lost original of Jerome and the Codex Amiatinus, which was hitherto the earliest known witness of the Vulgate text. The total impression of the writing suggests further that in these two manuscripts we have copies which were executed with incomparable concern and devotion, which is itself the best guarantee of textual quality and fidelity."[3]

1. A. Dold 1931.
2. *Ibid.*, IL.
3. *Ibid.*, LVII.

BORAETBARAACHESTICIASUN

SEMIIIII QUIIIIIASIIIIPRAE

CEPSABARAIKUIIISCIIIGERI

DIIIISOCONTRASCRIBENDISCNA

ANIMORUMREPERIA

CONTEKATIOR

QUAEHABITASINTEROUOSTERII

MOSITIAUDIASSIENHOTORECUM

DICITSOCONTRASCRIBENTISCNA

LANIMORUMREPERIA

CONTENTIOEST

EXTATILTRANSTORONEMQUIES

AGEHATELDANUAGABAINAUIBUS

ASERHABITABATINLITOREMARIS

ETINIORTIBUSMORABATUR

NULLONUIEROMINEIIALIN

OBTCHERETUISANIMASABSUAS

43. CODEX AMIATINUS

Illustration (Ps. 22[ᵭ 21]:25–25[24]:5) from a photograph kindly provided by the Biblioteca Medicea-Laurenziana.

This well-known and highly valued codex of the Vulgate, which is named after the Abbey of Monte Amiata where it once belonged, is of English origin. It was commissioned by Ceolfrid, abbot of the monasteries of Jarrow and Wearmouth in Northumberland, which were under the direct control of the Holy See. Ceolfrid intended to take it on his last journey to Rome as a gift to the Pope. The abbot died on his journey at Langres (A.D. 716), but some of his companions delivered the codex to Rome. It is the only codex to survive of the three which Ceolfrid commissioned to be written in his monasteries between 690 and 716: all three were in "the new translation," i.e., the translation by Jerome.[1]

In its outer form and in its artistic decoration Codex Amiatinus follows the example of the great codex of Cassiodorus, an illuminated manuscript with illustrations and tables which contained Jerome's revision of the Hexaplar text in the Old Testament. It was bought by Benedict Biscop and Ceolfrid while in Rome in 678, and brought to Jarrow. Contrary to earlier belief, neither the text nor the auxiliary material in Amiatinus is related to Cassiodorus.[2]

Bonifatius Fischer says of the text of Amiatinus:

> Several different manuscripts served as exemplars. A demonstrably inferior Irish text served for the Psalms, a good Neapolitan manuscript for the Gospels, and one with local color for the Catholic Epistles; for most books of the Bible there were good manuscripts available, probably from Italy. The monks at Jarrow edited their material deliberately. They were quite capable of recognizing good texts and choosing their models. Where only inferior texts were available they would attempt to improve them; cf. especially Tobit, also Psalms and Acts, and occasionally even books with good texts.
>
> These corrections of the biblical text may be understood in connection with the commentaries of the Venerable Bede, who was also among the monks at Jarrow when Amiatinus and its sister codices were in production there.[3]

---

1. Single leaves of one of these two lost codices have been found since 1909 (some had been used as "wrappers for estate papers") and are now in the British Library.
2. Cf. also B. Fischer 1962: 57-79.
3. *Ibid.,* 78f.

qm̄nondispexitneqcontempsit\
modestiampauperis\
etnonabsconditfaciemsuamabeo\
etcumclamaretadeumexaudiuit\
apudtelausmeainecclesiamulta\
uotameareddaminconspectu\
timentiumeum\
comedentmitesetsaturabuntur\
laudabuntdnmquaerenteseum\
uiuetcorduestruminsempiternum\
recordabunturetconuertentur\
addnmomnesfinesterrae\
etadorabuntcorameouniuerse\
cognationesgentium\
quiadniestregnumetdomina\
bitur gentium\
comederunt etadorauerunt\
omnespingues'terrae\
antefaciemeiuscurbabuntgenu\
uniuersiquidiscenduntinpuluere\
etanimaeiusipsiuiuet\
etsemenseruietei\
narrabunturdnoingeneratione\
uenientetadorabunturiustitiae\
populoquinasciturquasfecit\
psalmusdauiduoxecclesiae\
postbaptismum\
22 dnspascitmeetnihilmihideerit\
inpascuisherbarumadlocauitme\
superaquasrefectionis\
enutriuitme\
animammeamrefecit\
duxitmesupersemitasiustitiae\
propternomenuumsuum\
sedetsiambulaueroinualleoguas\
nontimeromalumqmtumecum\
circauiaetbaculustuusipsa\
consolabunturme\
ponescorammemensamin\
aduersohistrium...\
inpinguastiooleoexpudmitum...\
calixmeusinebrians...\
sedetpbenignitasetmisericor\
diasubsequiturme...

omnibusdiebusuitemeae\
ethabitaboindomodni\
inlongitudineinedierum\
psalmusprimasabbati\
confirmauxtiopopulicredentis\
portaequasdicitpeccatauel\
infernuuoxxpidiligentibusse\
23 dniestterraetplenitudoekis\
orbiset habitatoreseius\
quiipsesupermaria fundauiteum\
etsuperfluminxstabiliuitillm̄\
quisascendetinmontemdni\
etquisstabitinlocosicoeius\
innocensmanibetmundocorde\
quinonacceauitfrustra\
animamsuam\
etnoniurauitdoloso\
accipietbenedictionemadno\
etmisericordiamadosalutari\
haecestgeneratioquaerentumeu\
quaerentiumfaciemiacobsemper\
leuateportaecapituaestiras\
eteleuamini ianuaesempiternae\
etingrediaturrexgloriae\
quisestiste rexgloriae\
dnsfortisetpotensdns\
fortisinproelio\
leuateportaecapitagestra\
eteregitoianuaesempiternae\
etingrediaturrexgloriae\
quisestisterexgloriae\
dnsexercituumipseestrexgloriae\
psalmusdauidcanticum\
24 adtednecanimammeamleuaui\
dsmeusinteconfisussum\
neconfundar\
nelaetenturinimicidei\
seduniuersiquisperantinte\
nonconfundantur\
confundanturquiiniquagerunt\
frustra\
uiastuasdneostendemihi\
semitastuasdoceme\
deducmeinueritatetua

44. A COPTIC PAPYRUS CODEX

Cf. pp. 100f. Illustration (Deut. 34:11f.; Jonah 1:1-4) from E. A. Wallis Budge 1912.

In 1911 the British Museum acquired this papyrus codex found in Upper Egypt; it contains extensive parts of Deuteronomy, the whole book of Jonah, and the larger part of the Acts of the Apostles. It is to be dated in the fourth century A.D., and is thus of very great age.

The illustration shows the conclusion of the book of Deuteronomy: the title is written in large letters at the end of the book. Following it is a blessing in Greek on scribe and reader, and then the beginning of the book of Jonah.

ⲧⲙ̄ⲯⲁⲗⲧⲏⲣ ⲟⲩ.....ⲩⲕⲁⲍⲏ
ⲛⲟϭ ⲛ̄ϣⲡⲏⲣⲉ ⲁ.....ⲟⲓⲭⲉⲧ
ⲭⲟⲟⲩ ⲉⲛⲧⲁⲙ̄ⲯⲩ ⲥ̄ⲛⲥⲁⲗⲩⲙ
ⲡⲉⲙⲧⲟ ⲉⲃⲟⲗ ⲙ̄ⲡⲓⲥⲣⲁⲏⲗ
ⲧⲏⲣⲩ̄ ⲋⲋⲋⲋⲋⲋⲋⲋⲋ

⳥⳥⳥⳥⳥⳥⳥⳥⳥   ⳥⳥⳥⳥⳥⳥⳥⳥

ⲇⲧⲉⲩⲧⲉ
ⲣⲟⲛⲟⲙⲓⲟⲛ
ⲉⲓⲣⲏⲛⲏ ⲛⲧⲱ ⲅⲣⲁⳤⲁⲛⲧⲓ
ⲕⲁⲓⲧⲱ
ⲁⲛⲁⲅⲓⲛⲱⲥⲕⲟⲛⲧⲓ

ⲓⲱⲛⲁⲥ

ⲡϣⲁϫⲉ ⲙ̄ⲡϫⲟⲉⲓⲥ ⲁⲩϣⲱⲡⲉ ϣⲁ
ⲓⲱⲛⲁⲥ ⲉⲡϣⲏⲣⲉ ⲛ̄ⲁⲙⲁⲑⲟⲥ ⲉϥϫⲱ
ⲙ̄ⲙⲟⲥ ϫⲉ ⲧⲱⲟⲩ ⲛⲅ̄ⲃⲱⲕ ⲉⲅⲣⲁ
ⲉⲧ ⲛⲓⲛⲉⲩⲏ ⲧⲛⲟϭ ⲙ̄ⲡⲟⲗⲉⲓⲥ ⲛⲅ̄
ⲕⲏⲣⲩⲭⲉ ⲉⲅⲣⲁ ⲛ̄ϩ̄ⲏⲧⲥ̄ ϫⲉ ⲁⲡⲉ ⲑⲟ
ⲉⲓⲱ ⲛ̄ⲧⲉⲥⲕⲁⲕⲓⲁ ⲉⲓ ⲉⲅⲣⲁⲓ ⲙ̄ⲡⲁⲙ̄
ⲧⲟ ⲉⲃⲟⲗ· ⲁⲩⲱ ⲁϥⲧⲱⲟⲩⲛ ⲛ̄ϭⲓ
ⲓⲱⲛⲁⲥ ⲉⲡⲱⲧ ⲉⲑⲁⲣ ⲥⲉⲓⲥ ⲛ̄ϩⲁ
ⲣⲙ̄ ⲡⲓⲧⲟ ⲙ̄ⲡϫⲟⲉⲓⲥ· ⲁⲩ ⲱ ⲁϥⲃⲱⲕ
ⲉⲅⲣⲁⲓ ⲉⲓⲟⲡⲡⲏ ⲁϥϭⲛ̄ ⲟⲩ ⲭⲟⲉⲓ ⲉϥ ⲛⲁ
ⲥⲟ ⲛ̄ ⲣⲉ ⲃⲁ ⲣ ⲥⲉⲓⲥ ⲁ ⲩ ⲱ ⲧⲉ ⲧ ϩ ⲏ ⲗ ⲉ ⲧ
ϯ ⲗ ⲉ ⲃ ⲣ ⲟ ⲩ ⲉ ⲥⲟ ⲛ̄ ⲣ ⲏ ⲙ̄ ⲙ ⲓ ⲉ ⲃ ⲁ ⲣⲥⲉ
ⲙ ⲛ ⲁ ⲣ ⲏ ⲙ̄ ⲡ ϫ ⲟ ⲓ ⲙ̄ ⲡ ϫ ⲟ ⲉ ⲓ ⲥ· ⲁ ⲩ ⲱ ⲁ
ⲉ ⲓ ⲁ ⲗ ⲏ ⲧ ⲁ ⲩ ⲙ ⲉ ⲟ ⲩ ⲛ ⲟ ϭ ⲛ̄ ⲧ ⲏ ⲟ
ⲉ ⲅ ⲣ ⲁ ⲓ ⲥ ⲓ ⲉ ⲃ ⲁ ⲗ ⲗ ⲁ ⲉ ⲥ ⲁ ⲁ ⲅ ⲛ ⲟ ⲥ ϥ

45. AN ETHIOPIC MANUSCRIPT
(Paris, Bibliothèque Nationale, Eth. 11, fol. 70a)
Cf. p. 102. Illustration (Sus. 1–5) from O. Löfgren 1927.

The manuscript from which this illustration is taken contains the books of Job and Daniel. Löfgren describes it in this way: "Palaeographically this manuscript is of great interest. Its general appearance and many details bespeak its antiquity. The large (about 6 mm. high) angular script which differs little from the lapidary style of the inscriptions; the simple decoration, limited to rows of dots, St. Anthony's cross, and similar designs in the margin; the two-column page format — these all place S (i.e., this manuscript) in the relatively small group of ancient Ethiopic manuscripts which was succeeded about the middle of the fifteenth century by a new type with a more beautiful style of writing and a richer ornamentation" (O. Löfgren 1927: xxii). It was probably written between 1300 and 1400. "The care with which this manuscript was written, and its freedom from any substantial correction or revision suggests that we have in it a valuable witness to the text as it circulated about 1300, probably not yet revised" (Löfgren 1927: xxv).

While this manuscript preserves the original Ethiopic version, in later manuscripts the traces of various processes of revision may be observed: some indicate revision from Syro-Arabic sources, beginning in the fourteenth century (a popular recension); some point to a Hebrew base for revision in the fifteenth or sixteenth century (an academic recension). Naturally for the textual criticism of the Septuagint only those manuscripts are significant which preserve the original, Old Ethiopic form of this daughter text of the Septuagint.

ዘደነ ኤ ልነ	ደ አኅ ጠልጎሬ
ቢ ይ᎓	ቤቹ
ወህሎ አሐዪ	ወይልጽሎነ
ኅእሪ ዘዌነ	ቢሁ አዬሁዉ
ብሪ ባቢሎ፤	እክዉ ወእቺ
ወከዉ ኢሁአ	ይክብሪ አሙ፠
ቄም ወእወከ	ሎዉ
ቡ ዘእኪተ ኧ	ወአከተሪአዪ
ነተክዉ ስክ፫	ክልኤቱ ሪባና
ወለቱ ኪልዊ	ተ መድልዋንዘ
ዪ ዉሠ ጕዬቱ	ወእቱ ባጭቱ
ጠቄ ወትፈሪ ሁ	እ ለ በእንቲ አህ
እግዚ ለ ብሐ	ዉ᎓ ነገሪ እግ
ሪ᎓᎓ ወእዝ ጣዊ	ዚ ኢ᎓ ብ ሐሪ᎓
ሃ፫᎓ ጸ ድቃነ᎓	ክዉ አይ ባቢ
ወጠሁሪ ዋ በ	ሎነ᎓ ወ ይ እቱ᎓
ወ በ ጮ᎓ ሰሪ	ነ ዊ እቱ᎓ ኢዉ
ተ ዉ ኤ ወ ኢ ይ	ሪ ባ ና ተ መ ደ ል
ዋ ቿ ም ፡ በ ኅ ል ᎓	ዋ ነ ᎓ እ ለ ይ ብ ᎌ
ጠ ቄ ወ በ ᎓ ዐ ጸ	ያ ዐ ቅ በ ዉ ለ

46. AN ARABIC MANUSCRIPT
(British Museum arab. 1475 [Add. 26116])

Cf. p. 104. Illustration (Job 22:12–23:2) from W. Wright 1875-1883.

The variety of Arabic versions of Job, of which a page of the oldest is shown here, is representative of Arabic versions of the Bible as a whole.

There are at least four different versions of Job, one of which is among the earliest documents of Christian Arabic literature. The manuscript Brit. Mus. arab. 1475, which contains extensive portions of it, was written in the first half of the ninth century, probably at the monastery of St. Sabas. The version itself is from a Syro-Hexaplar base.

The author of another version of Job is known: Pethion (Fatyun ibn Aiyub), who was active as a translator in Baghdad probably about the middle of the ninth century; he is also credited with translations of Sirach and the Prophets. Pethion's text of Job is divided into fifteen chapters and (according to the London manuscript) claims to be translated from the Hebrew; actually the translator worked from a Syriac exemplar. Other versions of Job go back to the Peshitta and to the Coptic (G. Graf 1944: 126).

العلماء حكمه والديرينقلبوز بالعزه يدلهم واب ملت
مزايرتك ردبالهويد وصنفت ارالصواب حول سلك
وسرالفط وان البحاب كل سر اعمالك لا زلا نزيد
ولد لما طراف الارص مزيد وسالكي العسقه
مزلحط الديد لمتى كم الصاكيز ولم يدرد
بانك نوحربلا وقت مز الديكمل الانقاد على
اجبال حدلك يمنك المتمير الدين يهمولوا
ما الديز يصنع بها الرب واسرحلب علينا الك بك
كل الديز ملو ايو تهم مز الجير وموا مرد اتمه
يعمر بعده مزالرب وارطاكيز سطا وں
البهم ويصحكوا ومزكاز عبر هد بك لسمه
لهم بار سرمع ملك كواممم وبرکنهم زادل
النار كاطرح مز قمك ما لا ينبغا واكد قول
الرب على ملبك لانك رحمت وحمعه مريد
الرب يبما عد مزصعا مك الاوجام وكسمك
ملي محمره هوبه وتحوطبك اوديه الجيم ويعسد
بانك الكل وحلصد مزالعد واو نصوك
نيعا سله قصه مسلوكه ولعوم مريدى الرب
مسلمحمر وسطر الى السما هوكك صية واذا
طلب البه ليسمعك ويعطك وبسره الانذار
وبردعليك طعام الصلاح ولكور الصوادى
للعمر ى طوفك بانك ابصع بكسك بزيديه
وبطرج عند الجوه وبطا مرعسد بزيديه
وهو ليسمك وهوسلم الركى ورد عليك مواند
احاب ايوب وقال
اما اعلم بان نوحى بزيد يد هم صادت زميله

47. THE COMPLUTENSIAN POLYGLOT

Illustration (Gen. 21:28–22:3) from the Bodleian copy, with the kind permission of the Bodleian Library, Oxford.

The polyglots formed a useful tool for textual criticism by printing the original text with translations of the Bible in parallel columns to facilitate their comparison. The earliest polyglot, named the Complutensian after Complutum (Alcala de Henares), its place of publication, was edited in 1514-17 by Francisco Ximenez, archbishop of Toledo and founder of the University of Alcala; it was not published until 1522 due to a delay of papal authorization. Jewish converts were engaged to work on the Old Testament because at that time they alone had the training necessary for the work: among them was the renowned Alfonso de Zamora, professor of Oriental languages at Alcala from 1512.

The Hebrew text of the Complutensian Polyglot reveals some interesting deviations from normal usage. The Tiberian accent system is represented only by the athnach, yet here it is not used for the principal caesura alone, so that it may occur more than once in any verse (e.g., Gen. 22:3 [cf. illustration, lines 24-26]); nor is it written with the accented syllable, but after the word. The maqqeph is completely lacking. Hatephs appear only rarely: usually the vowel is written without the shewa; cf. in the illustration אֱלֹהִים, אֲשֶׁר [line 27], אֲצִי [line 26], etc. These peculiarities do not reflect any editorial caprice, as might be suspected. Rather it is the usage of ancient manuscripts that the editors appeal to as their precedent. Since the peculiarities mentioned are characteristic of the simple Babylonian pointing system (cf. p. 22), we may infer that the editors of the polyglot made use of Hebrew manuscripts of the Bible with Babylonian pointing along with manuscripts of the Ben Asher tradition. These may have been intended by the "*vetustissima exemplaria* (very ancient copies)" used by the editors, which have influenced the form of the Hebrew text printed in the polyglot.[1] These manuscripts are now lost: they were probably destroyed in ignorance of their value. For the Greek text of the Complutensian polyglot, cf. p. 75.

Of the later polyglots, the most comprehensive is the London Polyglot, edited by Brian Walton in 1654-57.

---

1. P. E. Kahle 1954b: 749f.

Trāsla. Gre. lxx. cū interp. latina.

et statuit abraā septē agnas ouiū
καὶ ἔστησεν ἀβραὰμ ἑπτὰ ἀμνάδας προβάτων
solas. et dixit abimelech abraam. quid
μόνας. καὶ εἶπεν ἀβιμέλεχ τῷ ἀβραάμ. τί εἰ-
sunt septē agne ouiū harū: quas
σιν αἱ ἑπτὰ ἀμνάδες τῶν προβάτων τούτων, ἃς
statuisti solas. et dixit qz septē agnas
ἔστησας μόνας. καὶ εἶπεν ὅτι τὰς ἑπτὰ ἀμνά-
accipies a me: vt sint mihi in testimoniū:
δας λήψῃ παρ' ἐμοῦ, ἵνα ὦσί μοι εἰς μαρτύριον,
qz ego fodi puteū hunc. ꝓpter hoc vo-
ὅτι ἐγὼ ὤρυξα τὸ φρέαρ τοῦτο. διὰ τοῦτο ἐπω-
cauit nomē loci illius: puteū iu-
νόμασε τὸ ὄνομα τοῦ τόπου ἐκείνου, φρέαρ ὁρ-
ramenti. qz illic iurauerūt ambo: et posuerūt
κισμοῦ. ὅτι ἐκεῖ ὤμοσαν ἀμφότεροι, καὶ ἔθηκαν
fedus sup puteū iuramēti. surrexit aūt abi
διαθήκην ἐπὶ τὸ φρέαρ τοῦ ὁρκισμοῦ. ἀνέστη δὲ ἀβι-
melech et ochozad pronubus eius et phi
μέλεχ καὶ ὀχοζὰθ ὁ νυμφαγωγὸς αὐτοῦ καὶ ὁ φι-
chol princeps exercitus eius: et re
χὼλ ὁ ἀρχιστράτηγος τῆς δυνάμεως αὐτοῦ, καὶ ἀ-
uersi sunt in terrā philisthijm. et plan-
πέστρεψαν εἰς τὴν γῆν τῶν φυλιστιείμ. καὶ ἐφύ-
tauit abraam agrū sup puteū iu
τευσεν ἀβραὰμ ἄρουραν ἐπὶ τῷ φρέατι τοῦ ὅρ-
ramēti. et inuocauit ibi nomē dñi: deus
κου. καὶ ἐπεκαλέσατο ἐκεῖ τὸ ὄνομα κυρίου, θεὸς
eternus. habitauit aūt abraā in terra phi-
αἰώνιος. παρῴκησε δὲ ἀβραὰμ ἐν τῇ γῇ τῶν φυ-
listiim dies multos.
λιστιείμ ἡμέρας πολλάς.

Ca. 22.

A Et factū ē post verba hec: deus
Καὶ ἐγένετο μετὰ τὰ ῥήματα ταῦτα, ὁ θεὸς
tentauit abraā. et dixit ei: abraam
Judith 8.c. Heb. 11 d. ἐπείρασε τὸν ἀβραάμ. καὶ εἶπεν αὐτῷ, ἀβραὰμ
abraā. et dixit. ecce ego. et dixit: accipe fi-
ἀβραάμ. καὶ εἶπεν, ἰδοὺ ἐγώ. καὶ εἶπεν, λάβε τὸν υἱ-
liū tuū dilectū: quē dilexisti isaac: et
όν σου τὸν ἀγαπητόν, ὃν ἠγάπησας τὸν ἰσαάκ, καὶ
vade in terrā excelsā. et offer eū
πορεύθητι εἰς τὴν γῆν τὴν ὑψηλήν. καὶ ἀνένεγκε αὐ-
ibi in holocaustū sup vnū montiū: quos
τὸν ἐκεῖ εἰς ὁλοκάρπωσιν ἐφ' ἓν τῶν ὀρέων, ὧν ἄν
tibi dixero. surgēs aūt abraā mane strauit
σοι εἴπω. ἀναστὰς δὲ ἀβραὰμ τὸ πρωῒ ἐπέσαξεν
asinū suū. assumpsit aūt secū duos pue-
τὴν ὄνον αὐτοῦ. παρέλαβε δὲ μεθ' ἑαυτοῦ δύο παῖ-
ros: et isaac filiū suū. et scindēs ligna in
δας, καὶ ἰσαὰκ τὸν υἱὸν αὐτοῦ. καὶ σχίσας ξύλα εἰς
holocaustū: surgens abijt. et venerūt in
ὁλοκάρπωσιν, ἀναστὰς ἐπορεύθη. καὶ ἦλθον εἰς
locū quē dixit ei deus: die
τὸν τόπον ὃν εἶπεν αὐτῷ ὁ θεός, τῇ ἡμέρᾳ

Trāsla. B. Hiero.

Et statuit abraam septem agnas gregis seorsū. Cui dixit abimelech. Quid sibi volunt septem agne iste: quas stare fecisti seorsum? At ille. Septem inquit agnas accipies de manu mea: vt sint mihi in testimoniū: qm̄ ego fodi puteū istū. Idcirco vocatus ē locus ille bersabee: quia ibi vterqꝫ iurauit. Et inierunt fedus ꝓ puteo iuramēti. Surrexit aūt abimelech et phicol princeps exercitus eius: reuersiqꝫ sūt ī terrā palestiorū. Abraā vero plātauit nemus in bersabee: et inuocauit ibi nomen dñi dei eterni: et fuit colonus terre palestiorū diebus multis.

Ca. 22.

Que postquā gesta sunt: tentauit deus abraam: et dixit ad eū. Abraam abraam. At ille rñdit. ad sū. ait illi. Tolle filiū tuū vnigenitum quem diligis isaac: et vade in terrā visionis: atqꝫ ibi offeres eū in holocaustum sup vnū montiū: quem monstrauero tibi. Igitur abraā de nocte consurgens strauit asinū suum ducens secum duos iuuenes et isaac filiū suum. Cumqꝫ concidisset ligna in holocaustum: abiit ad locum quem preceperat ei deus. Die autem

Tex. Heb. Gen. Ca. xxi.

וַיַּצֵּב אַבְרָהָם אֶת שֶׁבַע כִּבְשֹׂת |
הַצֹּאן לְבַדְּהֶן: וַיֹּאמֶר אֲבִימֶלֶךְ אֶל | בָּדַד
אַבְרָהָם מָה הֵנָּה שֶׁבַע כְּבָשֹׂת |
הָאֵלֶּה אֲשֶׁר הִצַּבְתָּ לְבַדָּנָה: | יָצַב
וַיֹּאמֶר כִּי אֶת שֶׁבַע כְּבָשֹׂת תִּקַּח |
מִיָּדִי בַּעֲבוּר תִּהְיֶה לִּי לְעֵדָה כִּי | עֵד הָיָה
חָפַרְתִּי אֶת הַבְּאֵר הַזֹּאת: עַל כֵּן |
קָרָא לַמָּקוֹם הַהוּא בְּאֵר שָׁבַע כִּי | קוּם
שָׁם נִשְׁבְּעוּ שְׁנֵיהֶם: וַיִּכְרְתוּ | שָׁבַע
בְרִית בִּבְאֵר שָׁבַע וַיָּקָם אֲבִימֶלֶךְ | קוּם
וּפִיכֹל שַׂר צְבָאוֹ וַיָּשֻׁבוּ אֶל אֶרֶץ | שׂוּר שׁוּב
פְּלִשְׁתִּים: וַיִּטַּע אֶשֶׁל בִּבְאֵר | נָטַע
שָׁבַע וַיִּקְרָא שָׁם בְּשֵׁם יְהוָה אֵל | קָרָא
עוֹלָם: וַיָּגָר אַבְרָהָם בְּאֶרֶץ | צָלַם גּוּר
פְּלִשְׁתִּים יָמִים רַבִּים: | יוֹם רָבָה

Cap. xxii.

וַיְהִי אַחַר הַדְּבָרִים הָאֵלֶּה |
וְהָאֱלֹהִים נִסָּה אֶת אַבְרָהָם | הָיָה
וַיֹּאמֶר אֵלָיו אַבְרָהָם וַיֹּאמֶר הִנֵּנִי: | אָמַר
וַיֹּאמֶר קַח נָא אֶת בִּנְךָ אֶת יְחִידְךָ | לָקַח יָחַד
אֲשֶׁר אָהַבְתָּ אֶת יִצְחָק וְלֶךְ לְךָ אֶל | הָלַךְ
אֶרֶץ הַמֹּרִיָּה וְהַעֲלֵהוּ שָׁם לְעֹלָה | עָלָה
עַל אַחַד הֶהָרִים אֲשֶׁר אֹמַר | הָרַר
אֵלֶיךָ: וַיַּשְׁכֵּם אַבְרָהָם בַּבֹּקֶר | שָׁכַם
וַיַּחֲבֹשׁ אֶת חֲמֹרוֹ וַיִּקַּח אֶת שְׁנֵי | חָבַשׁ שָׁנָה
נְעָרָיו אִתּוֹ וְאֵת יִצְחָק בְּנוֹ וַיְבַקַּע | בָּקַע
עֲצֵי עֹלָה וַיָּקָם וַיֵּלֶךְ אֶל הַמָּקוֹם | קוּם כּוּם
אֲשֶׁר אָמַר לוֹ הָאֱלֹהִים: בַּיּוֹם |

Transla. Chal.

וַאֲקִים אַבְרָהָם יָת שְׁבַע חוּרְפָאן דְעָאן בִּלְחוֹדֵיהוֹן: וַאֲמַר אֲבִימֶלֶךְ לְאַבְרָהָם מָה
אִינִין שְׁבַע חוּרְפָאן הָאִלֵּין דַּאֲקֵימְתָּא בִּלְחוֹדֵיהוֹן: וַאֲמַר אֲרֵי יָת שְׁבַע חוּרְפָאן תִּסַּב
מִן יְדִי בְּדִיל דִּתְהֵא לִי לְסָהִיד אֲרֵי חֲפָרִית יָת בֵּירָא הָדֵין: עַל כֵּן קְרָא לְאַתְרָא
הַהוּא בְּאֵר שָׁבַע אֲרֵי תַמָּן קַיִּימוּ תַּרְוֵיהוֹן: וּגְזָרוּ קְיָם בִּבְאֵר שָׁבַע וְקָם אֲבִימֶלֶךְ
וּפִיכֹל רַב חֵילֵיהּ וְתָבוּ לְאַרְעָא פְלִשְׁתָּאֵי: וּנְצַב נִצְבָא בִּבְאֵר שָׁבַע וְצַלִּי תַמָּן בִּשְׁמָא
דַּייָ אֱלָהּ עָלְמָא: וְאִתּוֹתַב אַבְרָהָם בְּאַרַע פְּלִשְׁתָּאֵי יוֹמִין סַגִּיאִין:

Ca. xxij.

וַהֲוָה בָּתַר פִּתְגָמַיָּא הָאִלֵּין וַייָ נַסִּי יָת אַבְרָהָם וַאֲמַר לֵיהּ אַבְרָהָם וַאֲמַר הָא אֲנָא:
וַאֲמַר דְּבַר כְּעַן יָת בְּרָךְ יָת יְחִידָךְ דִּרְחֵימְתָּא יָת יִצְחָק וְאִיזֵיל לָךְ לְאַרְעָא פּוּלְחָנָא
וְאַסְּקֵיהּ קֳדָמַי תַּמָּן לַעֲלָתָא עַל חַד מִן טוּרַיָּא דְּאֵימַר לָךְ: וְאַקְדֵּים אַבְרָהָם בְּצַפְרָא
וְזָרֵיז יָת חֲמָרֵיהּ וּדְבַר יָת תְּרֵין עוּלֵימוֹהִי עִמֵּיהּ וְיָת יִצְחָק בְּרֵיהּ וְצַלַּח אָעֵי דַעֲלָתָא
וְקָם וַאֲזַל לְאַתְרָא דַּאֲמַר לֵיהּ יְיָ: בְּיוֹמָא

Interp. chal.

Et statuit abraham septē agnas ouium seorsum. Dixitqꝫ abimelech ad abraham. Que sunt iste septem agne quas statuisti seorsum. Et ait. Quoniaꝫ septem agnas accipies de manu mea: vt sit mihi in testimonium quoniā fodi puteuꝫ istum. Propterea vocauit locum illū bersabee: quia ibi iurauerūt ambo: et inierunt pactū in bersabee. Surrexitqꝫ abimelech et phicol princeps exercitus eius: et reuersi sunt in terram philistinorum. Et plantauit plantationem in bersabee: et orauit ibi in nomine domini dei eterni. Et peregrinatus est abraham in terra philistinorum diebus multis.

Cap. 22.

Et factū est post verba hec: et deus tentauit abraham: et dixit ei. Abraham. Et ait: ecce ego. Et dixit. Tolle nunc filium tuū vnicum tuū queꝫ diligis isaac: et vade in terram diuini cultus: et offer illum coram me ibi in holocaustum super vnū montium quē dixero tibi. Et surrexit abraham mane et strauit asinum suum: et tulit duos pueros suos secum: et isaac filium suum: et concidit ligna in holocaustum: et surrexit et abijt in locum quē dixerat ei deus. Die autem

Priuatiua chal.
קוּם חַד
אֲלַף נְסַב
הֲוָה
קוּם קוּם
דְּבַר תּוּב צְלָא
יְתַב
אֲלַף נְסָה
אֲזַל
נְסַק עֲלָה קֳדָם
אָעָא
קוּם

48. A CHART OF THE OLD HEBREW ALPHABET

Illustration adapted from D. Diringer 1958 and 1962, with the kind permission of the author. Cf. p. 2.

	Gezer	Inscriptions	Cursive	Literary	Coins	Samaritan	Square
1							א
2							ב
3							ג
4							ד
5							ה
6							ו
7							ז
8							ח
9							ט
10							י
11							כ
12							ל
13							מ
14							נ
15							ס
16							ע
17							פ
18							צ
19							ק
20							ר
21							ש
22							ת

A. Sylvester

49. THE IZBET ṢARṬAH ABECEDARY[1]

Cf. p. 2. Photo by Moshe Weinberg in A. Demsky and M. Kochavi 1978: 22, with the kind permission of *Biblical Archaeology Review*.

In 1974, during the excavations at Izbet Ṣarṭah (the biblical Ebenezer?) sponsored by Tel Aviv University and Bar Ilan University, an ostracon in two pieces preserving the longest Old Hebrew inscription yet discovered was found by Aryeh Bornstein, a Tel Aviv University student. It measures 8.8 × 15 cm., and contains five lines of writing. The first four lines appear to be random letters (a writing exercise?), but the last line presents an abecedary with minor variations, written from left to right, evidently witnessing to a period before the right-to-left direction of Hebrew writing became established.

Archaeologically the find may be dated 1200-1000 B.C., but the writing has been ascribed on palaeographic grounds to the twelfth/eleventh century B.C., making it a century older than the Gezer calendar, and the oldest Hebrew abecedary yet discovered, as well as the most complete (the מ is no longer fully visible, although a trace of the letter remains).

It is interesting to note that the order of the letters עפ agrees with the pattern found in Pss. 9f. and Lam. 2–4, in contrast to the more usual order found in Pss. 25, 34, 37, 111f., 119, 145, Prov. 31, and Lam. 1.

For discussion, see M. Kochavi 1977; A. Demsky 1977; also A. Demsky and M. Kochavi 1978.

---

1. Added by the translator.

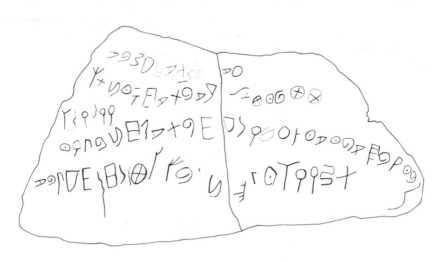

List of Sigla

BHS differs from BHK by not always citing manuscripts individually, but rather indicating them by the group sigla which include the individual witnesses. These group sigla are shown parenthetically for the individual witnesses in the following list.

BHS	**BHK**	
𝔐	𝔐	The Samaritan Pentateuch according to A. von Gall
𝔐$^{Ms(s)}$		Samaritan Pentateuch manuscript(s) according to the critical apparatus of A. von Gall
𝔐^T	𝔐^T	Samaritan Targum
𝔐^W		Samaritan Pentateuch according to B. Walton's London Polyglot
α′	A	Aquila
ε′	E′	Origen's Quinta
θ′	Θ	Theodotion
ο εβρ	ḥ^o	Origen's Hebrew text
οι γ′ ⎫ οι λ′ ⎭		the three later Greek versions
σ′	Σ	Symmachus
𝔄	𝔄	Arabic version
𝔄̈	𝔄̈	Ethiopic version
Ambr		Ambrose
Arm	Arm	Armenian version
𝔅	𝔅	Second Rabbinic Bible by Jacob ben Chayyim
Bo		Bohairic version

232

C	C	Codex Cairensis of the Prophets
𝕮		Cairo Geniza Hebrew codex fragment
𝕮²·³ ᵉᵗᶜ·		Two (three, etc.) Cairo Geniza Hebrew codex fragments
(𝕮)	Ea 1-27	
(𝕮)	Eb 1-30	} Fragments with simple Babylonian pointing
(𝕮)	Ec 1-24	
(𝕮)	Ka 1-22	
(𝕮)	Kb 1-15	} Fragments with complex Babylonian pointing
(𝕮)	Kc 1-14	
cit(t)		Quotations in rabbinic and medieval Jewish literature, according to V. Aptowitzer
Cyr	𝕲ᶜʸʳ	Septuagint, according to Cyril of Alexandria
Ed(d)		Editions of B. Kennicott, J. B. de Rossi, C. D. Ginsburg, etc., see Ms(s)
Eus		Eusebius Pamphilius of Caesarea (260/65-339)
Eus Onom		Eusebius, *Onomasticon* (= an index of biblical sites)
G	Ginsb(urg Mass)	C. D. Ginsburg 1880-1905
Ga		Psalterium Gallicanum
Gn R		Genesis Rabba, see cit(t)
𝕲	𝕲	Septuagint
𝕲*		Original Greek text, i.e., the unrevised form in contrast to the recensions
𝕲ᴬ	𝕲ᴬ	Codex Alexandrinus
𝕲ᴮ	𝕲ᴮ	Codex Vaticanus
𝕲ᴮ*		Codex Vaticanus, original hand
	𝕲ᴮᵉᵃᵗᵗʸ	Chester Beatty papyri
𝕲ᶜ	𝕲ᶜ	Codex Ephraemi Syri rescriptus
𝕲ᶜ		Greek text of the Catenae
	𝕲ᶜ⁽ᵒᵐ⁾ᵖˡ	Septuagint of the Complutensian Polyglot
𝕲ᶠ	𝕲ᶠ	Codex Ambrosianus
𝕲ᴸ	𝕲ᴸᵘᶜ	Lucian's recension
𝕲ᴸ·ᴵ·ᴵᴵ		Lucian's subgroups I and II
𝕲ᴸᵖ		Lucian's recension, in part
	𝕲ᴸ	Lagarde's edition
𝕲ᴹ	𝕲ᴹ	Codex Coislinianus

𝕲^{maj}		Greek uncial (majuscule) manuscripts
(𝕲^{maj})	𝕲^{XI}	Holmes-Parsons' Greek uncial no. XI
𝕲^{min}		Greek minuscule manuscripts
(𝕲^{min})	𝕲$^{62.147(Parsons)}$	Holmes-Parsons' Greek minuscules nos. 62, 147
𝕲$^{Ms(s)}$	𝕲$^{Mss(Holmes-)Parsons}$	Manuscripts according to Holmes-Parsons' edition
(𝕲^{Ms})	𝕲^{Γ}	Codex rescriptus Cryptoferratensis
(𝕲^{Ms})	𝕲^{Θ}	Codex Freer
(𝕲^{Ms})	𝕲^{D}	Codex Cottonianus Geneseos
(𝕲^{Ms})	𝕲^{E}	Codex Bodleianus Geneseos
(𝕲^{Ms})	𝕲^{G}	Codex Colberto-Sarravianus
(𝕲^{Ms})	𝕲^{K}	Codex Lipsiensis
(𝕲^{Ms})	𝕲^{W}	Codex Atheniensis
𝕲^{N}	𝕲^{N}	Codex Basiliano-Vaticanus
𝕲^{O}	𝕲^{h}	Hexaplaric recension of the Septuagint
𝕲^{Op}		= 𝕲^{O}, in part
𝕲^{Q}	𝕲^{Q}	Codex Marchalianus
𝕲^{R}		Codex Veronensis
𝕲^{S}	𝕲^{ℵ}	Codex Sinaiticus
𝕲^{U}	𝕲$^{Pap Lond}$	British Library Papyrus 37
𝕲^{V}	𝕲^{V}	Codex Venetus
	𝕲^{Vn}	Aldine edition
𝕲^{W}		Fragment 1 Sam. 18:8-25, according to H. Hunger's edition
𝕲$^{22.26\ etc.}$		Minuscule manuscripts in A. Rahlfs 1914
𝕲$^{-S}$ etc.		Greek tradition, except for 𝕲^{S} etc.
𝕲$^{S1.2.3}$	𝕲$^{ℵ\ c.a,c.b,c.c}$	Correctors of Codex Sinaiticus
Hier	Hie(r)	Jerome
Hill	Hill	Codex Hillel
	Jeric	Codex Jericho
jJeb		Jerushalmi Jebamot, see cit(t)
Jos Ant		Flavius Josephus, *Antiquitates Judaicae*
Just		Justin (martyred *ca.* A.D. 167)
K	K	Kethib
K^{Occ}	K^{Occ}	Kethib of the Western Masoretes
K^{Or}	K^{Or}	Kethib of the Eastern Masoretes
ϰ	ϰ	Coptic version
L	L	Codex Leningradensis
𝔏	𝔏	Old Latin versions
𝔏^{91}		Codex Legionensis

$\mathfrak{L}^{93}$		Copy of $\mathfrak{L}^{91}$
$\mathfrak{L}^{94}$		Incunabulum 54 marginalia
$\mathfrak{L}^{115}$		Naples Codex lat 1 (formerly Vindob. 17)
$\mathfrak{L}^{116}$		Fragmenta Quedlinburgensia and Magdeburgensia
$\mathfrak{L}^{117}$		Fragmenta Vindobonensia
	$\mathfrak{L}^{(Berger)}$	Old Latin version, edited by S. Berger
$\mathfrak{L}^{CY}$		Cyprian, *Testimonia*
	$\mathfrak{L}^{D}$	Old Latin version, edited by A. Dold
$\mathfrak{L}^{G}$		Codex Parisinus Latinus
$\mathfrak{L}^{gl}$		8th/9th cent. Old Latin glossarium "probably derived from a glossed Bible," edited by D. de Bruyne (see BHS XLVI)
	$\mathfrak{L}^{h}$	Old Latin version in the Würzburg palimpsests
	$\mathfrak{L}^{L}$	Codex Lugdunensis
$\mathfrak{L}^{Lg}$	$\mathfrak{L}^{Lg}$	Old Latin marginalia in Codex Legionensis
$\mathfrak{L}^{R}$		Codex Veronensis
$\mathfrak{L}^{S}$		Fragments from St. Gall
$\mathfrak{L}^{TE}$		Tertullian (*ca.* 160 — after 220), *Adversus Marcionem*
	$\mathfrak{L}^{Vind}$	Palimpsestus Vindobonensis
$\mathfrak{M}$	$\mathfrak{M}$	Masora, Masoretic text
	Mas	Masora of Codex Leningradensis
Mm	Mm, Mas.M	Masora magna
Mp	Mp	Masora parva
Ms(s), Ed(d)	MSS	Hebrew manuscripts cited in the editions of B. Kennicott, J. B. de Rossi, and C. D. Ginsburg
Mur		Manuscripts found at Wadi Muraba'at
Naft		Ben Naftali
Occ	Occ	Western Masoretes
Okhl	Ochla	*Okhla weOkhla,* S. Frensdorff's edition
Or	Or	Eastern Masoretes
Orig	Orig	Origen
Pes R		Pesiqta Rabba, see cit(t)
Q	Q	Qere
Q^{Occ}	Q^{Occ}	Qere of the Western Masoretes
Q^{Or}	Q^{Or}	Qere of the Eastern Masoretes
$\mathbb{Q}$		Qumran manuscripts
$\mathbb{Q}^{a}$		1QIs^{a}

ß[b]		1QIs[b]
1QGen Ap		Genesis Apocryphon from Qumran Cave 1
1QM		Milḥamah (War Scroll) from Qumran Cave 1
4QPs[b]		Fragmentary Psalm scroll (Ps. 91:5–118:26) published by P. W. Skehan 1964
S	S	Syriac Peshitta: agreement of S[W] and S[A]; in 1/2 Sm agreement of S[ABCD Jac edess Bar Hebr]
	S (S[W])	Syriac Peshitta in S[W]; but Pentateuch in Barnes 1914
S[A]	S[A]	Syriac Peshitta Codex Ambrosianus
	S[Aphr]	Syriac biblical quotations by Aphraates
S[B]		Codex British Library Add. 14,431
S[C]		Codex Leningradensis Public Library No. 2
S[D]		Codex British Library Add. 14,442
S[L]	S[L]	Syriac Peshitta edited by S. Lee
S[M]		Syriac Peshitta, Mosul edition
S[Mss]		Syriac Peshitta manuscripts
S[U]	S[U]	Syriac Peshitta, Urmia edition
S[W]		Syriac Peshitta in B. Walton's London Polyglot
S[Jac edess]		Syriac version of Jacob of Edessa
S[Bar Hebr]		Readings in the scholia of Bar Hebraeus
Sa	Sah	Sahidic version
Samar		Samaritan pronunciation according to P. E. Kahle 1959: 318-335
Seb	Seb	Sebir
	Sev	Codex Severi
Sor	Sor	Soraei (Masoretes of Sura)
Syh	S[h]	Syrohexaplar
𝕿	𝕿	Targum according to A. Sperber 1-3, 1959-62, and P. A. de Lagarde 1873
	𝕿[B]	Targum in the Second Rabbinic Bible
𝕿[Buxt]		Targum, J. Buxtorf edition
𝕿[ed princ]		Targum, editio princeps, Leiria 1494
𝕿[f]		Targum, Codex Reuchlinianus according to the apparatus of A. Sperber's edition
𝕿[J]	𝕿[J]	Targum Pseudo-Jonathan
𝕿[JII]	𝕿[JII]	Targum Jerušalmi
	𝕿[L]	Targum, P. A. de Lagarde edition, for the Kethubim

	𝔗ᴹ	A. Merx, *Chrestomathia Targumica*
𝔗ᴹˢ⁽ˢ⁾,ᴱᵈ⁽ᵈ⁾		Targum manuscripts or editions in A. Sperber's critical apparatus
(𝔗)	𝔗ᴼ	Targum Onkelos
𝔗ᴾ	𝔗ᴾ	Palestinian Targum
	𝔗ᴾʳ	Targum, F. Praetorius edition (Joshua, Judges)
	𝔗ᵂ	Targum in B. Walton's London Polyglot
Tert		Tertullian
Tiq soph	Tiq soph	Tiqqune sopherim
Tyc		Tyconius
𝔙	𝔙	Latin Vulgate
	𝔙ᴬ	Vulgate Codex Amiatinus
	Varᴮ	Variants cited in S. Baer's edition
	Varᴱ ¹·²·³	Variants in the three Erfurt codices
	V(ar)ᶠ	Variants in the first A. Firkowitsch collection
	V(ar)ᴳ	Variants cited in C. D. Ginsburg's edition
	V(ar)ᴶ	Variants in R. Hörning 1889
	V(ar)ᴷᵃ	Variants in Babylonian manuscripts cited by P. E. Kahle 1913, 1928
Vᴷᵉⁿ ⁶⁹ ᵉᵗᶜ·	V(ar)ᴷᵉⁿ	Variants cited in B. Kennicott's edition
	V(ar)ᴹ	Variants cited in J. H. Michaelis' edition
	V(ar)ᴼ	Variants of the Scholastic Odo cited by J. Fischer 1934, 1936
Vᴾ	V(ar)ᴾ	Variants in the Petersburg Prophets Codex
	V(ar)ᵖᵃˡ	Variants in manuscripts with Palestinian pointing
Vˢ	Varˢ	Variants in unpublished manuscripts cited in H. L. Strack 1921
	V(ar)ᵂ	Variants cited in W. Wickes 1881-87
Vrs		Many or all versions
c ast	c ast	with asterisk
c ob	c ob	with obelos
	conj	conjecture
dttg	dittogr	dittography
gl	gl(oss)	gloss
hpgr	haplogr	haplography
	Hex, hex	Hexapla, hexaplaric
homark		homoioarcton
homtel	homoeotel	homoioteleuton

Abbreviations

AASF	Annales academiae scientiarum Fennicae
AAWG	Abhandlungen der Akademie der Wissenschaften in Göttingen
ALBO	Analecta lovaniensia biblica et orientalia
ALGHJ	Arbeiten zur Literatur und Geschichte des hellenistischen Judentums
AnBib	Analecta biblica
ANET	J. B. Pritchard, ed., *Ancient Near Eastern Texts,* 3rd ed.
AOAT	Alter Orient und Altes Testament
AOS	American Oriental Series
ASOR	American Schools of Oriental Research
ASTI	*Annual of the Swedish Theological Institute*
ATAbh	Alttestamentliche Abhandlungen
ATANT	Abhandlungen zur Theologie des Alten und Neuen Testaments
BA	*Biblical Archaeologist*
BANE	G. E. Wright, ed., *The Bible and the Ancient Near East*
BAR	*Biblical Archaeology Review*
BASOR	*Bulletin of the American Schools of Oriental Research*
BBB	Bonner biblische Beiträge
Bib	*Biblica*
BJRL	*Bulletin of the John Rylands University Library of Manchester*
BOS	Bonner orientalistische Studien
BW	G. Rendsburg, *et al.,* eds., *The Bible World*
BWAT	Beiträge zur Wissenschaft für die alttestamentliche Wissenschaft
BZ	*Biblische Zeitschrift*

BZAW	Beihefte zur *ZAW*
CATSS	Computer Assisted Tools for Septuagint Studies
CBL	Collectanea biblica Latina
CBQ	*Catholic Biblical Quarterly*
CHB	*The Cambridge History of the Bible*
CNFI	*Christian News From Israel*
ConBOT	Coniectanea biblica, Old Testament Series
CSCO	Corpus scriptorum christianorum orientalium
CSEL	Corpus scriptorum ecclesiasticorum latinorum
DBSup	*Dictionnaire de la Bible, Supplément*
DJD	Discoveries in the Judaean Desert
Est Bib	*Estudios bíblicos*
HSM	Harvard Semitic Monographs
HTR	*Harvard Theological Review*
HTS	Harvard Theological Studies
HUCA	*Hebrew Union College Annual*
IDBSup	Supplementary volume to *The Interpreter's Dictionary of the Bible*
IEJ	*Israel Exploration Journal*
IOSOT	International Organization for the Study of the Old Testament
IZBG	*Internationale Zeitschriftenschau für Bibelwissenschaft und Grenzgebiete*
JBL	*Journal of Biblical Literature*
JEOL	*Jaarbericht ex oriente lux*
JITL	*Jahresbericht der israelitisch-theologischen Lehranstalt*
JJS	*Journal of Jewish Studies*
JNES	*Journal of Near Eastern Studies*
JQR	*Jewish Quarterly Review*
JSOTSup	Journal for the Study of the Old Testament—Supplement Series
JSS	*Journal of Semitic Studies*
JTS	*Journal of Theological Studies*
LCP	Latinitas Christianorum primaeva
MBE	Monumenta biblica et ecclesiastica
MSU	Mitteilungen des Septuaginta-Unternehmens der Gesellschaft/Akademie der Wissenschaften in Göttingen
NAWG	Nachrichten der Akademie der Wissenschaften zu Göttingen
NedTTs	*Nederlands theologisch tijdschrift*
NGWG	Nachrichten der Gesellschaft der Wissenschaften zu Göttingen

NJKA	Neue Jahrbucher für das klassische Altertum
OBO	Orbis biblicus et orientalis
OLCR	M. Black and W. A. Smalley, eds., *On Language, Culture, and Religion*
OLZ	*Orientalistische Literaturzeitung*
OTS	*Oudtestamentische Studiën*
PBA	*Proceedings of the British Academy*
PEQ	*Palestine Exploration Quarterly*
PIRHT	Publications de l'Institut de recherche et d'histoire des textes
PTA	Papyrologische Texte und Abhandlungen
QHBT	F. M. Cross, S. Talmon, eds., *Qumran and the History of the Biblical Text*
RAPH	Recherches d'archéologie, de philologie, et d'histoire
RB	*Revue biblique*
RBén	*Revue bénédictine*
RGG	*Religion in Geschichte und Gegenwart*
SANT	Studien zum Alten und Neuen Testament
SAWW	Sitzungsberichte der Akademie der Wissenschaften in Wien
SBAW	Sitzungsberichte der Bayerischen Akademie der Wissenschaften
SBLMasS	Society of Biblical Literature Masoretic Studies
SBLRBS	Society of Biblical Literature Resources for Biblical Study
SBLSCS	Society of Biblical Literature Septuagint and Cognate Studies
SPap	*Studia papyrologica*
SPAW	Sitzungsberichte der Preussischen Akademie der Wissenschaften
ScrHier	*Scripta hierosolymitana*
SSN	Studia semitica neerlandica
SVTG	*Septuaginta: Vetus Testamentum graece,* Göttingen
TAB	Texte und Arbeiten, Erzabtei Beuron
TBl	Theologische Blätter
TDNT	*Theological Dictionary of the New Testament*
TEstCisn	Textos y Estudios "Cardenal Cisneros"
TLZ	*Theologische Literaturzeitung*
TRE	Theologische Realenzyklopädie
TRev	*Theologische Revue*
TRu	*Theologische Rundschau*
TSK	*Theologische Studien und Kritiken*
TU	Texte und Untersuchungen

TWNT	*Theologisches Wörterbuch zum Neuen Testament*
TZ	*Theologische Zeitschrift*
UUÅ	Uppsala universitetsårsskrift
VT	*Vetus Testamentum*
VTS	Supplements to *Vetus Testamentum*
WO	*Die Welt des Orients*
ZAH	*Zeitschrift für Althebraistik*
ZAW	*Zeitschrift für die alttestamentliche Wissenschaft*
ZDMG	*Zeitschrift der deutschen morgenländischen Gesellschaft*
ZDMGSup	Supplements to *Zeitschrift der deutschen morgenländischen Gesellschaft*
ZDPV	*Zeitschrift des deutschen Palästina-Vereins*
ZNW	*Zeitschrift für die neutestamentliche Wissenschaft*

Bibliography

Aberbach, Moses, and Bernard Grossfeld
1982   *Targum Onkelos to Genesis: A Critical Analysis with an English Translation of the Text.* New York: KTAV.

Aejmelaeus, Anneli
1987   "What Can We Know about the Hebrew Vorlage of the Septuagint?" *ZAW* 99:58-89.

Alba Cecilia, Amparo
1980   *Biblia babilónica: Ezequiel. Edición critica según manuscritos hebreos de puntuación babilónica.* TEstCisn 27.
1980   *Biblia babilónica: Isaias. Edición critica según manuscritos hebreos de puntuación babilónica.* TEstCisn 28.

Albrektson, Bertil
1978   "Reflections on the Emergence of a Standard Text of the Hebrew Bible," *VTS* 29:50-65.
1981   "Difficilior lectio probabilior. A Rule of Textual Criticism and its Use in Old Testament Studies," *OTS* 21:5-18.

Albright, William Foxwell
1937   "A Biblical Fragment from the Maccabean Age: The Nash Papyrus," *JBL* 56:145-176.
1948   "The Early Alphabetic Inscriptions from Sinai and their Development," *BASOR* 110:6-22.
1949   *Archaeology of Palestine.* Harmondsworth: Penguin.
1949a   "On the Date of the Scrolls from ʿAin Feshka and the Nash Papyrus," *BASOR* 115:10-19.
1966   *The Proto-Sinaitic Inscriptions and their Decipherment,* HTS 22.
1969   "Palestinian Inscriptions," *ANET,* 320-22, 568f.

Alexander, Philip S.
1988   "Jewish Aramaic Translations of Hebrew Scriptures," in Mulder 1988:217-253.

Allegro, John Marco, and Arnold A. Anderson
1968   *Qumran Cave 4 I (4Q158-4Q186).* DJD 5. Oxford: Oxford University Press.

Allgeier, Arthur
1948   "Haec vetus et vulgata editio: Neue wort- und begriffsgeschichtliche
            Beiträge zur Bibel auf dem Tridentinum," *Bib* 29:353-390.

Alonso-Schökel, Luis
1990   Diccionario Bíblico Hebreo-Español: א — דָּמַם. Valencia: Institución
            San Jerónimo.
1991   "The Diccionario bíblico hebreo-español," *ZAH* 4/1: 76-84.

Aly, Zaki, and Ludwig Koenen
1980   *Three Rolls of the Early Septuagint: Genesis and Deuteronomy,* PTA 27.
            Bonn: Habelt.

Aptowitzer, Victor
1906-15   *Das Schriftwort in der rabbinischen Literatur.* SAWW, Phil.-hist. Kl.
            153/6 (1906); 160/7 (1908); *JITL* 18 (1911): 1-173; 22 (1915): 1-82.
            Prolegomenon, 1 Samuel, 2 Samuel, Joshua, Judges. Repr. New York:
            KTAV, 1970.

Avigad, Naḥman
1958   "The Palaeography of the Dead Sea Scrolls and Related Documents,"
            ScrHier 4:56-87. Repr. 1965.

———, and Yigael Yadin
1956   *A Genesis Apocryphon.* Jerusalem: Magnes and Hekhal ha-Sefer.

Baars, Willem
1968   *New Syro-Hexaplaric Texts, edited, commented upon and compared with
            the Septuagint.* Leiden: Brill.

Bacher, Wilhelm
1899   *Die exegetische Terminologie der jüdischen Traditionsliteratur* 1. Leip-
            zig: Hinrichs. Repr. Hildesheim: Olms, 1965.

Baer, Seligmann, and Franz Delitzsch
1869-1895   *Textum Masoreticum accuratissime expressit e fontibus Masorae codi-
            cumque varie illustravit.* Leipzig: Tauchnitz.

Baer, Seligmann, and Hermann L. Strack
1879   *Die Dikduke ha-Tᵉʿamim des Ahron ben Moscheh ben Ascher.* Leipzig:
            Fernau. Repr. with a new preface by David S. Loewinger, Jerusalem:
            Makor, 1970.

Baillet, Maurice
1982   *Qumran Grotte 4. III (4Q482–4Q520).* DJD 7. Oxford: Clarendon.
1982a   "Corrections à l'édition de von Gall du Pentateuque Samaritain," *Fest-
            schrift J. P. M. van der Ploeg.* AOAT 211:23-35.

———, Józef T. Milik, Roland de Vaux, and H. Wright Baker
1962   *Les 'Petites Grottes' de Qumrân: exploration de la falaise, les grottes
            2Q, 3Q, 5Q, 6Q, 7Q, à 10Q: Le Rouleau de cuivre.* DJD 3. Oxford:
            Clarendon.

Bardtke, Hans
1953-61   *Die Handschriftenfunde am Toten Meer.* Berlin: Evangelische Haupt-
            Bibelgesellschaft. 1: ²1953; 2: ²1961.
1953a   "Die Parascheneinteilung der Jesajarolle I von Qumran," *Festschrift Franz
            Dornseiff,* ed. Horst Kusch. Leipzig: Bibliographisches Institut, 33-75.

Barnes, William Emery
1904 *The Peshitta Psalter according to the West Syrian Text edited with an Apparatus Criticus.* Cambridge: Cambridge University Press.

————, **Charles W. Mitchell, and John Pinkerton**
1914 *Pentateuchus Syriace post Samuelum Lee, recognovit, emendavit, edidit G. E. Barnes, adiuvantibus C. W. Mitchell, I. Pinkerton.* London: British and Foreign Bible Society.

Barr, James
1966/67 "St. Jerome's Appreciation of Hebrew," *BJRL* 49:281-302.
1968 *Comparative Philology and the Text of the Old Testament.* Oxford: Clarendon. Repr. Winona Lake: Eisenbrauns, 1987.
1981 "A New Look at the Kethib-Qere," *OTS* 21:19-37.
1986 Review of Barthélemy 1982, *JTS* N.S. 37:444-450.

Barthélemy, Dominique
1953 "Redécouverte d'un chaînon manquant de l'histoire de la Septante," *RB* 60:18-29. Repr. Jellicoe 1974: 226-238; OBO 21 (1978): 38-50.
1963 *Les Devanciers d'Aquila: Première publication intégrale du texte des fragments du dodécapropheton trouvés dans le desert de Juda, précédée d'une étude sur les traductions et recensions greques de la Bible réalisées au premier siècle de notre ère sous l'influence du rabbinat palestinien.* VTS 10.
1974 "Pourquoi la Torah a-t-elle été traduite en Grec?" *OLCR,* 23-41. Repr. OBO 21 (1978): 322-340.
1974a "Qui est Symmaque?" *CBQ* 36:451-465. Repr. OBO 21 (1978): 307-321.
1976-80 (ed.) *Preliminary and Interim Report on the Hebrew Old Testament Text Project* (English and French), 5 vols. London: United Bible Societies.
1982 *Critique Textuelle de l'Ancien Testament,* 1: *Josué, Juges, Ruth, Samuel, Rois, Chroniques, Esdras, Néhémie, Ester.* OBO 50/1. Fribourg: Universitetsverlag and Göttingen: Vandenhoeck und Ruprecht.
1986 *Critique Textuelle de l'Ancien Testament,* 2: *Isaïe, Jérémie, Lamentations.* OBO 50/2. Fribourg: Universitetsverlag and Göttingen: Vandenhoeck und Ruprecht.
1986a "Texte, massores et facsimilé du manuscrit d'Alep," in *Salvacion en la Palabra . . . en memoria Alejandro Díez Macho.* Madrid: Ediciones Cristiandad, 53-63.

————, **and Józef T. Milik**
1955 *Qumran Cave I.* DJD 1. Oxford: Clarendon.

Bauer, Hans, and Pontus Leander
1922 *Historische Grammatik der hebräischen Sprache des Alten Testaments,* Halle: Niemeyer. Repr. Hildesheim: Olms, 1991.

Baumstark, Anton
1931 "Peschitta und palästinisches Targum," *BZ* 19:257-270.
1935 "Neue orientalische Probleme biblischer Textgeschichte," *ZDMG* 89:89-118.

Belsheim, Johannes Engebretsen
1885 *Codex Vindobonensis membranaceus purpureus.* Leipzig: Weigel.

Ben-David, Abba
1972   *Parallels in the Bible.* Jerusalem: Carta.

Benedictine Monastery of St. Jerome, Rome
1926-86 *Biblia Sacra iuxta latinam vulgatam versionem ad codicum fidem iussu Pii PP. XI cura et studio Monachorum Abbatiae Pontificiae S. Hieronymi in urbe ordinis S. Benedicti edita.* Rome: Typis Polyglottis Vaticanis.

1959   *Biblia Sacra Vulgatae Editionis: Editio emendatissima apparatu critico instructa cura et studio Abbatiae Pontificiae S. Hieronymi in Urbe Ordinis S. Benedicti.* Turin: Marietti.

Ben-Ḥayyim, Zeev
1958   "Traditions in the Hebrew Language, with Special Reference to the Dead Sea Scrolls," ScrHier 4 (1965^2): 200-214.

1977   *The Words of the Pentateuch.* The Literary and Oral Traditions of Hebrew and Aramaic amongst the Samaritans 4. Jerusalem: Academy of the Hebrew Language.

Benoit, Pierre, Józef T. Milik, and Roland de Vaux
1961   *Les Grottes de Murabbaʿat.* DJD 2. Oxford: Clarendon.

Ben-Zvi, Izhak
1960   "The Codex of Ben Asher," *Textus* 1:1-16. Repr. Leiman 1974: 757-772.

Berger, Samuel
1893   *Notices et Extraits des Manuscrits de la Bibliothèque Nationale et autres Bibliothèques* 34/2:119-152.

Berliner, Abraham
1877   *Die Masorah zum Targum Onkelos.* Leipzig: Hinrichs.
1884-86 *Targum Onkelos,* 2 vols. Berlin: Gorzelanczyk.

Bertram, Georg
1936   "Das Problem der Umschrift und die religionsgeschichtliche Bedeutung der Septuaginta," *BZAW* 66:97-109.

1938   "Zur Septuagintaforschung," *TRu* N.S. 10:69-80, 133-167.

1939   "Der Sprachschatz der Septuaginta und der des hebräischen Alten Testaments," *ZAW* N.S. 16:85-101.

1957   "Praeparatio evangelica in der Septuaginta," *VT* 7:225-249.

1969-71 "Das Problem der griechischen Umschrift des hebräischen Alten Testaments: Ein Beitrag zur Geschichte der Septuaginta-Forschung," *WO* 5-6:237-264.

Beyer, Klaus
1969   *Althebräische Grammatik: Laut- und Formenlehre.* Göttingen: Vandenhoeck und Ruprecht.

Birnbaum, Solomon A.
1954-57 *The Hebrew Scripts,* 2: *The Plates.* London: Palaeographia.
1971   *The Hebrew Scripts,* 1: *The Texts.* Leiden: Brill.

Black, Matthew
1957   "Die Erforschung der Muttersprache Jesu," *TLZ* 82:653-668.

———, **and William A. Smalley, eds.**
1974   *On Language, Culture, and Religion: In Honor of Eugene A. Nida.* The Hague: Mouton.

Blau, Ludwig

1902   *Studien zum althebräischen Buchwesen und zur biblischen litera-turgeschichte.* Budapest: Landes Rabbinerschule and Strasbourg: Trübner.

Boer, P. A. H. de

1981   "Towards an Edition of the Syriac Version of the Old Testament," *VT* 31:346-357.

Borger, Rykle

1987   "NA[26] und die neutestamentliche Textkritik," *TRu* 52:1-58.

Bornkamm, Heinrich

1933   *Das Wort Gottes bei Luther.* Munich: Kaiser.

Botte, Bernard

1949   "Itala," *DBSup* 4:777-782.

1957   "Latines (Versions) Anterieures à S. Jérôme," *DBSup* 5:334-39.

1960   "Versions Coptes," *DBSup* 6:818-825.

Bowker, John

1969   *The Targums and Rabbinic Literature: An Introduction to Jewish Inter-pretations of Scripture.* Cambridge: Cambridge University Press.

Brock, Sebastian P.

1978   Review of K. Hyvärinen 1977, *Society for Old Testament Study Booklist.* Sheffield.

1980   "Bibelübersetzungen," *TRE* 6:160ff.

————, **Charles T. Fritsch, and Sidney Jellicoe**

1973   *A Classified Bibliography of the Septuagint.* ALGHJ 6.

Brooke, Alan E., Norman McLean, and Henry St. John Thackeray

1906-1940 *The Old Testament in Greek according to the Text of Codex Vaticanus.* 3 vols. in 9. Cambridge: Cambridge University Press.

Brown, Francis, Samuel Rolles Driver, and Charles A. Briggs, eds.

1907   *Hebrew and English Lexicon of the Old Testament.* Oxford: Oxford University Press. Corrected ed. 1952.

Bruyne, Donatien de

1930   "Le problème du psautier romain," *RBén* 42:101-126.

Budge, Ernest Alfred Wallis

1912   *Coptic Biblical Texts in the Dialect of Upper Egypt.* London: British Museum.

Burkitt, Francis Crawford

1897   *Fragments of the Books of Kings according to the Translation of Aquila.* Cambridge: Cambridge University Press.

Burrows, Millar

1949   "Variant Readings in the Isaiah Manuscript," *BASOR* 113:24-32.

1950   *The Isaiah Manuscript and the Habakkuk Commentary.* The Dead Sea Scrolls of St. Mark's Monastery 1. New Haven: American Schools of Oriental Research.

1951   *Plates and Transcription of the Manual of Discipline.* The Dead Sea Scrolls of St. Mark's Monastery 2. New Haven: American Schools of Oriental Research.

Busto-Saiz, José Ramón

1978   *La Traduccion de Simaco en el Libro de los Salmos.* Diss., Madrid: Alcalà. Repr. Madrid: Consejo Nazionale Investigaciones Cientificas, 1985.

Cassuto, Moshe David [Umberto], ed.

1953   *Torah, Prophets and Scriptures: Jerusalem Edition, Corrected on the Basis of the Masora of Ben Asher.* Jerusalem: Magnes.

Ceriani, Antonius Maria

1874   *Monumenta Sacra et Profana* 7. Milan: Biblioteca Ambrosiana.

1876   *Translatio Syra Pescitto Veteris Testamenti ex codice Ambrosiano sec. fere VI photolithographice edita.* Milan: della Croce.

Chiesa, Bruno

1978   *L'Antico Testamento Ebraico secondo la tradizione <u>palestinese.</u>* Turin: Bottega d'Erasmo.

1979   *The Emergence of Hebrew Biblical Pointing: The Indirect Sources.* Judentum und Umwelt 1. Frankfurt/Main: Lang.

Clines, David J. A.

1990   "The Dictionary of Classical Hebrew," *ZAH* 3/1:73-80.

Coggins, Richard J.

1975   *Samaritans and Jews: The Origins of Samaritanism Reconsidered.* Atlanta: John Knox.

Cook, Stanley Arthur

1903   "A Pre-Massoretic Biblical Papyrus," *Proceedings of the Society of Biblical Archaeology* 25:34-56.

Cowley, Arthur Ernest

1919   *Jewish Documents of the Time of Ezra.* London: SPCK and New York: Macmillan.

1923   *Aramaic Papyri of the Fifth Century B.C.* Repr. Osnabrück: Zeller, 1976.

Cox, Claude E.

1981   *The Armenian Translation of Deuteronomy.* Armenian Texts and Studies 2. Chico, CA: Scholars Press.

1986   *Hexaplaric Materials Preserved in the Armenian Version.* Atlanta: Scholars Press.

Cross, Frank Moore

1954   "The Evolution of the Proto-Canaanite Alphabet," *BASOR* 134:15-24.

1955   "The Oldest Manuscripts from Qumran," *JBL* 74:147-172. Repr. *QHBT*, 147-176.

1961   *The Ancient Library of Qumran and Modern Biblical Studies.* Garden City, NY: Doubleday. 1st ed. 1958. Repr. Grand Rapids: Baker, 1980.

1961a   "The Development of the Jewish Scripts," *BANE,* 133-202.

1964   "History of the Biblical Text in the Light of the Discoveries of the Judaean Desert," *HTR* 57:281-299. Repr. *QHBT,* 177-195.

1966   "The Contribution of the Qumran Discoveries to the Study of the Biblical Text," *IEJ* 16:81-95. Repr. Leiman 1974: 334-348; *QHBT,* 278-292.

1975   "The Evolution of a Theory of Local Texts," *QHBT,* 306-320.

———, **and David Noel Freedman**

1952   *Early Hebrew Orthography.* AOS 36.

————, and Shemaryahu Talmon, eds.

1975   *Qumran and the History of the Biblical Text.* Cambridge, MA: Harvard University Press.

David, C. Joseph, and G. Ebed-Jesus Khayyath

1887-1891 *Biblia Sacra juxta versionem simplicem quae dicitur Pschitta.* Mosul: Dominican.

Davies, Graham I., et al.

1991   *Ancient Hebrew Inscriptions.* Cambridge: Cambridge University Press.

Deissmann, Adolf

1903   "Die Hellenisierung des semitischen Monotheismus," *NJKA* 11:161-177.

Deist, Ferdinand E.

1988   *Witnesses to the Old Testament: Introducing Old Testament Textual Criticism.* Pretoria: N. G. Kerkboekhandel.

Delekat, Lienhard

1957   "Die syrolukianische Übersetzung des Buches Jesaja," *ZAW* 69:21-54.

1957a   "Die syropalästinische Jesaja-Übersetzung," *Bib* 38: 185-199, 321-335.

Delitzsch, Friedrich

1920   *Die Lese- und Schreibfehler im Alten Testament.* Berlin: de Gruyter.

Demsky, Aaron

1977   "A Proto-Canaanite Abecedary Dating from the Period of the Judges and its Implications for the History of the Alphabet," *Tel Aviv* 4:14-27.

————, and Moshe Kochavi

1978   "An Alphabet from the Days of the Judges," *BAR* 4/3:22-30.

Dexinger, Ferdinand, and Reinhard Pummer

1992   *Die Samaritaner.* Darmstadt: Wissenschaftliche Buchgesellschaft.

Diaz Esteban, Fernando

1975   *Sefer 'Oklah we-'Oklah.* Textos y Estudios 4. Madrid: Consejo Superior de Investigaciones Cientificas.

Dietrich, Manfried

1968   *Neue palästinisch punktierte Bibelfragmente: Veröffentlicht und auf Text und Punktation hin untersucht.* Leiden: Brill.

Díez Macho, Alejandro

1954   "Tres nuevos manuscritos biblicos 'palestinenses'," *Est Bib* 13:247-265.

1956   "Una copia de todo el Targum jerosolimitano en la Vaticana," *Est Bib* 15:446f.

1960   "The recently discovered Palestinian targum: Its antiquity and relationship with the other targums," *VTS* 7:222-245.

1962   "Palestinian Targum," *CNFI* 13/2: 19-25.

1963   "A New List of So-called 'Ben Naftali' Manuscripts, Preceded by an Inquiry into the True Character of these Manuscripts," *Hebrew and Semitic Studies.* Festschrift G. R. Driver, 16-52.

1968-79 *Neophyti 1 Targum Palestinense Ms de la Biblioteca Vaticana,* vol. 1-6. Madrid: Consejo Superior de Investigaciones Cientificas.

1977, 1980 *Targum Palestinense in Pentateuchum: Additur Targum Pseudojonatan eiusque Hispanica Versio.* Biblia Polglota Matritense, ser. 4. 2: *Exodus* (1980); 3: *Leviticus;* 5: 4: *Numeri* (1977); *Deuteronomium* (1980).

————, and Angeles Navarro Peiro

1987   *Biblia babilónica: fragmentos de Salmos, Job y Proverbios (MS. 508 A del Seminario Teológico Judío de Nueva York).* TEstCisn 42.

Díez Merino, Luis

1975   *La Biblia Babilónica.* Madrid: Sección Targúmica.

Diringer, David

1958   *The Story of the Aleph Beth.* New York: Philosophical Library and London: Lincolns-Praeger.

1958a   "Inscriptions," in Tufnell 1958: 127-133.

1962   *Writing.* New York: Praeger and London: Thames and Hudson.

1968   *The Alphabet: A Key to the History of Mankind.* 3rd ed. New York: Funk and Wagnalls.

1970   "The Biblical Scripts," *CHB* 1:11-29.

Dirksen, Peter B.

1985   "East and West, Old and Young, in the Text Tradition of the Old Testament Peshitta," *VT* 35:468-484.

1988   "The Old Testament Peshitta," in Mulder 1988: 255-297.

1989   *An Annotated Bibliography of the Peshitta of the Old Testament.* Monograph of the Peshitto Institute, 5. Leiden: Brill.

Dörrie, Heinrich

1940   "Zur Geschichte der LXX im Zeitalter Konstantins," *ZNW* 39:57-110.

Dold, Alban

1923   *Konstanzer altlateinische Propheten- und Evangelienbruchstücke mit Glossen.* Leipzig: Harrassowitz.

1931   *Zwei Bobbienser Palimpseste mit frühestem Vulgatatext, herausgegeben und bearbeitet.* TAB I, 19/20. Leipzig: Erzabtei Beuron.

1940   *Neue St. Galler vorhieronymianische Propheten-Fragmente der St. Galler Sammelhandschrift 1398b zugehörig.* TAB 31. Leipzig: Erzabtei Beuron.

Donner, Herbert, and W. Röllig

1971-76 *Kanaanäische und aramäische Inschriften.* 2nd ed. 3 vols. Wiesbaden: Harrassowitz.

Dotan, Aron

1957   "?האמנם היה בן אשר קראי," *Sinai* 41:280-312, 350-362. Repr. Leiman 1974: 710-745. English trans. *Ben Asher's Creed: A Study of the History of the Controversy* (Missoula: Scholars Press, 1977).

1964/65 "Was the Aleppo Codex Actually Vocalized by Aharon ben Asher?" *Tarbiz* 34:136-155 [Hebrew].

1973   (ed.) *Torah, Nevi'im u-Khetuvim* [Codex Leningradensis, diplomatic edition]. Tel Aviv: Huts'ah 'Edi.

Drazin, Israel

1982   *Targum Onkelos to Deuteronomy: An English Translation of the Text with Analysis and Commentary.* New York: KTAV.

Driver, Godfrey Rolles

1950   "L'interprétation du texte masorétique à la lumière de la lexicographie hebraique," *ALBO,* 2, ser. 18.

1960   "Abbreviations in the Masoretic Text," *Textus* 1:112-131.

1964   "Abbreviations in the Masoretic Text," *Textus* 4:76-94.

1976   *Semitic Writing from Pictograph to Alphabet.* Schweich Lectures 1944. Oxford: Oxford University Press. Rev. ed. 1954; revised by S. A. Hopkins 1976.

Dunand, Françoise

1966   *Papyrus Grecs Bibliques (Papyrus F. Inv. 266): Volumina de la Genèse et du Deuteronome.* RAPH 27.

Ecker, Roman

1962   "Die arabische Job-Übersetzung des Gaon Saadja ben Josef-al-Fajjumi," *SANT* 4.

Edelmann, Rafael

1953   "The Arabic Versions of the Pentateuch," *Studia Orientalia J. Pedersen dicata.* Copenhagen: Munksgaard, 71-75.

1968   "Soferim — Masoretes, 'Masoretes' — Nakdanim: In memoriam P. Kahle," *BZAW* 103:116-123.

Eissfeldt, Otto

1949   "Ansetzung der Rollen nach paläographischen Kriterien," *TLZ* 74:221-26.

1949a   "Der gegenwärtige Stand der Erforschung der in Palästina neu gefundenen hebräischen Handschriften. 7: Der Anlass zur Entdeckung der Höhle und ihr ähnliche Vorgänge aus ältere Zeit," *TLZ* 74: 597-600. Repr. *Kleine Schriften* III (Tübingen: Mohr, 1966): 71-74.

Elbogen, Ismar

1962   *Der jüdische Gottesdienst in seiner geschichtlichen Entwicklung.* 4th ed. Hildesheim: Olms.

Elliger, Karl

1953   *Studien zum Habakuk-Kommentar vom Toten Meer.* Tübingen: Mohr.

Emerton, J. A.

1956   "The Purpose of the Second Column of the Hexapla," *JTS* N.S. 7:79-87. Repr. Jellicoe 1974: 347-355.

1962   "Unclean Birds and the Origin of the Peshitta," *JSS* 7:204-211.

1970   "Were Greek Transliterations of the Hebrew O.T. Used by Jews before the Time of Origen?" *JTS* N.S. 21:17-31.

1971   "A Further Consideration of the Purpose of the Second Column of the Hexapla," *JTS* N.S. 22:15-28.

Even-Shoshan, Abraham

1989   *A New Concordance of the Old Testament: Using the Hebrew and Aramaic Text.* Grand Rapids: Baker.

Fernandez-Galliano, M.

1971   "Nuevas páginas del códice 967 del A.T. griego (Ez. 28,19–43,9)," *SPap* 10:1-79.

Fernández Tejero, Emilia

1983   (ed.) *Estudios Masoreticos.* Proceedings of the Fifth Congress of the International Organization for the Study of the Old Testament. Madrid: Instituto "Arias Montano."

1983a   "Report on the Cairo Codex Edition," in 1983: 79-86.

Field, Frederick

1875   *Origenis Hexaplorum quae supersunt.* 2 vols. Oxford: Oxford University Press. Repr. Hildesheim: Olms, 1964.

Fischer, Bonifatius
1949   *Vetus Latina, 1: Sigla.* Freiburg: Herder.
1951-54   *Vetus Latina, 2: Genesis.* Freiburg: Herder.
1957   *Die Alkuin-Bibel.* Aus der Geschichte der lateinischen Bibel 1. Freiburg:
            Herder.
1962   "Codex Amiatinus und Cassiodor," *BZ* N.S. 6:57-79.
1977   *Novae Concordantiae Bibliorum Sacrorum iuxta Vulgatam Versionem
            Critice Editam, quas digessit Bonifatius Fischer OSB.* 5 vols. Stuttgart:
            Fromann-Holzboog.

Fischer, Johann
1930   *In welcher Schrift lag das Buch Isaias den LXX vor?* BZAW 56.
1934   "Die hebräischen Bibelzitate des Scholastikers Odo," *Bib* 15:50-93.
1936   "Einige Proben aus den hebräischen Bibelzitaten des Scholastikers
            Odo," *Werden und Wesen des Alten Testaments.* Festschrift Claus Wes-
            termann. BZAW 66:198-206.

Fishbane, Michael
1976   "Abbreviations, Hebrew Texts," *IDBSup* 3f.

Fitzmyer, Joseph A.
1990   *The Dead Sea Scrolls: Major Publications and Tools for Study.* Revised
            ed. SBLRBS 20. Atlanta: Scholars Press.

Fohrer, Georg
1951   "Die Glossen im Buche Ezechiel," *ZAW* 63:33-53.

Franchi de' Cavalieri, Pio Pietro, and Hans Lietzmann
1929   *Specimina Codicum Graecorum Vaticanorum.* 2nd ed. Berlin: de Gruyter.

**Freedman, David Noel, and Kenneth A. Mathews (with contributions by
Richard S. Hanson)**
1985   *The Paleo-Hebrew Leviticus Scroll (11Q paleo Lev).* Winona Lake:
            Eisenbrauns.

Frensdorff, Salomon
1864   *Das Buch Ochlah W'ochlah.* Hannover: Hahn. Repr. Tel Aviv: Zion,
            1969; New York: KTAV, 1972.

Fritsch, Charles Theodore
1943   *The Anti-Anthropomorphisms of the Greek Pentateuch.* Princeton:
            Princeton University Press.

von Gall, August Freiherr
1914-18   *Der hebräische Pentateuch der Samaritaner.* Giessen: Töpelmann. Repr.
            1966.

Galling, Kurt, ed.
1950   *Textbuch zur Geschichte Israels.* Tübingen: Mohr. 2nd ed. 1968; 3rd ed.
            1979.

Geiger, Abraham
1857   *Urschrift und Übersetzungen der Bibel in ihrer Abhängigkeit von der
            inneren Entwicklung des Judenthums.* Breslau: Hainauer. Repr. Frank-
            furt: Madda, 1928.

Geissen, Angelo, ed.
1968   *Der Septuaginta-Text des Buches Daniel: Kap. 5–12 sowie Esther 1–
            2,15.* Papyrologische Texte und Arbeiten 5. Bonn: Habelt.

Gerleman, Gillis

1948   *Synoptic Studies in the Old Testament.* Lund: Gleerup.

Gertner, M.

1960   "The Masorah and the Levites," *VT* 10:241-284.

Gese, Hartmut

1957   "Die hebräischen Bibelhandschriften zum Dodekapropheton nach der Variantensammlung des Kennicott," *ZAW* 69:55-69.

Gesenius, Wilhelm

1815   *De Pentateuchi Samaritani origine, indole et auctoritate commentatio philologica-critica.* Halle: Libraria Rengerianae.

1829-58   *Thesaurus philologicus criticus linguae Hebraeae et Chaldaeae Veteris Testamenti.* Leipzig: Vogel. 17th ed., revised by Frants Buhl, 1921.

————, **Emil Kautzsch, and Arthur Ernest Cowley**

1910   *Gesenius' Hebrew Grammar as edited and enlarged by the late E. Kautzsch, Second English edition revised by A. E. Cowley.* Oxford: Clarendon. Revised and enlarged 1980.

Gibson, John C. L.

1971-82   *Textbook of Syrian Semitic Inscriptions,* 1: *Hebrew and Moabite Inscriptions* (1971); 2: *Aramaic Inscriptions including Inscriptions in the Dialect of Zenjirli* (1975); 3: *Phoenician Inscriptions including Inscriptions in the Mixed Dialect of Arslan Tash (1982).* Oxford: Clarendon.

Ginsburg, Christian David

1880-1905 *The Massorah Compiled from Manuscripts Alphabetically and Lexically Arranged.* Vols. 1-4,1. London: Brög. Repr. New York: KTAV, 1968, with prolegomenon by A. Dotan.

1897   *Introduction to the Massoretico-Critical Edition of the Hebrew Bible.* London: Trinitarian Bible Society. New edition with prolegomenon by Harry M. Orlinsky. New York: KTAV, 1966.

1908-26   *Textum Masoreticum accuratissime expressit e fontibus Masorae codicumque varie illustravit.* London: British and Foreign Bible Society.

Ginsburger, Moses

1899   *Das Fragmenten-Targum (Targum Jeruschalmi zum Pentateuch).* Berlin: Kohlhammer.

1903   *Targum Pseudo-Jonathae (Thargum Jonathan ben Usiel zum Pentateuch): Nach der Londoner Hs. B. Mus. add. 27031.* Berlin: Kohlhammer.

Giron Blanc, Luis-F.

1976   *Pentateuco Hebreo-Samaritano: Genesis.* Biblia Poliglota Matritense, ed. Federico Pérez Castro. Madrid: Fundación Universitaria Española.

Glaue, Paul, and Alfred Rahlfs

1911   *Fragmente einer griechischen Übersetzung des samaritanischen Pentateuchs.* MSU 2. Göttingen: Vandenhoeck und Ruprecht.

Gordis, Robert

1937   *The Biblical Text in the Making: A Study of the Kethib-Qere.* New York. Repr. with new introduction, New York: KTAV, 1981.

Goshen-Gottstein, Moshe H.

1956   "Neue Syrohexaplafragmente," *Bib* 37:175-183.

1960   "The Authenticity of the Aleppo Codex," *Textus* 1:17-58. Repr. Leiman 1974: 773-814 (= Goshen-Gottstein 1960a: 1-42).

1960a   *Text and Language in Bible and Qumran.* Jerusalem/Tel Aviv: Orient.

1962   "Biblical Manuscripts in the United States," *Textus* 2:28-59.

1963   "The Rise of the Tiberian Bible Text," in *Biblical and Other Studies,* ed. Alexander Altmann. Cambridge, MA: Harvard University Press, 79-122. Repr. Leiman 1974: 666-709.

1963a   "Theory and Practice of Textual Criticism. The Text-critical Use of the Septuagint," *Textus* 3:130-158.

1963/64 "The Aleppo Codex and Ben Buyaʿa the Scribe," *Tarbiz* 33:149-156.

1965-81 *The Book of Isaiah.* The Hebrew University Bible Project. Jerusalem: Magnes. *Sample Edition with Introduction* (1965); 1: *Is 1:1–22:10* (1975); 2: *Is 22:11–44:28* (1981).

1966   "The Psalms Scroll (11QPsᵃ): A Problem of Canon and Text," *Textus* 5:22-33.

1966a   "A Recovered Part of the Aleppo Codex," *Textus* 5:53-59.

1967   "Hebrew Biblical Manuscripts: Their History and their Place in the HUBP Edition," *Bib* 48:243-290. Repr. *QHBT*, 42-89.

1972   (ed.) *Biblia Rabbinica: A Reprint of the 1525 Venice Edition.* Jerusalem: Makor.

1976   (ed.) *The Aleppo Codex, Provided with Massoretic Notes and Pointed by Aaron ben Asher, the Text Considered Authoritative by Maimonides.* Jerusalem: Magnes.

1979   "The Aleppo-Codex and the Rise of the Massoretic Bible Text," *BA* 42:145-163.

1991   "Exercises in Targum and Peshitta I," *Textus* 16: 117ff.

Graf, Georg
1944   *Geschichte der christlichen arabischen Literatur,* 1: *Die Übersetzungen.* Studi e Testi 118.

Gray, John
1974   "The Masoretic Text of Job, the Targum and the Septuagint Version in the Light of the Qumran Targum (11QtargJob)," *ZAW* 86:331-350.

Greenberg, Moshe
1977   "The Use of the Ancient Versions for Interpreting the Hebrew Text," *VTS* 29:131-148.

Gressmann, Hugo
1926-27 *Altorientalische Texte zum Alten Testament.* Berlin: de Gruyter.

Grossfeld, Bernard
1972-78 *A Bibliography of Targum Literature.* 2 vols. Cincinnati: Hebrew Union College and New York: KTAV.

Grossouw, Wilhelm Karel Maria
1938   *The Coptic Versions of the Minor Prophets: A Contribution to the Study of the Septuagint.* MBE 3. Rome: Pontifical Biblical Institute.

Groves, J. Alan
1989   "Correction of Machine-Readable Texts by Means of Automatic Comparison: Help with Method." *Bible and Computer: Methods, Tools, Results. Jerusalem, 9-13, 1988.* Paris: Champion and Geneva: Slatkine, 271-295.

Gunkel, Hermann
1928 "Glosse," *RGG*[2], 2:1230.

Hadas, Moses
1951 *Aristeas to Philocrates.* New York: Harper.

Haefeli, Leo
1927 *Die Peshitta des AT mit Rücksicht auf ihre textkritische Bearbeitung und Herausgabe.* ATAbh 11/1. Münster: Aschendorff.

Halperin, David J.
1982 "Merkabah Midrash in the Septuagint," *JBL* 101:351-363.

Hamm, Winfried
1969 "Der Septuaginta-Text des Buches Daniel Kap. 1–2," *PTA* 10. Bonn: Habelt.

Hanhart, Robert
1959 *Maccabaeorum liber II.* SVTG 9/2. Revised ed. 1976.
1960 *Maccabaeorum liber III.* SVTG 9/3. Revised ed. 1980.
1962 "Fragen um die Entstehung der Septuaginta," *VT* 12:139-163.
1966 *Esther.* SVTG 8/3. Revised ed. 1983.
1967 "Die Bedeutung der Septuaginta-Forschung für die Theologie," *Drei Studien zum Judentum.* Theologische Existenz heute 38-64. Repr. Jellicoe 1974: 583-609.
1974 *I Esdras.* SVTG 8/1.
1974a *Text und Textgeschichte des 1. Esrabuches.* MSU 12. Göttingen: Vandenhoeck und Ruprecht.
1978 Review of Dunand 1966, *OLZ* 73:40-45.
1979 *Judith.* SVTG 8/4.
1979a *Text und Textgeschichte des Buches Judith,* MSU 14. Göttingen: Vandenhoeck und Ruprecht.
1979b "Jüdische Tradition und christliche Interpretation: Zur Geschichte der Septuagintaforschung in Göttingen," *Kerygma und Logos.* Festschrift Carl Andresen, 280-297.
1981 "Das Neue Testament und die griechische Überlieferung des Judentums: Überlieferungsgeschichtliche Untersuchungen," *TU* 125:293-303.
1983 *Tobit.* SVTG 8/5.
1984 *Text und Textgeschichte des Buches Tobit,* MSU 17. Göttingen: Vandenhoeck und Ruprecht.
1984b "Zum gegenwärtigen Stand der Septuagintaforschung," in Pietersma and Cox 1984, 3-18.

———, **and John W. Wevers**
1977 *Das Göttinger Septuaginta-Unternehmen,* Festschrift Joseph Ziegler. Göttingen: Vandenhoeck und Ruprecht.

Hanson, Richard Simon
1964 "Palaeo-Hebrew Script in the Hasmonean Age," *BASOR* 175: 26-42.

Haran, Menahem
1982 "Book-Scrolls in Israel in Pre-Exilic Times," *JJS* 33: 161-173.
1983 "Book-Scrolls at the Beginning of the Second Temple Period: The Transition from Papyrus to Skins," *HUCA* 54:111-122.

Harding, G. Lankester
1949   "The Dead Sea Scrolls," *PEQ:*112-16 (illustrated).

Harkavy, Albert, and Hermann Leberecht Strack
1875   *Catalog der hebräischen Bibelhandschriften der kaiserlichen öffentlichen Bibliothek in St. Petersburg.* Leipzig: Hinrichs.

Harnack, Adolf von
1902   "Der Brief des Ptolemäus an die Flora," SPAW, 507-545.

Hatch, Edwin, and Henry Redpath
1897   *A Concordance to the Septuagint.* 2 vols. Oxford: Clarendon. Supplement, 1906. Repr. Graz: Akademische Verlag, 1954; Grand Rapids: Baker, 1983.

Hempel, Johannes
1930   "Chronik (Bericht über die textkritische Forschung und ihre Problematik)," *ZAW* 48:187-202.
1934   "Innermasoretische Bestätigungen des Samaritanus," *ZAW* 52:254-274.
1937   "Zum griechischen Deuteronomiumtext des II. Jahrhunderts a. C.," *ZAW* 55:115-127.
1938   "Die Ostraka von Lakiš," *ZAW* 56:126-139.
1959   "Der textkritische Wert des Konsonantentextes von Kairener Genizafragmenten in Cambridge und Oxford zum Deuteronomium," *NAWG* 1: 207-236.
1965   "Die Texte von Qumran in der heutigen Forschung," 290-95. Offprint from *NAWG* 1/10, 1961.

Herrmann, Johannes, and Friedrich Baumgärtel
1923   "Beiträge zur Entstehungsgeschichte der Septuaginta," BWAT N.S. 5.

Holl, Karl
1948   "Luthers Bedeutung für den Fortschritt der Auslegungskunst," *Gesammelte Aufsätze zur Kirchengeschichte,* 1:544-582. Darmstadt: Wissenschaftliche Buchgesellschaft.

Holmes, Robert, and James Parsons
1798-1827 *Vetus Testamentum Graecum cum variis lectionibus.* Oxford: Clarendon.

Hyvärinen, Kyosti
1977   *Die Übersetzung von Aquila.* ConBOT 10. Lund: Gleerup.

Jaroš, Karl
1982   *Hundert Inschriften aus Kanaan und Israel.* Fribourg: KBW.

Jellicoe, Sidney
1968   *The Septuagint and Modern Study.* Oxford: Clarendon. Repr. Winona Lake: Eisenbrauns, 1989.
1974   (ed.) *Studies in the Septuagint: Origins, Recensions, and Interpretations.* New York: KTAV.

Jepsen, Alfred
1963   "Von den Aufgaben der alttestamentlichen Textkritik," *VT* 9: 332-341.

Jeremias, Joachim
1964   "γραμματεύς," *TDNT* 1:740-42 (= 1933 *TWNT* 1:740-42).
1967   "παῖς θεοῦ," *TDNT* 5:677-717 (= 1951 *TWNT* 5:653-713).

Johnson, Allan Chester, Henry Snyder Gehman, and Edmund Harris Kase, Jr.
1938   *The John H. Scheide Biblical Papyri: Ezekiel.* Princeton University Studies in Papyrology 3. Princeton: Princeton University Press.

Johnson, Bo
1968   *Die armenische Bibelübersetzung als hexaplarischer Zeuge im 1. Samuelbuch.* ConBOT 2. Lund: Gleerup.

Joüon, Paul
1923   *Grammaire de l'Hebreu biblique.* Rome: Pontificio Istituto Biblico. Repr. 1987.

Kahle, Paul E.
1901   "Zur Geschichte der hebräischen Punktation," *ZAW* 21:273-317.
1902   *Der masoretische Text des Alten Testaments nach der Überlieferung der Babylonischen Juden.* Leipzig: Hinrichs. Repr. Hildesheim: Olms, 1966.
1913   *Masoreten des Ostens: Die ältesten punktierten Handschriften des Alten Testaments und der Targume.* BWAT 15. Leipzig: Hinrichs. Repr. Olms, 1984.
1915   "Untersuchungen zur Geschichte des Pentateuchtextes," *TSK* 88: 399-439. Repr. Kahle 1956: 3-37.
1922   H. Bauer and P. Leander 1922, §§6-9.
1925   "Die Punktation der Masoreten," *BZAW* 41:167-172. Repr. Kahle 1956: 48-53.
1928   "Die hebräischen Bibelhandschriften aus Babylonien," *ZAW* 46:113-137, with an appendix of 70 facsimiles.
1927-30 *Masoreten des Westens,* 2 vols. Stuttgart: Kohlhammer. Repr. in 1 vol., Hildesheim: Olms, 1984.
1947   "Die Septuaginta: Prinzipielle Erwägungen," *Festschrift Otto Eissfeldt,* ed. Johann Fück. Halle: Niemeyer, 161-180. Repr. 1961.
1947a   "Felix Pratensis — à Prato, Felix: Der Herausgeber der ersten Rabbinerbibel, Venedig 1516-17," *WO* 1:32-36.
1950   "Zur Aussprache des Hebräischen bei den Samaritanern," *Festschrift Alfred Bertholet.* Tübingen: Mohr, 281-86. Repr. Kahle 1956: 180-85.
1951   *Die hebräischen Handschriften aus der Höhle.* Franz Delitzsch-Vorlesungen. Stuttgart: Kohlhammer.
1951a   "The Hebrew Ben Asher Bible Manuscripts," *VT* 1:161-67.
1953   "The Abisha' Scroll of the Samaritans," *Studia Orientalia J. Pedersen dicata.* Copenhagen: Munksgaard, 188-192.
1953a   Review of *"The New Hebrew Bible,* Jerusalem 1953," *VT* 3:416-420.
1954   "Die im August 1952 entdeckte Lederrolle mit dem griechischen Text der Kleinen Propheten und das Problem der Septuaginta," *TLZ* 79:81-94. Repr. Kahle 1956: 113-127, in English.
1954a   "Zwei durch Humanisten besorgte, dem Papst gewidmete Ausgaben der hebräischen Bibel," *Festschrift Leo Baeck.* London: East and West Library, 50-74. Repr. Kahle 1956: 128-150.
1954b   "The Hebrew Text of the Complutensian Polyglot," *Homenaje a Millás-Vallicrosa.* Barcelona: Consejo Superior de Investigaciones Cientificas, 1:741-751.
1954c   Review of Cassuto 1953, *VT* 4:109f.

1956   *Opera Minor: Festgabe zum 21. Januar 1956.* Leiden: Brill.

1958   "Das palästinische Pentateuchtargum und das zur Zeit Jesu gesprochene Aramäisch," *ZNW* 49:100-115.

1959   *The Cairo Geniza.* Rev. ed. London: Blackwell.

1960   "The Greek Bible Manuscripts used by Origen," *JBL* 79: 111-18.

1961   *Der hebräische Bibeltext seit Franz Delitzsch.* Franz Delitzsch-Vorlesung 1958. Stuttgart: Kohlhammer.

Kahle, P. E., Jr., ed.

1954   *Bala'iza: Coptic Texts from Deir el-Bala'izah in Upper Egypt.* Oxford: Oxford University Press.

Kappler, Werner

1936   *Maccabaeorum Liber I.* SVTG 9/1. Göttingen: Vandenhoeck und Ruprecht. Rev. ed. 1968.

Karo, Georg Heinrich, and Hans Lietzmann

1902   *Catenarum Graecarum Catalogus.* NGWG, Phil.-hist. Kl.

Kasser, Rodolphe

1965   "Les dialectes coptes et les versions coptes bibliques," *Bib* 46:287-310.

————, and Michel Testuz

1967   *Papyrus Bodmer XXIV.* Cologny-Geneva: Bibliotheca Bodmeriana.

Katsh, Abraham I.

1959   "Hebraica Collections in the U.S.S.R.," *Akten des XXIV. Internationalen Orientalistenkongresses München 1957* 24:202-5.

Katz, Eliezer

1992   *A Topical Concordance of the Old Testament: Using the Hebrew and Aramaic Text.* Grand Rapids: Baker.

Katz, Peter (W. P. M. Walters)

1949   "Das Problem des Urtextes der Septuaginta," *TZ* 5/1:1-24.

1950   *Philo's Bible: The Aberrant Text of Bible Quotations in Some Philonic Writings and Its Place in the Textual History of the Greek Bible.* Cambridge: Cambridge University Press.

1956   "Septuagintal Studies in the Mid-century: Their Links with the Past and Their Present Tendencies," *The Background of the New Testament and Its Eschatology.* Festschrift C. H. Dodd. Cambridge: Cambridge University Press, 176-208.

1957   "Frühe hebraisierende Rezensionen der Septuaginta und die Hexapla," *ZAW* 69:77-84.

Kautzsch, Emil Friedrich

1900   *Die Apokryphen und Pseudepigraphen des Alten Testaments.* Tübingen: Mohr. Repr. Hildesheim: Olms, 1962.

Kedar-Kopfstein, Benjamin

1968   *The Vulgate as a Translation.* Diss., Hebrew University, Jerusalem.

1988   "The Latin Translations," in Mulder 1988: 299-338.

Kellermann, Diether

1977   "Bemerkungen zur Neuausgabe der Biblia Hebraica," *ZDMGSup* 3/1: 128-138.

1980   "Korrektur, Variante, Wahllesart? Ein Beitrag zu dem Verständnis der K l'/Q lw," *BZ* 24:55-75.

Kennedy, James

1928 *An Aid to the Textual Amendment of the Old Testament*, ed. Nahum Levison. Edinburgh: Clark.

Kennicott, Benjamin

1776-80 *Vetus Testamentum Hebraicum cum variis lectonibus.* 2 vols. Oxford: Clarendon.

Kenyon, Frederic George

1933-37, *The Chester Beatty Biblical Papyri.* 7 vols. London: Walker.
1958

1949 *Bible and Archaeology.* 2nd ed. New York: Harper.

1975 *The Text of the Greek Bible.* 3rd ed., revised by Arthur W. Adams. London: Duckworth.

Kilpatrick, George Dunbar

1951 Review of P. Katz 1950, *JTS* N.S. 2: 89f.

Kippenberg, Hans G.

1971 *Garizim und Synagoge.* Religionsgeschichtliche Versuche und Vorarbeiten 30. Berlin: de Gruyter.

Kittel, Rudolf

1902 *Über die Notwendigkeit und Möglichkeit einer neuen Ausgabe der hebräischen Bibel: Studien und Erwägungen. Leipzig: Edelmann, 1901. Einladung zur Feier des Reformationsfestes und des Übergangs des Rektorats der Universität Leipzig . . . durch den designierten Dekan der theol. Fakultät.* Leipzig: Deichert.

Klein, Michael L.

1980 *The Fragment Targums of the Pentateuch According to Their Extant Sources.* AnBib 76.

1986 *Genizah Manuscripts of Palestinian Targum to the Pentateuch.* 2 vols. Cincinnati: Hebrew Union College Press.

Kochavi, Moshe

1977 "An Ostracon of the Period of the Judges from Izbet Sartah," *Tel Aviv* 4:1-13.

Köhler, Ludwig, and Walter Baumgartner

1958 *Lexikon in Veteris Testamenti Libros.* 2nd ed. Leiden: Brill. Repr. Leiden: Brill and Grand Rapids: Eerdmans, 1985.

1990 *Hebräisches und aramäisches Lexikon zum Alten Testament.* 3rd ed. Leiden: Brill.

Kohlenberger, John R.

1987 *The NIV Interlinear Hebrew-English Old Testament.* Grand Rapids: Zondervan.

van der Kooij, Arie

1981 *Die alten Textzeugen des Jesajabuches.* OBO 35. Fribourg: Universitetsverlag and Göttingen: Vandenhoeck und Ruprecht.

1988 "Symmachus, de vertaler der Joden," *NedTTs* 42:1-20.

Kosack, W.

1973 *Proverbia Salomonis, Achmimisch, sahidisch, bohairisch und arabisch.* Vetus Testamentum Coptice 1. Bonn: Habelt.

Koster, M. D.

1977   *The Peshitta of Exodus: The Development of its Text in the Course of Fifteen Centuries.* SSN 19. Assen: van Gorcum.

Kraeling, Emil G.

1953   *The Brooklyn Museum Aramaic Papyri.* Brooklyn: Brooklyn Museum and New Haven: Yale University Press. Repr. New York: Arno, 1969.

1958   "Elephantine," *RGG*³, 2:415-18.

Kuhn, Karl Georg

1958   *Ruckläufiges Hebräisches Wörterbuch.* Göttingen: Vandenhoeck und Ruprecht.

Lagarde, Paul A. de

1863   *Anmerkungen zur griechischen Übersetzung der Proverbien.* Leipzig: Brockhaus.

1872   *Prophetae Chaldaice: Paulus de Lagarde e fide codicis reuchliniani edidit.* Leipzig: Teubner.

1873   (ed.) *Hagiographa Chaldaice.* Leipzig: Teubner.

1883   *Librorum Veteris Testamenti canonicorum pars prior graece.* Göttingen: Hoyer.

1891   *Septuagintastudien.* AAWG 37.

1892   *Bibliothecae Syriacae.* Göttingen: Horstmann.

Landauer, Samuel

1896   *Die Massorah zum Onkelos nach neuen Quellen.* Amsterdam: Van Ess en Joachimathal.

Le Déaut, Roger J.

1966   *Introduction à la Littérature Targumique.* Rome: Pontifical Biblical Institute.

1978-82   *Targum du Pentateuque: Traduction des deux recensions palestiniennes complètes avec introduction, parallèles, notes et index.* 5 vols. Paris: Éditions du Cerf.

Lee, Samuel

1823   *The Syriac Old and New Testament.* London: British and Foreign Bible Society. Repr. 1979.

Lehman, I. O.

1967   "A Forgotten Principle of Biblical Textual Tradition Rediscovered," *JNES* 26:93-101.

Leiman, Sid Z., comp.

1974   *The Canon and Masorah of the Hebrew Bible: An Introductory Reader.* New York: KTAV.

Leloir, Louis

1960   "Versions Arméniennes," *DBSup* 6:810-18.

Lemaire, André

1981   *Les Écoles et la formation de la bible dans l'Ancien Israel.* OBO 39. Fribourg: Universitetsverlag and Göttingen: Vandenhoeck und Ruprecht.

Leveen, Jacob

1949   "Newly Found Hebrew Scrolls from Palestine," *The Listener.* London, August 25, 323.

Levine, Etan
1982 "The Transcription of the Torah Scroll," *ZAW* 94:99-105.
1982a "The Biography of the Aramaic Bible," *ZAW* 94:353-379.
1988 *The Aramaic Versions of the Bible: Contents and Context.* BZAW 174.

Levy, Kurt
1936 *Zur masoretischen Grammatik: Texte und Untersuchungen.* BOS 15. Stuttgart: Kohlhammer.

Lietzmann, Hans
1897 *Catenen: Mitteilungen über ihre Geschichte und handschriftliche Über-lieferung.* Tübingen: Mohr.

Lifshitz, B.
1962 "Greek Documents from the Cave of Horror," *IEJ* 12:201-7.

———, and J. Schiby
1968 "Une synagogue samaritaine à Thessalonique," *RB* 75:368-378.

Lipschütz, Lazar
1962 "Mishael ben Uzziel's Treatise on the Differences between Ben Asher and Ben Naftali," *Textus* 2:3-58 [Hebrew, English summary]. See 1965.
1964 "Kitāb al-Khilaf: The Book of the Ḥillufim," *Textus* 4:1-29. See 1965.
1965 *Kitāb al-Khilaf.* Jerusalem: Magnes. Repr. of 1962 and 1964.

Lisowsky, Gerhard
1958 *Konkordanz zum hebräischen Alten Testament.* Stuttgart: German Bible Society. 2nd ed. 1966; 3rd ed. 1990, reduced format 1993.

Löfgren, Oscar
1927 *Die äthiopische Übersetzung des Propheten Daniels.* Paris: Geuthner.

Loewe, Raphael J.
1969 "The Medieval History of the Latin Vulgate," *CHB* 2:102-154.

Loewinger, David Samuel
1960 "The Aleppo Codex and the Ben Asher Tradition," *Textus* 1:59-111.
1970 *Pentateuch, Prophets and Hagiographa: Codex Leningrad B19A: The Earliest Complete Bible Manuscript.* Jerusalem: Makor.
1971 *Codex Cairensis of the Bible from the Karaite Synagogue at Abbasiya.* Jerusalem: Makor.

Lund, Shirley, and Julia A. Foster
1977 *Variant Versions of Targumic Traditions within Codex Neofiti I.* Aramaic Studies 2. Missoula: Scholars Press.

Maas, Paul
1958 *Textual Criticism.* Oxford: Clarendon.

McCarthy, Carmel
1981 *The Tiqqune Sopherim and Other Theological Corrections in the Ma-soretic Text of the Old Testament.* OBO 36. Fribourg: Universitetsverlag and Göttingen: Vandenhoeck und Ruprecht.

McNamara, Martin
1966 *The New Testament and the Palestinian Targum to the Pentateuch.* AnBib 27. Rome: Pontifical Biblical Institute.

Macuch, Rudolf
  1969   *Grammatik des samaritanischen Hebräisch.* Studia Samaritana 1. Berlin: de Gruyter. Repr. 1982.
Maher, Michael
  1990   *Targum Pseudo-Jonathan: Genesis.* Collegeville: Liturgical.
————, *et al.*
  1987   *The Aramaic Bible: The Targum.* Wilmington: Glazier.
Maier, Johann
  1978   *Die Tempelrolle vom Toten Meer.* Uni-Taschenbücher 829. Munich: Reinhardt.
  1982   *Jüdische Auseinandersetzung mit dem Christentum in der Antike.* Ertrag der Forschung 177. Darmstadt: Wissenschaftliche Buchgesellschaft.
  1985   *The Temple Scroll: An Introduction, Translation and Commentary.* JSOTSS 34.
Mandelkern, Solomon
  1896   *Veteris Testamenti Concordantiae Hebraicae atque Chaldaicae.* Leipzig: Veit. 2nd ed., corrected by F. Margolin. Berlin, 1925. Repr. Graz: Akademische Druk und Verlagsanstalt, 1955. 6th ed., corrected by Moshe Goshen-Gottstein. Tel Aviv: Schocken, 1964.
Manson, Thomas Walter
  1945   Review of Fritsch 1943, *JTS* 46:78f.
Maori, Yeshayahu
  1975   *The Peshitta Version of the Pentateuch in its Relation to the Sources of Jewish Exegesis.* Diss., Hebrew University, Jerusalem. [Hebrew]
Margolis, Max Leopold
  1931-38 *The Book of Joshua in Greek.* 4 vols. Paris: Geuthner. 5: Winona Lake: Eisenbrauns, 1992.
Martin, M. Fitzmaurice
  1963   "The Palaeographical Character of Codex Neofiti I," *Textus* 3:1-35.
Meershoek, G. Q. A.
  1966   *Le Latin Biblique d'après Saint Jérôme.* LCP 20. Nijmegen: Dekker en Van de Vegt.
Mercati, Giovanni
  1947   "Il problema delle colonna II dell'Esaplo," *Bib* 28:1-30, 173-215.
  1958   *Psalterii Hexapli reliquiae.* Codices ex ecclesiasticis Italiae bybliothecis delecti phototypice expressi 8. Rome: Bibliotheca Vaticana.
  1965   *Osservazioni, Commento critico al Testo dei Frammenti Esaplari.* Rome: Bibliotheca Vatican.
Merx, Adalbert
  1888   *Chrestomathia Targumica.* Berlin: Reuther and New York: Westermann.
Meyer, Rudolf
  1950   "Zur Sprache von ʿAin Feschcha," *TLZ* 75:721-26.
  1961   "Die Bedeutung von Deuteronomium 32,8f.43 (4Q) für die Auslegung des Moseliedes," *Verbannung und Heimkehr.* Festschrift Wilhelm Rudolph, ed. Arnulf Kuschke. Tübingen: Mohr, 197-209.

1963 "Die Bedeutung des Codex Reuchlinianus für die hebräische Sprachgeschichte," *ZDMG* 113:51-61.

1966 *Hebräische Grammatik,* 1. 3rd ed. Sammlung Göschen 763. Berlin: de Gruyter.

————, and Herbert Donner

1987 *Wilhelm Gesenius Hebräisches und Aramäisches Handwörterbuch über das Alte Testament.* 18th ed. 1: *Aleph-Gimel,* Berlin: Springer.

Michaelis, Johann Heinrich

1720 *Biblia Hebraica ex aliquot manuscriptis et compluribus impressis codicibus, item Masora tam edita, quam manuscripta aliisque hebraeorum criticis diligenter recensita . . .* Halle: Orpha.

Migne, Jacques-Paul

1844-64 *Patrologia latina.* 221 vols. Paris: Migne. Supplement, 5 vols. Paris: Garnier Freres, 1958-74.

Milik, Józef Tadeusz

1959 *Ten Years of Discovery in the Wilderness of Judaea.* Naperville: Allenson.

Milne, H. M., and Theodore Cressy Skeat

1938 *Scribes and Correctors of the Codex Sinaiticus.* London: British Museum.

Min, Young-Jin

1977 *The Minuses and Pluses of the LXX Translation of Jeremiah as Compared with the Massoretic Text: Their Classification and Possible Origins.* Diss. Hebrew University, Jerusalem.

Möhle, August

1934 "Ein neuer Fund zahlreicher Stücke aus den Jesaia-Übersetzung des Akylas, Symmachos und Theodotion," *ZAW* N.S. 11:176-183.

Morag, Shelomo

1959 "The Vocalization of Codex Reuchlinianus: Is the 'Pre-Masoretic' Bible Pre-Masoretic?" *JSS* 4:216-237.

Müller, Karlheinz

1978 "Aristeasbrief," *TRE* 3:719-725.

Mulder, Martin Jan

1988 (ed.) *Mikra: Text, Translation, Reading and Interpretation of the Hebrew Bible in Ancient Judaism and Early Christianity.* Compendia Rerum Iudaicarum ad Novum Testamentum 2/1. Assen: van Gorcum and Philadelphia: Fortress.

1988a "The Transmission of the Biblical Text," in Mulder 1988: 87-135.

Muraoka, Takemitsu

1991 *A Grammar of Biblical Hebrew.* Rome: Pontifical Biblical Institute.

Murtonen, Aimo Edward

1958-62 *Materials for a Non-Masoretic Hebrew Grammar.* Diss., Helsinki, 1 (1958), 2 (1960), 3 (1962).

Nautin, Pierre

1986 "Hieronymus," *TRE* 15:304-315.

Navarro Peiro, Angeles

1976 *Biblia babilónica: Proverbios. Edición critica según manuscritos hebreos de puntuación babilónica.* TEstCisn 13.

————, and Federico Pérez Castro

1977   *Biblia babilónica: Profetas menores. Edición crítica según manuscritos hebreos de puntuación babilónica.* TEstCisn 16.

Naveh, Joseph

1987   *Early History of the Hebrew Alphabet.* 2nd ed. Jerusalem: Hebrew University and Leiden: Brill.

Noth, Martin

1963   *Geschichte Israels.* Göttingen: Vandenhoeck und Ruprecht. English trans. of 2nd ed. Peter R. Ackroyd, *The History of Israel.* New York: Harper and London: Black, 1960.

Nyberg, Hendrik Samuel

1934   "Das textkritische Problem des Alten Testaments am Hoseabuch demonstriert," *ZAW* 52:241-254.

1935   *Studien zum Hoseabuch, zugleich ein Beitrag zur Klärung des Problems der AT Textkritik.* UUÅ 6. Uppsala.

O'Connell, Kevin G.

1976   "Greek Versions (Minor)," *IDBSup,* 377-381.

Oesch, Josef M.

1979   *Petucha und Setuma.* OBO 27. Fribourg: Universitetsverlag and Göttingen: Vandenhoeck und Ruprecht.

Orlinsky, Harry Meyer

1946   "The Septuagint — Its Use in Textual Criticism," *BA* 9:21-34.

1960   "The Origin of the Kethib-Qere System: A New Approach," *VTS* 7:184-192. Repr. Leiman 1974: 407-415.

1961   "The Textual Criticism of the Old Testament," *BANE:* 113-132. Repr. Jellicoe 1974: 239-258.

Pasquali, Georgio

1952   *Storia della tradizione e critica del testo.* Florence: Le Monnier. 1st ed. 1932.

Penkower, Jordan S.

1988-89   "A Tenth Century Pentateuchal Manuscript from Jerusalem (Ms. C3) Corrected by Mishael ben Uzziel," *Tarbiz* 58:49-74 [Hebrew].

Pérez Castro, Federico

1959   (ed.) *Séfer Abišaʿ.* Madrid: Consejo Superior de Investigaciones Cientificas.

1960   "Das Kryptogramm des Sefer Abischaʾ," *VTS* 7:52-60.

1979-   (ed.) *El Codice de Profetas de El Cairo.* 7: *Profetas Menores* (1979); 1: *Josue-Jueces* (1980); 2: *Samuel* (1983); 3: *Reyes* (1984); 4: *Isaias* (1986); 5: *Jeremias* (1987); 6: *Ezequiel* (1988). Textos y Estudios "Cardinal Cisneros." Madrid: Consejo Superior de Investigaciones Cientificas.

Perkins, J., ed.

1852   *Kᵉtābâ qaddîšâ hā(naw): dᵉ-diyatîqî ʿattîqtâ sûryāʾît wᵉ-pušqâ dᵉ-men ʿebrāʾît,* Urmia: American Board of Commissioners for Foreign Missions. Repr. 1854.

Perles, Felix

1895   *Analekten zur Textkritik des Alten Testaments.* Munich: Ackermann.

1922 *Analekten zur Textkritik des Alten Testaments: Neue Folge.* Leipzig: Engel.

Perrella, Gaetano Maria

1949 *Introduzione Generale alla Sacra Biblia.* Turin: Marietti. 2nd ed. 1952.

Petermann, Julius Heinrich, and Carl Vollers

1872-91 *Pentateuchus Samaritanus ad fidem librorum manuscriptorum apud Nablusianos repertum.* Berlin: Moeser.

Peters, Curt

1935 "Peschitta und Targumim des Pentateuchs," *Muséon* 48:1-54.

1939 "Peschitta Psalter und Psalmentargum," *Muséon* 52:275ff.

Peters, Melvin K. H.

1979 *An Analysis of the Textual Character of the Bohairic of Deuteronomy.* SBLSCS 9. Missoula: Scholars Press.

1983– *A Critical Edition of the Coptic (Bohairic) Pentateuch.* 1: *Genesis* (1985); 2: *Exodus* (1986); 5: *Deuteronomy* (1983). Atlanta: Scholars Press.

Pietersma, Albert

1984 "Kyrios or Tetragram: A Renewed Quest for the Original Septuagint," in Pietersma and Cox 1984: 85-101.

1985 "Septuagint Research: A Plea for a Return to Basic Issues," *VT* 35:296-311.

————, **and Claude Cox, eds.**

1984 *De Septuaginta.* Festschrift John Williams Wevers. Mississauga, Ont.: Benben.

Ploeg, J. P. M. van der, and Adam Simon van der Woude

1971 *Le Targum de Job de la Grotte XI de Qumran.* Leiden: Brill.

Porten, Bezalel

1968 *Archives from Elephantine: The Life of an Ancient Jewish Military Colony.* Berkeley: University of California Press.

Praetorius, Franz

1899 *Das Targum zu Jesaja in jemenischer Überlieferung.* Berlin: Reuther und Reichard and London: Williams and Norgate.

1900 *Targum zum Buch der Richter in jemenischer Überlieferung.* Berlin: Reuther und Reichard.

Preuschen, Erwin

1889 *ZAW* 9:303.

Prijs, Josef

1957 "Über Ben Naftali-Bibelhandschriften und ihre paläographischen Besonderheiten," *ZAW* 69:171-184.

Prijs, Leo

1948 *Jüdische Tradition in der Septuaginta.* Leiden: Brill. Repr. Hildesheim: Olms, 1987 (with *Die grammatikalische Terminologie des Abraham Ibn Ezra*).

Pritchard, James B., ed.

1969 *Ancient Near Eastern Texts Relating to the Old Testament.* 3rd ed. Princeton: Princeton University Press.

Procksch, Otto

1935 "Tetraplarische Studien," *ZAW* N.S. 12:240-269.

Pummer, Reinhard
1976-77　　"The Present State of Samaritan Studies," *JSS* 21:39-61; 22:24-47.
Purvis, James D.
1968　　*The Samaritan Pentateuch and the Origin of the Samaritan Sect.* HSM 2.
van Puyvelde, C.
1960　　"Versions Syriaques," *DBSup* 6:834-884.
Rabin, Chaim
1955　　"The Dead Sea Scrolls and the History of the Old Testament Text," *JTS* N.S. 6:174-182.
1968　　"The Translation Process and the Character of the Septuagint," *Textus* 6:1-26.
Rahlfs, Alfred
1914　　*Verzeichnis der griechischen Handschriften des Alten Testaments.* NGWGPH Beiheft. Berlin: Weidmann. Continued by Göttingen: Septuaginta-Unternehmen.
1922　　*Das Buch Ruth griechisch, als Probe einer kritischen Handausgabe der Septuaginta.* Stuttgart: Württembergische Bibelanstalt.
1926　　*Genesis.* Stuttgart: Württembergische Bibelanstalt.
1928　　*Paul de Lagardes wissenschaftliches Lebenswerk im Rahmen einer Geschichte seines Lebens dargestelle.* MSU 4/1. Berlin: Weidmann.
1931　　*Psalmi cum Odis,* SVTG 10. Göttingen: Vandenhoeck und Ruprecht. 3rd ed. 1979.
1935　　(ed.) *Septuaginta, Id est Vetus Testamentum graece iuxta LXX interpretes.* 2 vols. Stuttgart: Württembergische Bibelanstalt. Editio minor in 1 vol. 1984.
Ranke, Ernst
1871　　*Par Palimpsestorum Wirceburgensium Antiquissimae Veteris Testamenti Versionis Latinae Fragmenta.* Vienna: Braumüller.
Reider (Rieder), David, ed.
1974　　*Pseudo-Jonathan: Targum Jonathan ben Uziel on the Pentateuch, based on London, British Library Add. 27031.* Jerusalem: Rieder.
Reider (Rieder), Joseph, and Turner, Nigel
1966　　*An Index to Aquila. VTS* 12.
Rendsburg, Gary, et al., eds.
1980　　*The Bible World. Festschrift Cyrus H. Gordon.* New York: KTAV.
Rengstorf, Karl Heinrich
1960　　*Hirbet Qumran und die Bibliothek vom Toten Meer.* Studia Delitzschiana 5. Stuttgart: Kohlhammer. English tr. *Ḥirbet Qumrân and the Problem of the Library of the Dead Sea Caves.* Leiden: Brill, 1963 (without endnotes and indexes). Leiden: Brill.
Revell, Ernest John
1969　　"A New Biblical Fragment with Palestinian Vocalization," *Textus* 7:59-75.
1977　　*Biblical Texts with Palestinian Pointing and Their Accents.* SBLMasS 4. Missoula: Scholars Press.
1990　　(ed.) *VIII International Congress of the International Organization for Masoretic Studies.* Atlanta: Scholars Press.

Reymond, Philippe
1989   "Vers la publication d'un Dictionnaire Hébreu-Français," *ZAH* 3/1:81-83.

Robert, Ulysse
1881   *Pentateuchi versio latina antiquissima e codice Lugdunensi.* Paris: Librairie de Firmin-Didot.
1900   *Heptateuchi partis posterioris versio latina antiquissima e codice Lugdunensi.* Lyon: Rey.

Roberts, Bleddyn Jones
1951   *The Old Testament Text and Versions: The Hebrew Text in Transmission and the History of the Ancient Versions.* Cardiff: University of Wales Press.
1959/60   "The Second Isaiah Scroll from Qumrân (IQIsb)," *BJRL* 42/1: 132-144.
1964   "The Hebrew Bible Since 1937," *JTS* N.S. 15: 253-264. Repr. Leiman 1974: 821-832.

Roberts, Colin Henderson
1936   *Two Biblical Papyri in the John Rylands Library, Manchester.* Manchester: Manchester University Press.
1954   "The Codex," *PBA* 40:169-204.
1970   "Books in the Graeco-Roman World and in the New Testament," *CHB* 1:48-66.

————, and Theodor Cressy Skeat
1987   *The Birth of the Codex.* London: British Academy.

Roberts, J. J. M.
1989   "The Princeton Classical Hebrew Dictionary Project," *ZAH* 3/1:84-89.

Robertson, Edward
1962   Review of Pérez Castro 1959, *VT* 12:228-235.

Rosenmüller, Ernst Friedrich Karl
1797   *Handbuch für die Literatur der biblischen Kritik und Exegese* 1. Göttingen: Vandenhoeck und Ruprecht.

Rosenthal, Franz
1939   *Die aramaistische Forschung seit Th. Nöldekes Veröffentlichungen.* Leiden: Brill. Repr. 1974.

de Rossi, Giovanni Bernardo
1784-88   *Variae Lectiones Veteris Testamenti, ex immensa MMS. Editorumq. Codicum Congerie haustae et ad Samar. Textum, ad vetustiss. versiones, ad accuratiores sacrae criticae fontes ac leges examinatae opera ac studio Johannis Bern. de Rossi.* 4 vols. Parma: Regius. Repr. with 1798 Supplement, 5 vols. in 2. Amsterdam: Philo, 1969-70.
1798   *Scholia critica in V. T. libros seu supplementa ad varias sacri textus lectiones.* Parma: Regius. Repr. Amsterdam: Philo, 1969-70.

Rost, Leonhard
1970   "Vermutungen über den Anlass zur griechischen Übersetzung der Tora," in *Wort — Gebot — Glaube.* Festschrift Walther Eichrodt, ed. Hans Joachim Stoebe. ATANT 59: 39-44.

Rowley, Harold Henry
1961   "Papyri from Elephantine," in Thomas 1961: 256-269.

Rubinstein, Arie
1959 "A Kethib-Qere Problem in the Light of the Isaiah-Scroll," *JSS* 4:127-133.
Rüger, Hans Peter
1983 *An English Key to the Latin Words and Abbreviations and the Symbols of Biblia Hebraica Stuttgartensia.* Stuttgart: German Bible Society.
Sabatier, Pierre
1739-49 *Bibliorum Sacrorum latinae versiones antiquae, seu vetus italica, et caetera quaecunque in codicibus mss. et antiquorum libris reperiri potuerunt quae cum Vulgata latina et cum textu graeco comparantur.* Rheims: Florentein. Repr. Turnhout: Herder, 1976.
Sachau, Eduard
1911 *Aramäische Papyrus und Ostraca aus einer jüdischen Militärkolonie zu Elephantine.* Leipzig: Hinrichs.
Sadaka, Abraham
1959 *Samaritan Version of the Pentateuch, Copied by Hand.* Tel Aviv: TaSH-YaT.
————, **and Ratson Sadaka**
1961-65 *Jewish Version, Samaritan Version of the Pentateuch, with Particular Stress on the Differences Between Both Texts.* Tel Aviv: Mass.
de Sainte Marie, Henri
1954 *Sancti Hieronymi Psalterium iuxta Hebraios.* CBL 11. Rome.
Sanders, Henry Arthur, and Carl Schmidt
1927 *The Minor Prophets in the Freer Collection and the Berlin Fragment of Genesis.* University of Michigan Studies, Humanistic Series 21. New York: Macmillan.
Sanders, James A.
1965 *The Psalms Scroll of Qumrân Cave 11 (11QPs^a).* DJD 4, Oxford: Oxford University Press.
1967 *The Dead Sea Psalms Scroll.* Ithaca: Cornell University Press.
1975 "Palestinian Manuscripts (1947-1972)," *QHBT,* 401-413.
Sanderson, Judith E.
1986 *An Exodus Scroll from Qumran: 4QpaleoExod^m and the Samaritan Tradition.* Atlanta: Scholars Press.
dos Santos, Elmar Camilo
1973 *An Expanded Hebrew Index for the Hatch-Redpath Concordance to the Septuagint.* Jerusalem: Dugith.
Sass, Benjamin
1991 *Studia Alphabetica.* OBO 102. Fribourg: Universitetsverlag and Göttingen: Vandenhoeck und Ruprecht.
Scanlin, Harold P.
1993 *The Dead Sea Scrolls and Modern Translations of the Old Testament.* Wheaton: Tyndale.
Schäfer, Peter
1980 "Bibelübersetzungen II. Targumim," TRE 6:216-228.
Schenker, A.
1975 *Hexaplarische Psalmenbruchstücke: Die hexaplarischen Psalmenfragmente der Handschriften Vaticanus Graecus 752 und Canonicus Grae-*

cus 62. OBO 8. Fribourg: Universitetsverlag and Göttingen: Vanden-hoeck und Ruprecht.

Schmitt, Armin

1966   *Stammt der sogenannte "Θ" — Text bei Daniel wirklich von Theodo-tion?* NAWG, Phil.-hist. Kl. 8.

Schneider, Heinrich

1949/50   "Wenig beachtet Rezensionen der Peshitta," *ZAW* N.S. 21:168-199.

1954   *Der Text der Gutenbergbibel.* BBB 7.

Schoeps, Hans Joachim

1950   "Aus frühchristlicher Zeit," *Religionsgeschichtliche Untersuchungen,* 82-119.

Schubart, Wilhelm

1918   *Einführung in die Papyruskunde.* Berlin: Weidmann.

1921   *Das Buch bei den Griechen und Römern.* Berlin: de Gruyter. 3rd ed. Heidelberg: Schneider, 1962.

Schwarz, Werner

1955   *Principles and Problems of Biblical Translation: Some Reformation Controversies and Their Background.* Cambridge: Cambridge University Press.

Scott, William R.

1990   *A Simplified Guide to BHS.* 2nd ed., Berkeley: BIBAL.

Sed-Rajna, Gabrielle

1988   *Lisbon Bible, 1482: British Library Or, 2626,* with introduction. Tel-Aviv: Nahar-Miskal.

Seeligmann, Isac Leo

1948   *The Septuagint Version of Isaiah: A Discussion of Its Problems.* Leiden: Brill.

1990   "Problems and Perspectives in Modern Septuagint Research," *Textus* 15:169-232. English translation of "Problemen en perspectieven in het moderne Septuagintaonderzoek," *JEOL* 2/7 (1940): 359-390e, 763-766.

Segal, Moses H.

1953   "The Promulgation of the Authoritative Text of the Hebrew Bible," *JBL* 72:35-47. Repr. Leiman 1974: 285-297.

Segall, J.

1910   *Travels Through Northern Syria.* London: The London Society for Promoting Christianity Amongst the Jews.

Sellin, Ernst, and Georg Fohrer

1968   *Introduction to the Old Testament.* 10th ed., trans. David E. Green. Nashville: Abingdon.

1968a   *Einleitung in das Alte Testament.* 11th ed. Heidelberg: Quelle und Meyer.

Shehadeh, Hasheeb

1978   *The Arabic Translation of the Samaritan Pentateuch. Prolegomena to a Critical Edition.* Diss. Hebrew University, Jerusalem.

Shutt, R. J. H.

1985   "Letter of Aristeas: A New Translation and Introduction," in Charlesworth 1985: 2:7-34.

Siegel, Jonathan Paul

1975   *The Severus Scroll and IQIsª*. SBL Masoretic Studies 2. Missoula: Scholars Press.

Simon, Leon

1954   "The Jerusalem Bible," *VT* 4:109f.

Skeat, Theodor Cressy

1969   "Early Christian Book-Production: Papyri and Manuscripts," *CHB* 2:54-79.

Skehan, Patrick W.

1954   "A Fragment of the 'Song of Moses' (Deut. 32) from Qumran," *BASOR* 136:12-15.

1955   "Exodus in the Samaritan Recension from Qumran," *JBL* 74:182-87.

1957   "The Q Mss. and Textual Criticism (ed. 4Q LXX Lev 26,2-16)," *VTS* 4:148-160.

1959   "Qumran and the Present State of Old Testament Text Studies: The Masoretic Text," *JBL* 78:21-25.

1964   "A Psalm Manuscript from Qumran (4Q Ps^b)," *CBQ* 26:313-322.

1965   "The Biblical Scrolls from Qumran and the Text of the Old Testament," *BA* 28:87-100. Repr. *QHBT* 1975: 264-277.

————, **Ernest Charles Ulrich, and Judith Sanderson, eds.**

1992   *Qumran Cave 4. 4: Palaeo-Hebrew and Greek Biblical Manuscripts*. DJD 9. Oxford: Clarendon Press.

Smolar, Leivy, Moses Aberbach, and Pinkhas Churgin

1983   *Studies in Targum Jonathan to the Prophets*. New York: KTAV.

Snaith, Norman H.

1957   "New Edition of the Hebrew Bible," *VT* 7:207f.

1961   "The Siloam Inscription," in Thomas 1961: 209-211.

1962   "The Ben Asher Text," *Textus* 2:8-13.

Sokoloff, Michael

1974   *The Targum to Job from Qumran Cave XI*. Ramat Gan: Bar-Ilan University.

Sonderlund, Sven

1985   *The Greek Text of Jeremiah: A Revised Hypothesis*. JSOTSS 47.

Sperber, Alexander

1956   *Codex Reuchlinianus, no. 3 of the Badische Landesbibliothek in Karlsruhe . . . with a General Introduction: Masoretic Hebrew*. Corpus Hebraicorum Medii Aevi 2/1. Copenhagen: Munksgaard.

1959-73   *The Bible in Aramaic*. 4 vols. Leiden: Brill.

1969   *The Prophets According to the Codex Reuchlinianus*. Leiden: Brill.

Sprengling, Martin, and William Creighton Graham

1931   *Barhebraeus' Scholia on the Old Testament. 1: Genesis–II Samuel*. Chicago: Oriental Institute.

Stamm, Johann Jakob

1953   "Zu Hiob 19,24," *ZAW* 65: 302.

Stauffer, Ethelbert, *et al.*

1965   "θεός," *TDNT* 3:65-119 (= *TWNT* 3 [1938]: 65-120).

Stern, Madeleine B., and Leona Rostenberg

1982   "The Libri Affair: A Study in Bibliokleptomania," *The 1982 Book-man's Yearbook* 2:25-28 (= *AB Bookman's Weekly,* June 22, 1981, 67\25: 4901-5).

Stier, Ewald Rudolf, and K. G. W. Theile

1847-55   *Polyglotten-Bibel zum praktischen Handgebrauch.* Bielfeld: Velhagen und Klasing. 4th ed. 1875.

Strack, Hermann Leberecht

1876   *Prophetarum posteriorum Codex Babylonicus Petropolitanus.* Petrograd: Bibliotheca publica imperialis. Repr. *The Hebrew Bible — Latter Prophets: The Babylonian Codex of Petrograd.* New York: KTAV, 1971.

1921   *Grammatik des Biblisch-Aramäischen.* 6th ed. Munich: Beck.

————, and Paul Billerbeck

1922-28   *Kommentar zum Neuen Testament aus Talmud und Midrasch.* 6 vols. in 7. Munich: Beck. Repr. 1961.

Stricker, Bruno Hugo

1956   *De brief van Aristeas: De hellenistische codificaties der praehelleense godsdiensten.* Amsterdam: Noord-Hollandsche.

Stummer, Friedrich

1928   *Einführung in die lateinische Bibel: Ein Handbuch für Vorlesungen und Selbstunterricht.* Paderborn: Schöningh.

1936   "Hauptprobleme der Erforschung der alttestamentliche Vulgata," *BZAW* 66:233-39.

1940/41   "Griechisch-römische Bildung und christliche Theologie in der Vulgata des Hieronymus," *ZAW* N.S. 17:251-269.

Suder, Robert W.

1984   *Hebrew Inscriptions: A Classified Bibliography.* Selinsgrove, PA: Susquehanna University.

Sukenik, Eleazar Lipa

1950   *Megillot genuzot* 2. Jerusalem: Bialik.

1954   *Otzer ha-megillot ha-genuzot.* Jerusalem: Bialik Foundation and the Hebrew University.

1955   *The Dead Sea Scrolls of the Hebrew University.* English trans. ed. Naḥman Avigad and Yigael Yadin. Jerusalem: Hebrew University and Magnes.

Sutcliffe, Edmund F.

1948   "The Name 'Vulgate,' " *Bib* 29:345-352.

Swete, Henry Barclay

1887-91   *The Old Testament in Greek.* 3 vols. Cambridge: Cambridge University Press.

1914   *An Introduction to the Old Testament in Greek.* 2nd ed. Cambridge: Cambridge University Press. Repr. New York: KTAV, 1968.

Szyszman, Simon

1959   "Un siècle après les découvertes de Firkowicz," *Akten des XXIV. Internationalen Orientalistenkongresses München 1957* 24: 194-96.

1975   "Centenaire de la mort de Firkowicz," *VTS* 28:196-216.

Tal (Rosenthal), Abraham

1980-83   *The Samaritan Targum of the Pentateuch: A Critical Edition.* 3 vols. Tel
           Aviv: Tel Aviv University.

1988   "The Samaritan Targum of the Pentateuch," in Mulder 1988: 189-216.

Talmon, Shemaryahu

1951   "The Samaritan Pentateuch," *JJS* 2:144-150.

1960   "Double Readings in the Masoretic Text," *Textus* 1:144-184.

1961   "Synonymous Readings," *ScrHier* 8:335-383.

1962   "DSIa as a Witness to Ancient Exegesis of the Book of Isaiah," *ASTI*
           1:62-72. Repr. *QHBT,* 116-126.

1964   "Aspects of the Textual Transmission of the Bible in the Light of
           Qumran Manuscripts," *Textus* 4:95-132. Repr. *QHBT,* 226-263.

1969   Prolegomenon to Romain Francis Butin, *The Ten Nequdoth of the Torah.*
           Diss., Catholic University, 1904. Repr. New York: KTAV, 1969.

1970   "The Old Testament Text," *CHB* 1:159-199. Repr. *QHBT,* 1-41.

1975   "The Textual Study of the Bible — A New Outlook," *QHBT,* 306-400.

1981   "The Ancient Hebrew Alphabet and Biblical Text Criticism," Mélanges
           D. Barthélemy. OBO 38:498-530. Fribourg: Universitetsverlag and
           Göttingen: Vandenhoeck und Ruprecht.

1985   "The Ancient Hebrew Alphabet and Biblical Criticism," Mélanges
           Mathias Delcor. AOAT 215:387-402.

Talstra, Eep

1989   *Computer Assisted Analysis of Biblical Texts: Papers Read on the Occasion
           of the "Werkgroep Informatica" Faculty of Theology, Vrije Universiteit,
           Amsterdam, November, 5-6, 1987.* Amsterdam: Free University Press.

Taylor, Charles F.

1900   *Hebrew-Greek Cairo Geniza Palimpsests from the Taylor-Schechter Col-
           lection.* Cambridge: Cambridge University Press.

Thackeray, Henry St. John

1921   *The Septuagint and Jewish Worship.* The Schweich Lectures, 1920.
           London: Milford.

Thomas, David Winton, ed.

1961   *Documents from Old Testament Times.* New York: Harper and Row.

Tisserant, Eugene

1914   *Specimina Codicum Orientalium.* Bonn: Marcus and Weber.

**Torczyner, Naphtali Harry, G. Lankester Harding, Agnes Lewis, and John L.
Starkey**

1938   *Lachish I (Tell ed-Duweir).* 1: *The Lachish Letters.* Oxford: Oxford
           University Press.

1940   "תעודות לכיש," *Yediʿot* 15/17. [Not available to the author.]

Tov, Emanuel

1971   "Pap. Giessen 13, 19, 22, 26: A Revision of the Septuagint?" *RB* 78:355-
           383.

1976   *The Septuagint Translation of Jeremiah and Baruch: A Discussion of
           an Early Revision of the LXX Jeremiah 29–52 and Baruch 1,1–3,8.* HSM
           8. Missoula: Scholars Press.

1981   *The Text-Critical Use of the Septuagint in Biblical Research.* Jerusalem Biblical Studies 3. Jerusalem: Sinor.

1982   "A Modern Textual Outlook Based on the Qumran Scrolls," *HUCA* 53:11-28.

1982a   "Criteria for Evaluating Textual Readings: The Limitation for Textual Rules," *HTR* 75:429-448.

1984   "Did the Septuagint Translators Always Understand Their Hebrew Text?" in Pietersma and Cox 1984, 53ff.

1986   *A Computerized Data Base for Septuagint Studies: The Parallel Aligned Text of the Greek and Hebrew Bible.* CATSS 2. Stellenbosch: Journal of Northwest Semitic Languages Supplement 1.

1988   "The Septuagint," in Mulder 1988: 161-188.

1989   *The Textual Criticism of the Bible: An Introduction.* Jerusalem: Bialik [Hebrew]. Philadelphia: Fortress, 1992 [English].

————, *et al.*

1990   *The Greek Minor Prophets Scroll from Naḥal Ḥever (8ḤevXIIgr).* DJD 8/1. Seiyal Collection 1. Oxford: Oxford University Press.

Trever, John C.

1972   *Scrolls from Qumran Cave I: The Great Isaiah Scroll, the Order of the Community, the Pesher to Habakkuk.* Jerusalem: Albright Institute of Archaeological Research and Shrine of the Book. Repr. black and white 1974.

Tufnell, Olga, *et al.*

1958   *Lachish IV (Tell ed-Duweir): The Bronze Age.* Oxford: Oxford University Press.

Ullendorff, Edward

1961   "The Moabite Stone," in Thomas 1961: 195-99.

1968   *Ethiopia and the Bible.* Schweich Lectures 1967. Oxford: Oxford University Press.

1980   "Hebrew, Aramaic and Greek: The Versions Underlying Ethiopic Translations of the Bible and Intertestamental Literature," *BW,* 249-257.

Vaccari, Alberto

1936   "Fragmentum Biblicum Saeculi II ante Christum," *Bib* 17:501-4.

Vannutelli, Primus

1931-34   *Libri synoptici Veteris Testamenti seu librorum Regum et Chronicorum loci paralleli.* 2 vols. Rome: Pontifical Biblical Institute.

Vasholz, Robert I.

1983   *Data for the Sigla of BHS.* Winona Lake: Eisenbrauns.

de Vaux, Roland Guerin

1953   "Les grottes de Murabba'at et leurs documents: Rapport préliminaire," *RB* 60:245-267.

1973   *Archaeology and the Dead Sea Scrolls.* Schweich Lectures 1959. Rev. ed. Oxford: Oxford University Press. 1st ed. 1961.

————, **and Józef Tadeusz Milik**

1977   *Qumran Grotte 4.* 1: *Archéologie;* 2: *Tefillin, Mezuzot et Targums* (4Q128–4Q157). DJD 6. Oxford: Oxford University Press.

Venetz, H. J.

1974   *Die Quinta des Psalteriums: Ein Beitrag zur Septuaginta- und Hexa-plaforschung.* PIRHT, Sect. Biblique et Masorétique I/2. Hildesheim: Gerstenberg.

Vermès, Géza

1973   *Scripture and Tradition in Judaism: Haggadic Studies.* 2nd ed. Leiden: Brill.

1982   *The Dead Sea Scrolls: Qumran in Perspective.* Philadelphia: Fortress.

Vööbus, Arthur

1958   *Peschitta und Targumim des Pentateuchs.* Stockholm: Etse.

1975   *The Pentateuch in the Version of the Syro-Hexapla: A Facsimile Edition of a Midyat Ms. Discovered in 1964.* CSCO 45. Rome.

Volz, Paul

1936   "Ein Arbeitsplan für die Textkritik des Alten Testaments," *ZAW* N.S. 13:100-113.

Waddell, W. G.

1944   "The Tetragrammaton in the LXX: With a Plate," *JTS* 45:158-161.

Waldman, Nahum M.

1989   *The Recent Study of Hebrew: A Survey of the Literature with a Selected Bibliography.* Cincinnati: Hebrew Union College Press and Winona Lake: Eisenbrauns.

Waltke, Bruce K., and Michael P. O'Connor

1990   *An Introduction to Biblical Hebrew Syntax.* Winona Lake: Eisenbrauns.

Warner, Sean

1980   "The Alphabet: An Innovation and Its Diffusion," *VT* 30:81-90.

Weber, Robert, ed.

1953   *Le Psautier Romain et les autres anciens Psautiers Latins.* CBL 10. Rome: Abbey St. Jerome.

1969   *Biblia Sacra iuxta Vulgatam Versionem: Adiuvantibus Bonifatio Fischer OSB, Johanne Gribomont OSB, Hadley Frederich Davis Sparks, Walter Thiele, Recensuit et brevi apparatu instruxit R. Weber OSB.* 2 vols. Stuttgart: German Bible Society. 3rd ed. 1975; Editio minor in 1 vol. 1983.

Weil, Gérard E.

1962   "Propositions pour une étude de la tradition massorétique babylonienne," *Textus* 2:103-119.

1963   "La nouvelle édition de la Massorah (BHK IV) et l'histoire de la Massorah," *VTS* 9:266-284.

1963a   "Quatre fragments de la Massorah Magna," *Textus* 3:74-120.

1963b   "La Massorah Magna Babylonienne des Prophetes," *Textus* 3:163-170.

1968   "Nouveaux fragments inédits de la Massorah Magna babylonienne," *Textus* 6:75-105.

1971   *Massorah Gedolah iuxta Codicem Leningradensem B 19a, elaboravit ediditque Gérard E. Weil.* 1: *Catalogi.* Rome: Pontifical Biblical Institute.

Weitzmann, Kurt, and Herbert L. Kessler

1986   *The Cotton Genesis.* The Illustrations in the Manuscripts of the Septuagint. 1: Genesis. Princeton: Princeton University Press.

Wellhausen, Julius
1871   *Der Text der Bücher Samuelis.* Göttingen: Vandenhoeck und Ruprecht.
Wellisch, Hans H.
1985-86   "Hebrew Bible Concordances, with a Biographical Study of Solomon Mandelkern," *Jewish Book Annual* 43:56-91.
Wendland, Paul, ed.
1900   *Aristeae ad Philocratèm epistula.* Leipzig: Teubner.
Wernberg-Møller, Preben
1962   "An Inquiry into the Validity of the Text-critical Argument for an Early Dating of the Recently Discovered Palestinian Targum," *VT* 12:313-330.
Wevers, John Williams
1952   "A Study in the Textual History of Codex Vaticanus in the Books of Kings," *ZAW* 64:178-189.
1954   "Septuaginta-Forschungen," *TRu* N.S. 22:85-138, 171-190.
1968   "Septuaginta-Forschungen seit 1954," *TRu* N.S. 33:18-76.
1974   *Genesis.* SVTG 1. Göttingen: Vandenhoeck und Ruprecht.
1974a   *Text History of the Greek Genesis.* MSU 11. Göttingen: Vandenhoeck und Ruprecht. Also AAWG, Göttingen.
1977   *Deuteronomy.* SVTG 3/2. Göttingen: Vandenhoeck und Ruprecht.
1978   *Text of the Greek Deuteronomy.* MSU 13. Göttingen: Vandenhoeck und Ruprecht.
1982   *Text History of the Greek Numbers,* MSU 16. Göttingen: Vandenhoeck und Ruprecht.
1986   *Leviticus.* SVTG 2/2. Göttingen: Vandenhoeck und Ruprecht.
1986a   *Text History of the Greek Leviticus.* MSU 19. Göttingen: Vandenhoeck und Ruprecht.
————, **and Udo Quast**
1977   *Numbers.* SVTG 3/1. Göttingen: Vandenhoeck und Ruprecht.
Wickes, William
1881-87   *A Treatise on the Accentuation of the Old Testament.* 2 vols. Oxford: Clarendon. Repr. with Prolegomenon by Aron Dotan. New York: KTAV, 1970.
Wieder, N.
1956/57   "The Qumran Sectaries and the Caraites," *JQR* 47:97-113, 269-292.
Wiseman, Donald John
1970   "Books in the Ancient Near East and in the Old Testament," *CHB* 1:30-48.
Wonneberger, Reinhard
1990   *Understanding BHS: A Manual for Users of Biblia Hebraica Stuttgartensia.* 2nd ed. Subsidia Biblica 8. Rome: Pontifical Biblical Institute.
Wright, George Ernest, ed.
1961   *The Bible and the Ancient Near East: Essays in Honor of William Foxwell Albright.* Garden City, NY: Doubleday. Repr. Winona Lake: Eisenbrauns, 1979.
Wright, William, ed.
1875-83   *Facsimiles of Manuscripts and Inscriptions.* Oriental Series. London: Palaeographical Society.

Wutz, Franz Xavier

1923 "Die ursprüngliche Septuaginta," *TBl* 2:111-16.

1937 *Systematische Wege von der Septuaginta zum hebräischen Urtext.* Stuttgart: Kohlhammer.

Yadin, Yigael

1966 "Another Fragment (E) of the Psalms Scroll from Qumran Cave 11 (11QPsª)," *Textus* 5:1-11.

1976 *Masada.* 2nd ed. New York: Random House.

1983 *Megillat ha-Miqdash.* 3 vols. Plates, transcription. Jerusalem: Israel Exploration Society. English trans. *The Temple Scroll,* 1984.

Yeivin, Israel

1962 "The Vocalization of Qere-Kethiv in A," *Textus* 2:146-49.

1963 "A Palestinian Fragment of Haftaroth and Other Mss with Mixed Pointing," *Textus* 3:121-27.

1969 "The Division into Sections in the Psalms," *Textus* 7:76-102.

1980 *Introduction to the Tiberian Masorah. Trans. and ed. Ernest John Revell.* SBLMasS 5. Missoula: Scholars Press.

Ziegler, Joseph

1934 *Die Einheit der Septuaginta zum Zwölfprophetenbuch.* Vorlesungsverzeichnis der Staats Akademie zu Braunsberg/Ostpr., 1-16. Repr. Ziegler 1971: 29-42.

1934a *Untersuchungen zur Septuaginta des Buches Isaias.* ATAbh 12/3.

1939 *Isaias.* SVTG 14. 3rd ed., 1982.

1943 *Duodecim Prophetae.* SVTG 13. Rev. ed. 1967.

1943/44 *Die jüngeren griechischen Übersetzungen als Vorlagen der Vulgata in den prophetischen Schriften.* Vorlesungsverzeichnis der Staats Akademie zu Braunsberg/Ostpr., 1-92. Repr. Ziegler 1971: 139-228.

1944 "Studien zur Verwertung der Septuaginta im Zwölfprophetenbuch," *ZAW* 60:107-131.

1944a "Beiträge zur koptischen Dodekapropheton-Übersetzung," *Bib* 25:105-142.

1944b "Der griechische Dodekapropheton-Text der Complutenser Polyglotte," *Bib* 25:297-310. Repr. Ziegler 1971: 229-242.

1945 "Der Text der Aldina im Dodekapropheton," *Bib* 26:37-51. Repr. Ziegler 1971: 306-320.

1945/48 "Die Bedeutung des Chester Beatty-Scheide Papyrus 967 für die Textüberlieferung der Ezechiel-Septuaginta," *ZAW* 61:76-94. Repr. Ziegler 1971: 321-339.

1952 *Ezechiel.* SVTG 16/1. Rev. ed. 1978.

1954 *Susanna, Daniel, Bel et Draco.* SVTG 16/2.

1957 *Jeremias, Baruch, Threni, Epistula Jeremiae.* SVTG 15. Rev. ed. 1976.

1960 *Antike und moderne lateinische Psalmenübersetzungen.* SBAW.

1962 *Sapientia Salomonis.* SVTG 12/1. Rev. ed. 1980.

1962a "Die Septuaginta: Erbe und Auftrag," Würzburger Universitätsreden 33, 5-29. Repr. Ziegler 1971: 590-614.

1962b Review of Vööbus 1958, *TRev* 58: 304-7.

1965 *Sapientia Iesu Filii Sirach.* SVTG 12/2. Rev. ed. 1980.

1971   *Sylloge: Gesammelte Aufsätze zur Septuaginta.* MSU 10. Göttingen: Vandenhoeck und Ruprecht.

1982   *Iob.* SVTG 9/4.

1985   *Beiträge zum griechischen Iob.* MSU 18. Göttingen: Vandenhoeck und Ruprecht.

Zlotowitz, Bernard M.

1981   *The Septuagint Translation of the Hebrew Terms in Relation to God in the Book of Jeremiah With an Introductory Essay: On Anthropomorphisms and Anthropopathisms in the Septuagint and Targum, by H. M. Orlinsky.* New York: KTAV.

Index of Authors

Aberbach, Moses, 83
Aejmelaeus, Anneli, 242
Alba Cecilia, Amparo, 23
Albrektson, Bertil, 13, 14, 119, 120
Albright, William Foxwell, 2, 3, 15, 34, 117, 136, 138, 140, 144, 152
Alexander, Philip S., 83, 89, 131, 146
Allegro, John Marco, 32
Allgeier, Arthur, 98
Alonso-Schökel, Luis, 129
Alt, Albrecht, 43
Aly, Zaki, 190
Aptowitzer, Victor, 19, 233
Avigad, Naḥman, 32, 34, 152

Baars, Willem, 59, 89, 90
Bacher, Wilhelm, 18
Baer, Seligmann, 41, 178
Baillet, Maurice, 32, 47
Baker, H. Wright, 32
Bardtke, Hans, 8, 20
Barnes, G. E., 89
Barnes, William Emery, 89
Barr, James, 17, 96, 105, 117, 120, 127
Barthélemy, Dominique, 4, 9, 36, 52, 54-57, 60, 120, 148, 192
Bauer, Hans, 22, 41
Baumgärtel, Friedrich, 53
Baumgartner, Walter, 116, 127, 129
Baumstark, Anton, 86
Belsheim, Johannes Engebretsen, 93
Benoît, Pierre, 32
Ben-David, Abba, 130

Ben-Hayim, Zeev, 27
Ben-Zvi, Izhak, 20, 36
Berger, Samuel, 92
Berliner, Abraham, 83
Bertram, Georg, 68, 69, 71
Beyer, Klaus, 27
Bidawid, R. J., 89
Birnbaum, Solomon A., 4, 152
Black, Matthew, 81, 240
Blau, Ludwig, 16, 158
Boer, P. H. A. de, 85, 89
Borger, Rykle, 119
Bornkamm, Heinrich, 122
Botte, Bernard, 246
Bowker, John, 79
Briggs, Charles A., 116, 127
Brock, Sebastian P., 48, 50, 55, 89
Brooke, Alan E., 76
Brown, Francis, 116, 127
Bruyne, Donatien de, 95
Budge, Ernest Alfred Wallis, 101, 220
Burkitt, Francis Crawford, 55
Burrows, Millar, 32, 35, 154, 158
Busto-Saiz, José Ramón, 56

Cassuto, Moshe David, 42
Ceriani, Antonius Maria, 59, 88, 89
Chiesa, Bruno, 21, 23
Churgin, Pinkhas, 83
Clines, David J. A., 127, 128
Coggins, Richard J., 45
Cook, Stanley Arthur, 34
Cowley, Arthur Ernest, 129, 142

Cox, Claude E., 103
Cross, Frank Moore, 2-4, 6, 15, 21, 53, 150, 152, 160, 240

David, C. Joseph, 89
Davies, Graham I., 130
Dedering, S., 90
Deissmann, Adolf, 69
Deist, Ferdinand E., 131
Delekat, Lienhard, 86
Delitzsch, Franz, 41
Delitzsch, Friedrich, 108
Demsky, Aaron, 230
Dexinger, Ferdinand, 45
Diaz Esteban, Fernando, 30
Dietrich, Manfried, 23
Díez Macho, Alejandro, 23, 26, 81, 82
Díez Merino, Luis, 23
Diringer, David, 3, 134, 138, 142, 228
Dirksen, Peter B., 85, 87-89, 131
Dold, Alban, 93, 212, 214, 216, 235
Donner, Herbert, 2, 127, 130, 136, 138
Dörrie, Heinrich, 60, 63
Dotan, Aron, 24, 30, 36, 126, 174
Drazin, Israel, 83
Driver, Godfrey Rolles, 2, 9, 110, 117, 136, 138, 170
Driver, Samuel Rolles, 116, 127
Dunand, Françoise, 190

Ecker, Roman, 104
Edelmann, Rafael, 10, 13, 104
Eissfeldt, Otto, 43, 148, 158
Elbogen, Ismar, 166
Elliger, Karl, ix, 10, 34, 117
Emerton, J. A., 22, 57, 86, 89
Even-Shoshan, Abraham, 124

Fernandez-Galliano, M., 72
Fernández Tejero, Emilia, 35, 131
Field, Frederick, 59
Fischer, Bonifatius, 92-94, 98, 99, 214, 218
Fischer, Johann, 67
Fishbane, Michael, 110
Fitzmyer, Joseph A., 32
Fohrer, Georg, 32, 112

Foster, Julia A., 81
Franchi, de' Cavalieri, Pio Petro, 204, 208
Freedman, David Noel, 3, 21
Frensdorff, Salomon, 30
Fritsch, Charles Theodore, 50, 69

Gall, August Freiherr von, 47
Galling, Kurt, 136, 138, 140
Gehman, Henry Snyder, 72
Geiger, Abraham, 45, 112
Geissen, Angelo, 72
Gelston, A., 89
Gerleman, Gillis, 17
Gertner, M., 10
Gese, Hartmut, 114
Gesenius, Wilhelm, 45, 116, 127, 129
Gibson, John C. L., 2, 6, 130, 136, 138
Ginsburg, Christian David, 10, 16, 30, 38, 39, 41, 42, 114, 176
Ginsburger, Moses, 82
Giron Blanc, Luis-F., 47
Glaue, Paul, 78
Gordis, Robert, 17
Goshen-Gottstein, Moshe H., 19-21, 24, 25, 27, 34-37, 39, 41, 44, 114, 118, 174
Gottlieb, Hans, 89
Graf, Georg, 224
Graham, William Creighton, 88
Gray, John, 80
Greenberg, Moshe, 105
Gressmann, Hugo, 136, 138
Grossfeld, Bernard, 79, 83
Grossouw, Wilhelm Karel Maria, 100
Groves, J. Alan, 126
Gunkel, Hermann, 112

Hadas, Moses, 51
Haefeli, Leo, 85
Halperin, David J., 70
Hamm, Winfried, 72
Hammershaimb, Erling, 89
Hanhart, Robert, 51-55, 60, 66, 69, 77, 190
Hanson, Richard Simon, 3
Haran, Menahem, 6

Harding, G. Lankester, 31, 146, 160, 162, 164
Harding, Stephen, 98
Harkavy, Albert, 31, 180
Harnack, Adolf von, 50
Hatch, Edwin, 76, 78, 125
Hayman, A. P., 89
Hempel, Johannes, 19, 32, 71, 108, 114, 140
Herrmann, Johannes, 53
Holl, Karl, 122
Holmes, H. E., 41
Holmes, Robert, 71, 73, 76
Hyvärinen, Kyosti, 55

Jansma, T., 89
Jaroš, Karl, 2
Jellicoe, Sidney, 50, 57, 60, 131
Jepsen, Alfred, 113
Jeremias, Joachim, 12, 80
Johnson, Allan Chester, 72
Johnson, Bo, 103
Joüon, Paul, 129

Kahle, Paul E., 13, 16, 20, 22-25, 27, 34, 37-39, 41-43, 45, 47, 55-58, 60, 63-65, 67, 71, 81, 82, 84, 86, 101, 104, 156, 158, 160, 166, 170, 172, 174, 176, 178, 180, 182, 184, 186, 190, 192, 194, 226
Kahle, Paul E., Jr., 100
Kappler, Werner, 77
Karo, Georg Heinrich, 208
Kase, Edmund Harris, Jr., 72
Kasser, Rodolphe, 72, 100
Katsh, Abraham, 31
Katz, Eliezer, 124
Katz, Peter (W. P. M. Walters), 55, 57, 63
Kautzsch, Emil Friedrich, 51, 129
Kedar-Kopfstein, Benjamin, 96, 131
Kellermann, Diether, 10, 17
Kennedy, James, 108
Kenyon, Frederic George, 56, 72, 136, 194
Kessler, Herbert L., 74
Khayyath, G. Ebed-Jesus, 89

Kilpatrick, George Dunbar, 55
Kippenberg, Hans G., 45
Kittel, Rudolf, 10, 39, 42, 43
Klein, Michael L., 82, 136
Kochavi, Moshe, 230
Kohlenberger, John R., 124
Köhler, Ludwig, 116, 127, 129
Kooij, Arie van der, 33, 56, 86, 87, 114
Kosack, W., 101
Koster, M. D., 86, 87, 89
Kraeling, Emil G., 142
Kuhn, Karl Georg, 125

Lagarde, Paul A. de, 19, 59, 61-66, 73, 76, 77, 83, 84, 115
Landauer, Samuel, 83
Lane, D. J., 89
Lebram, J. C. H., 89
Lee, Samuel, 89, 236
Lehman, I. O., 109
Leiman, Sid Z., 131
Lella, Alexander A. di, 89
Leloir, Louis, 103
Lemaire, André, 3
Leveen, Jacob, 162
Levine, Etan, 12, 79
Levy, Kurt, 25
Lewis, Agnes, 140
Le Déaut, Roger J., 79, 81, 82
Lietzmann, Hans, 204, 208
Lifshitz, B., 78, 192
Lipschütz, Lazar, 24, 35
Lisowsky, Gerhard, 116, 124
Loewe, Raphael J., 97
Loewinger, David Samuel, 24, 35, 36
Löfgren, Oscar, 222
Louw, Johannes P., 128
Lund, Shirley, 81

Maas, Paul, 113
Macuch, Rudolf, 47
Maher, Michael, 81
Maier, Johann, 4, 7
Mandelkern, Solomon, 116, 124
Manson, Thomas Walter, 69
Maori, Yeshayahu, 86
Margolis, Max Leopold, 78

Martin, M. Fitzmaurice, 81
Mathews, Kenneth A., 3
McCarthy, Carmel, 18
McNamara, Martin, 79, 81
Meershoek, G. Q. A., 97
Mercati, Giovanni, 58, 59, 200
Merx, Adalbert, 84, 236
Meyer, Rudolf, 25-27, 127, 150
Michaelis, Johann Heinrich, 37, 40
Migne, Jacques-Paul, 190
Milik, Józef Tadeusz, 6, 9, 32, 148, 150, 164
Milne, H. M., 198
Min, Young-Jin, 53
Mitchell, C. W., 89
Möhle, August, 59
Morag, Shelomo, 25, 26
Mulder, Martin Jan, 89, 131
Müller, Karlheinz, 51
Muraoka, Takemitsu, 129
Murtonen, Aimo Edward, 23, 47

Nautin, Pierre, 96
Navarro Peiro, Angeles 23
Naveh, Joseph, 1
Nida, Eugene A., 128
Noth, Martin, 142
Nyberg, Hendrik Samuel, 67

Oesch, Josef M., 20
Orlinsky, Harry Meyer, 17, 69, 70
O'Connell, Kevin G., 55

Parsons, James, 71, 73, 76
Pasquali, Georgio, 12
Penkower, Jordan S., 24
Pérez Castro, Federico, 23, 35, 47
Perkins, J., 89
Perles, Felix, 170
Perrella, Gaetano Maria, 202
Petermann, Julius Heinrich, 84
Peters, Curt, 86
Peters, M. K. H., 101
Pietersma, Albert, 56, 69, 188, 190
Pinkerton, I., 89
Ploeg, J. P. M. van der, 80
Porten, Bezalel, 142

Praetorius, Franz, 83, 237
Preuschen, Erwin, 41
Prijs, Josef, 26, 38, 70
Pritchard, James B., 238
Procksch, Otto, 59
Pummer, Reinhard, 45
Purvis, James D., 45
Puyvelde, C. van, 85

Quast, Udo, 77

Rabin, Chaim, 15, 67
Rahlfs, Alfred, 54-56, 59, 61, 62, 71, 73, 75-78, 208
Ranke, Ernst, 93
Redpath, Henry, 76, 78, 125
Reider (Rieder), David, 82
Reider (Rieder), Joseph, 55
Rendsburg, Gary, 238
Rengstorf, Karl Heinrich, 146
Revell, Ernest John, 23, 131
Reymond, Philippe, 128
Rignell, Lars G., 89
Robert, J., 82
Robert, Ulysse, 93, 214
Roberts, Bleddyn Jones, 14, 37, 130, 156
Roberts, Colin Henderson, 8, 71, 72, 188, 192
Roberts, Jimmy J. M., 128
Robertson, Edward, 47
Roediger, Ernst, 127
Röllig, W., 2, 130, 136, 138
Rosenmüller, Ernst Friedrich Karl, 19, 41
Rosenthal, Franz, 48, 49, 84
Rossi, Giovanni Bernardo de, 40, 114
Rost, Leonhard, 52, 109
Rostenberg, Leona, 214
Rowley, Harold Henry, 142
Rubinstein, Arie, 17
Rüger, Hans Peter, 106, 123

Sabatier, Pierre, 92, 214
Sachau, Eduard, 142
Sadaka, Abraham, 47
Sadaka, Ratson, 47

Sailhamer, John H., 124
Sainte Marie, Henri de, 99
Sanders, Henry Arthur, 57, 72, 75, 196
Sanders, James A., 32, 34
Sanderson, Judith E., 3, 32
Santos, Elmar Camilo dos, 125
Sass, Benjamin, 3
Scanlin, Harold P., 15, 32
Schäfer, Peter, 79, 82
Schenker, A., 59
Schiby, J., 78
Schmidt, Carl, 57, 72, 196
Schmitt, Armin, 56
Schneider, Heinrich, 90, 98
Schoeps, Hans Joachim, 56
Schubart, Wilhelm, 8, 192
Schwarz, Werner, 96
Scott, William R., 123
Sed-Rajna, Gabrielle, 42
Seeligmann, Isac Leo, 70
Segal, Moses H., 38
Segall, J., 36
Sellin, Ernst, 32
Seow, Choon-Leong, 128
Shehadeh, Hasheeb, 104
Shutt, R. J. H., 51
Siegel, Jonathan Paul, 38
Simon, Leon, 164
Skeat, Theodore Cressy, 5, 6, 8, 9, 198
Skehan, Patrick W., 3, 15, 32, 71, 150, 236
Smalley, William A., 240
Smolar, Leivy, 83
Snaith, Norman H., 42, 138
Sokoloff, Michael, 80
Sonderlund, Sven, 53
Sperber, Alexander, 25, 26, 83, 236
Sprengling, Martin, 88
Sprey, T., 89
Stamm, Johann Jakob, 9
Starkey, John L., 140
Stauffer, Ethelbert, 69
Stern, Madeleine B., 214
Stier, Ewald Rudolf, 76
Strack, Hermann Leberecht, 18, 31, 37, 178, 180, 237
Stricker, Bruno Hugo, 52

Stummer, Friedrich, 97, 98
Suder, Robert W., 130
Sukenik, Eleazar Lipa, 32, 33, 146, 148, 152, 156, 160
Sutcliffe, Edmund F., 98
Swete, Henry Barclay, 51, 76
Szyszman, Simon, 31

Tal (Rosenthal), Abraham, 84, 131
Talmon, Shemaryahu, 15, 16, 33, 46, 105, 108, 110, 240
Talstra, Eep, 126
Taylor, Charles F., 55
Testuz, Michel, 72
Thackeray, Henry St. John, 51, 53, 76
Theile, K. G. W., 76
Thomas, David Winton, 2, 140
Tisserant, Eugene, 206
Torczyner, Naphtali Harry, 140
Tov, Emanuel, 7, 15, 32, 53, 54, 67, 68, 71, 78, 105, 118, 125, 126, 131, 192
Trever, John C., 32, 152
Tufnell, Olga, 134
Turner, Nigel, 55

Ullendorff, Edward, 102
Ulrich, Eugene, 32

Vaccari, Alberto, 188
Vannutelli, Primus, 130
Vasholz, Robert I., 123
Vaux, Roland Guerin de, 6, 31, 32, 146, 148, 160, 164, 186
Venetz, H. J., 56
Vermès, Géza, 80, 82
Vliet, M. van, 89
Vollers, Carl, 84
Volz, Paul, 112, 122
Vööbus, Arthur, 59, 86

Waddell, W. G., 190
Waldman, Nahum M., 129
Walter, D. M., 89
Waltke, Bruce K., 129
Warner, Sean, 3
Weber, Robert, 95, 96, 99, 126

Weil, Gérard E., 28-30
Weitzmann, Kurt, 74
Wellhausen, Julius, 111
Wellisch, Hans H., 124
Wendland, Paul, 51
Wernberg-Møller, Preben, 37, 80
Wevers, John Wiulliams, 53, 58, 60,
    62, 65, 69, 77, 78
Whitaker, Richard E., 128
Wickes, William, 36, 237
Wieder, N., 24
Wiseman, Donald John, 5
Wonneberger, Reinhard, 106

Woude, A. S. van der, 80
Wright, George Ernest, 238
Wright, William, 210, 224
Wutz, Franz Xavier, 67

Yadin, Yigael, 7, 32, 34
Yeivin, Israel, 10, 16, 20, 23, 24, 26,
    28, 37

Ziegler, Joseph, 53, 56, 57, 60-62, 66,
    68, 70, 75-78, 86, 91, 96, 97, 100-
    102, 194, 204
Zlotowitz, Bernard M., 69

Index of Subjects

Abbreviations, 29, 30, 106, 110, 123, 170
  Masora, 29, 30, 123
  Masoretic text, 110, 170
Abisha scroll. *See* Samaritans
Abu al-Barakat scroll. *See* Samaritans
Abu Sa'id, 104
Adiabene, 86
Ahikar, 142
Ahiram, 2
Akhmimic, 100
Akiba, Rabbi, 13, 18, 55
Akkadian, 117
Aksum, 102
Alcuin, 97, 98
Alexander Jannaeus, 146
Alexandrian philologists, 12
Alphabet, 1-2
  Armenian, 103
  Coptic, 100
  Greek, 22
  Phoenician, 3
  Semitic, 1-3, 142, 228
Ambrose, 94
'Anan ben David, 23
Ancient Biblical Manuscripts Center, 126
Anthropomorphism, 69, 80
Antinoopolis. *See* Papyrus
Aphraates, 88
Apollinarius of Laodicea, 95
Aquila, 55. *See* Greek versions
Arabic, 34, 74, 102, 104, 186, 222, 224

Old South Arabic, 117
Arad, 2
Aramaic. *See* Targums
'Araq el-Emir. *See* Inscriptions
Aristarchan sigla, 58, 59, 74, 202
Aristarchus, 58
Aristeas, 6, 51, 52, 63-65
Armenian, 103
Asterisk, 58, 154, 202, 204, 206
Augustine, 50, 91, 96

Babylon, Babylonians, 2, 12, 140
Babylonian:
  Masora, 30
  Pointing, 22-24, 37, 166, 226
  Schools, 12, 20, 27
  Talmud, 4, 18, 21
  Targum. *See* Targums
  Text type, 15
Bar Kochba, 31, 164, 192
Barnabas, 56, 198
Baruch, 6
Basil the Great, 62
Bede, Venerable, 218
Ben Asher, 24-27, 30, 35-36, 41-43, 182, 226
  Aaron ben Asher, 13, 25, 26, 36, 37, 174, 176, 178, 180
  Moses ben Asher, 25, 26, 35, 36, 172
Ben Buya'a, Shelomo, 13, 174, 178
Ben Chayyim. *See* Hebrew editions
Ben Naphtali 24-27, 35, 37, 41, 43, 182

Ben 'Uzziel, Mishael, 24, 176
    Jonathan, 56
Berlin Genesis. *See* Papyrus
Biblia Hebraica, 42, 43, 106
    BHK, ix, 10, 39, 42, 43
    BHS, ix, 10, 43, 123
Biscop, Benedict, 218
Bodleian Library, Oxford, 20, 35, 182,
    184, 226
Bohairic, 100
Bomberg, Daniel, 10, 39, 184
Bornstein, Aryeh, 230
Buxtorf, Johan, 28, 84, 184
Byblos, 2

Caesarea, 59, 62, 96
Cairo, 35, 36, 174, 180
    Cairo Codex, 20, 44
    Cairo Geniza, 7, 8, 11, 19, 22, 31,
        34, 55, 81, 158
Cambridge University Library, 34, 35,
    47, 75, 166
Carbon-14, 31
Cassiodorus, 218
Catena, 58, 62, 208
    Catena text, 62, 76, 194
Center for the Computer Analysis of
    Texts (CCAT), 125
Centre 'Informatique et Bible', 126
Ceolfrid, Abbot, 218
Chapters, 20, 21, 98
Charlemagne, 98
Chester Beatty. *See* papyrus
China, 7
Chrysostom, 60, 62
Chufutkaleh, 37
Church Fathers, 51, 62, 72, 88, 91, 92,
    94
Clement VIII, Pope, 98
Codex, 7-8, 11
Colbert, Jean Baptiste, 202
Complutensian, 23, 75, 184, 226
Computer Assisted Tools for Septu-
    agint Studies, 126
Conjecture, 43, 68, 106, 113, 116, 119,
    120, 154, 160, 162
Copper scroll, 5

Coptic, 75, 100, 194, 220, 224
Crusaders, 35
Cyprian, 91, 94
Cyril of Alexandria, 62

Damascus Document. *See* Zadokite
    Document
Damasus I, Pope, 95
Dead Sea, 11, 31, 146
    Dead Sea Scrolls, 3, 20, 128, 131
    Dead Sea Scrolls Manuscript Project,
        131
Demetrius of Phaleron, 51
Diocletian, 60
Dittography, 14, 40, 109
Division, 41
    Book, 8
    Chapter, 21, 98
    Parashah (Parashoth), 20, 36
    Seder (Sedarim), 20
    Verse, 21
    Word, 14, 73, 110, 134, 188
Double readings, 110

Ebionite, 55, 56
Egypt, 5-7, 9, 12, 33, 34, 60, 69, 70,
    87, 100, 104, 142, 180
    Lower Egypt, 73, 100, 200
    Upper Egypt, 72, 100, 196, 220
Eleazar, High Priest, 51
Elephantine, 142
Emendation, 18, 33, 43, 70, 106, 116,
    119, 120, 154, 194
Ephraem Syrus, 74, 88
Epiphanius, 56
Erfurt, 37, 40
Essenes, 146
Ethiopic, 102, 222
Eusebius of Caesarea, 56, 57, 59, 60,
    62, 94
Ezra, 2, 79

Fatyun ibn Aiyub. *See* Pethion
Fayyum, 72, 188
Finchasiye. *See* Polyglot
Firkowitsch, Abraham, 30, 31, 37
Fouad. *See* Papyrus

Free scribal usage, 15, 18, 21, 27, 87, 110, 114
Free translation, 53, 68, 102

Gamaliel, 79
Genesis apocryphon, 32, 80
Geniza. *See* Cairo Geniza
Gerizim, 45, 46
Gezer, 2, 3, 230
Glosses, 93, 94, 112, 117, 128, 212
Greek codices
  Coislinianus, 59, 74
  Colberto-Sarravianus, 59, 73, 202
  Marchalianus, 59, 62, 74, 204
  Sinaiticus, 72, 73, 198
  Vaticanus, 62, 64, 73, 74, 76
  Venetus, 62, 74
Greek editions, 75-78
  Aldine, 76
  Cambridge Septuagint, 76, 77, 126
  Complutensian, 75, 226
  Göttingen Septuagint, 66, 71, 73, 75, 77, 78, 115, 126
  Holmes-Parsons, 71, 73, 76
  Rahlfs, 62, 77, 78
  Sixtine, 76, 98
  Swete, 76
Greek versions
  Aquila, 4, 55, 57, 83, 97, 158, 194, 204, 206
  Hesychius, 60, 62
  Lucian, 60, 62
  Septuagint, 50-78, *passim*
  Symmachus 55-57, 97, 194, 206
Gregory of Nazianzus, 95

Hadassi, 28
Hapax legomena, 28
Haphtarah, 166
Haplography, 14, 40, 109
Harding, Stephen, 98
Harris Papyrus. *See* Papyrus
Hebrew codices, 34-38
  Aleppo, 13, 20, 24, 30, 36, 37, 43, 44, 142, 174, 178
  Bodleian Genesis, 75
  Cairensis, 11, 24, 35, 172

Erfurt, 37, 40
Leningradensis, 10, 13, 36, 37, 43, 180
St. Petersburg Prophets, 37, 38, 166
Hebrew editions
  Baer, 41
  Ben Chayyim, 10, 26, 29, 30, 39, 41, 43, 84, 184
  Biblia Hebraica. *See* Biblia Hebraica
  Ginsburg, 10, 41, 114
  Hebrew University, 43, 44
  Hooght, van der, 40
  Jablonski, 40
  Michaelis, 37, 40
  Snaith, 42
Hebrew University, 32, 36, 126
Hebrew University Bible Project, 36, 43, 174
Hermas, Shepherd of, 56, 198
Hesychius. *See* Greek versions
Hexapla, 22, 55-60, 62, 74, 76, 85, 96, 100, 101, 103, 194, 198, 200, 202, 204, 206
Hodayot, 4
Homoioarcton, 110
Homoioteleuton, 109, 154, 204

Ibn Ezra, 39, 184
Ink, 2, 5-7, 9, 130, 140, 206, 208
Inscriptions, 3, 125, 128, 130, 142
  'Araq el-Emir, 1
  Mesha stele, 136
  Moabite stone, 2, 138
  Serabiṭ el-Ḥadem, 3
  Siloam, 2, 5, 21, 110, 138
International Organization for Masoretic Studies, 131
International Organization for Septuagint and Cognate Studies, 131, 132
'Ir-hammelach, 146
Isidore of Seville, 92, 216
Itala, 91
Itture sopherim, 17, 18
Izbet Ṣarṭa. *See* Ostraca

Jacobite, 85, 88
Jamnia, 13

Jehoiakim, 6
Jerome, 50, 56, 58, 60-62, 91, 95-99,
    190, 212, 216, 218
Jewish Theological Seminary, 23
John Hyrcanus, 45, 146
John Rylands. See Papyrus
Josephus, 12, 51, 60, 64, 77, 130
Justin Martyr, 51, 60
Justinian, Emperor, 55

Kaige, 55, 56
Karaite, 23, 24, 28, 30, 31, 35
Ketef Hinnom, 2
Kethib, 16, 17, 24, 184
Kimchi, 39
Kitab al-Khilaf, 24

Lachish 2, 3, 5, 9, 21, 108-10, 134, 140
Langton, Stephen, 21, 98
Latin, 26, 73, 125, 131
    Old Latin, 49, 75, 91-94, 99, 194,
        212, 214
    Vulgate, 21, 49, 95-99, 216, 218
Leather, 4-9, 33, 56, 60, 71, 152, 156,
    160
Lectio difficilior, 112, 119, 120, 162
Leningrad, 74, 75, 88, 202
Leningradensis. See Hebrew codices
Levita, Elias, 10
Ligatures, 72, 142
Literal, 23, 28, 51, 53, 55-57, 65, 69,
    80, 81, 83
Lucian. See Greek versions
Luther, Martin, 121, 122

Maimonides, 20, 26, 36, 174
Manual of Discipline, 35, 158
Mari, 117
Masada, 32
Masora, 10, 13, 18, 19, 23, 28-31, 36-
    39, 41, 44, 83, 123, 166, 172, 174,
    176, 178, 180, 184
Masoretes, 10, 12, 13, 20, 24-28, 30,
    35, 38, 121, 130
Matres lectionis, 15, 21
Meir, Rabbi, 56
Melito of Sardis, 72

Mesha. See Inscriptions
Mesrob, 103
Metobelos, 58
Midrash, 23, 35, 70, 80, 83
Milan, 58, 59, 74, 88, 94, 200
Mishna, 4, 23, 35, 128
Moabite stone. See Inscriptions
Moses of Nisibis, 87, 206
Murabba'at, 2, 6, 31, 164

Nablus, 47, 186
Nahal Hever, 4, 32, 54, 192
Nakdanim, 13, 250
Nash 1, 14, 30, 34, 144
Natronai II, Gaon, 27
Nehardea, 12
Nestorian, 88, 148
Nitrian desert, 206, 210
Nun inversum, 16

Obelos, 58, 202, 206
Odo, Scholastic, 237
Okhla weokhla, 29, 38
Old Hebrew. See Script
Old Latin, 49, 75, 91-94, 96, 98, 99,
    194, 212, 214
Oral tradition, 21, 49
Origen, 57-60, 62, 78, 96, 100, 101,
    154, 158, 196, 198, 202, 204
Ostraca, 5, 9
    Izbet Sarta, 2, 230
    Lachish, 2, 5, 21, 108-10, 140
    Samaritan, 2, 110

Palestine Archaeological Museum, 32,
    192
Palimpsests, 2, 6, 7, 55, 58, 74, 93,
    164, 212, 216
Pamphilus, 59, 60, 198
Paper, 6, 7, 31, 136
Papyrus, 5-9, 11, 12, 33, 68, 70, 71,
    142
    Antinoopolis Proverbs, 72
    Berlin Genesis, 72, 196
    Bodmer Library, 72
    British Library, 8, 72
    Chester Beatty, 71, 72, 194

Coptic, 220
Elephantine, 142
Fouad, 55, 69, 71, 190
John Rylands Greek, 458, 60, 71, 188
Murabba'at, 6, 164
Nash, 1, 14, 30, 34, 144
Parallel passages, 15, 17, 29, 40, 46, 130
Parallelismus membrorum, 116
Paraphrase, 80, 85
Parashoth, 20, 36, 174
Parchment, 7-9, 31, 81, 93, 166, 210, 212, 216
Patristic, 62, 71, 76, 85, 86, 88, 92, 208
Paul of Tella, 59, 101, 206
Pergamon, 7
Peshitta, 48, 85-89, 103, 104, 131, 210, 224
Pethion, 224
Pharisees, 14
Pharos, 51, 64
Philo, 51, 60, 64, 77
Philology, 27, 184
Pirqe Aboth, 18
Pliny the Elder, 146
Pointing, 10, 12, 13, 16, 21-28, 35-38, 41, 44, 116, 176, 180
  Babylonian, 22-23, 37, 166, 226
  Distinctive, 182
  Palestinian, 22-24, 27, 170
  Tiberian, 22-27, 35-38, 59, 174, 226
  Yemenite, 23, 166
Polyglots, 104, 226
  Complutensian, 23, 75, 184, 226
  London, 40, 47, 76, 84, 88, 89, 226
  Paris, 47, 84, 88
  Stier and Theile, 76
  Torah Finchasiye, 186
Pratensis, Felix, 39, 184
Prussian State Library, 37, 196
Psalterium gallicanum, 96
Psalterium romanum, 95
Ptolemy II Philadelphus, 51, 52
Pumbeditha, 12
Puncta extraordinaria, 16, 184

Qere, 16, 17, 24, 29, 160, 184

Quinta, 56, 58
Qumran, 8, 11, 31, 146, 148, 152
  Cave 1, 5, 14, 125, 146
  Caves 2-11, 32
  Cave 4, 15, 71, 80
  Cave 7, 71
  Copper scroll, 5
  Habakkuk Commentary, 158
  Ink, 9
  Targums, 80
  Temple scroll, 7
  Texts, 1, 18, 20, 31, 32, 34, 45-47, 53, 67, 130, 160
  Text types, 14, 18, 114, 164
  1QGenAp, 32, 80
  1QIsaᵃ, 27, 108-10, 114
  1QIsaᵇ, 14
  1QpHab, 33, 158
  4QDtn 32, 150
  4QJerᵃ, 2
  4QJerᵇ, 53
  4QLev aram, 79
  4Qpap Isᵖ, 6
  4QSamᵇ, 2, 150
  4Qtg Job, 79
  6Qpap Ps, 6
  7Qpap GrGen, 6
  11QPsᵃ, 34

Rabbinic Bibles, 29, 39, 84, 184
  Rabbinic literature, 13, 44, 56
  Rabbinic text, 3, 17
Rashi, 39, 184
Reuchlinianus, 25, 83
Rockefeller Museum, 32

Saadia Gaon, 104
St. Sabas monastery, 224
St. Petersburg, 10, 30, 44, 73, 198
Samaritans, 4, 22, 56, 104, 160
  Abisha scroll, 47
  Abu al-Barakat scroll, 47
  Manuscripts, 23, 40, 186
  Ostraca. See Ostraca
  Pentateuch, 14, 45-47, 78
  Pronunciation, 26, 27
  Script. See Script

Text type, 3, 19, 22, 40, 66-67
Samariticon, 78
Samuel ben Jacob, 13, 180
Sarrave, Claude, 202
Sassoon, David, 42
Scheide, John H., 72, 194
Script 1-5, 31, 44, 67, 136, 152, 154, 156
  Aramaic, 67, 142
  Cuneiform, 1, 5
  Cursive, 9, 196
  Ethiopic, 222
  Hebrew square, 1, 3, 4, 67, 108, 110, 158, 160, 190
  Latin uncial, 216
  Nabatean, 142
  Old Hebrew, 2-4, 27, 34, 45, 108, 109, 136, 138, 140, 142, 154, 158, 160, 164, 186, 228, 230
  Palmyrene, 142
  Phoenician. See Old Hebrew
  Proto-Palestinian, 3
  Samaritan, 4, 45, 47, 186
  Sinai, 3
  Syrian (Estrangela), 142, 210
Scriptio continua, 110
Scriptio defectiva, 28, 29, 172
Scriptio plena, 22, 158
Scriptorium, 98
Scroll, 3-8, 20
Sebirin, 16
Sedarim. See Division
Seder. See Division
Septima, 56
Septuagint. See Greek versions
Serabiṭ el-Ḥadem. See Inscriptions
Severus, Emperor, 38
Sexta, 56
Shechem, 3, 45-47, 84, 186
Shem Tob Bible, 42
Siloam. See Inscriptions
Simon ben Kosiba. See Bar Kochba
Sinai, 6, 27
  St. Catherine's Monastery, 73, 75, 198
Sinaiticus. See Greek codices
Sirach, 53

Arabic, 224
  Greek, 35, 72, 73, 74
  Hebrew, 35, 125
  Old Latin, 99
Sixtus V, Pope, 76, 98
Sopherim, 12, 16-19
Special points, 16, 184
Sura, 12, 104
Symmachus, 55-56
Synagogue, 11, 35, 37, 38, 66, 78, 79, 84, 170
Syriac, 22, 27, 34, 48, 59, 85, 86, 89, 102, 103, 206, 210, 224
Syrian St. Mark's Monastery, Jerusalem, 32
Syro-Hexapla, 59, 62, 85, 88, 101, 206, 224

Tablets (clay, stone, wood), 5
Talmud, 9, 19, 21, 23, 35, 56, 70, 170
  Babylonian, 4, 18, 21
  Jerusalem, 6
Targumic translation, 52, 53, 64-66
Targums, xiii, 23, 32, 37, 39, 63, 64, 70, 79-86, 166, 184
  Palestinian, 81-83, 86
  Samaritan, 47, 84, 131
  Yemenite, 83
Tattam, Henry, 206
Tell ed-Duweir, 5, 140
Tertullian, 91, 94
Tetragram(maton), 4, 69, 158, 190
Tetrapla, 58, 59
Textus receptus (Arabic), 104
Textus receptus (Hebrew), 26, 37, 39, 42, 182
Theodoret of Cyrrhus, 60, 62
Theodotion, 55-58, 83, 97, 194, 204, 206
Tiberias, 12, 24, 26, 35
Timothy I of Seleucia, Patriarch, 148
Tiqqune sopherim, 17
Tironian notes, 214
Tischendorf, Constantin von, 73-76, 198
Transliteration, 22, 26, 57, 58, 67, 130, 140

Transposition, 10, 14, 109, 162

Ugaritic, 3, 117

Versions, 33, 42, 44, 48-49, 53-60,
115, 118, 119, 123, 125, 206
Vulgate. *See* Latin

Wen Amon, 5
Writing implements, 4-7

Yemenite 23, 42, 83, 166

Zadokite Document, 35
Zamora, Alfonso de, 226
Zeitlin, Solomon, 152

Index of Scripture References

OLD TESTAMENT

Genesis

1:1	28, 29, 47
1:7	58
1:11	28
1:12	28
1:14	58
5	46
6:3	38
10:14	112
10:19	38
11	46
16:5	16
18:5	18
18:9	16
18:21	38
18:22	17
19:6	38
19:8	16
19:23	16
19:33	16
21:28–22:3	226
21:33b–22:4a	184
22:3	226
24:7	38
24:28	68
24:55	18
26:37–27:30	36
27:19	30
27:46–28:11	214
28:18–29:22	180
31:36	38

33:4	16
34:11-25	196
37:12	16
41:46	17
49:13	16

Exodus

1:18	68
4:10	68
5:6, 10, 13	70
5:11	68
5:13, 19	68
8:8	68
12:35	68
13:8-17	210
15:1-21	93
16:4	68
18:11, 14	68
18:16	68
18:22	68
19:3	69
20	144
20:2-17	34
20:17	3, 46
24:10	69
24:14	68
25:19	38
27:10-15	206
29:1	68
34:1	5

Leviticus

10:16	19

11:42	19
19:31-34	160
20:20-23	160
20:21	160
20:22	160
21:24–22:3	160
22:4, 5	160
23:13	38
26:9	38
26:39	38

Numbers

3:39	16
4:3	38
5:28	38
6:22-27	78
6:24-26	2
9:10	16
10:35	16
10:36	16
11:15	17
12:12	17
21:30	16
24:23	38
26:12-27	176
29:15	16
31:2	18

Deuteronomy

1:34	176
4:38–6:3	36
5	144
5:6-21	34

6:4f.	34	3:13	17, 18	*Job*	
9:15-23	178	8:34	17	1:1–15:24	216
11:30	46	9:40	17	1:5	18, 112
23:18	70	18:8-25	75	1:11	112
23:24–24:3	71, 188			2:5	112
25:1-3	71, 188	*2 Samuel*		2:9	18, 112
26:12	71, 188	2:8ff.	17	6:5	208
26:17-19	71, 188	4:4	17	7:20	18
27:2f.	5	5:16	17	19:24	4, 9
27:4	46	8:3	18	22:12–23:2	224
27:8	172	12:9, 14	18	32:3	18
27:15(?)	188	16:12	17	33:21	172
28:2(?)	188	16:23	18	37:17–38:15	166
28:31-33	71, 188	19:20	16		
29:14-18	162	20:1	18	*Psalms*	
29:28	16	22	16	9f.	230
30:20–31:5	162			10:2–18:6	72
31:1	162	*1 Kings*		13 Greek	54
31:3	28	1:2	17	14	16
31:15-19	186	8:6	112	17–118	72
31:28–32:6	190	9:8	18	18	16
31:28–32:14	174	12:16	18	19:5	108
32:1-44+31:30	93	18:19, 22, 40	112	20:14–34:6	72
32:8, 37-43	150	21	214	22[21]:25-25[24]:5	218
34:11f.	220			25	230
		2 Kings		27:4	172
Joshua		3:4-27	136	27:13	16
4:24	69	5:18	18	28(27):6f.	200
10:12-19	202	18:13–20:19	16	34	230
15:62	146	20:4	108	36:7	18
		20:20	138	37	230
Judges		24:18–25:30	16	40:8	5
5:15-18	216			40:14-18	16
7:8	108	*1 Chronicles*		45:2	9
18:30	19	8:33	17	53	16
		9:39	17	68:26	18
Ruth		14:7	17	70	16
2:11	18			80:14	19
3:5, 17	18	*2 Chronicles*		90:3	68
3:12	18	10:16	18	90:6	68
4:10	61	32:30	138	95 Greek	54
4:11-22	61	35:7–36:19	36	105:27–137:6	73
				106:20	18
1 Samuel		*Nehemiah*		107:21-26, 40	16
1:9	30	2:8	172	111f.	230
2:1-10	93	8:8	79	112:2–114:3	182
23:9-13	150			112:2	182

112:4	182	26:3f.	109	2:21		110, 119
112:5	182	28:1, 4	109	8:8		9
112:6, 7, 8	182	28:2	158	9:2f.		198
112:7	182	28:20	108	9:9f.		198
112:8	182	28:21	108	17:1		9
112:10	182	30:8	5	24:11-19 Greek		204
113:1	182	30:30	109	26:1		29
113:1, 9	182	30:33	108	27:1		29
113:9	182	31:18-24	70	28:1		29
114:2	182	32:19	109	29–52		53
119	230	33:1	108	29:32		172
145	34, 230	33:8	108	31:38		18
151	34	33:13	108	32:11		18
		34–66	33	32:14		7
Proverbs		36–39	16	35:11-19 Hebrew		204
31	230	37:29	109	36		6
		38:8–40:28	152	36:2ff.		5
Song		38:11	109	36:18		9
3:12	36	38:20	109	48:34		29
		39:1	111	50:29		18
Isaiah		40:6-20	154	51:3		18
1–33	33	40:7f.	109	52		16
1:4	110	42:1-4	64	Greek		53
1:17, 23	110	42:16	108	Letter		99
2:1-4	130	42:25	108			
2:2-4	16	44:9	16	**Lamentations**		
2:20	110	47:10	108	1		230
3:17	158	47:13	108	2–4		230
4:5f.	109	48:17–49:7	156	3:20		18
5:1-9	93	48:17	156			
5:8	109	48:18	156	**Ezekiel**		
5:29	108	48:21	156	2:9		5
6:11	158	49:4	156	2:10		6
7:11–9:8	170	49:5	156	3:1-3		5
7:14	54, 158	49:6	156	8:17		18
8:1	5, 9	49:7	156	16:57–17:1		194
8:11	109	50:7–51:8	156	20:43-47		212
8:19	109	50:11	156	26:17		172
9:7	158	51:9	108	40–48		67
9:8	108	52:13–53:12	80	41:20		16
9:18	109	62:8f.	166	46:22		16
11:6	108	63:7-16	166	48:16		18
11:12	178					
14:4	108	**Jeremiah**		**Daniel**		
16:8f.	109	1–28	53	3:51-90		93
21:16	158	2:11	18	8:9		180
23:15	109	2:16-33	172			

Hosea
4:7	18
13:14	68
14:2f.	166

Amos
2:7	110
6:12	110
8:11–9:15	164
8:11	164
8:14	164
9:5	164
9:6	164
9:8	164
9:12	164

Jonah
1:1-4	220
2:3-10	93

Micah
4:1-3	16

Habakkuk
1–2	33
1:8, 11	158
1:12	18
1:14–2:5	192
2:2	5
2:6	65
2:7-14	158
2:13-15	192
2:16	158

3:2-19	93
3:5	68
3:6b-7a	117

Zechariah
2:12	18
5:1f.	5

Malachi
1:13	18

NEW TESTAMENT

Matthew
5:18	1
12:18-20	64

Luke
1:46-55	93

Acts
7:4	46
7:32	46
8:26f.	54

Hebrews
9:3f.	46

1 Peter
2	214

DEUTEROCANON

Tobit
6:5-7	198
6:11f.	198

Sirach
Prologue	53
51:13-30	34

Susanna
1–5	222

1 Maccabees | 73
9:12f.	198
9:20-22	198

OTHER SOURCES

Aristeas
314-16	63
314	65

Megilla
1.9	6

Nedarim
37b	18

Pirqe Aboth
3:13	18